登場人物紹介 Character

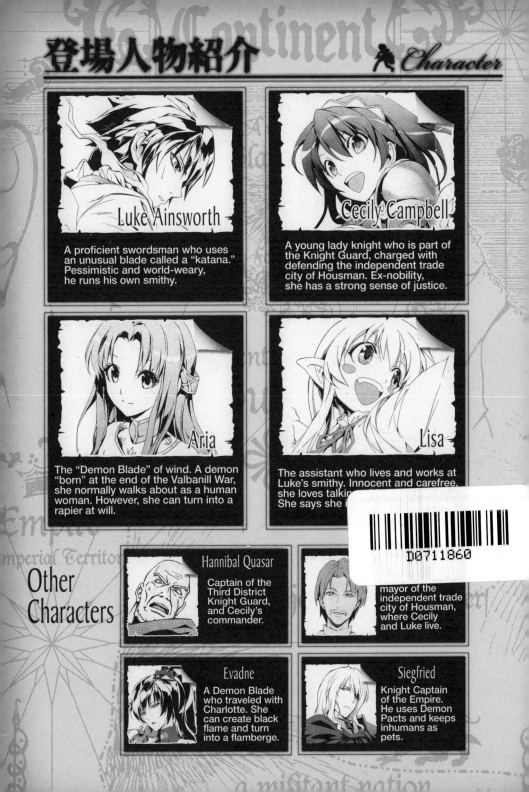

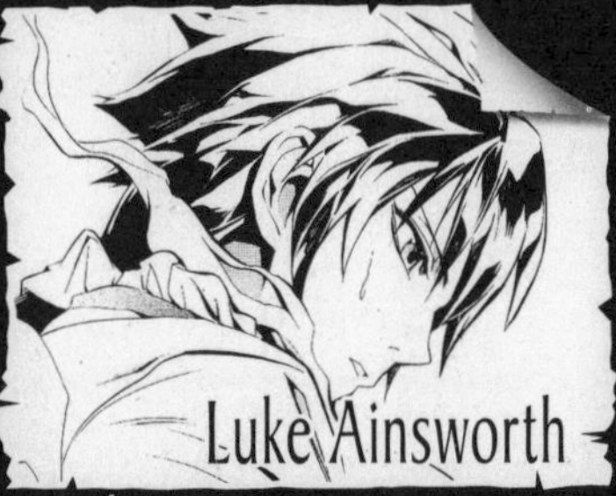
Luke Ainsworth

A proficient swordsman who uses an unusual blade called a "katana." Pessimistic and world-weary, he runs his own smithy.

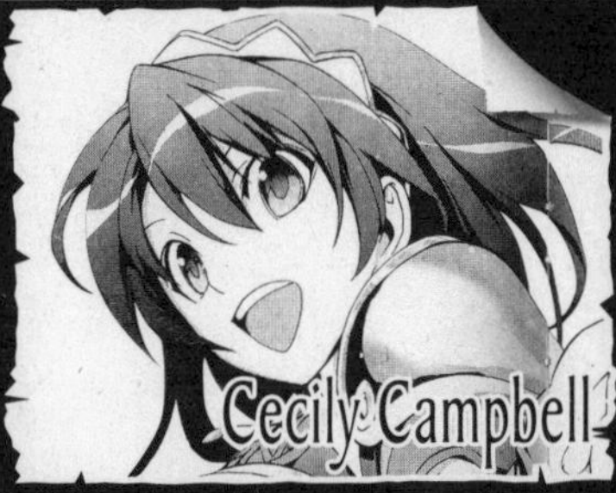
Cecily Campbell

A young lady knight who is part of the Knight Guard, charged with defending the independent trade city of Housman. Ex-nobility, she has a strong sense of justice.

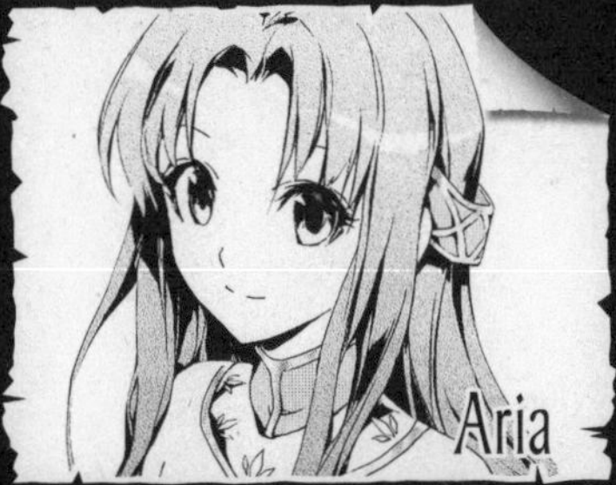
Aria

The "Demon Blade" of wind. A demon "born" at the end of the Valbanill War, she normally walks about as a human woman. However, she can turn into a rapier at will.

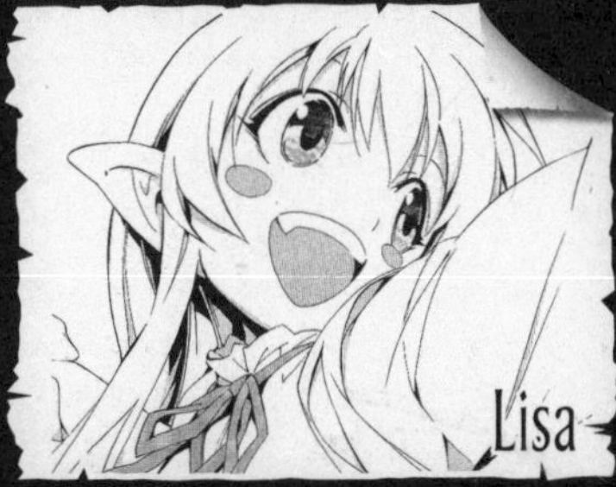
Lisa

The assistant who lives and works at Luke's smithy. Innocent and carefree, she loves talki
She says she i

Other Characters

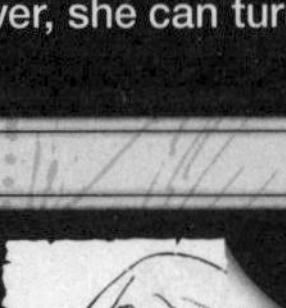

Hannibal Quasar

Captain of the Third District Knight Guard, and Cecily's commander.

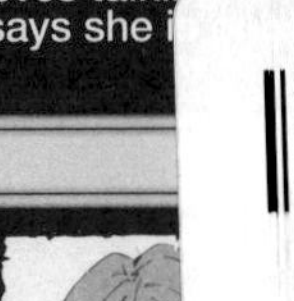

mayor of the independent trade city of Housman, where Cecily and Luke live.

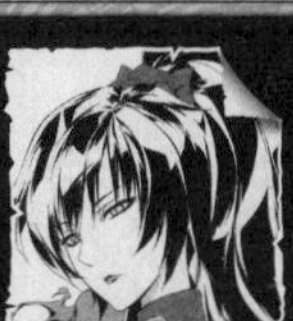

Evadne

A Demon Blade who traveled with Charlotte. She can create black flame and turn into a flamberge.

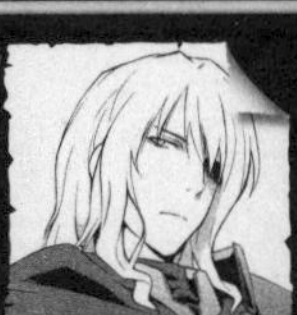

Siegfried

Knight Captain of the Empire. He uses Demon Pacts and keeps inhumans as pets.

I TRUST LUKE AINSWORTH.

Decades ago, a great war raged across the continent. Called the "Valbanill War," it saw the widespread use of powerful Demon Pacts. Forty-four years later, a young lady knight named Cecily Campbell meets a mysterious blacksmith named Luke Ainsworth, and asks him to forge for her a sword.

As the partner of the Demon Blade Aria, Cecily is asked to be a bodyguard for Siegfried, a Knight Captain of the Empire, when he comes to Housman to retrieve the corpse of an inhuman.

NOBODY IS GOING TO COME AND "SAVE" YOU.

HE WON'T.

Siegfried attempted to use the dark secret between Luke and Lisa to shake Cecily's beliefs, but Cecily held true to those she trusted. This angered Siegfried, and he finally showed his true colors...

あらすじ Story

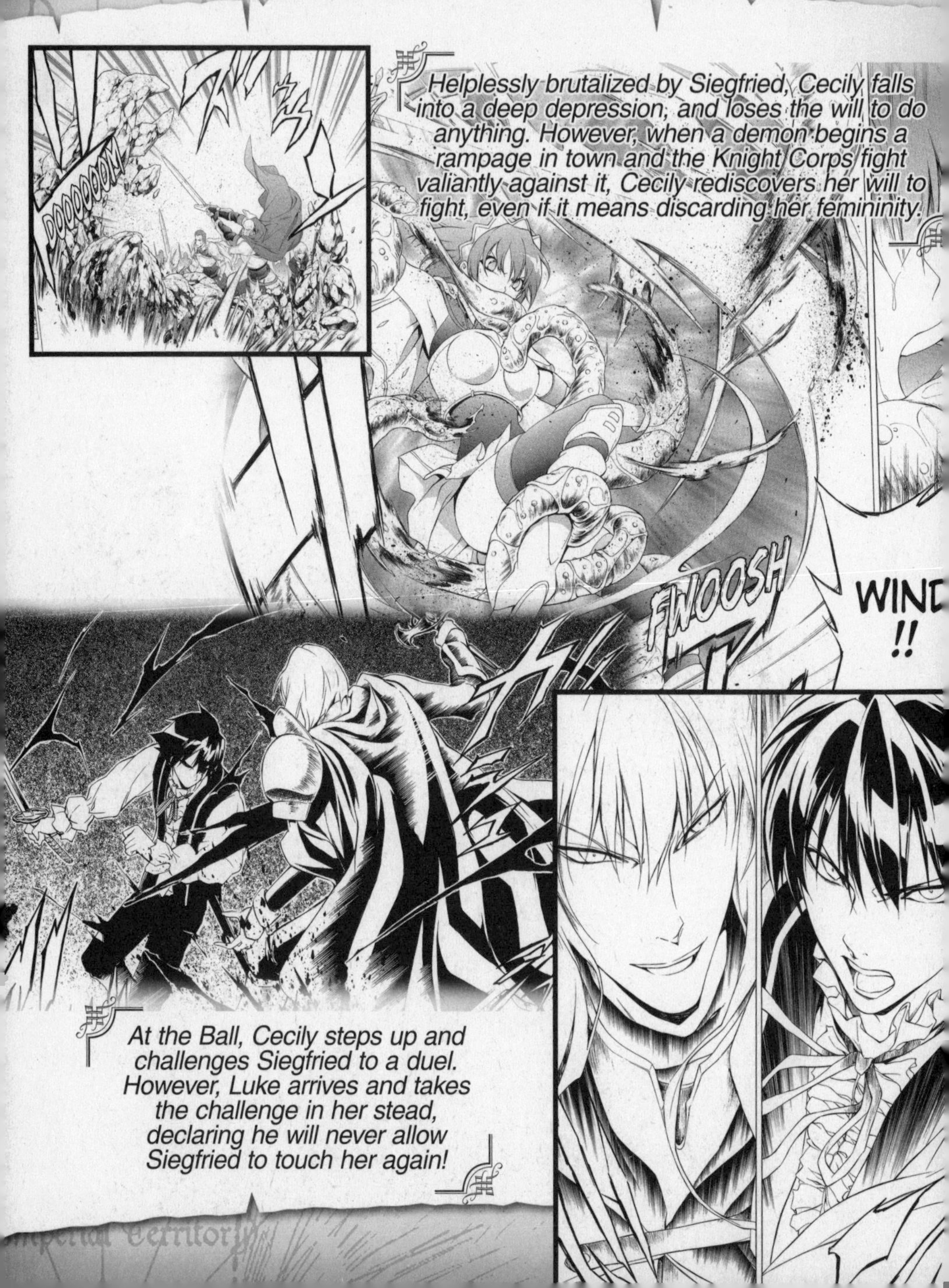
DOOOOOOM
FWOOSH
WIND !!

Helplessly brutalized by Siegfried, Cecily falls into a deep depression, and loses the will to do anything. However, when a demon begins a rampage in town and the Knight Corps fight valiantly against it, Cecily rediscovers her will to fight, even if it means discarding her femininity.

At the Ball, Cecily steps up and challenges Siegfried to a duel. However, Luke arrives and takes the challenge in her stead, declaring he will never allow Siegfried to touch her again!

The Sacred Blacksmith

聖剣の刀鍛治

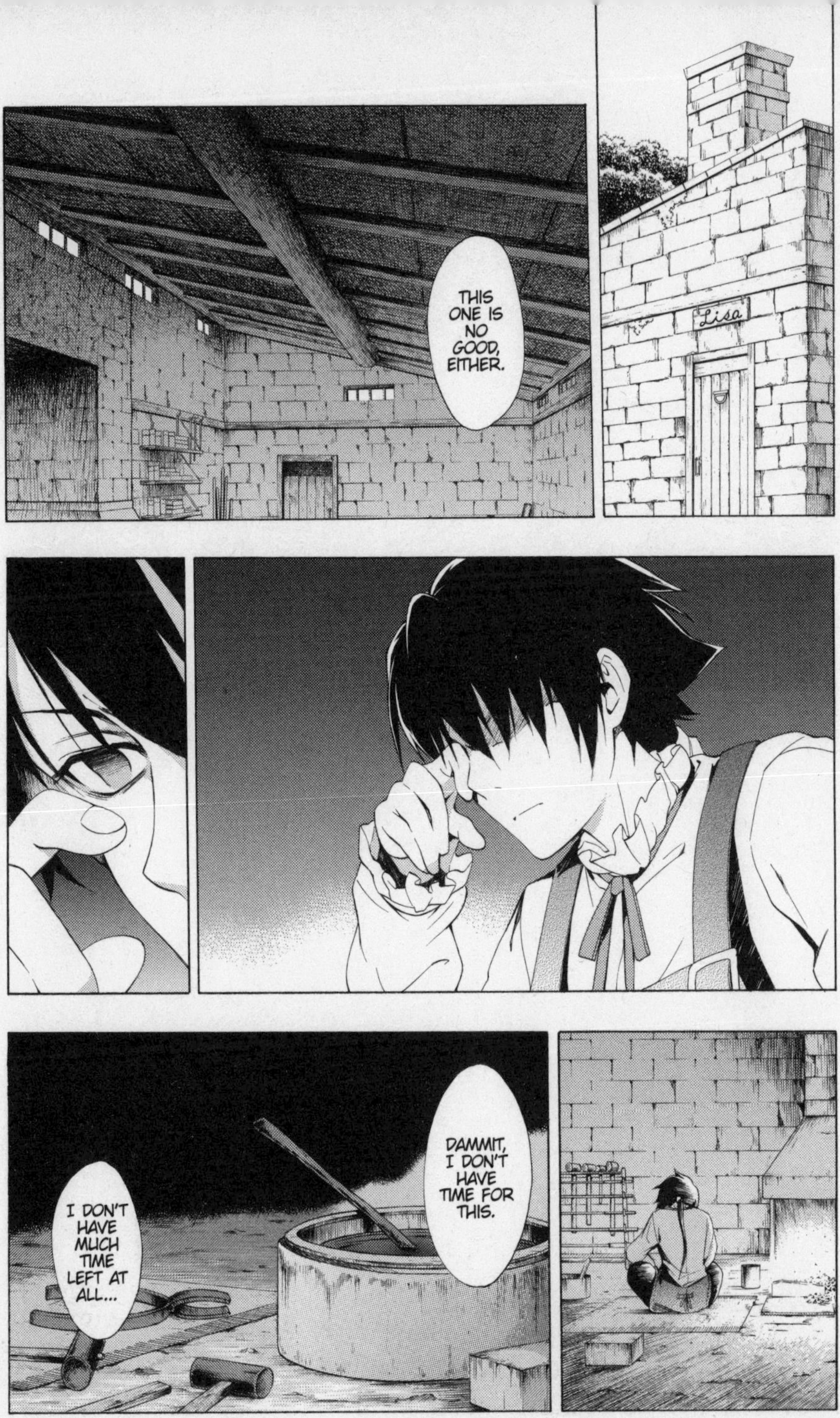
Lisa
THIS ONE IS NO GOOD, EITHER.
DAMMIT, I DON'T HAVE TIME FOR THIS.
I DON'T HAVE MUCH TIME LEFT AT ALL...

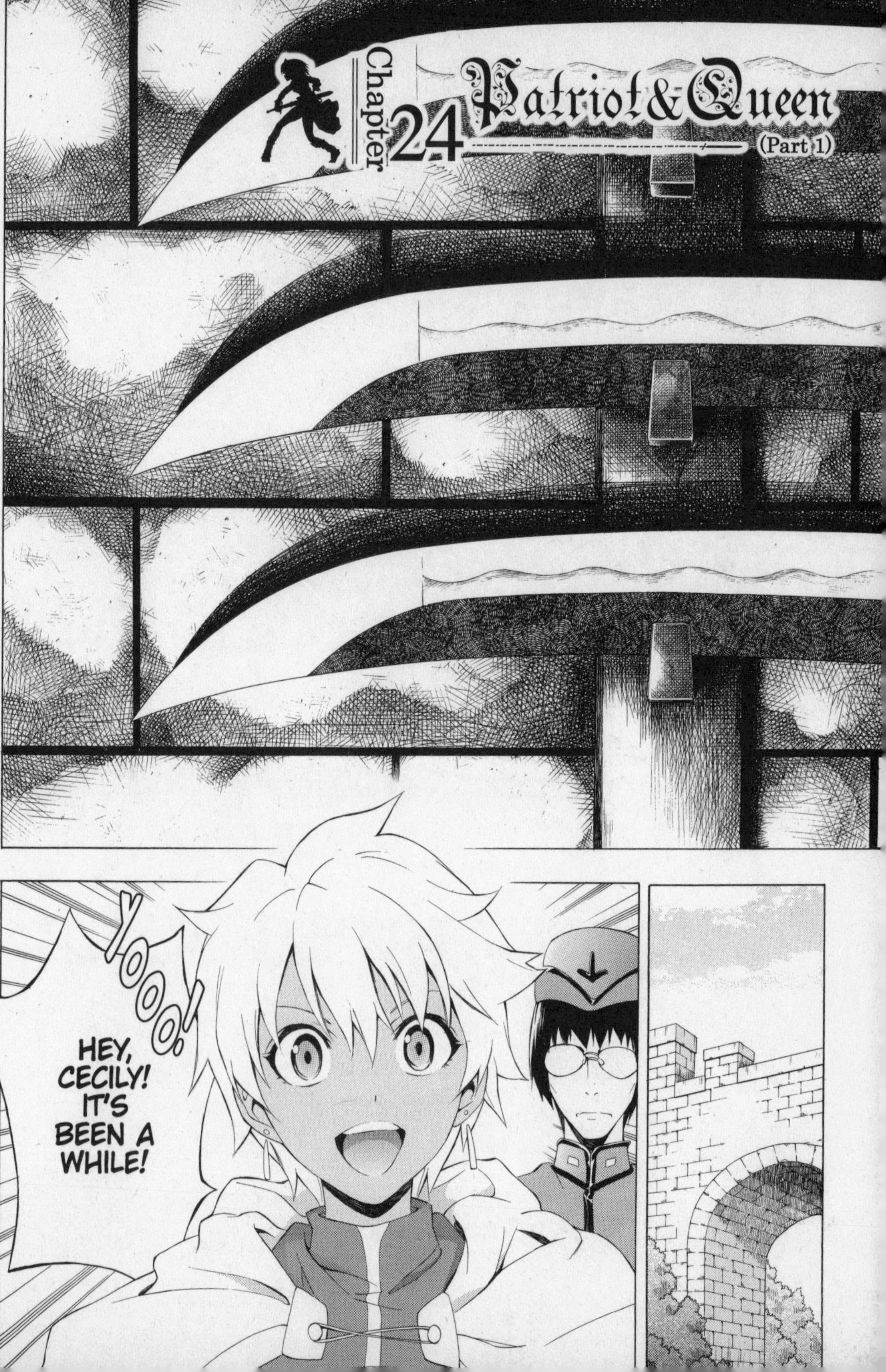
Chapter 24
Patriot & Queen
(Part 1)
YOOOO!
HEY, CECILY! IT'S BEEN A WHILE!

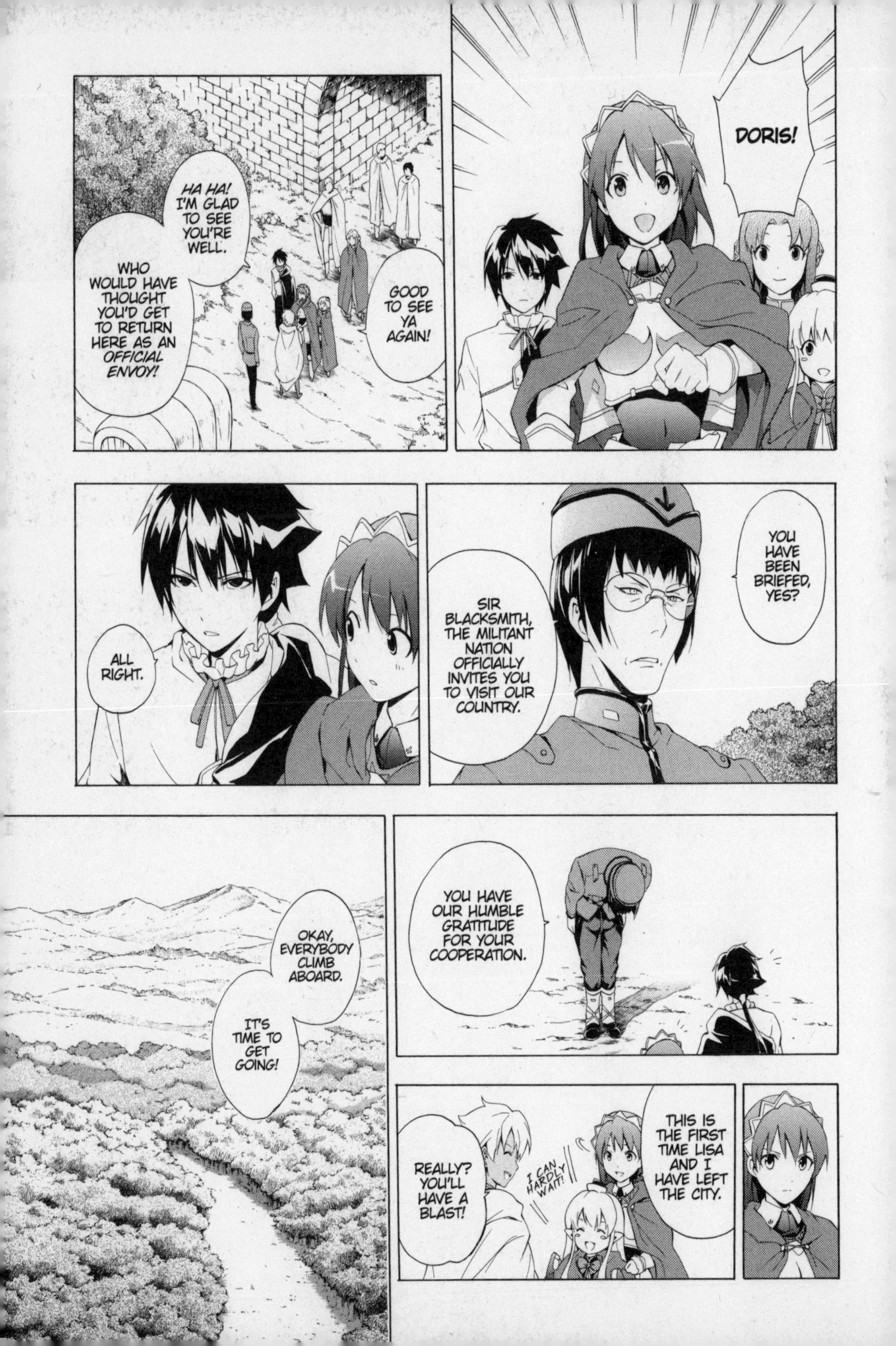
DORIS!
GOOD TO SEE YA AGAIN!
HA HA! I'M GLAD TO SEE YOU'RE WELL.
WHO WOULD HAVE THOUGHT YOU'D GET TO RETURN HERE AS AN OFFICIAL ENVOY!
YOU HAVE BEEN BRIEFED, YES?
SIR BLACKSMITH, THE MILITANT NATION OFFICIALLY INVITES YOU TO VISIT OUR COUNTRY.
ALL RIGHT.
YOU HAVE OUR HUMBLE GRATITUDE FOR YOUR COOPERATION.
THIS IS THE FIRST TIME LISA AND I HAVE LEFT THE CITY.
I CAN HARDLY WAIT!
REALLY? YOU'LL HAVE A BLAST!
OKAY, EVERYBODY CLIMB ABOARD.
IT'S TIME TO GET GOING!

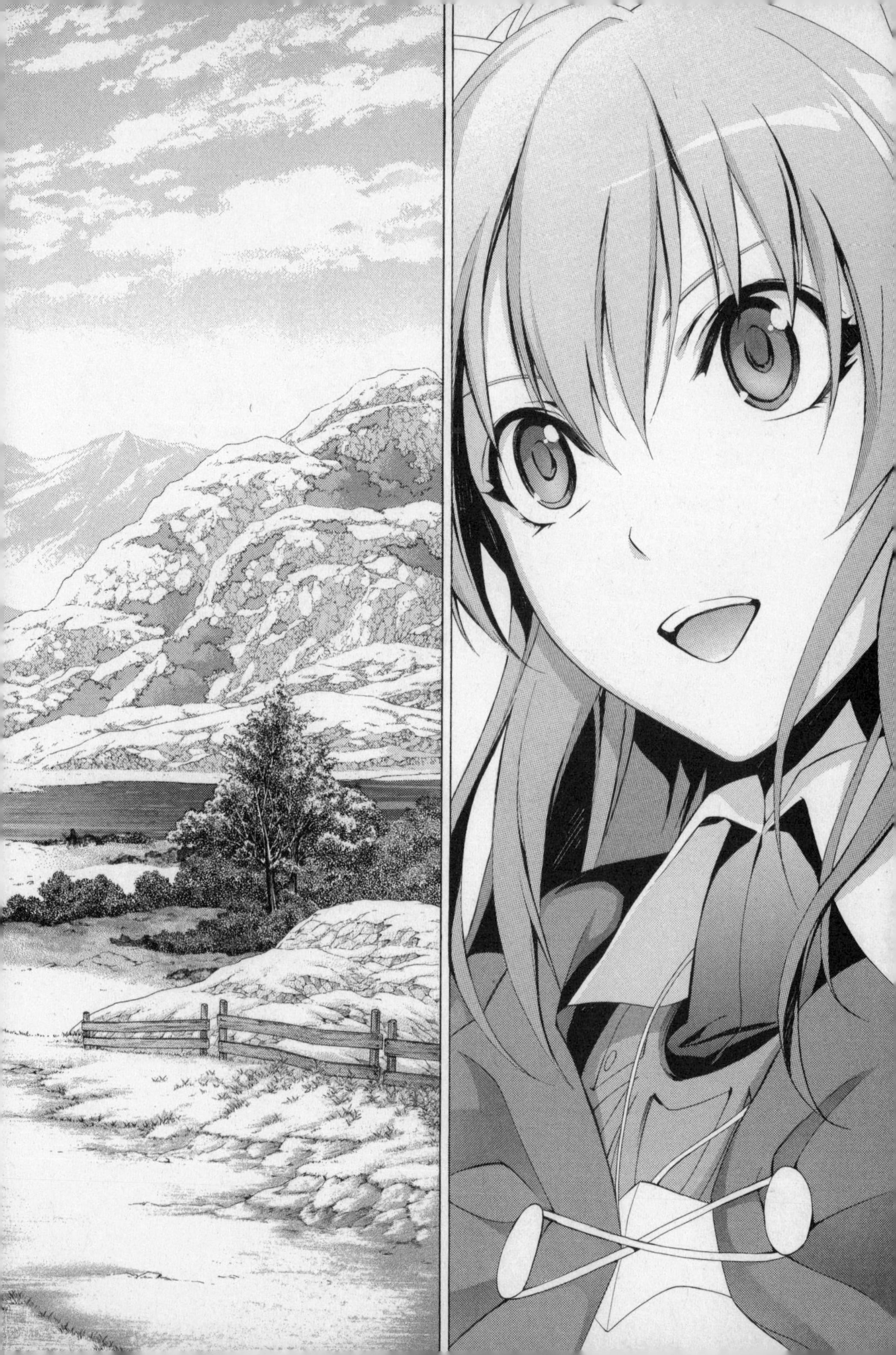

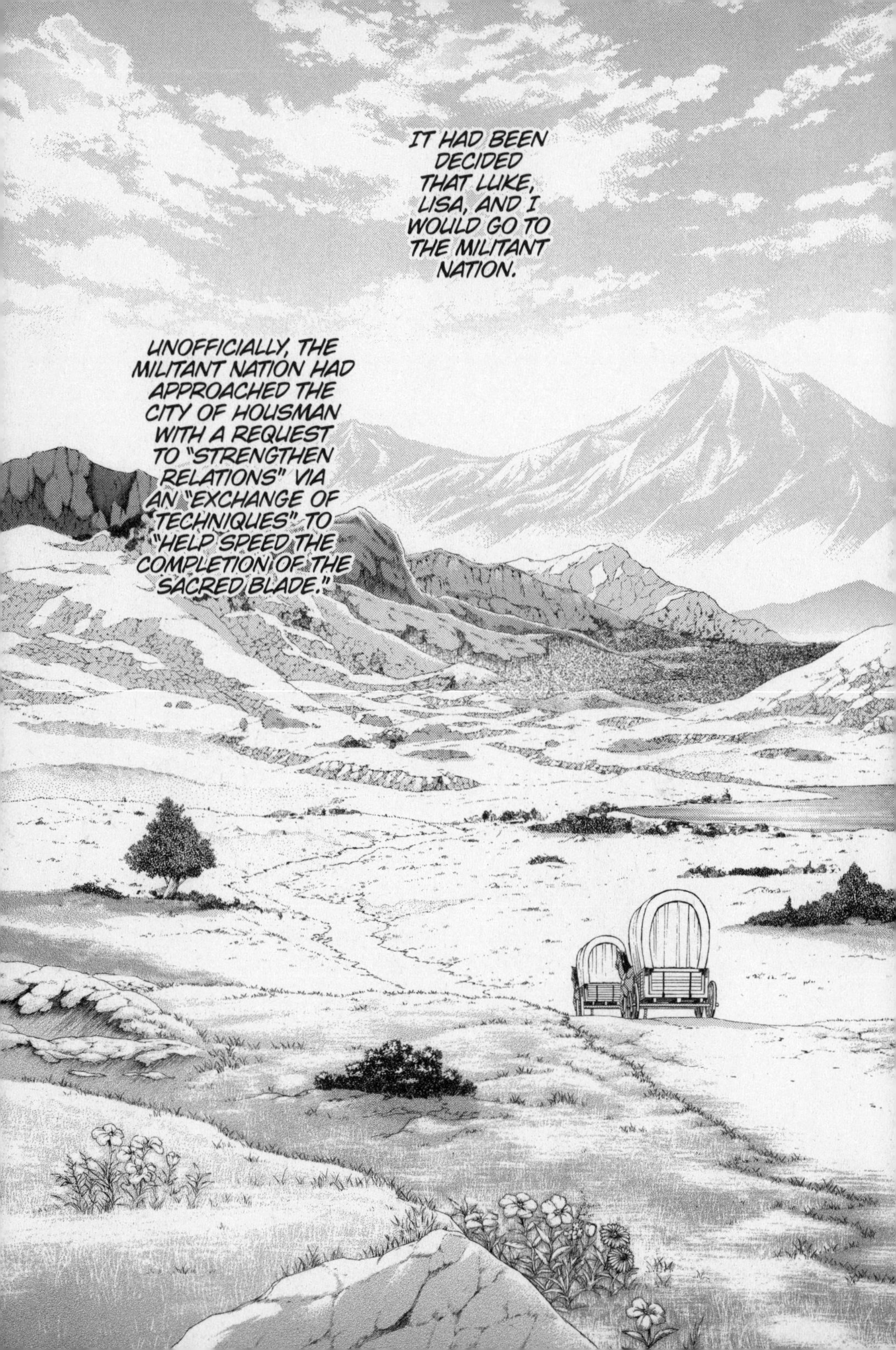
IT HAD BEEN DECIDED THAT LUKE, LISA, AND I WOULD GO TO THE MILITANT NATION.
UNOFFICIALLY, THE MILITANT NATION HAD APPROACHED THE CITY OF HOUSMAN WITH A REQUEST TO "STRENGTHEN RELATIONS" VIA AN "EXCHANGE OF TECHNIQUES" TO "HELP SPEED THE COMPLETION OF THE SACRED BLADE."

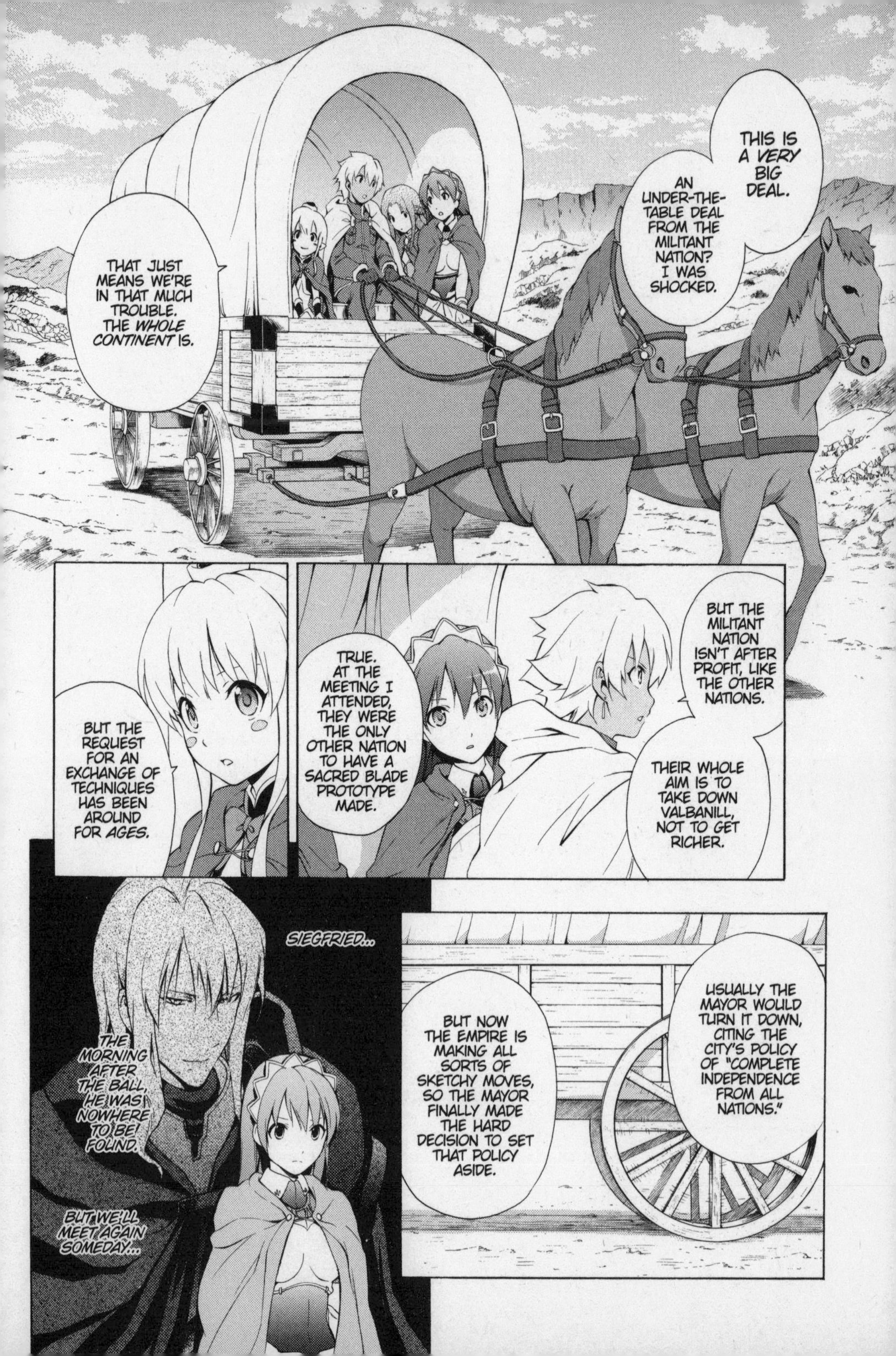
THIS IS A VERY BIG DEAL.
AN UNDER-THE-TABLE DEAL FROM THE MILITANT NATION? I WAS SHOCKED.
THAT JUST MEANS WE'RE IN THAT MUCH TROUBLE. THE WHOLE CONTINENT IS.
BUT THE MILITANT NATION ISN'T AFTER PROFIT, LIKE THE OTHER NATIONS.
THEIR WHOLE AIM IS TO TAKE DOWN VALBANILL, NOT TO GET RICHER.
TRUE. AT THE MEETING I ATTENDED, THEY WERE THE ONLY OTHER NATION TO HAVE A SACRED BLADE PROTOTYPE MADE.
BUT THE REQUEST FOR AN EXCHANGE OF TECHNIQUES HAS BEEN AROUND FOR AGES.
USUALLY THE MAYOR WOULD TURN IT DOWN, CITING THE CITY'S POLICY OF "COMPLETE INDEPENDENCE FROM ALL NATIONS."
BUT NOW THE EMPIRE IS MAKING ALL SORTS OF SKETCHY MOVES, SO THE MAYOR FINALLY MADE THE HARD DECISION TO SET THAT POLICY ASIDE.
SIEGFRIED...
THE MORNING AFTER THE BALL, HE WAS NOWHERE TO BE FOUND.
BUT WE'LL MEET AGAIN SOMEDAY...

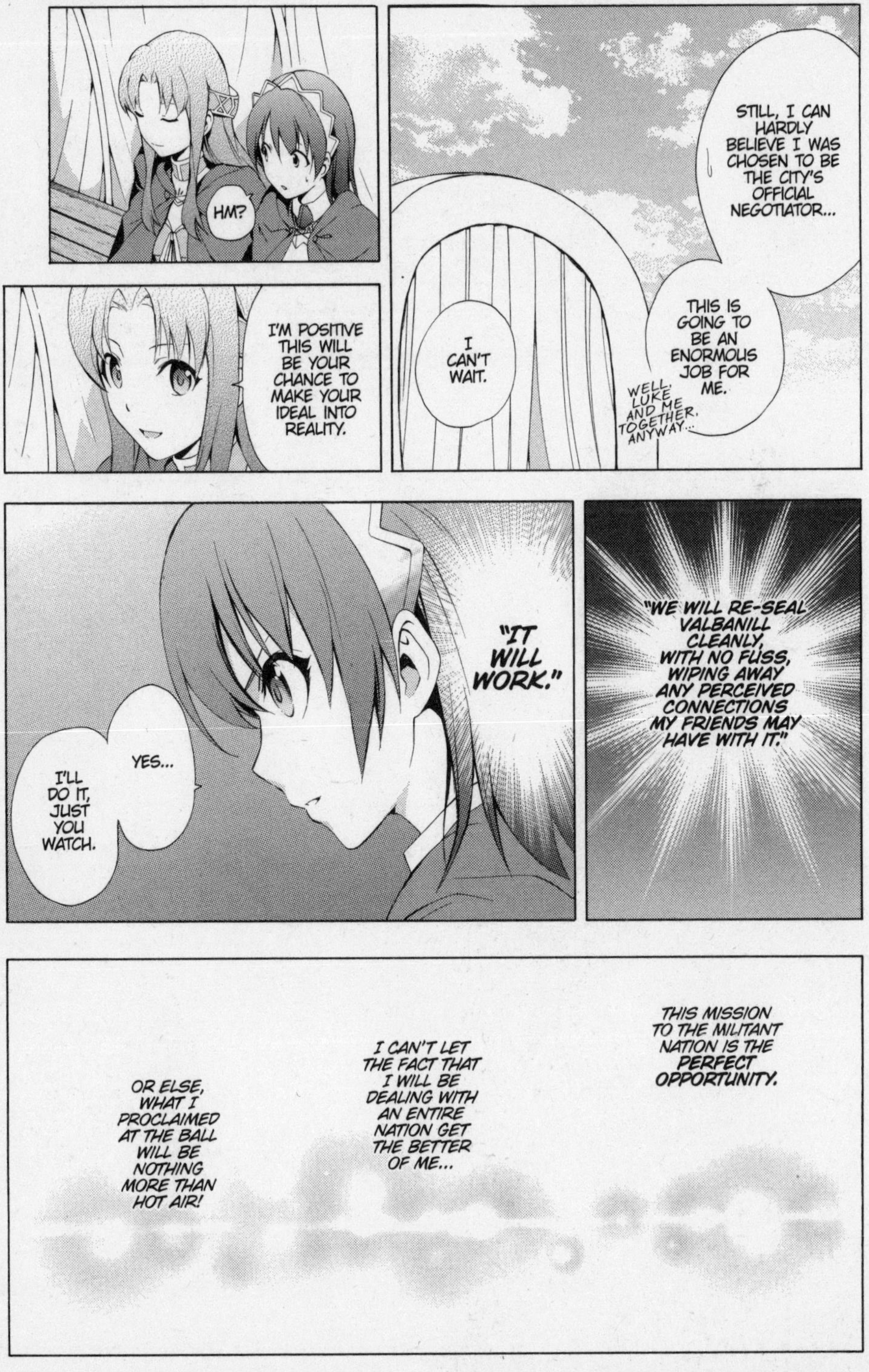
STILL, I CAN HARDLY BELIEVE I WAS CHOSEN TO BE THE CITY'S OFFICIAL NEGOTIATOR...
THIS IS GOING TO BE AN ENORMOUS JOB FOR ME.
WELL, LUKE AND ME TOGETHER, ANYWAY...
I CAN'T WAIT.
HM?
I'M POSITIVE THIS WILL BE YOUR CHANCE TO MAKE YOUR IDEAL INTO REALITY.
"WE WILL RE-SEAL VALBANILL CLEANLY, WITH NO FUSS, WIPING AWAY ANY PERCEIVED CONNECTIONS MY FRIENDS MAY HAVE WITH IT."
"IT WILL WORK."
YES...
I'LL DO IT, JUST YOU WATCH.
THIS MISSION TO THE MILITANT NATION IS THE PERFECT OPPORTUNITY.
I CAN'T LET THE FACT THAT I WILL BE DEALING WITH AN ENTIRE NATION GET THE BETTER OF ME...
OR ELSE, WHAT I PROCLAIMED AT THE BALL WILL BE NOTHING MORE THAN HOT AIR!

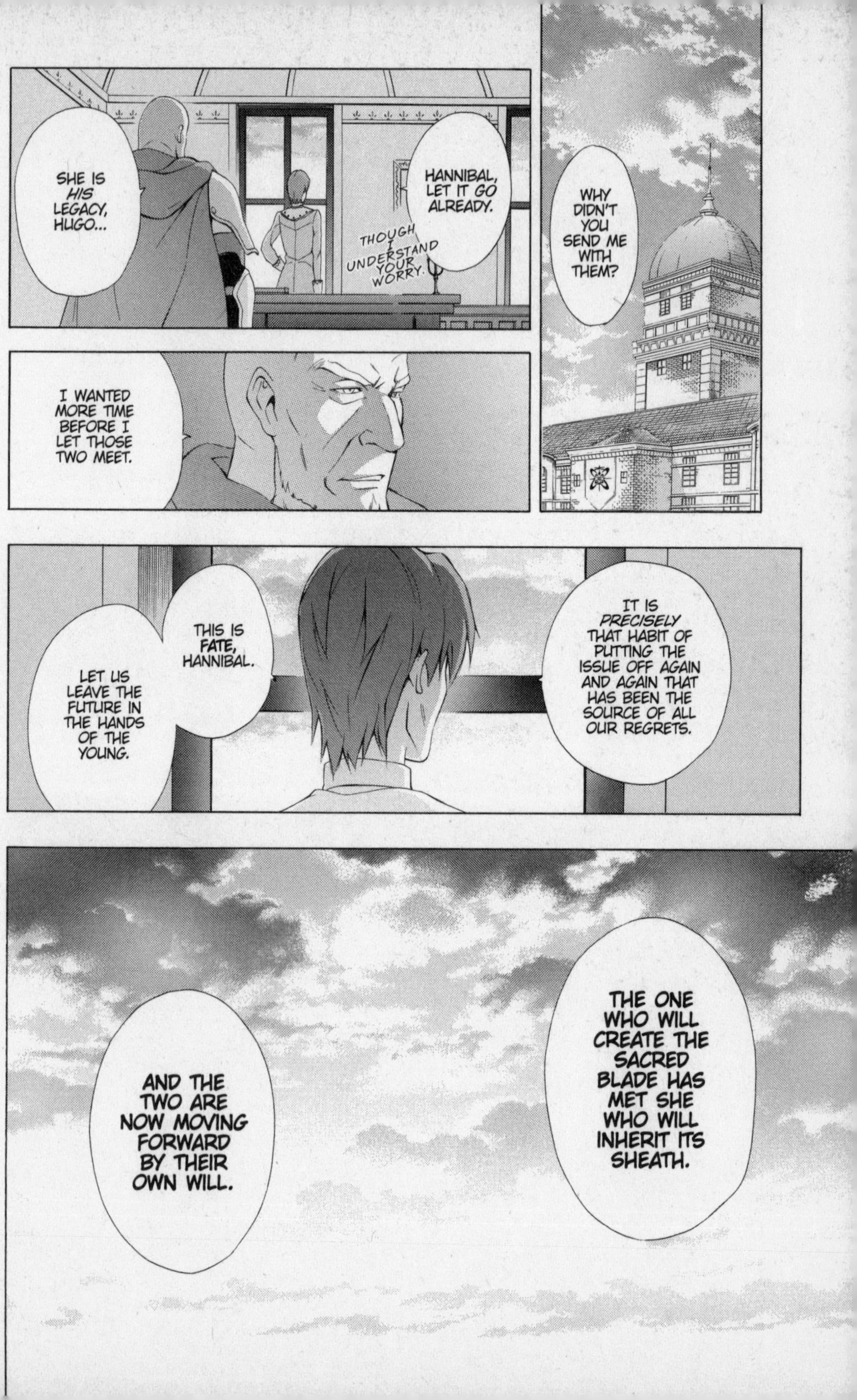
WHY DIDN'T YOU SEND ME WITH THEM?
HANNIBAL, LET IT GO ALREADY.
THOUGH I UNDERSTAND YOUR WORRY.
SHE IS *HIS* LEGACY, HUGO...
I WANTED MORE TIME BEFORE I LET THOSE TWO MEET.
IT IS *PRECISELY* THAT HABIT OF PUTTING THE ISSUE OFF AGAIN AND AGAIN THAT HAS BEEN THE SOURCE OF ALL OUR REGRETS.
THIS IS FATE, HANNIBAL.
LET US LEAVE THE FUTURE IN THE HANDS OF THE YOUNG.
THE ONE WHO WILL CREATE THE SACRED BLADE HAS MET SHE WHO WILL INHERIT ITS SHEATH.
AND THE TWO ARE NOW MOVING FORWARD BY THEIR OWN WILL.

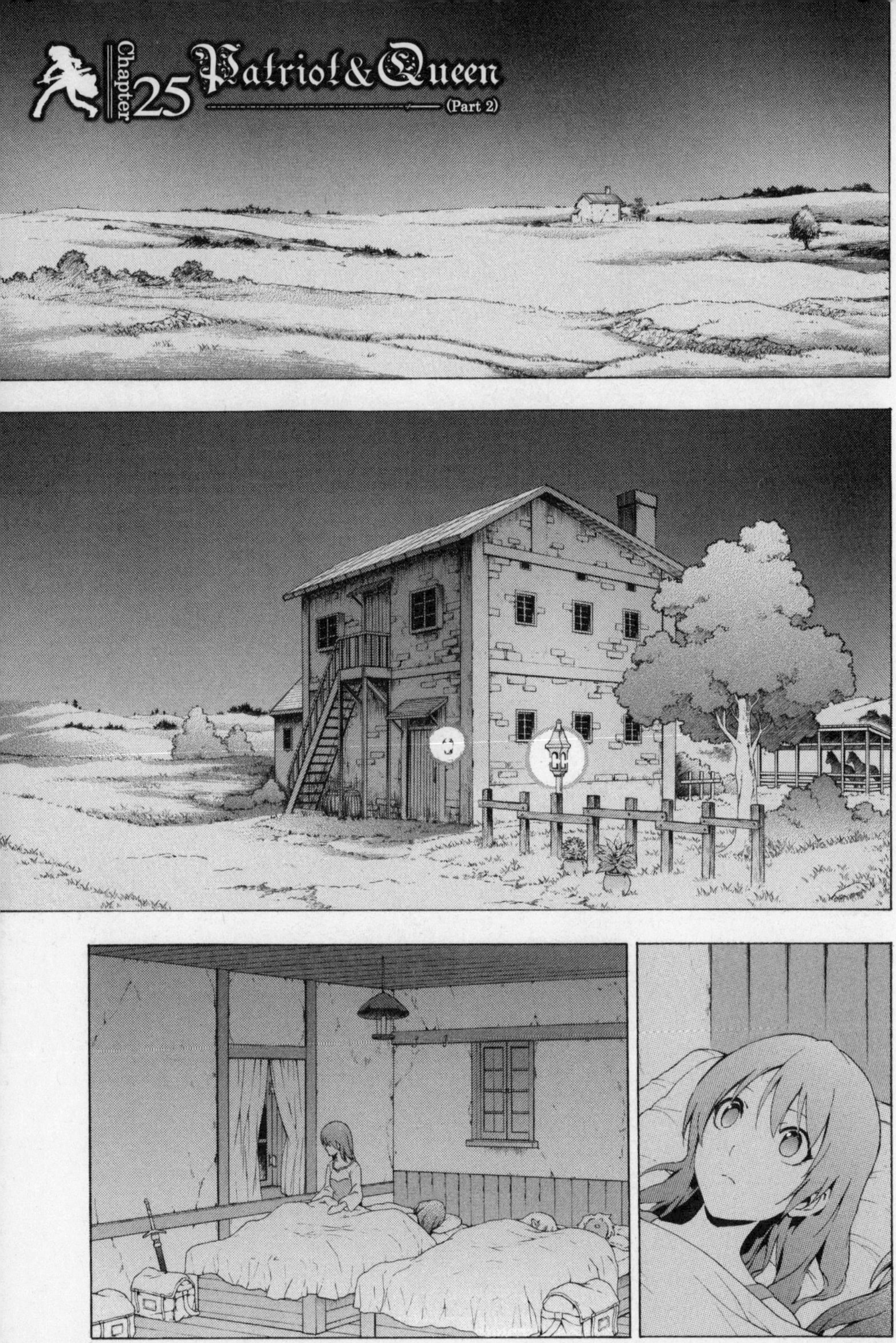
Chapter 25 Patriot & Queen
(Part 2)

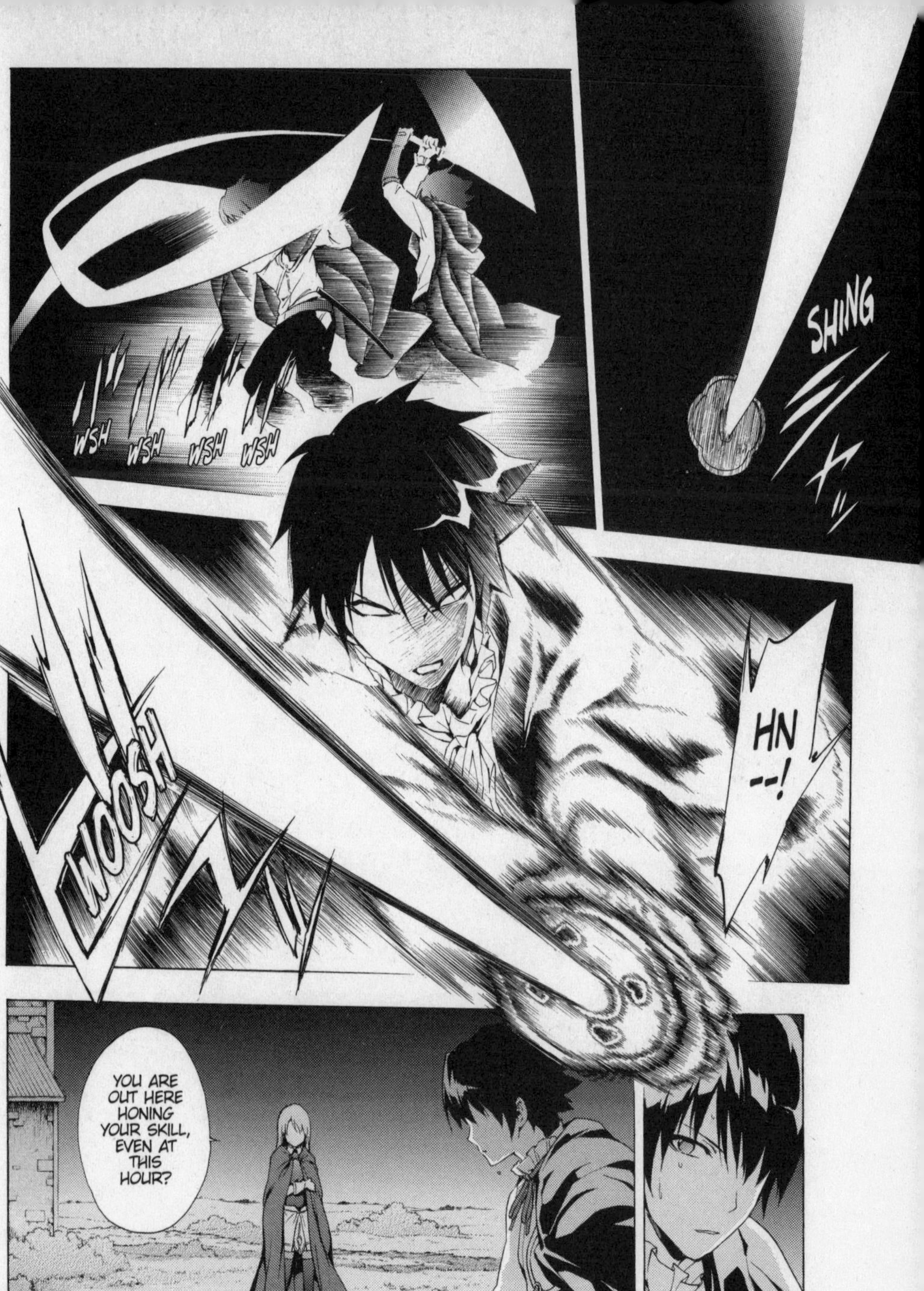
SHING
WSH WSH WSH WSH
HN--!
WOOSH
YOU ARE OUT HERE HONING YOUR SKILL, EVEN AT THIS HOUR?

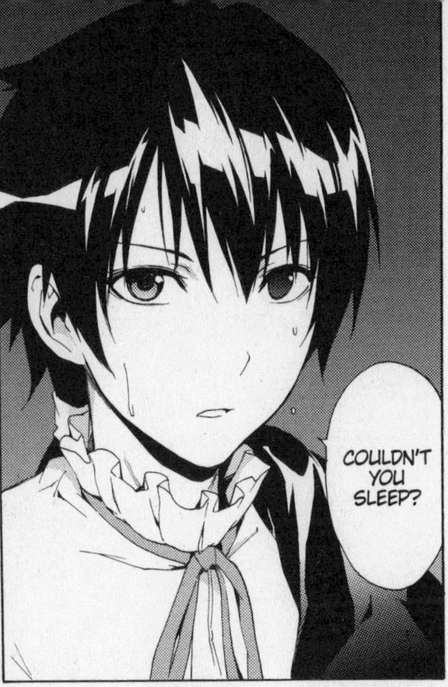
COULDN'T YOU SLEEP?
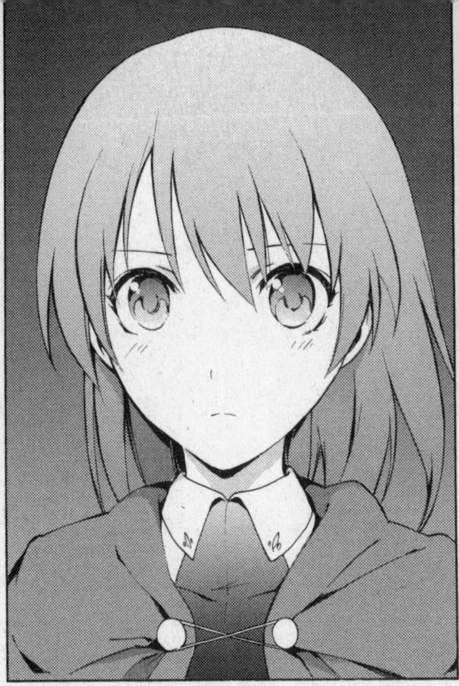

Chapter 25 Patriot & Queen (Part 2)

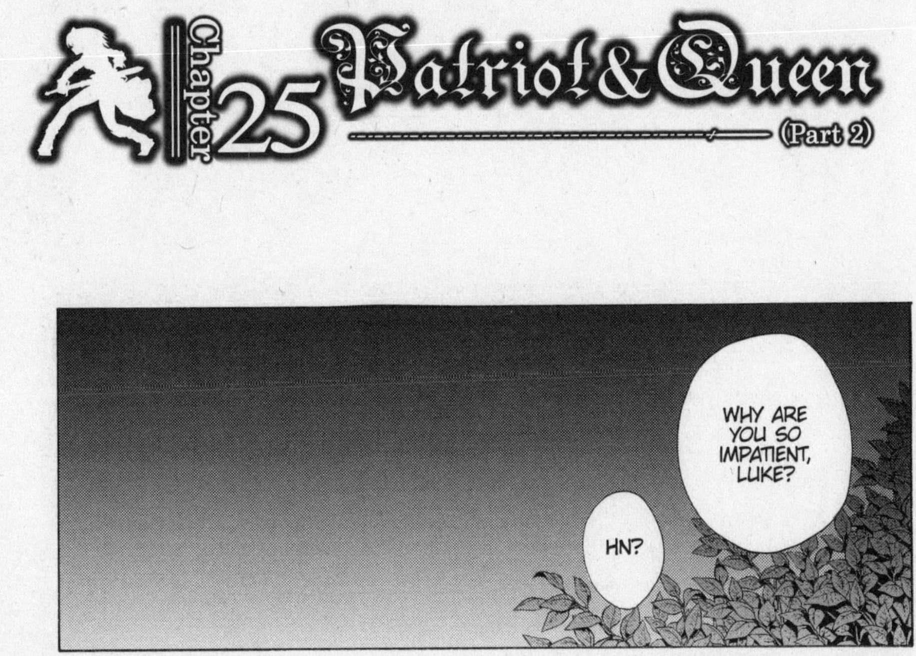
WHY ARE YOU SO IMPATIENT, LUKE?
HN?

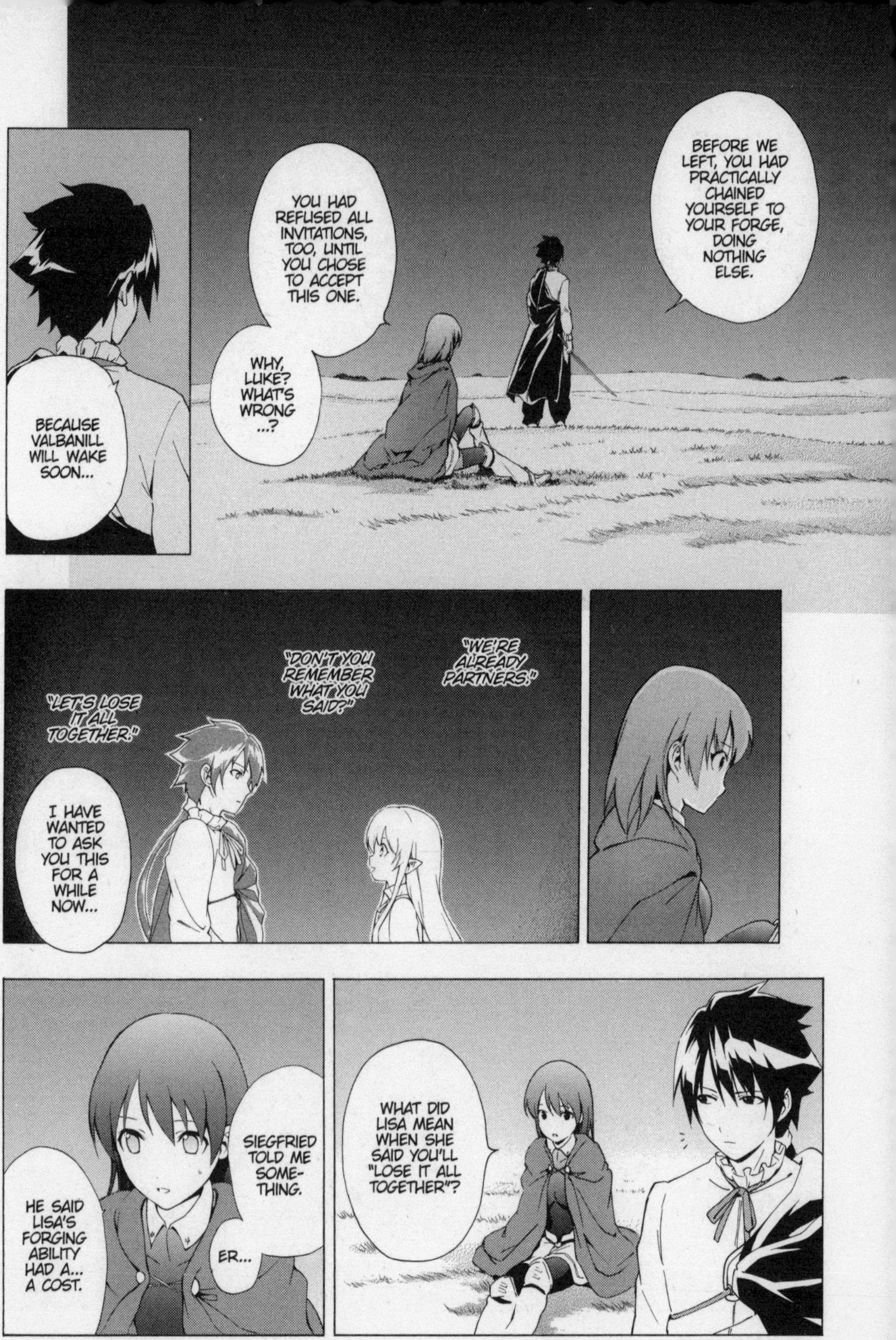

BEFORE WE LEFT, YOU HAD PRACTICALLY CHAINED YOURSELF TO YOUR FORGE, DOING NOTHING ELSE.
YOU HAD REFUSED ALL INVITATIONS, TOO, UNTIL YOU CHOSE TO ACCEPT THIS ONE.
WHY, LUKE? WHAT'S WRONG ...?
BECAUSE VALBANILL WILL WAKE SOON...
"WE'RE ALREADY PARTNERS."
"DON'T YOU REMEMBER WHAT YOU SAID?"
"LET'S LOSE IT ALL TOGETHER."
I HAVE WANTED TO ASK YOU THIS FOR A WHILE NOW...
WHAT DID LISA MEAN WHEN SHE SAID YOU'LL "LOSE IT ALL TOGETHER"?
SIEGFRIED TOLD ME SOME-THING.
ER...
HE SAID LISA'S FORGING ABILITY HAD A... A COST.

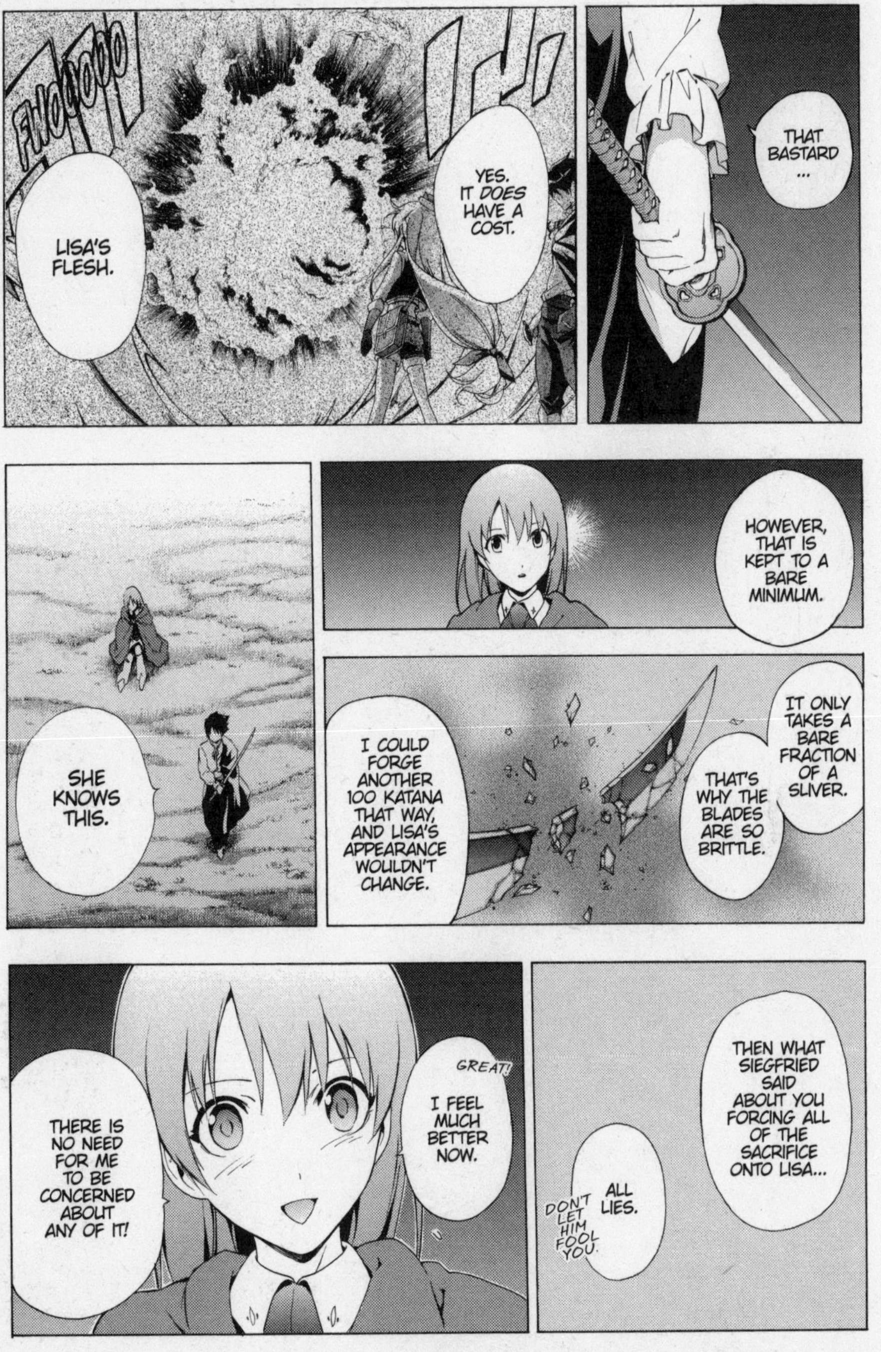
THAT BASTARD ...
YES. IT *DOES* HAVE A COST.
FWOOOOO
LISA'S FLESH.
HOWEVER, THAT IS KEPT TO A BARE MINIMUM.
IT ONLY TAKES A BARE FRACTION OF A SLIVER.
THAT'S WHY THE BLADES ARE SO BRITTLE.
I COULD FORGE ANOTHER 100 KATANA THAT WAY, AND LISA'S APPEARANCE WOULDN'T CHANGE.
SHE KNOWS THIS.
THEN WHAT SIEGFRIED SAID ABOUT YOU FORCING ALL OF THE SACRIFICE ONTO LISA...
ALL LIES.
DON'T LET HIM FOOL YOU.
GREAT!
I FEEL MUCH BETTER NOW.
THERE IS NO NEED FOR ME TO BE CONCERNED ABOUT ANY OF IT!

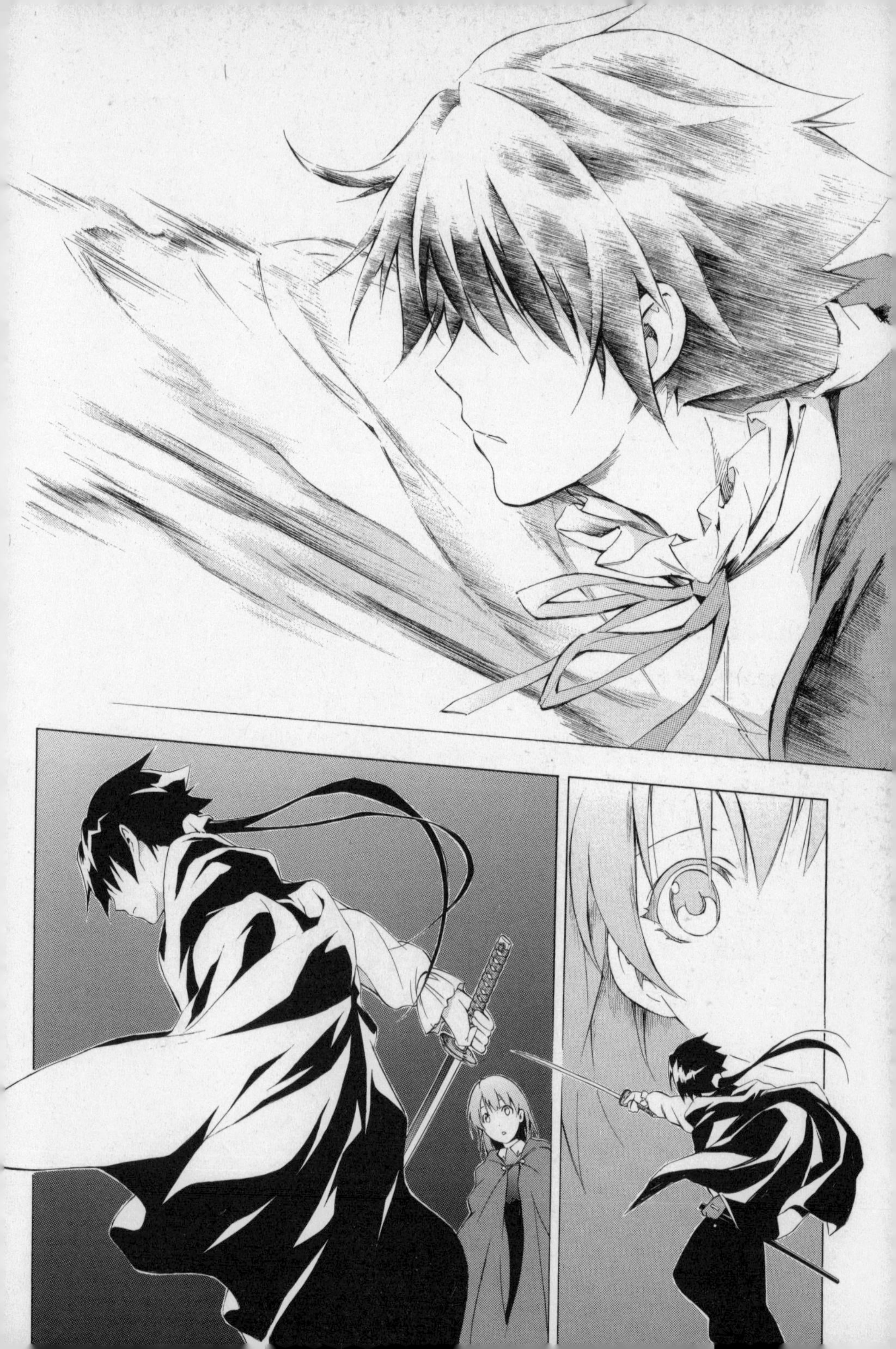

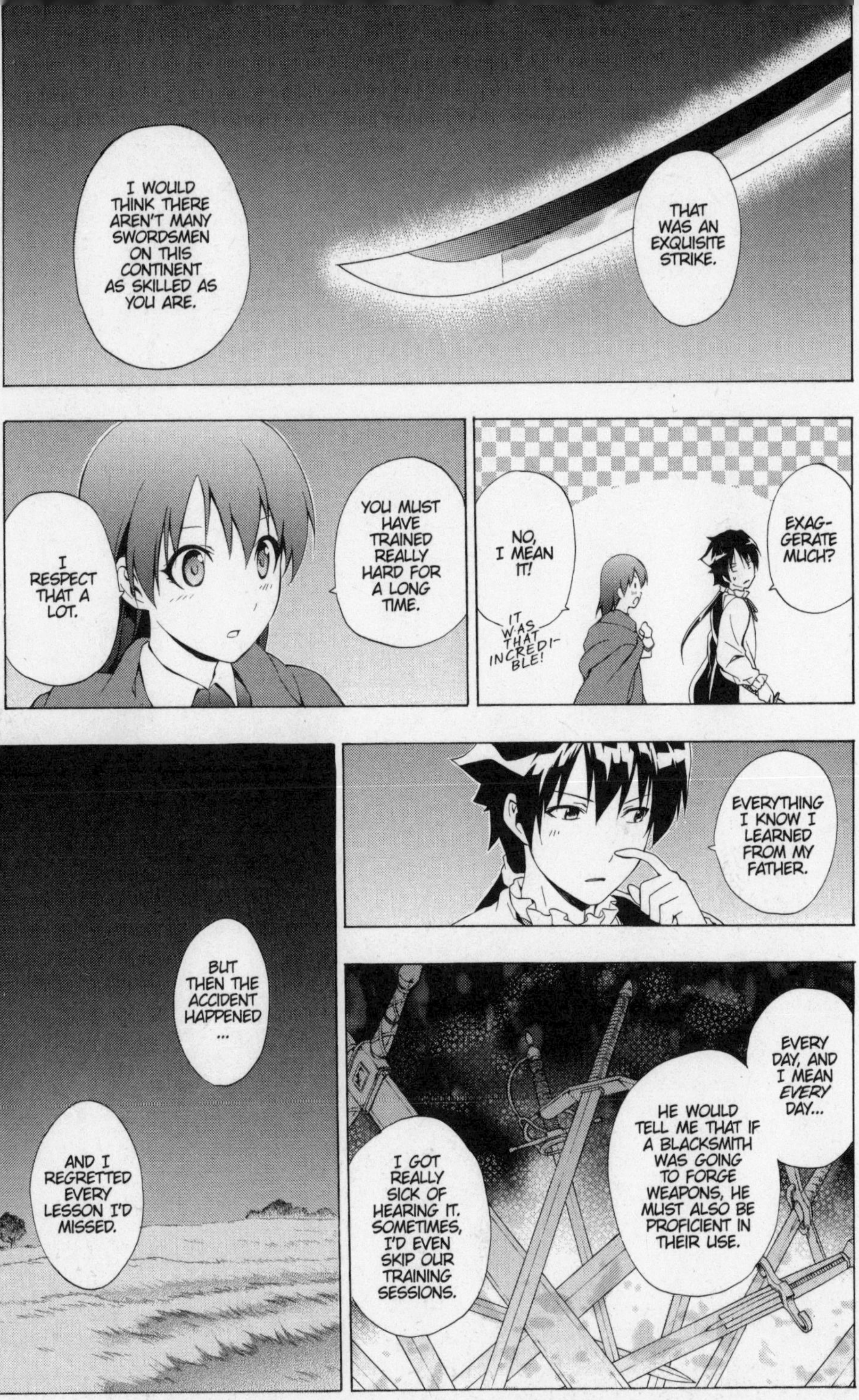
THAT WAS AN EXQUISITE STRIKE.
I WOULD THINK THERE AREN'T MANY SWORDSMEN ON THIS CONTINENT AS SKILLED AS YOU ARE.
EXAGGERATE MUCH?
NO, I MEAN IT!
IT WAS THAT INCREDIBLE!
YOU MUST HAVE TRAINED REALLY HARD FOR A LONG TIME.
I RESPECT THAT A LOT.
EVERYTHING I KNOW I LEARNED FROM MY FATHER.
EVERY DAY, AND I MEAN *EVERY* DAY...
HE WOULD TELL ME THAT IF A BLACKSMITH WAS GOING TO FORGE WEAPONS, HE MUST ALSO BE PROFICIENT IN THEIR USE.
I GOT REALLY SICK OF HEARING IT. SOMETIMES, I'D EVEN SKIP OUR TRAINING SESSIONS.
BUT THEN THE ACCIDENT HAPPENED...
AND I REGRETTED EVERY LESSON I'D MISSED.

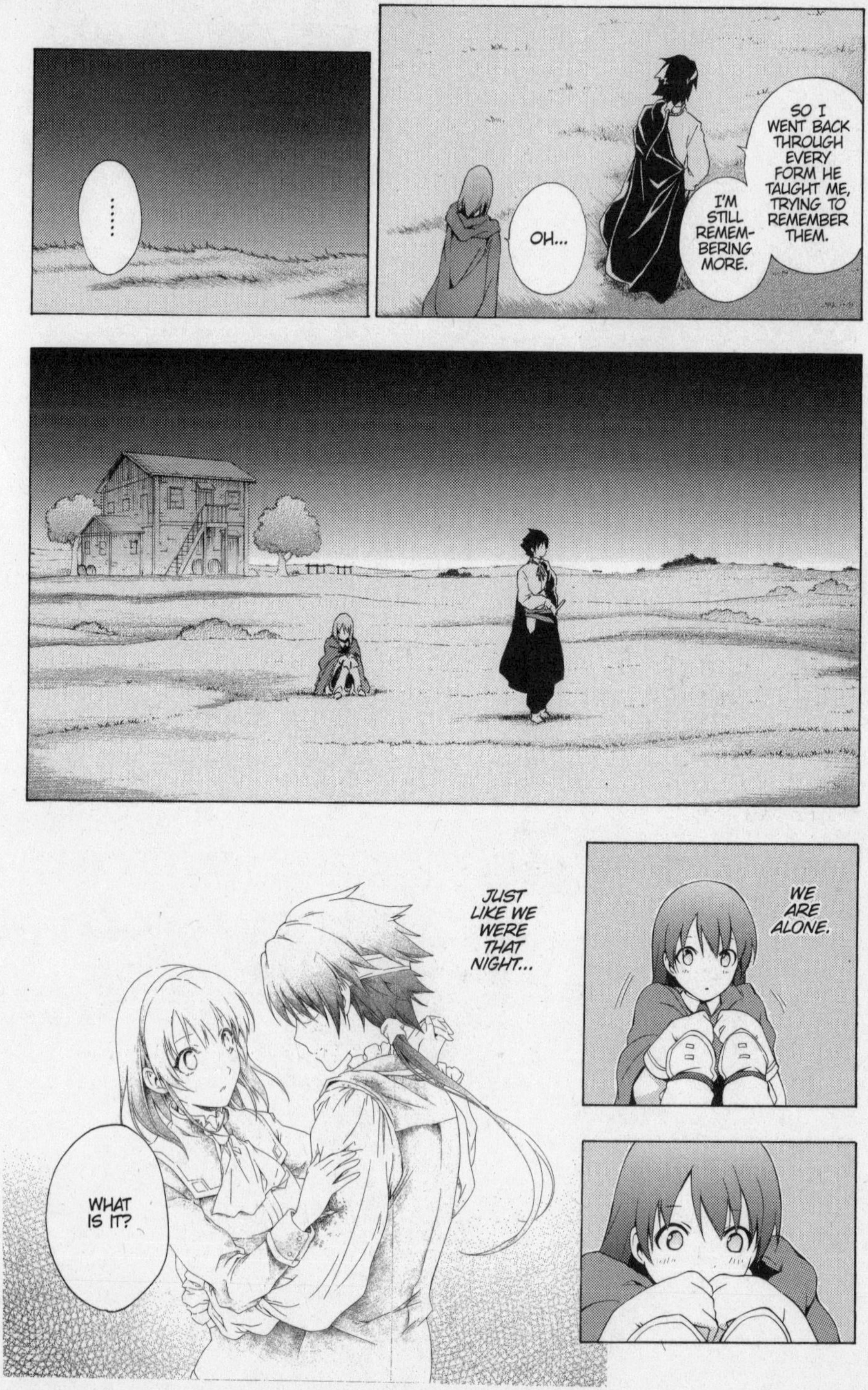
SO I WENT BACK THROUGH EVERY FORM HE TAUGHT ME, TRYING TO REMEMBER THEM.
I'M STILL REMEMBERING MORE.
OH...
......
WE ARE ALONE.
JUST LIKE WE WERE THAT NIGHT...
WHAT IS IT?

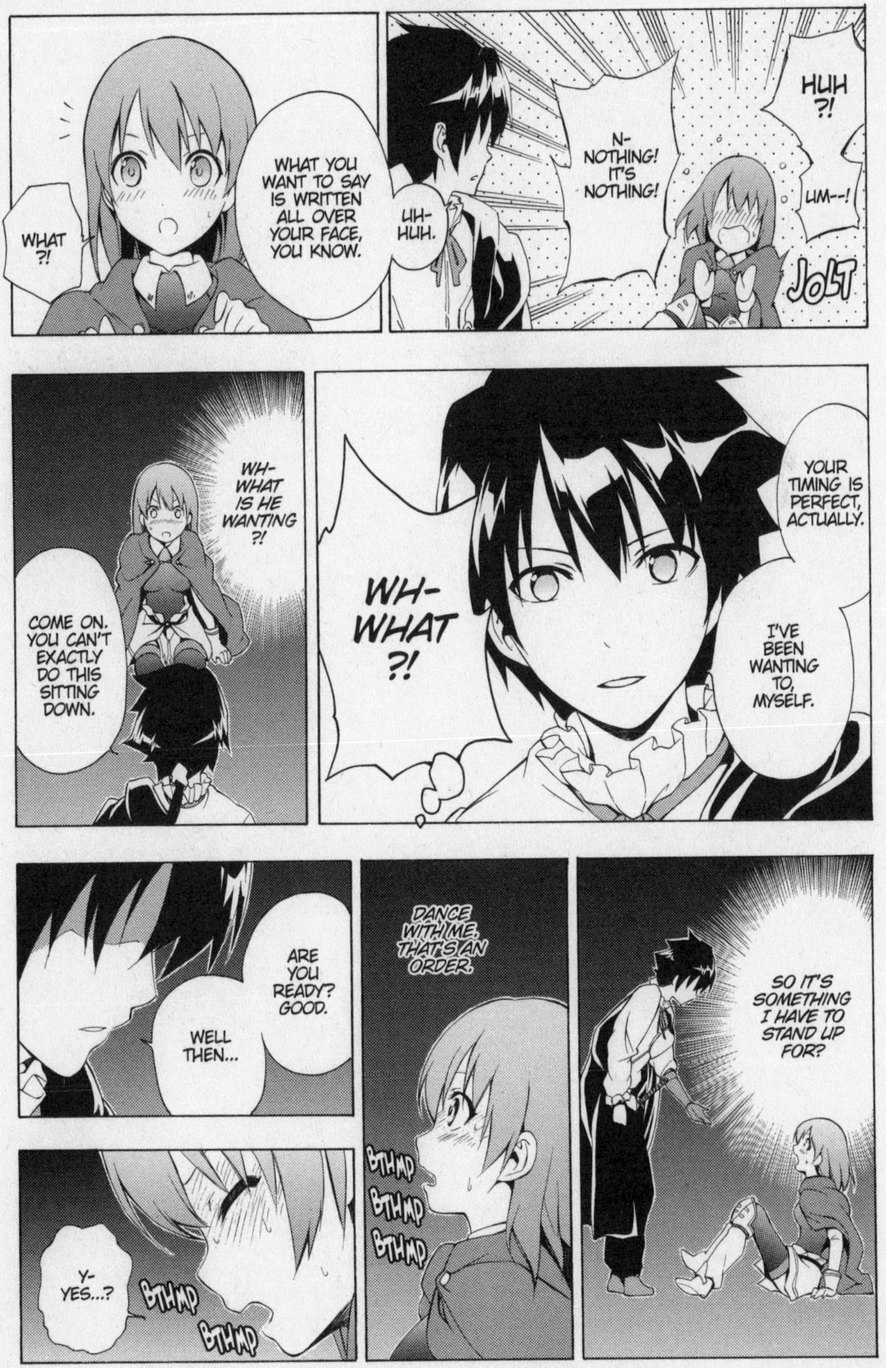
HUH ?!
UM--!
N-NOTHING! IT'S NOTHING!
JOLT
UH-HUH.
WHAT YOU WANT TO SAY IS WRITTEN ALL OVER YOUR FACE, YOU KNOW.
WHAT ?!
YOUR TIMING IS PERFECT, ACTUALLY.
I'VE BEEN WANTING TO, MYSELF.
WH-WHAT ?!
WH-WHAT IS HE WANTING ?!
COME ON. YOU CAN'T EXACTLY DO THIS SITTING DOWN.
SO IT'S SOMETHING I HAVE TO STAND UP FOR?
DANCE WITH ME. THAT'S AN ORDER.
BTHMP
BTHMP
BTHMP
ARE YOU READY? GOOD.
WELL THEN...
BTHMP
BTHMP
Y-YES...?

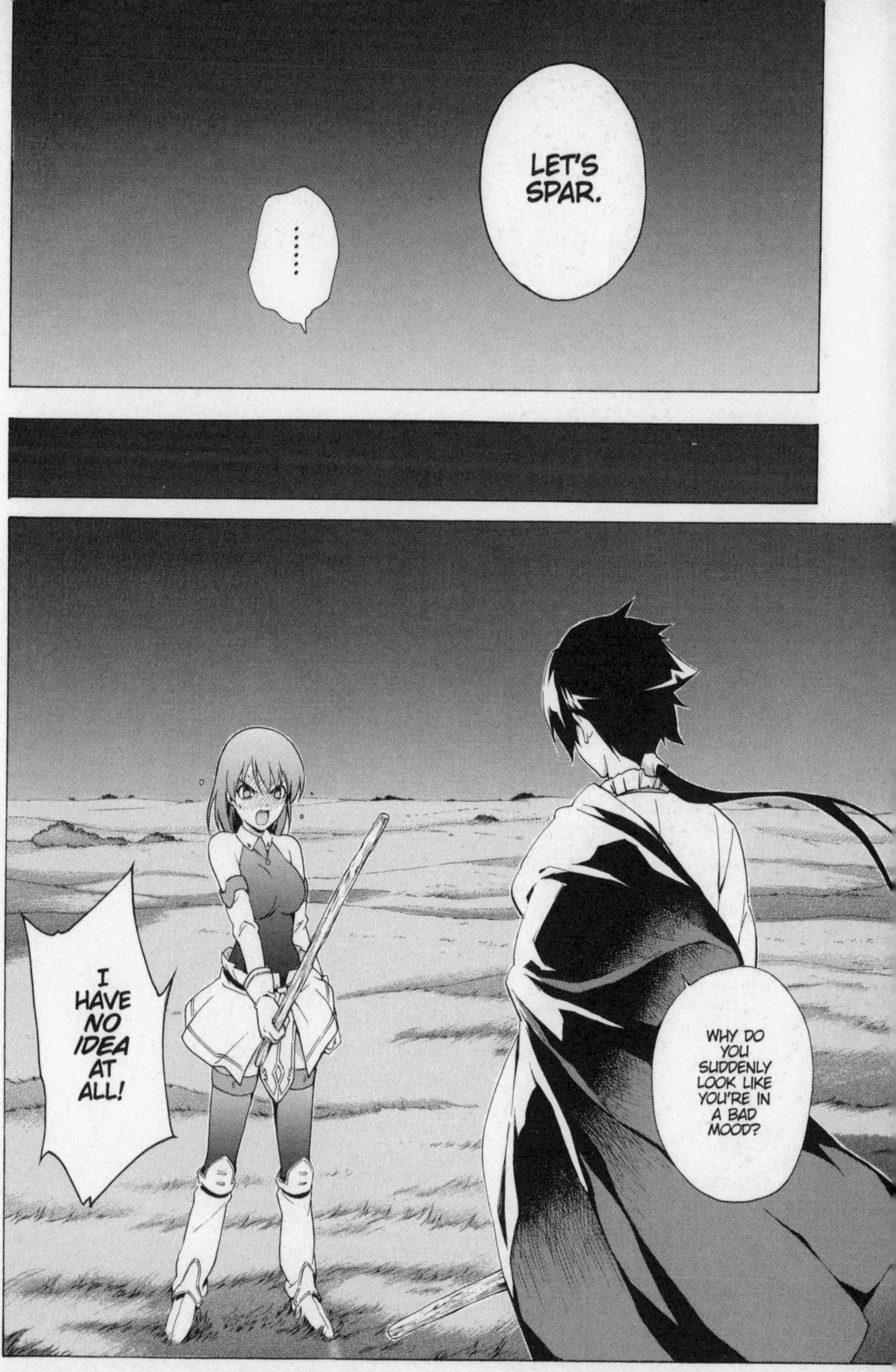
LET'S SPAR.
......
WHY DO YOU SUDDENLY LOOK LIKE YOU'RE IN A BAD MOOD?
I HAVE NO IDEA AT ALL!

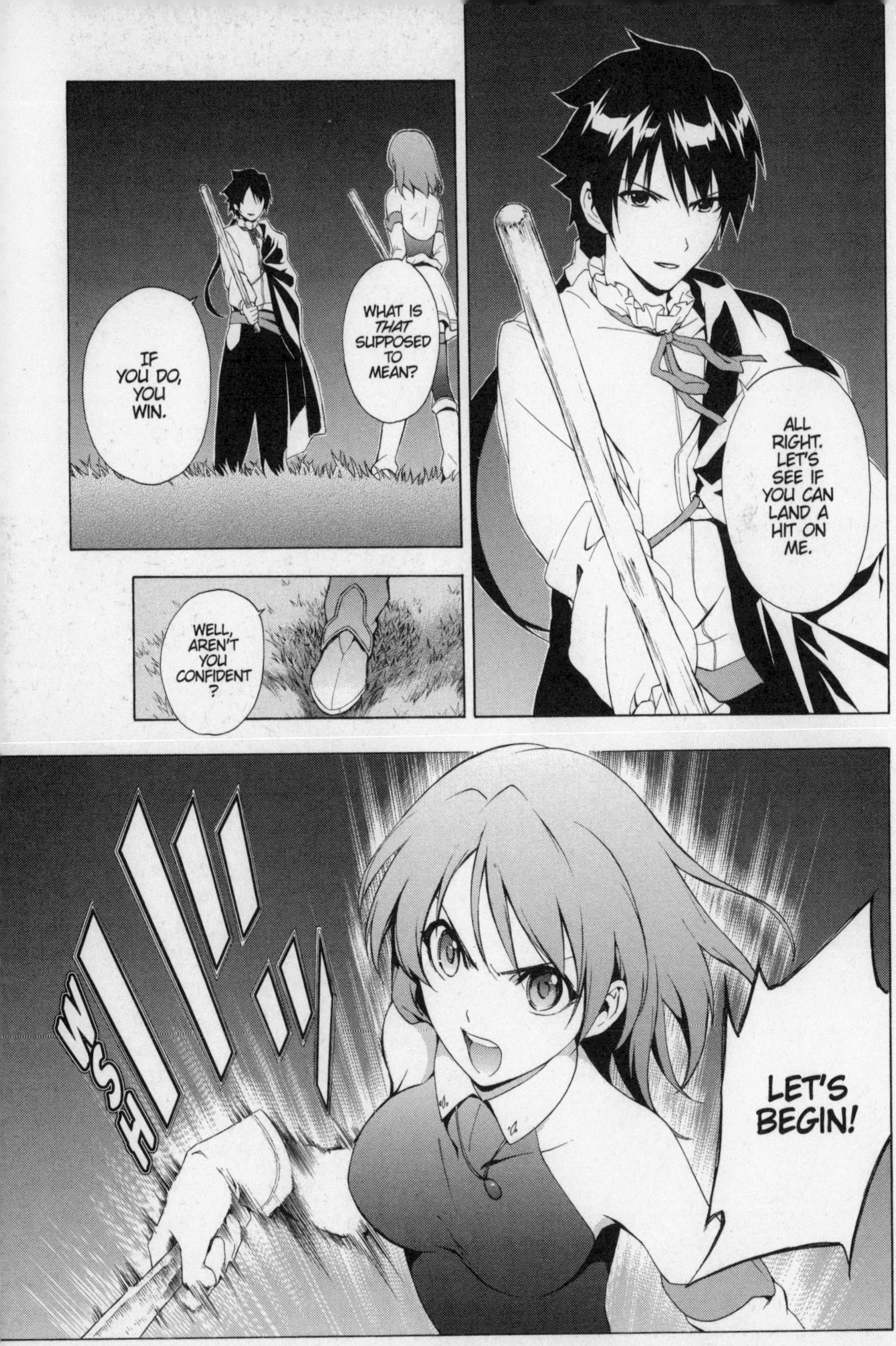
ALL RIGHT. LET'S SEE IF YOU CAN LAND A HIT ON ME.
WHAT IS *THAT* SUPPOSED TO MEAN?
IF YOU DO, YOU WIN.
WELL, AREN'T YOU CONFIDENT?
LET'S BEGIN!
WSH

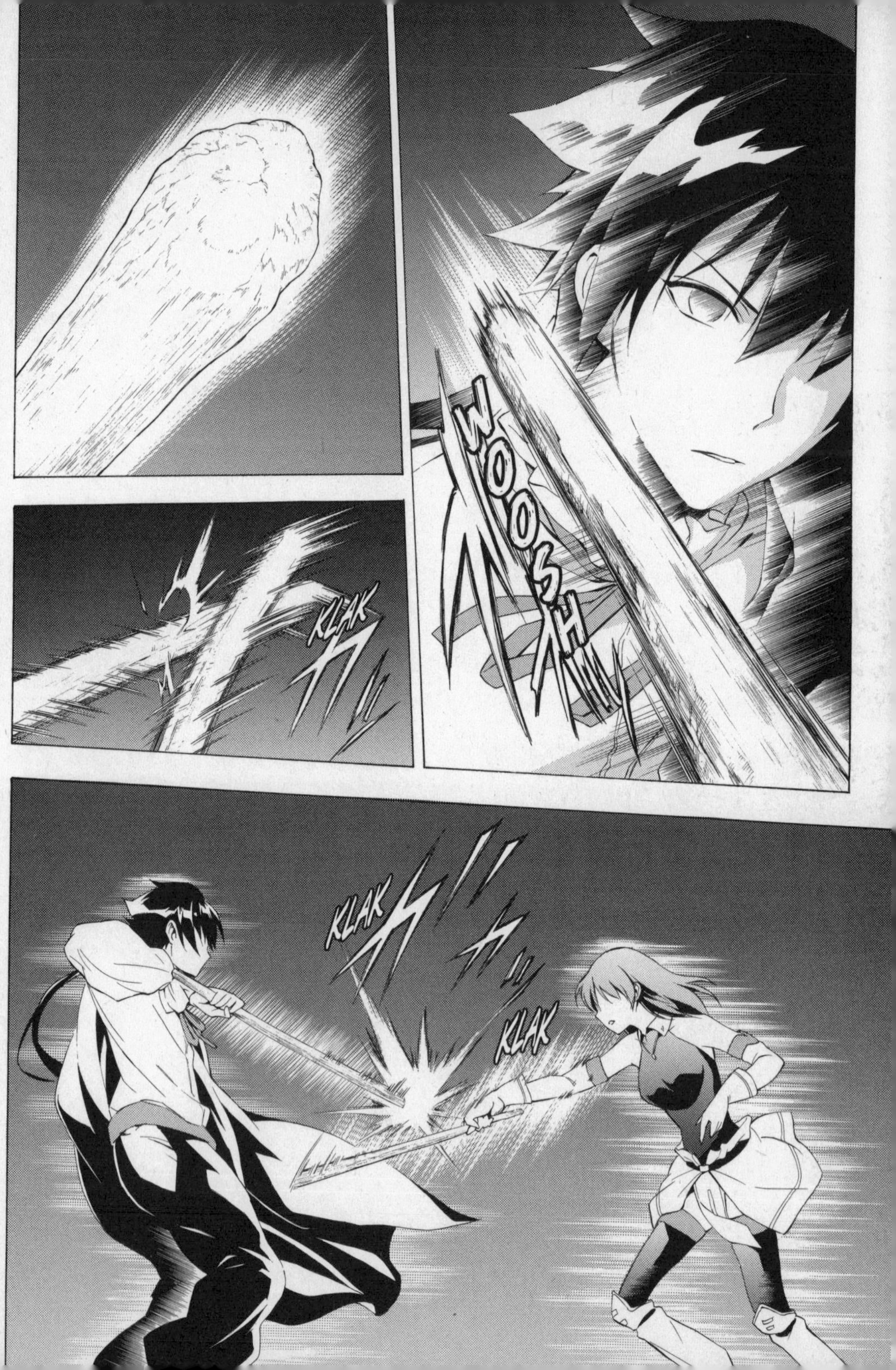
WOOSH
KLAK
KLAK
KLAK

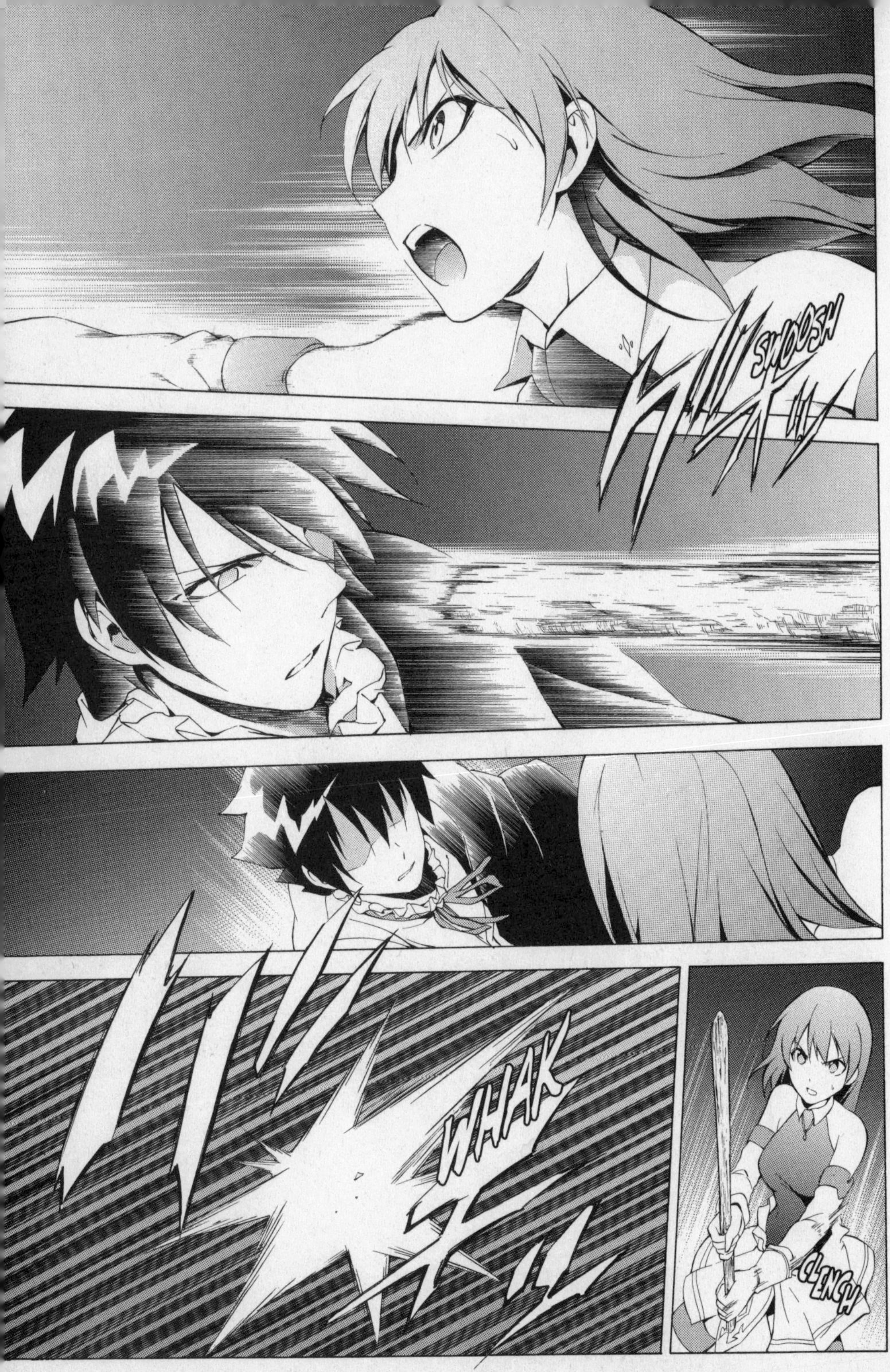
SWOOSH
WHAK
CLENCH

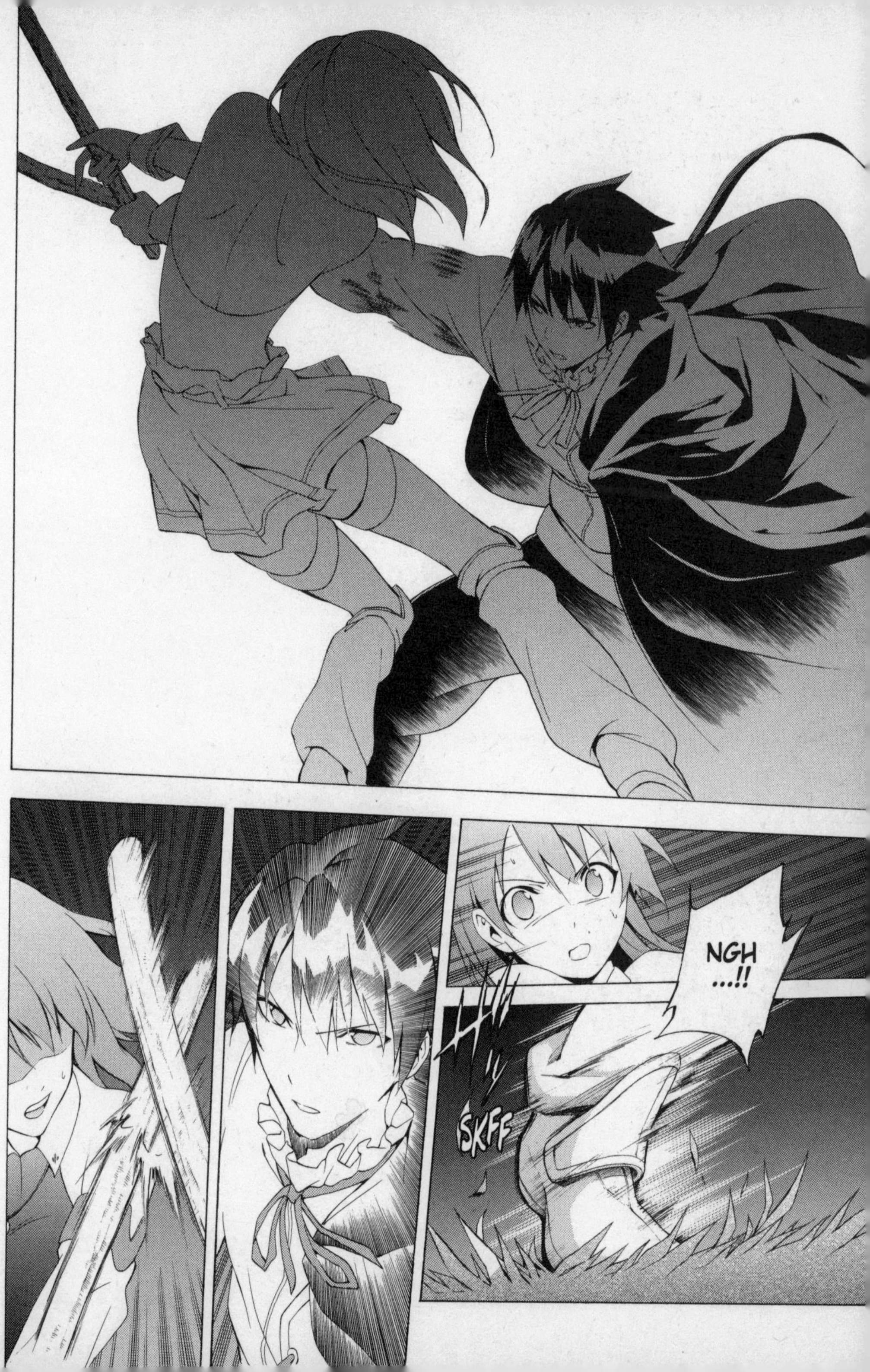
NGH ...!!
SKFF

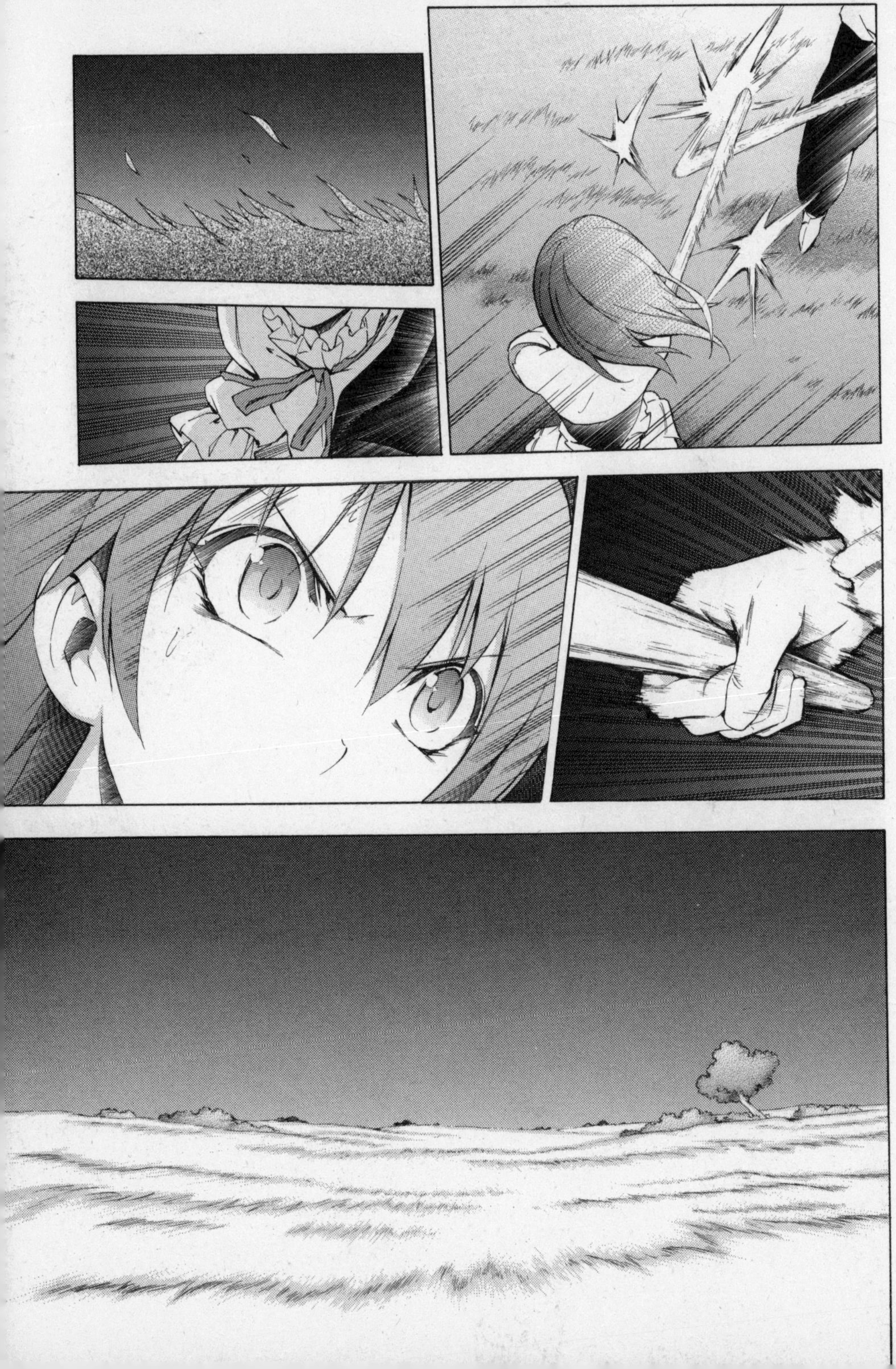

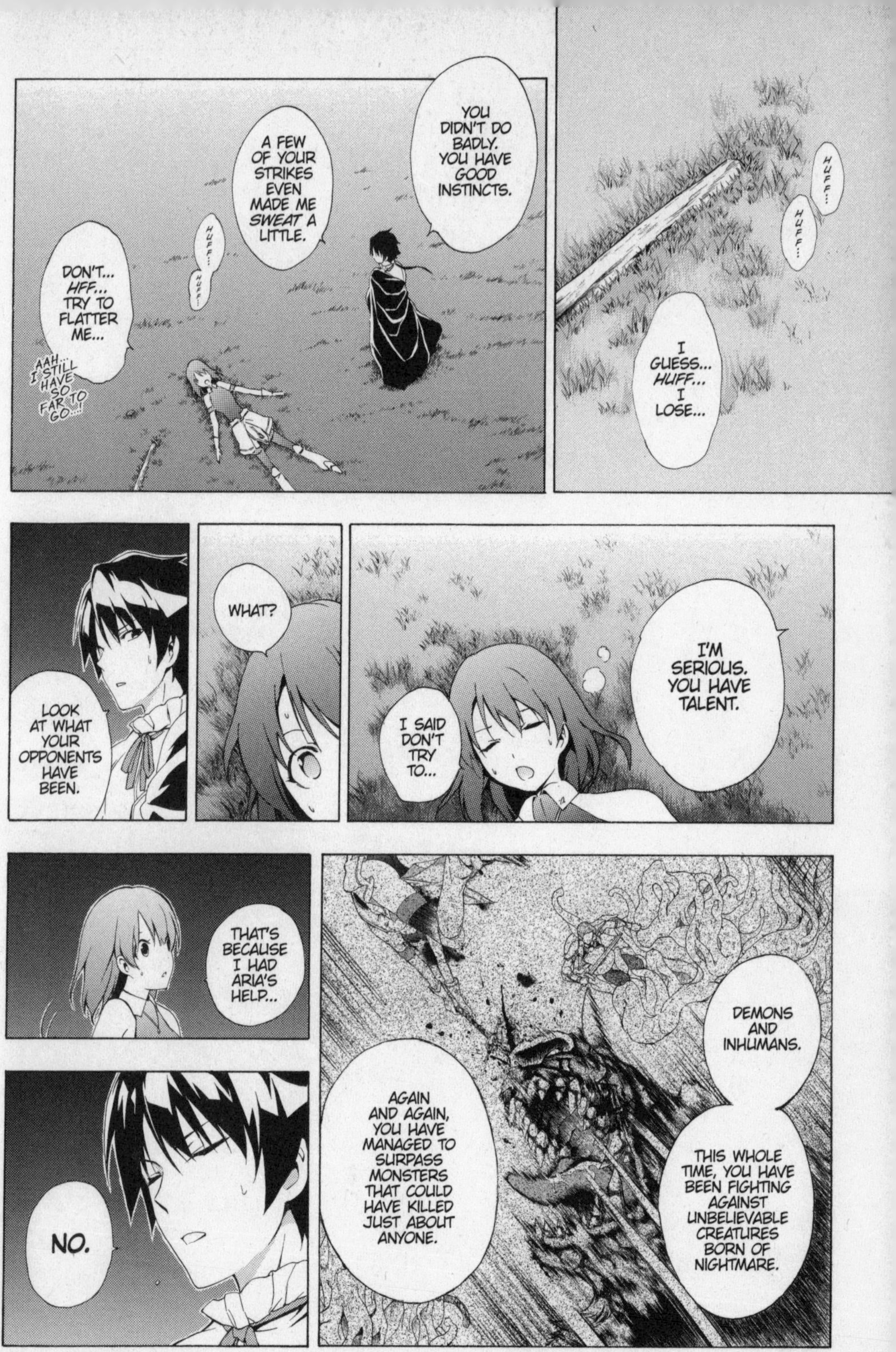
HUFF...
HUFF...
I GUESS... HUFF... I LOSE...
YOU DIDN'T DO BADLY. YOU HAVE GOOD INSTINCTS.
A FEW OF YOUR STRIKES EVEN MADE ME SWEAT A LITTLE.
HUFF...
HUFF...
DON'T... HFF... TRY TO FLATTER ME...
AAH... I STILL HAVE SO FAR TO GO...!
I'M SERIOUS. YOU HAVE TALENT.
I SAID DON'T TRY TO...
WHAT?
LOOK AT WHAT YOUR OPPONENTS HAVE BEEN.
DEMONS AND INHUMANS.
THIS WHOLE TIME, YOU HAVE BEEN FIGHTING AGAINST UNBELIEVABLE CREATURES BORN OF NIGHTMARE.
AGAIN AND AGAIN, YOU HAVE MANAGED TO SURPASS MONSTERS THAT COULD HAVE KILLED JUST ABOUT ANYONE.
THAT'S BECAUSE I HAD ARIA'S HELP...
NO.

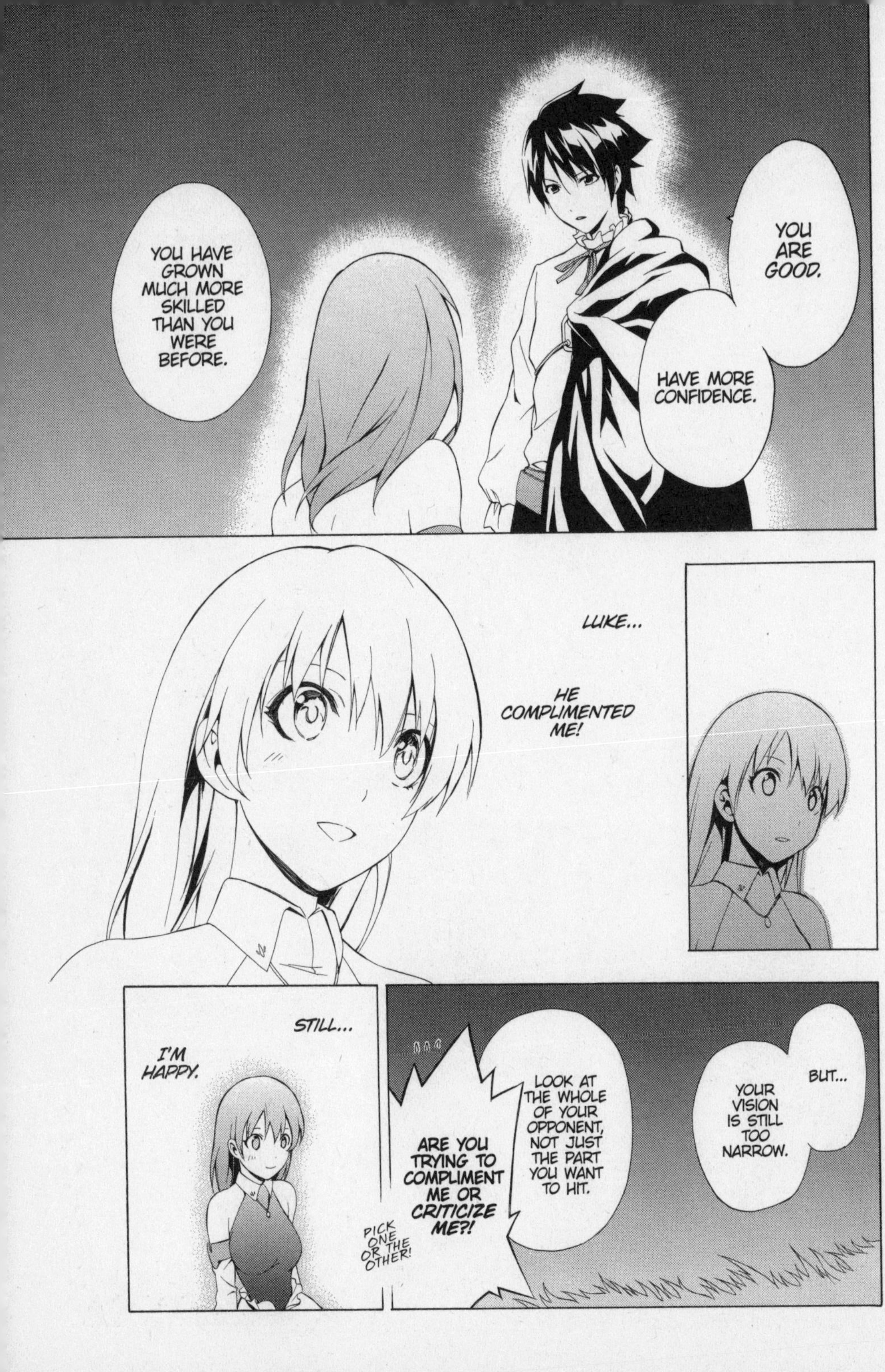
YOU ARE GOOD.
HAVE MORE CONFIDENCE.
YOU HAVE GROWN MUCH MORE SKILLED THAN YOU WERE BEFORE.
LUKE...
HE COMPLIMENTED ME!
BUT...
YOUR VISION IS STILL TOO NARROW.
LOOK AT THE WHOLE OF YOUR OPPONENT, NOT JUST THE PART YOU WANT TO HIT.
ARE YOU TRYING TO COMPLIMENT ME OR CRITICIZE ME?!
PICK ONE OR THE OTHER!
STILL...
I'M HAPPY.

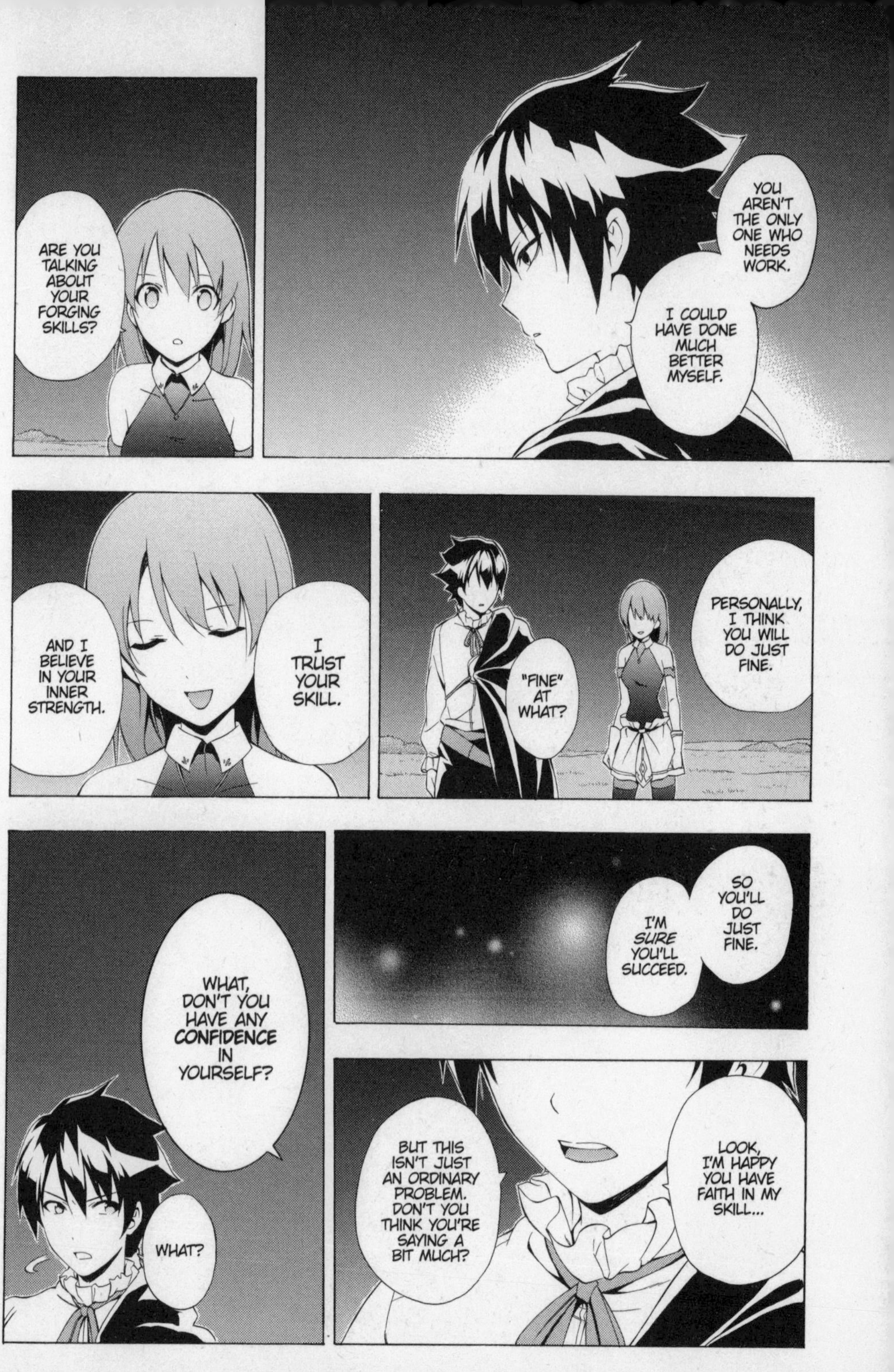
YOU AREN'T THE ONLY ONE WHO NEEDS WORK.
I COULD HAVE DONE MUCH BETTER MYSELF.
ARE YOU TALKING ABOUT YOUR FORGING SKILLS?
PERSONALLY, I THINK YOU WILL DO JUST FINE.
"FINE" AT WHAT?
I TRUST YOUR SKILL.
AND I BELIEVE IN YOUR INNER STRENGTH.
SO YOU'LL DO JUST FINE.
I'M SURE YOU'LL SUCCEED.
LOOK, I'M HAPPY YOU HAVE FAITH IN MY SKILL...
BUT THIS ISN'T JUST AN ORDINARY PROBLEM. DON'T YOU THINK YOU'RE SAYING A BIT MUCH?
WHAT, DON'T YOU HAVE ANY CONFIDENCE IN YOURSELF?
WHAT?

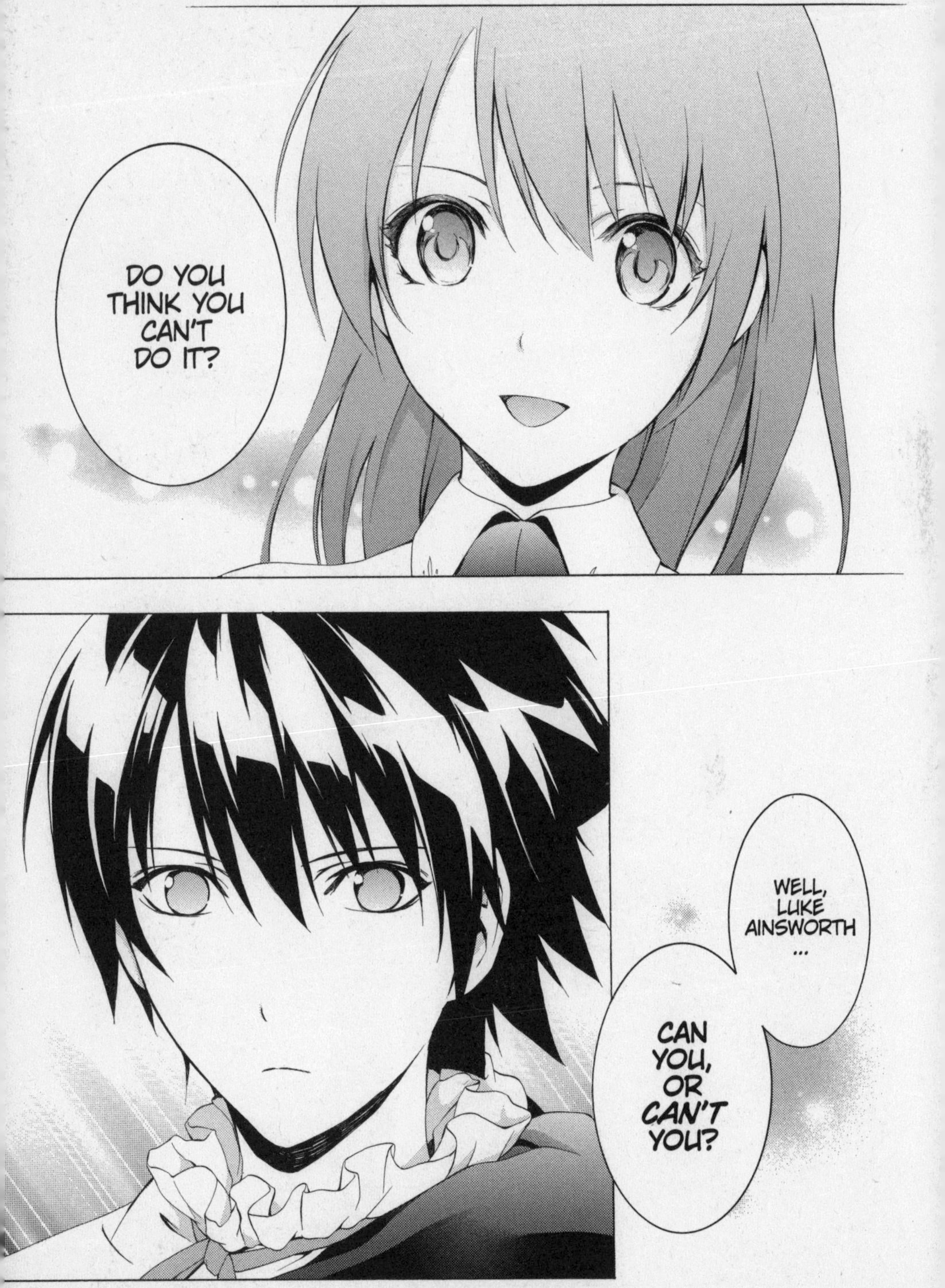
DO YOU THINK YOU CAN'T DO IT?
WELL, LUKE AINSWORTH ...
CAN YOU, OR CAN'T YOU?

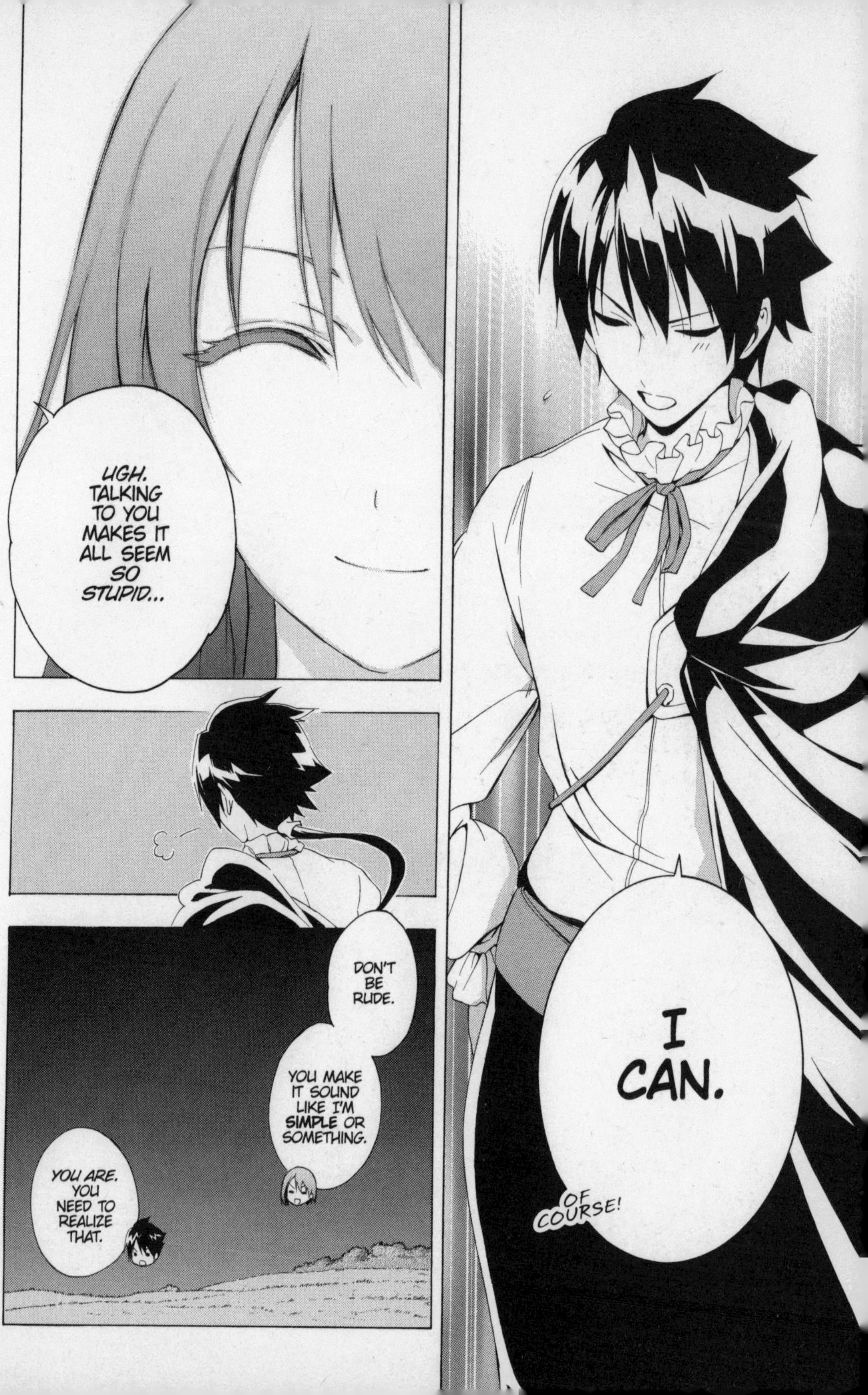

I CAN.
OF COURSE!
UGH. TALKING TO YOU MAKES IT ALL SEEM SO STUPID...
DON'T BE RUDE.
YOU MAKE IT SOUND LIKE I'M **SIMPLE** OR SOMETHING.
YOU ARE. YOU NEED TO REALIZE THAT.

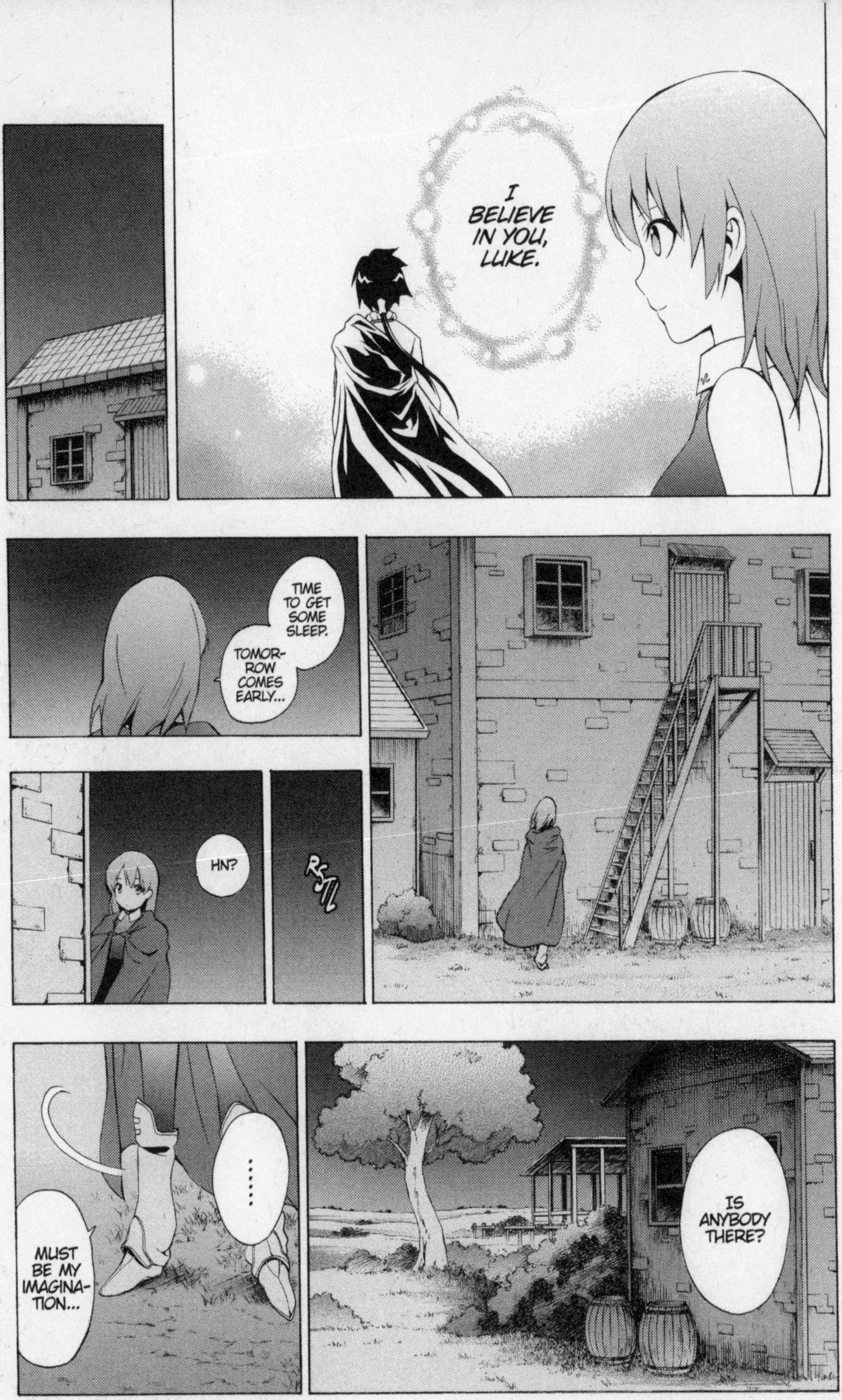
I BELIEVE IN YOU, LUKE.
TIME TO GET SOME SLEEP.
TOMOR-ROW COMES EARLY...
RSTL
HN?
IS ANYBODY THERE?
......
MUST BE MY IMAGINA-TION...

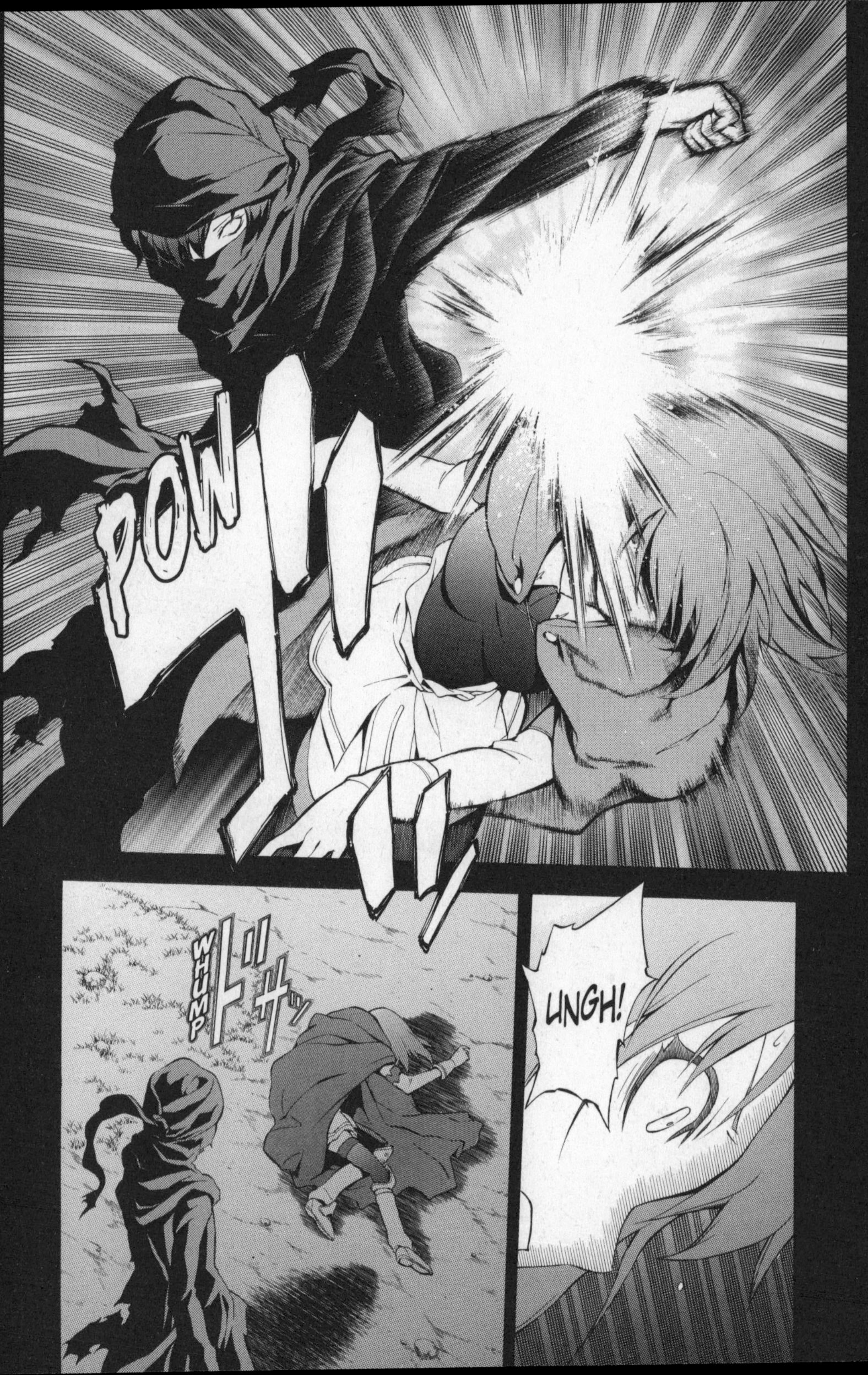
POW
UNGH!
WHUMP
ドザッ

Chapter 26 Patriot & Queen (Part 3)

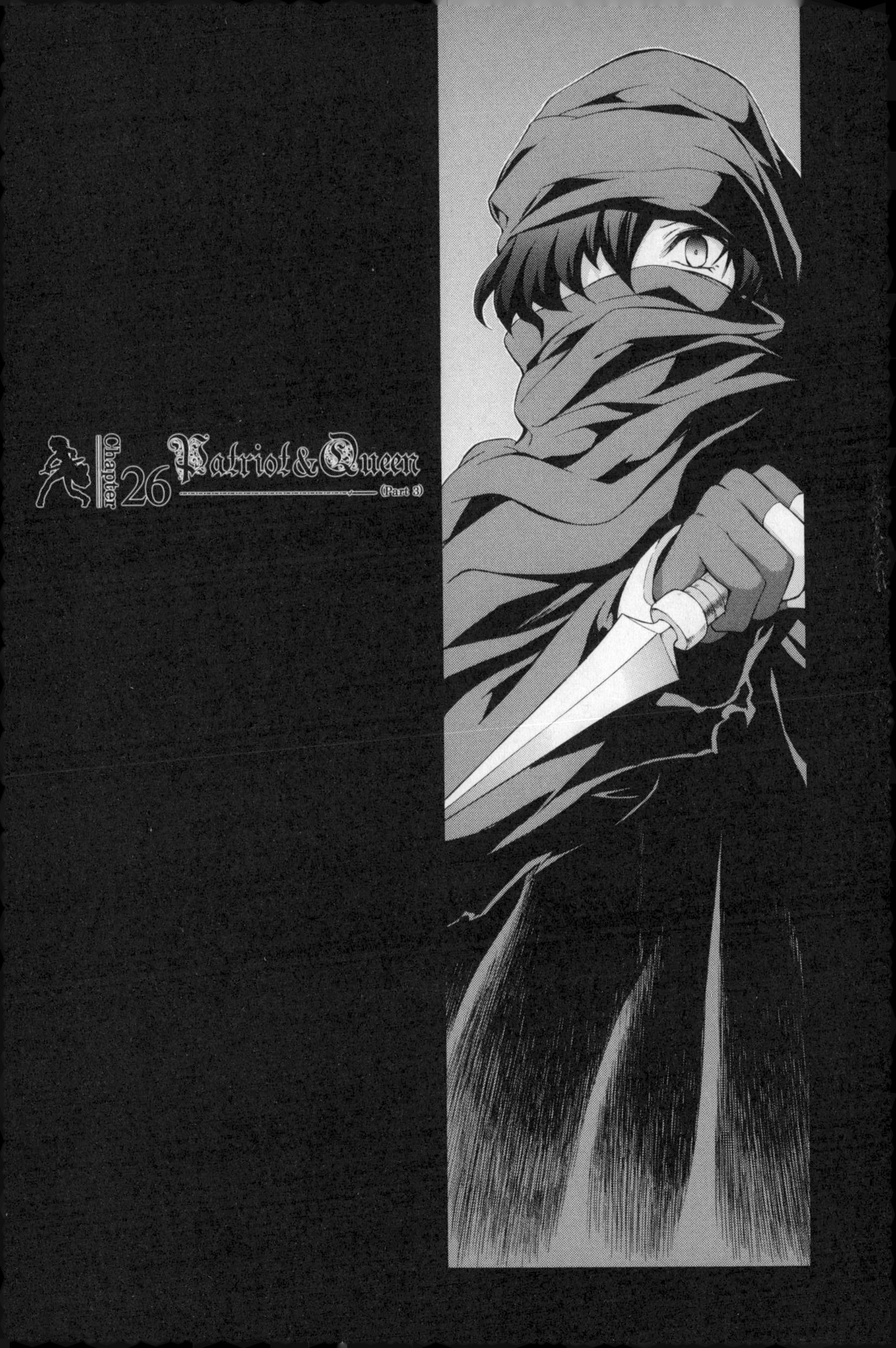

The Sacred Blacksmith

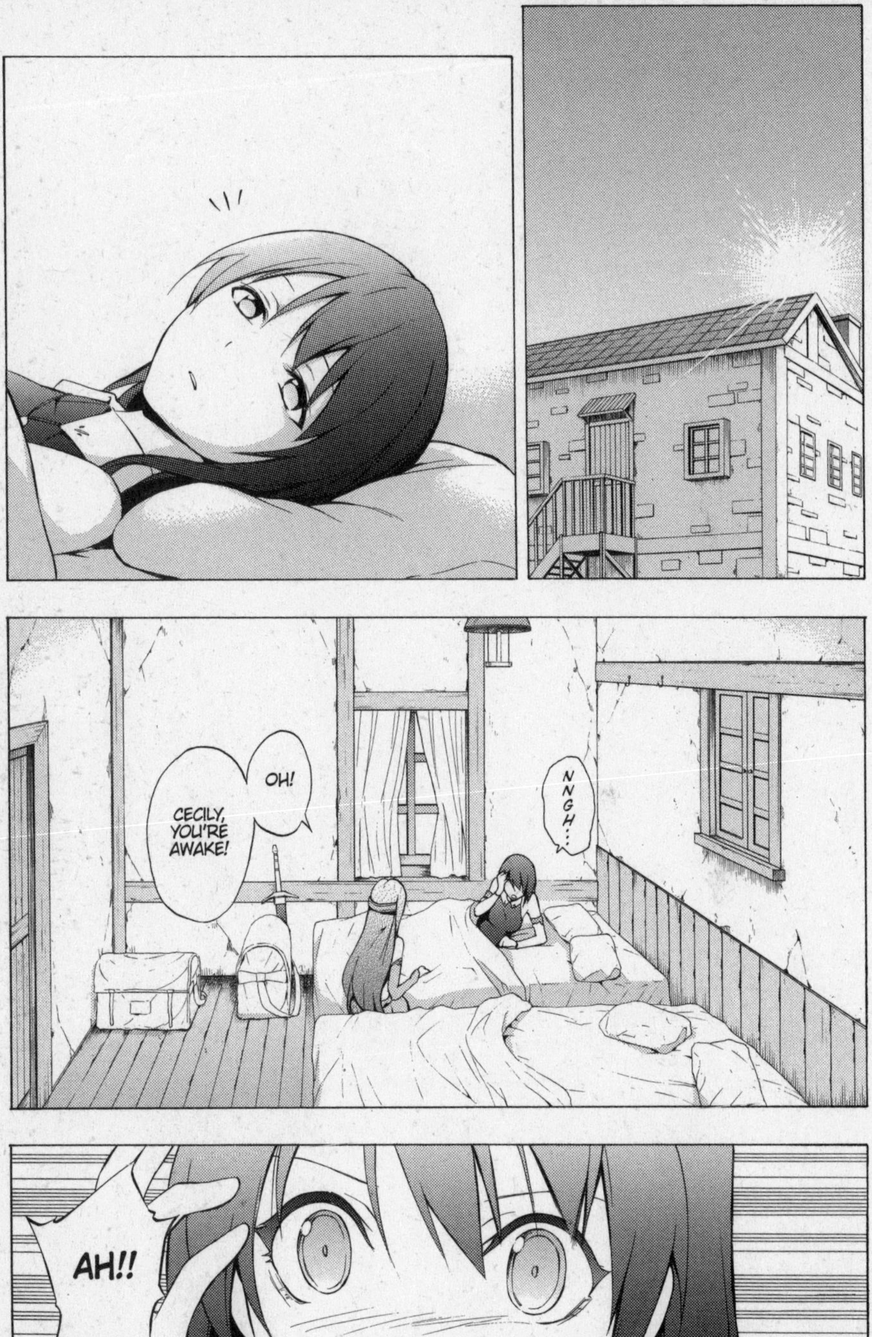
NNGH...
OH!
CECILY, YOU'RE AWAKE!
AH!!

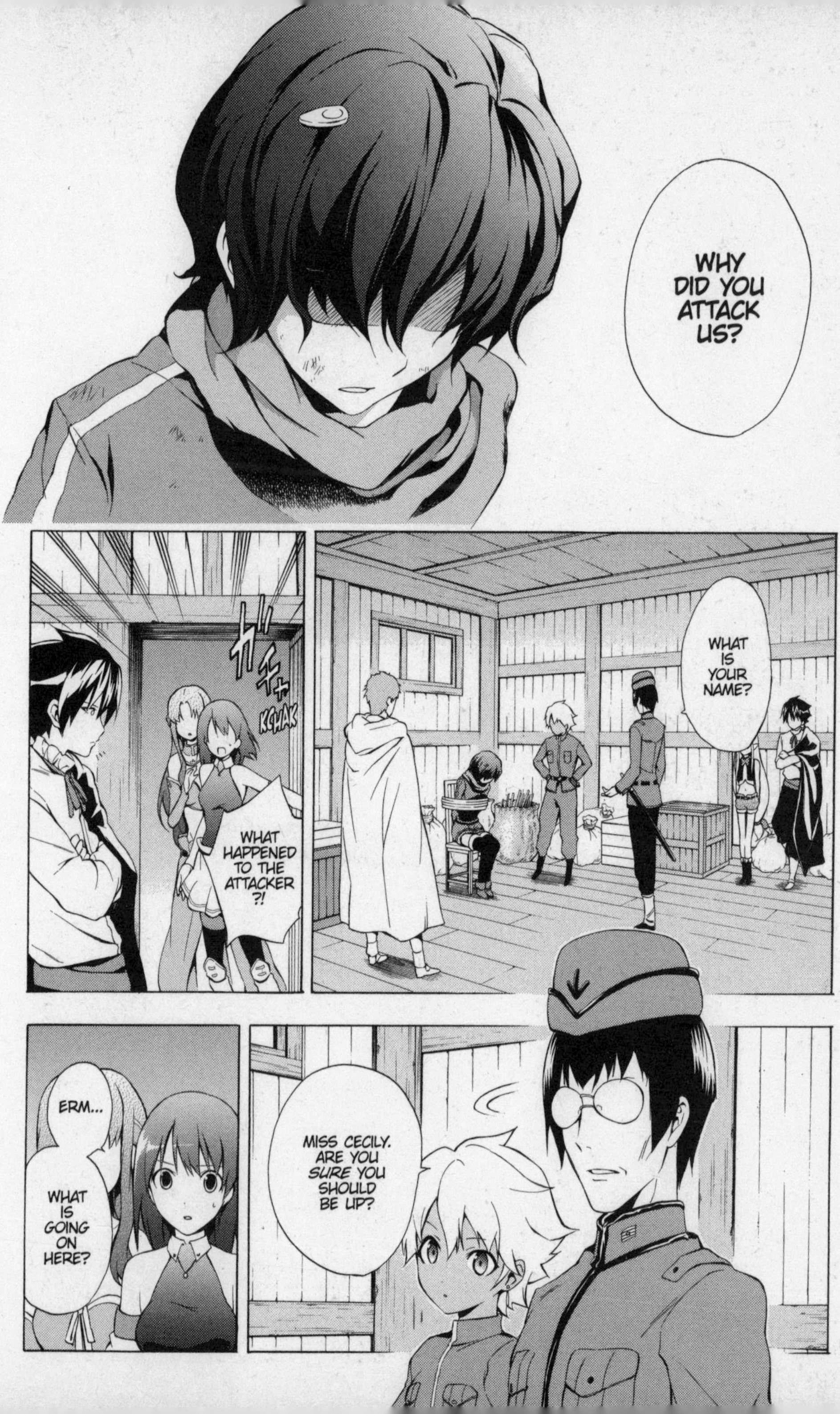
WHY DID YOU ATTACK US?
WHAT IS YOUR NAME?
ガチャ
KCHAK
WHAT HAPPENED TO THE ATTACKER?!
MISS CECILY. ARE YOU *SURE* YOU SHOULD BE UP?
ERM...
WHAT IS GOING ON HERE?

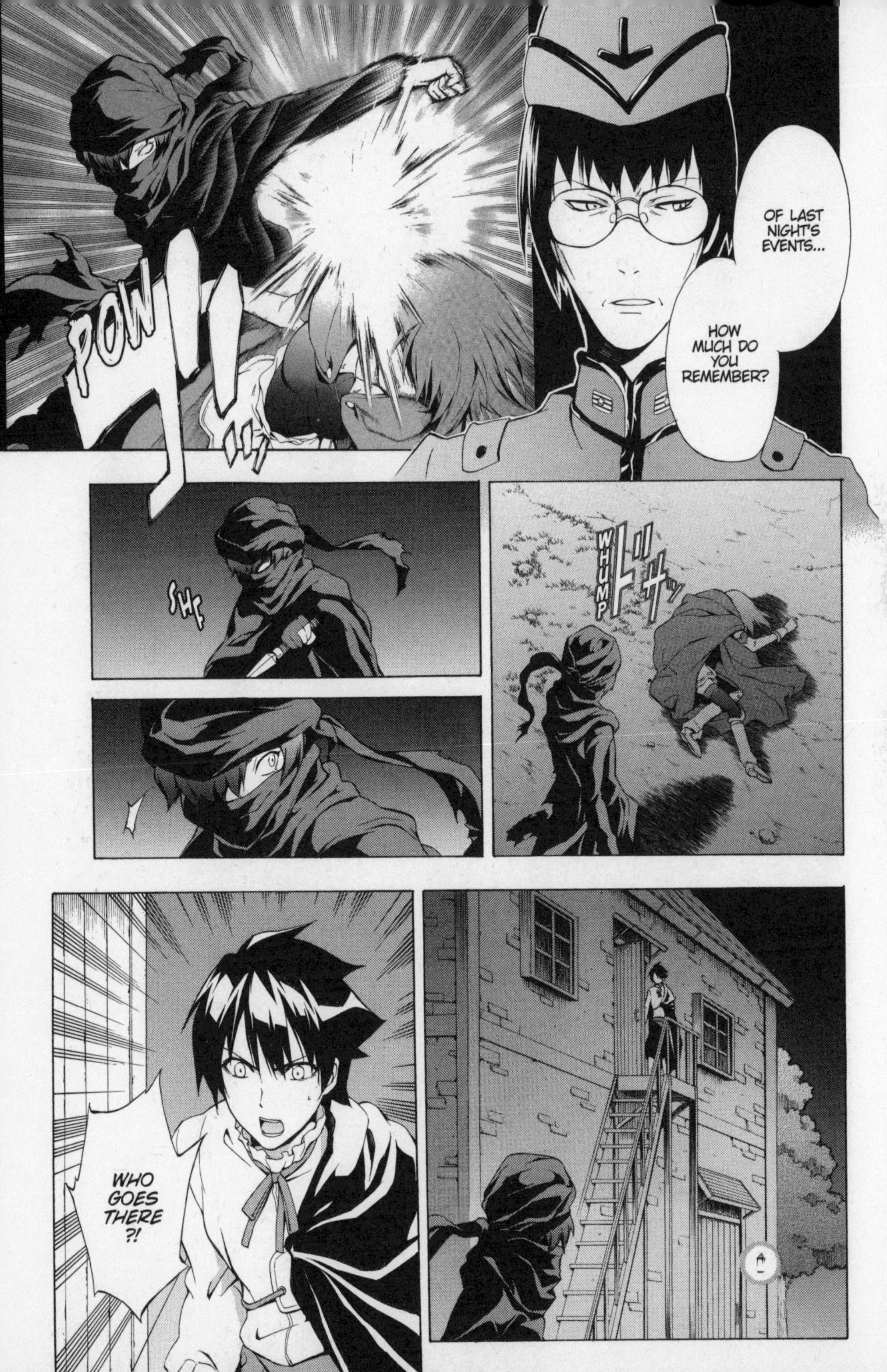
OF LAST NIGHT'S EVENTS...
HOW MUCH DO YOU REMEMBER?
POW
WHUMP
SHF
!
WHO GOES THERE ?!

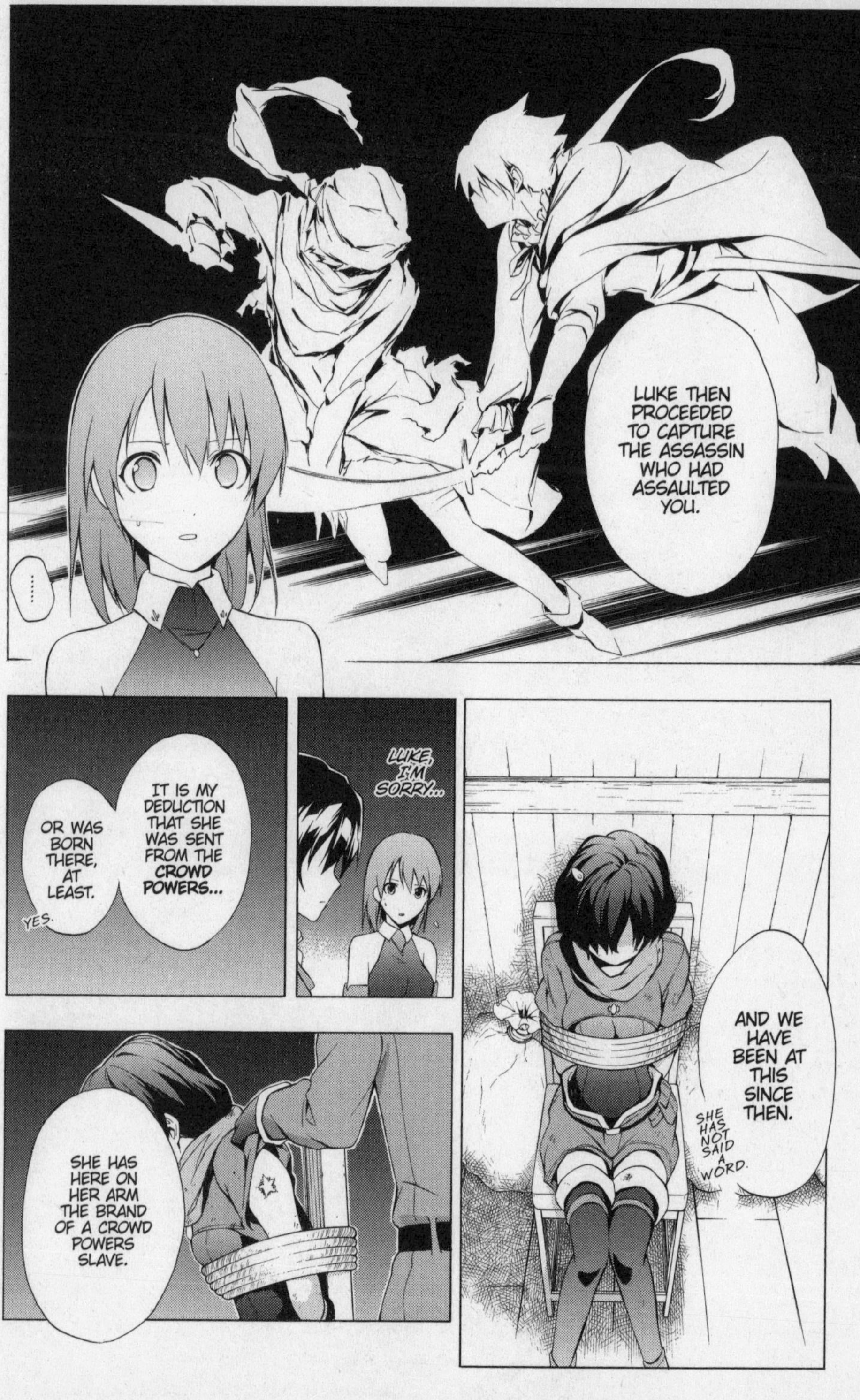
LUKE THEN PROCEEDED TO CAPTURE THE ASSASSIN WHO HAD ASSAULTED YOU.
......
AND WE HAVE BEEN AT THIS SINCE THEN.
SHE HAS NOT SAID A WORD.
LUKE, I'M SORRY...
IT IS MY DEDUCTION THAT SHE WAS SENT FROM THE CROWD POWERS...
OR WAS BORN THERE, AT LEAST.
YES.
SHE HAS HERE ON HER ARM THE BRAND OF A CROWD POWERS SLAVE.

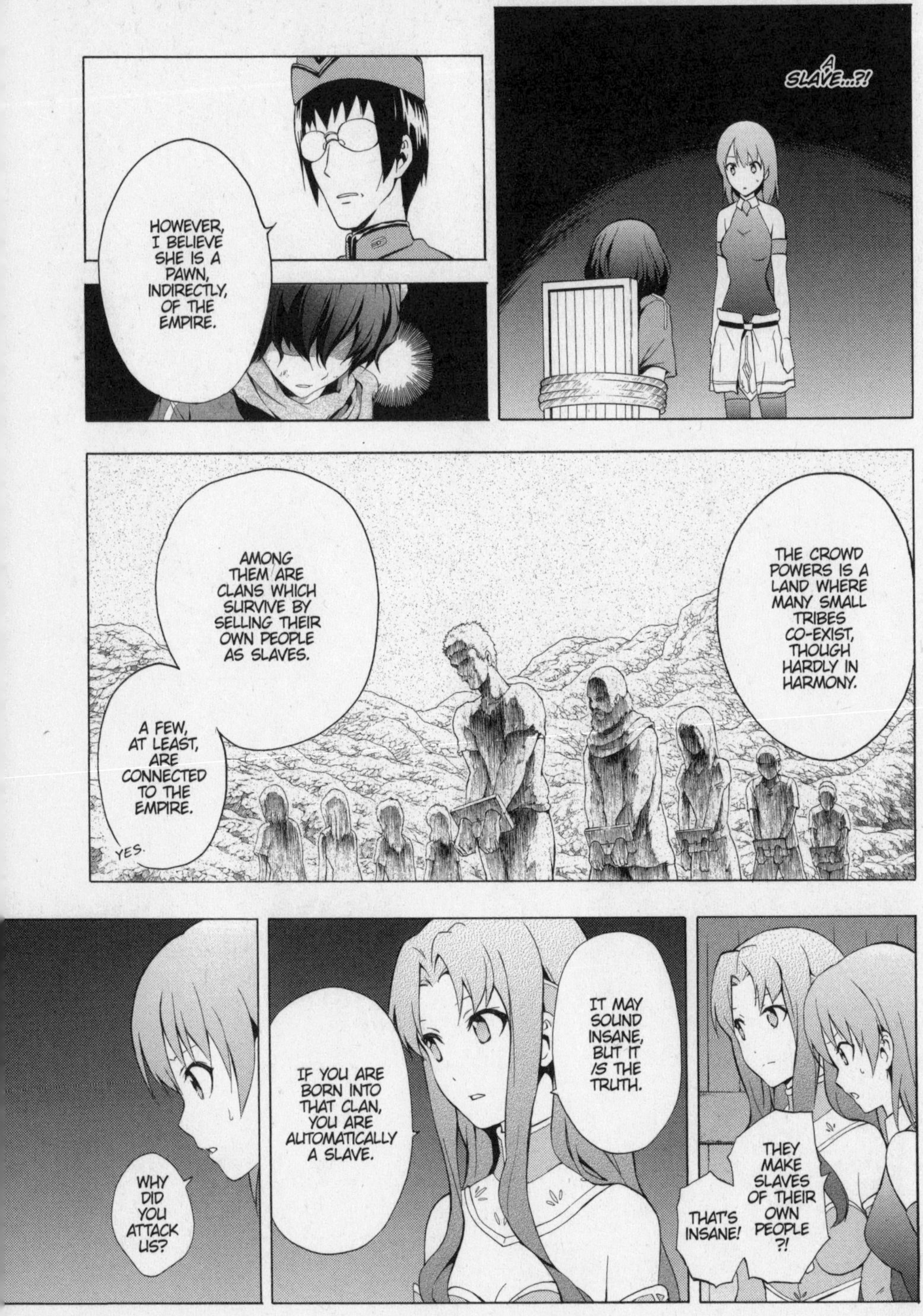
A SLAVE...?!
HOWEVER, I BELIEVE SHE IS A PAWN, INDIRECTLY, OF THE EMPIRE.
THE CROWD POWERS IS A LAND WHERE MANY SMALL TRIBES CO-EXIST, THOUGH HARDLY IN HARMONY.
AMONG THEM ARE CLANS WHICH SURVIVE BY SELLING THEIR OWN PEOPLE AS SLAVES.
A FEW, AT LEAST, ARE CONNECTED TO THE EMPIRE.
YES.
THEY MAKE SLAVES OF THEIR OWN PEOPLE?!
THAT'S INSANE!
IT MAY SOUND INSANE, BUT IT IS THE TRUTH.
IF YOU ARE BORN INTO THAT CLAN, YOU ARE AUTOMATICALLY A SLAVE.
WHY DID YOU ATTACK US?

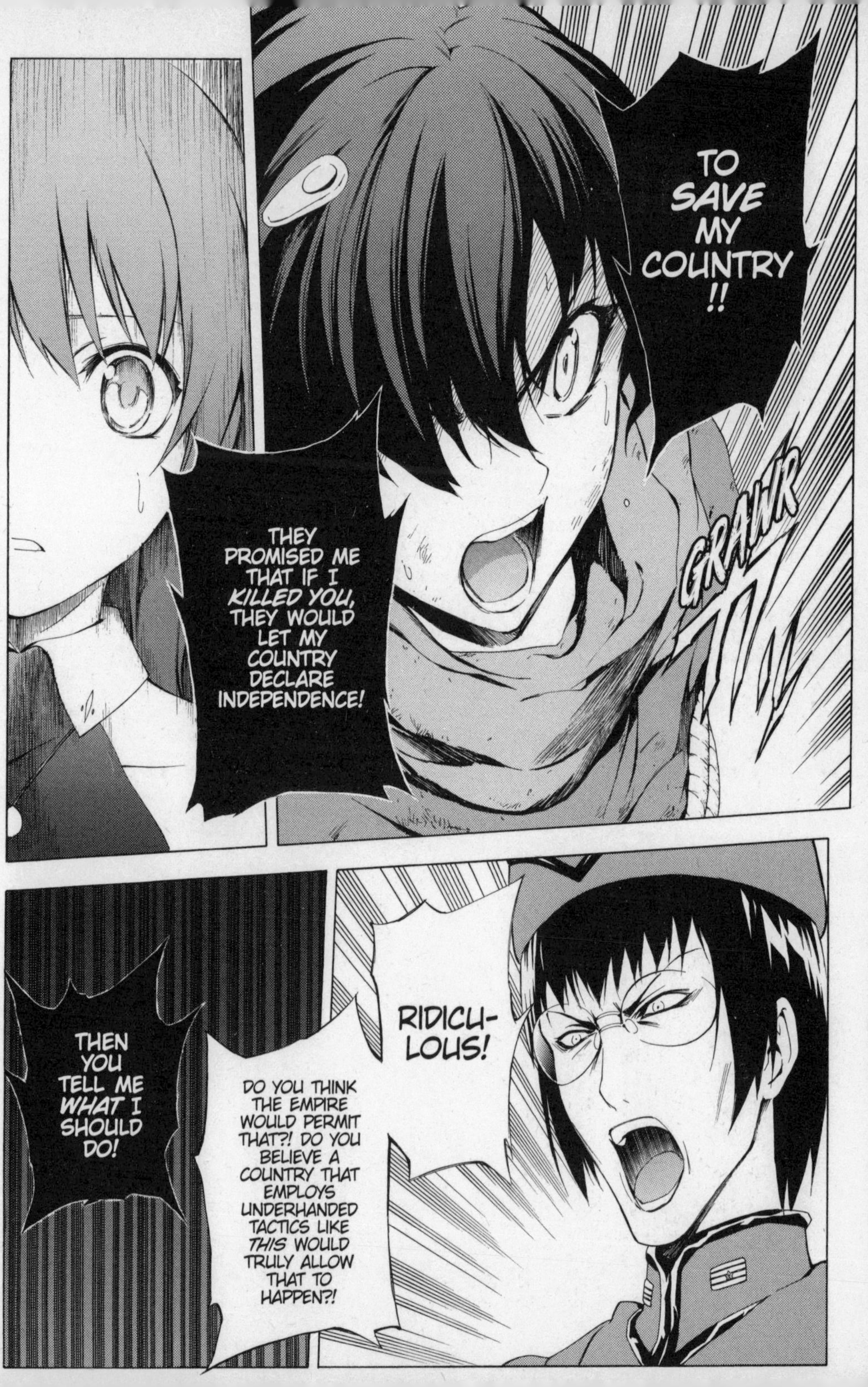
TO *SAVE* MY COUNTRY !!
THEY PROMISED ME THAT IF I *KILLED YOU*, THEY WOULD LET MY COUNTRY DECLARE INDEPENDENCE!
GRAWR
RIDICU-LOUS!
DO YOU THINK THE EMPIRE WOULD PERMIT THAT?! DO YOU BELIEVE A COUNTRY THAT EMPLOYS UNDERHANDED TACTICS LIKE *THIS* WOULD TRULY ALLOW THAT TO HAPPEN?!
THEN YOU TELL ME *WHAT* I SHOULD DO!

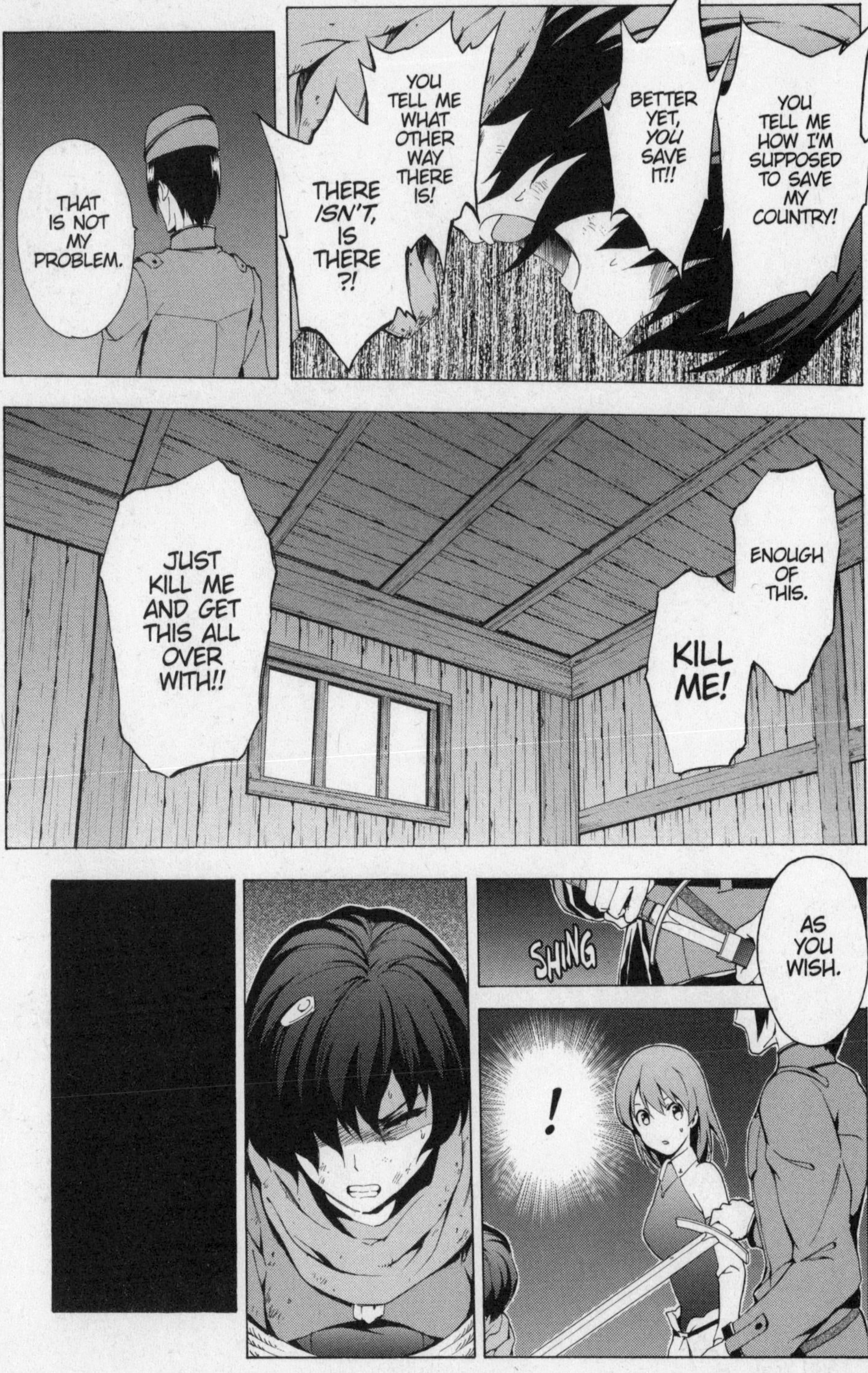
YOU TELL ME HOW I'M SUPPOSED TO SAVE MY COUNTRY!
BETTER YET, *YOU* SAVE IT!!
YOU TELL ME WHAT OTHER WAY THERE IS!
THERE *ISN'T*, IS THERE ?!
THAT IS NOT MY PROBLEM.
ENOUGH OF THIS.
KILL ME!
JUST KILL ME AND GET THIS ALL OVER WITH!!
AS YOU WISH.
SHING
!

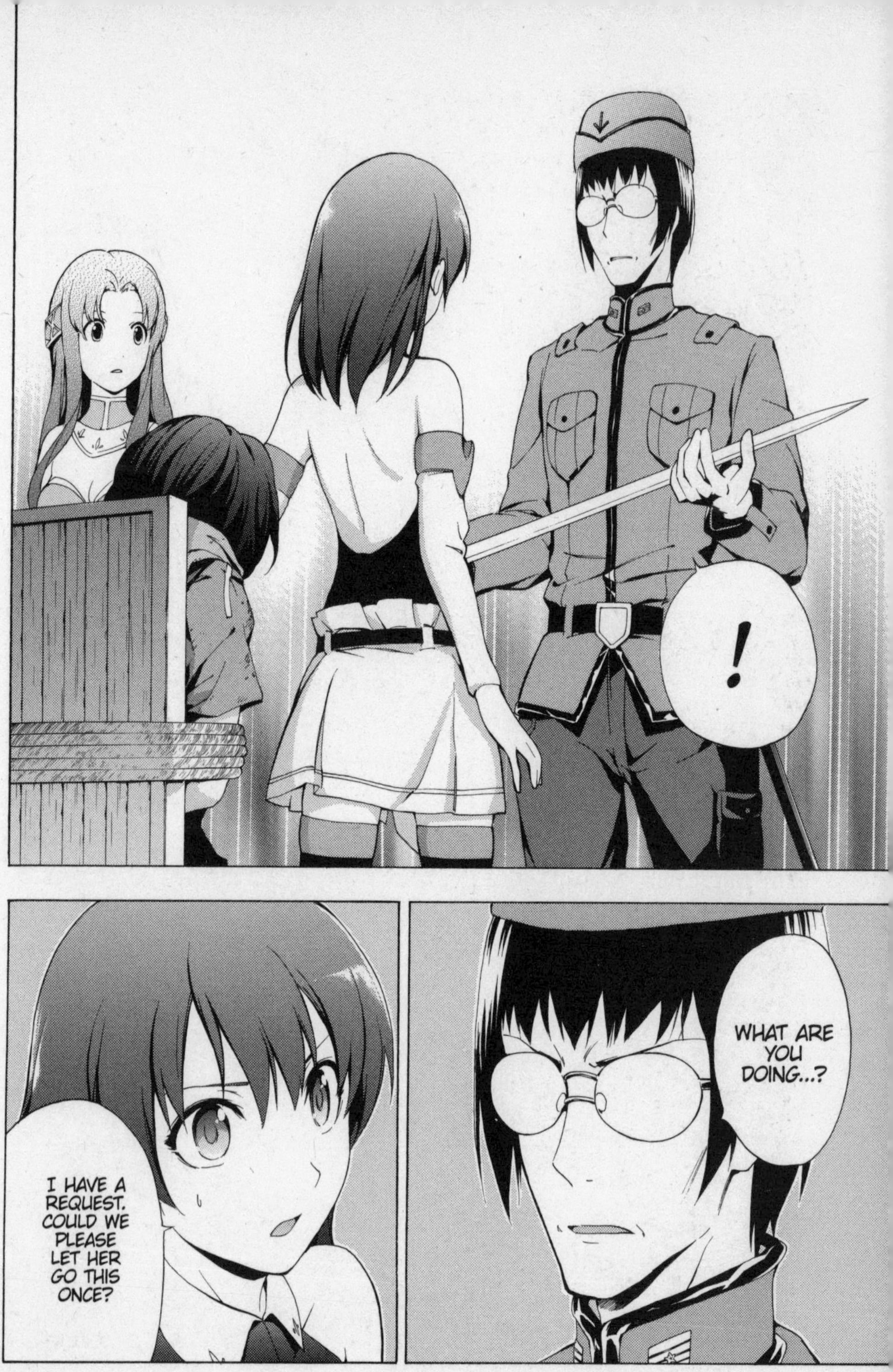
!
WHAT ARE YOU DOING...?
I HAVE A REQUEST. COULD WE PLEASE LET HER GO THIS ONCE?

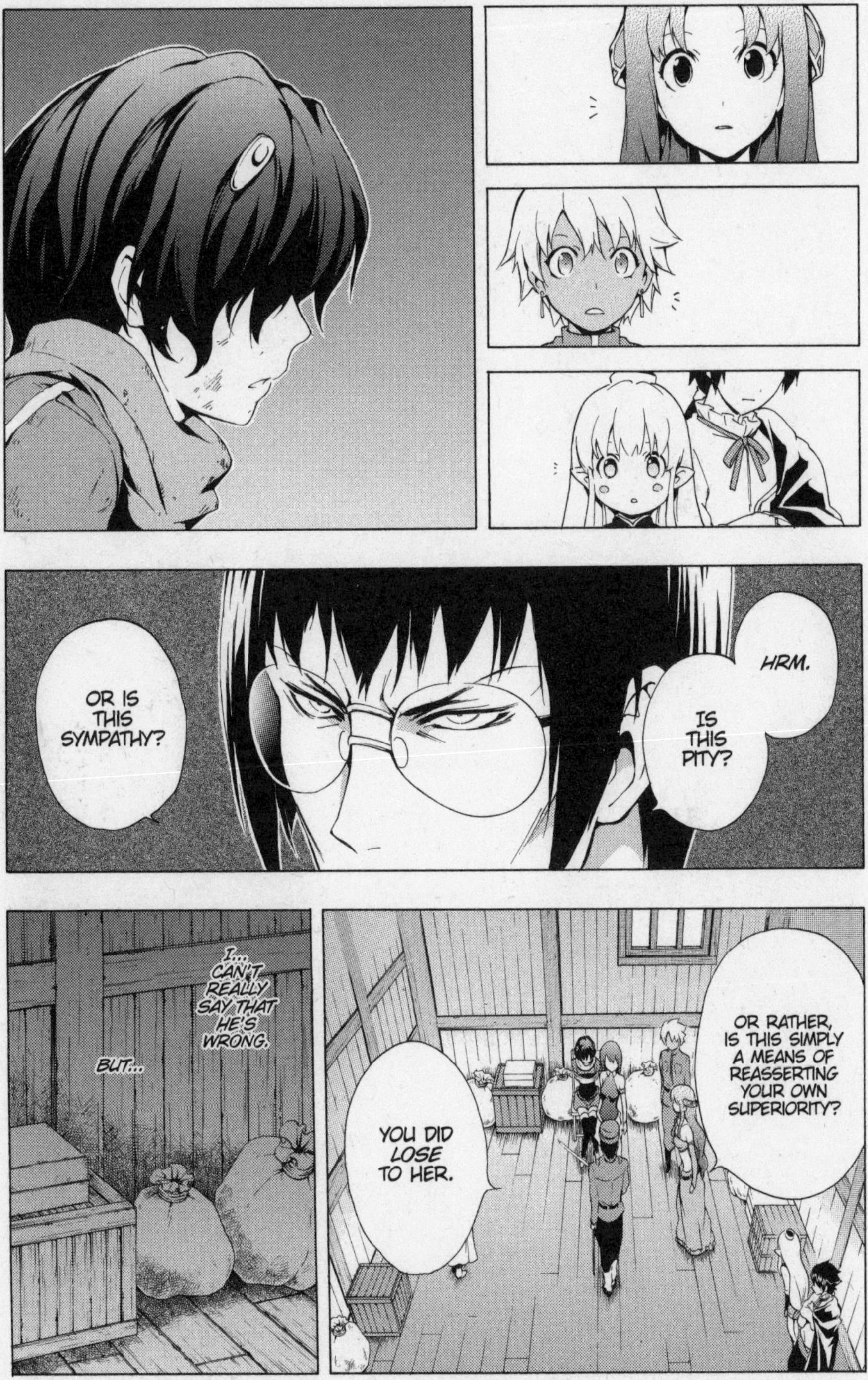
HRM. IS THIS PITY?
OR IS THIS SYMPATHY?
OR RATHER, IS THIS SIMPLY A MEANS OF REASSERTING YOUR OWN SUPERIORITY?
YOU DID LOSE TO HER.
I... CAN'T REALLY SAY THAT HE'S WRONG.
BUT...

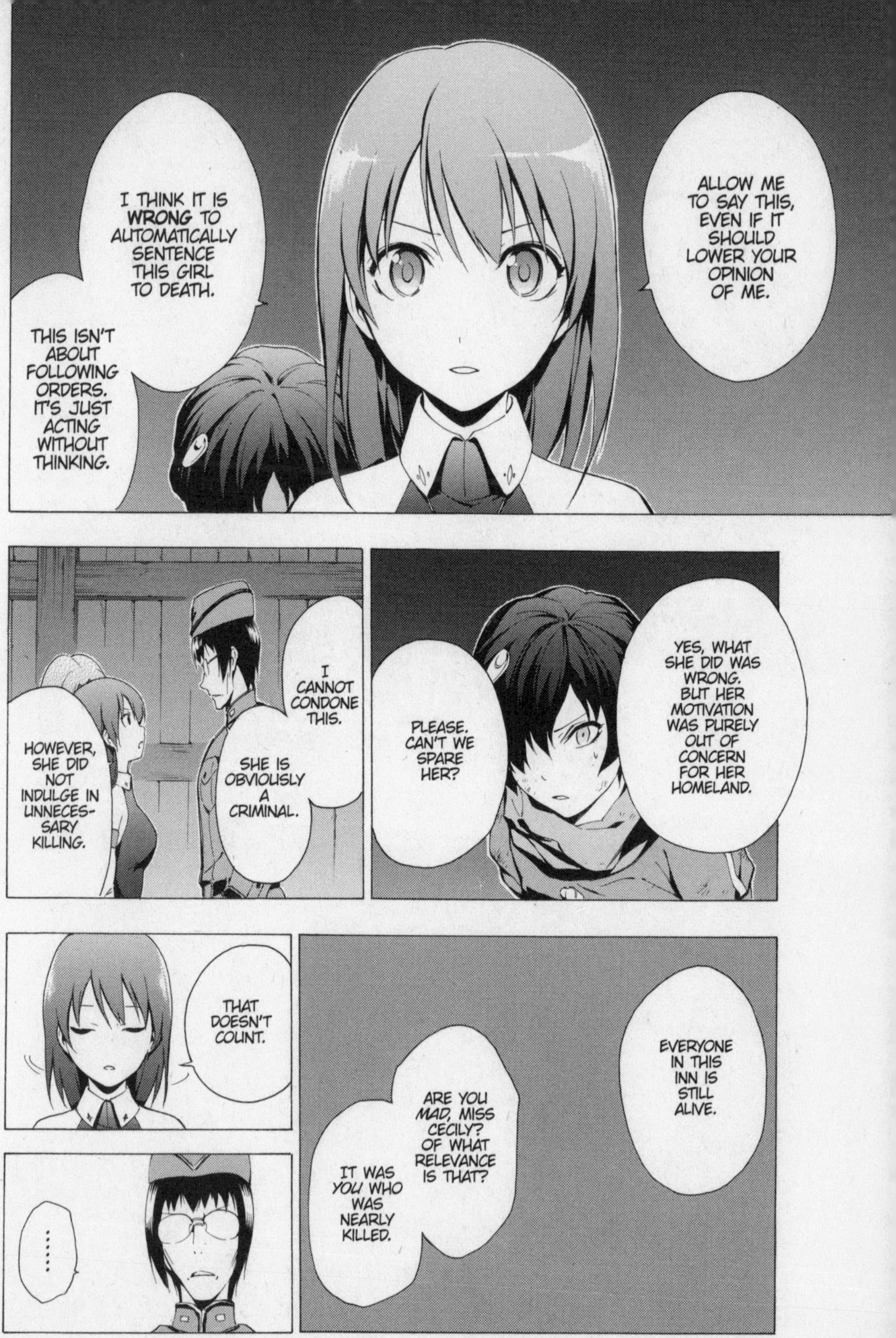
ALLOW ME TO SAY THIS, EVEN IF IT SHOULD LOWER YOUR OPINION OF ME.
I THINK IT IS **WRONG** TO AUTOMATICALLY SENTENCE THIS GIRL TO DEATH.
THIS ISN'T ABOUT FOLLOWING ORDERS. IT'S JUST ACTING WITHOUT THINKING.
YES, WHAT SHE DID WAS WRONG. BUT HER MOTIVATION WAS PURELY OUT OF CONCERN FOR HER HOMELAND.
PLEASE. CAN'T WE SPARE HER?
I CANNOT CONDONE THIS.
SHE IS OBVIOUSLY A CRIMINAL.
HOWEVER, SHE DID NOT INDULGE IN UNNECES-SARY KILLING.
EVERYONE IN THIS INN IS STILL ALIVE.
ARE YOU *MAD*, MISS CECILY? OF WHAT RELEVANCE IS THAT?
IT WAS *YOU* WHO WAS NEARLY KILLED.
THAT DOESN'T COUNT.
......

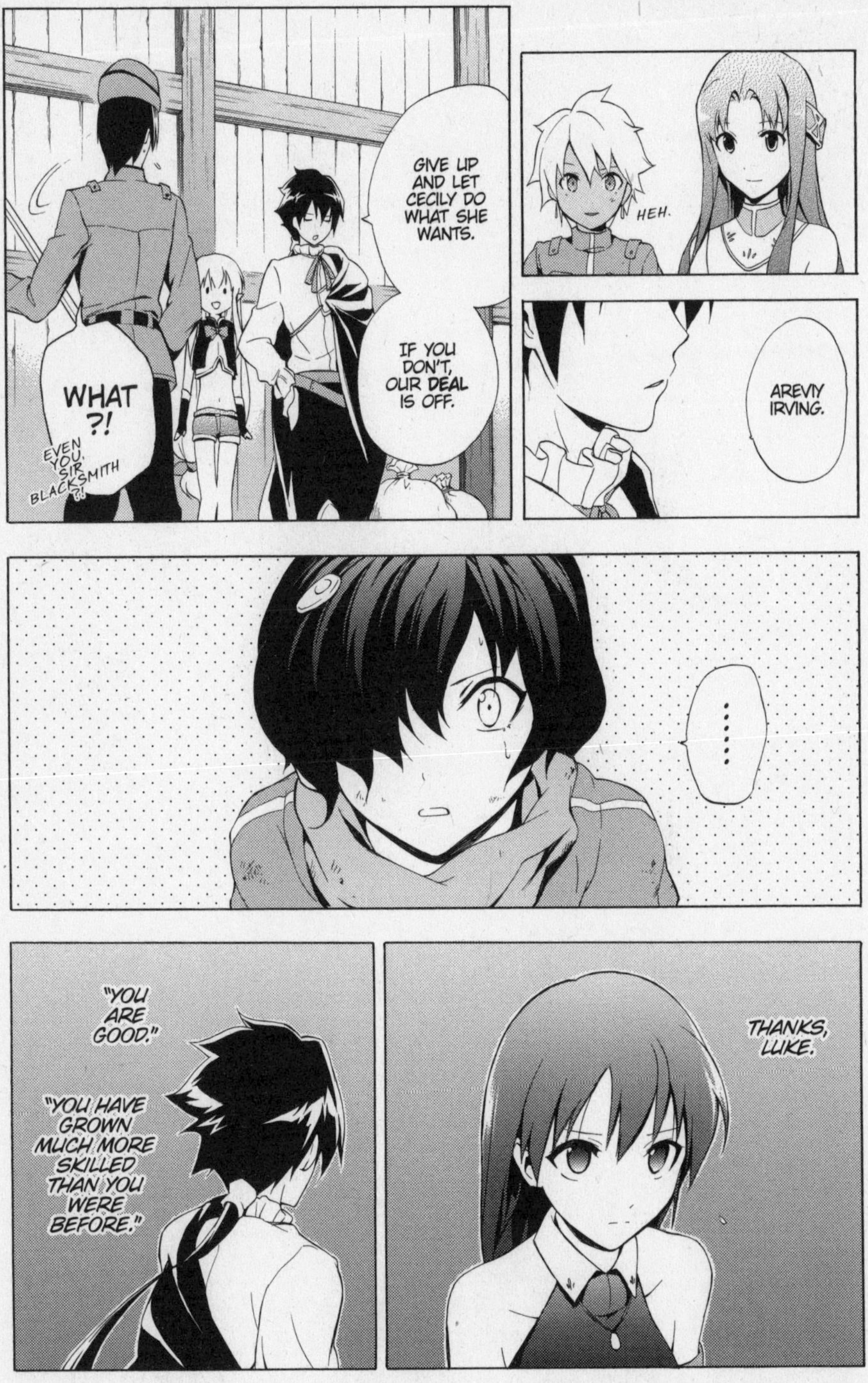
HEH.
AREVIY IRVING.
GIVE UP AND LET CECILY DO WHAT SHE WANTS.
IF YOU DON'T, OUR DEAL IS OFF.
WHAT ?!
EVEN YOU, SIR BLACKSMITH ?!
......
THANKS, LUKE.
"YOU ARE GOOD."
"YOU HAVE GROWN MUCH MORE SKILLED THAN YOU WERE BEFORE."

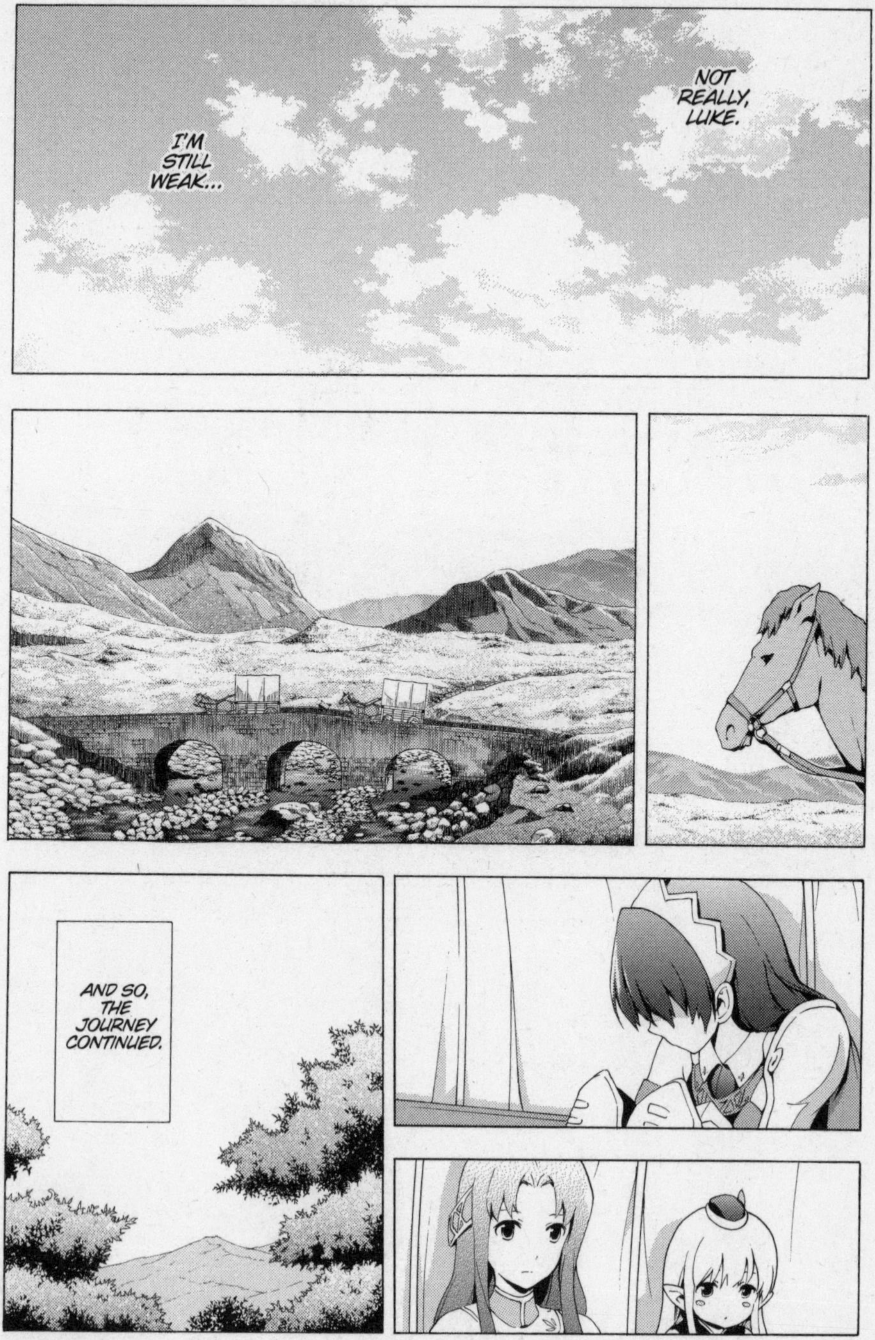
NOT REALLY, LUKE.
I'M STILL WEAK...
AND SO, THE JOURNEY CONTINUED.

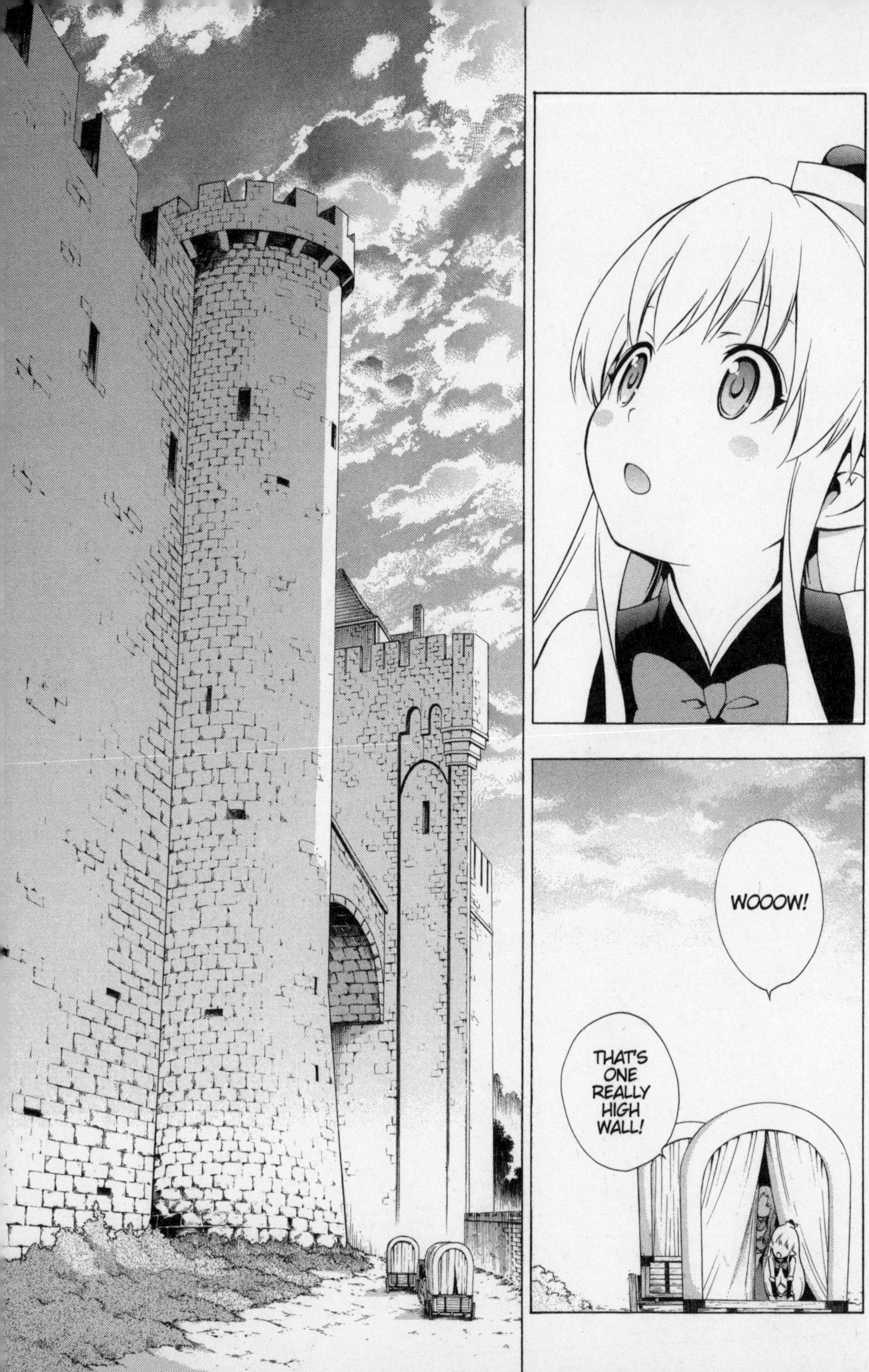
WOOOW!
THAT'S ONE REALLY HIGH WALL!

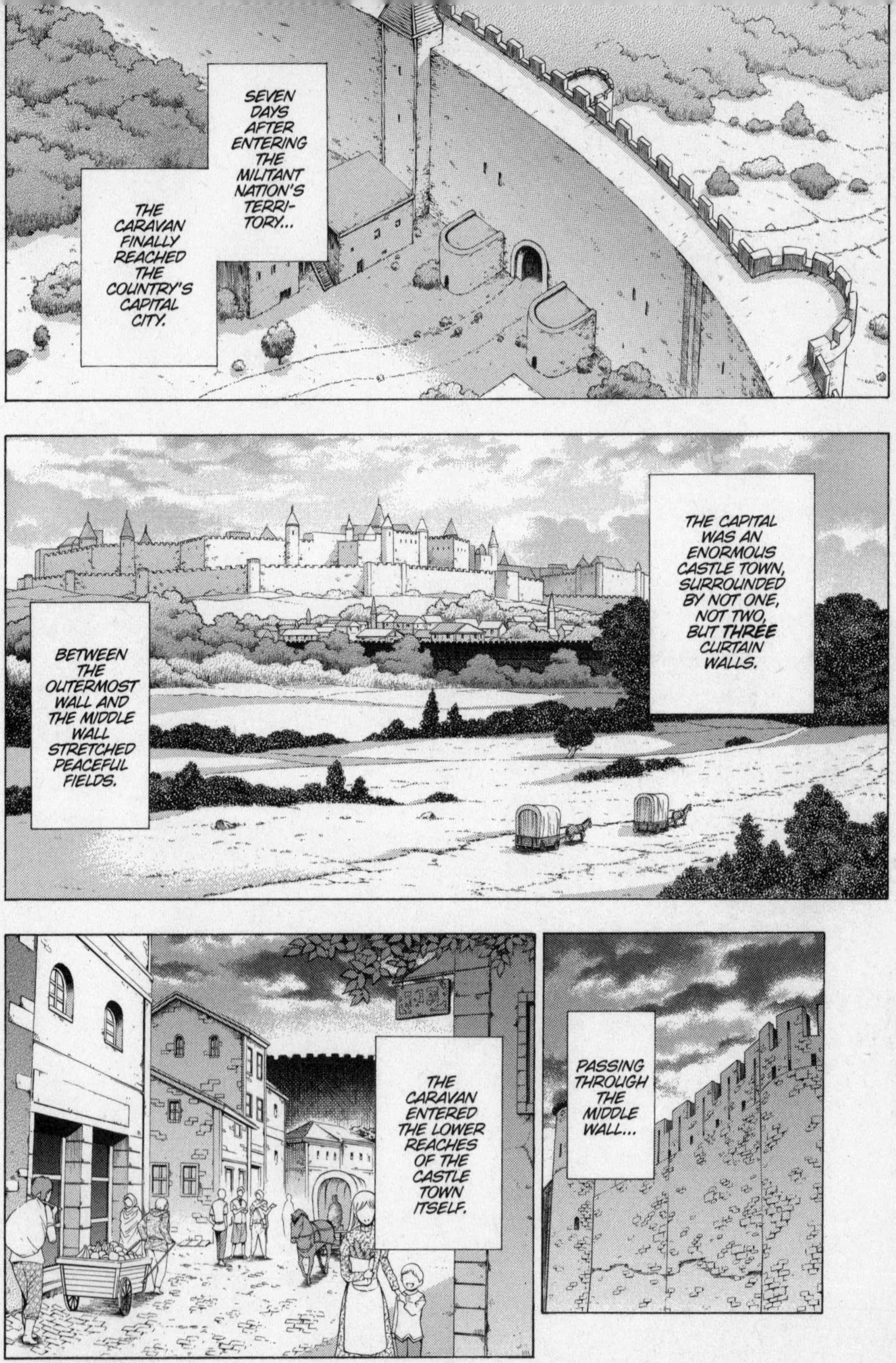
SEVEN DAYS AFTER ENTERING THE MILITANT NATION'S TERRI-TORY...
THE CARAVAN FINALLY REACHED THE COUNTRY'S CAPITAL CITY.
THE CAPITAL WAS AN ENORMOUS CASTLE TOWN, SURROUNDED BY NOT ONE, NOT TWO, BUT THREE CURTAIN WALLS.
BETWEEN THE OUTERMOST WALL AND THE MIDDLE WALL STRETCHED PEACEFUL FIELDS.
PASSING THROUGH THE MIDDLE WALL...
THE CARAVAN ENTERED THE LOWER REACHES OF THE CASTLE TOWN ITSELF.

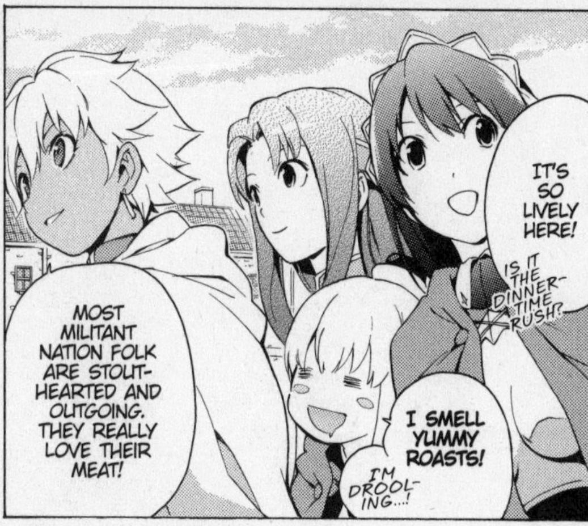
IT'S SO LIVELY HERE!
IS IT THE DINNER-TIME RUSH?
I SMELL YUMMY ROASTS!
I'M DROOLING...!
MOST MILITANT NATION FOLK ARE STOUT-HEARTED AND OUTGOING. THEY REALLY LOVE THEIR MEAT!

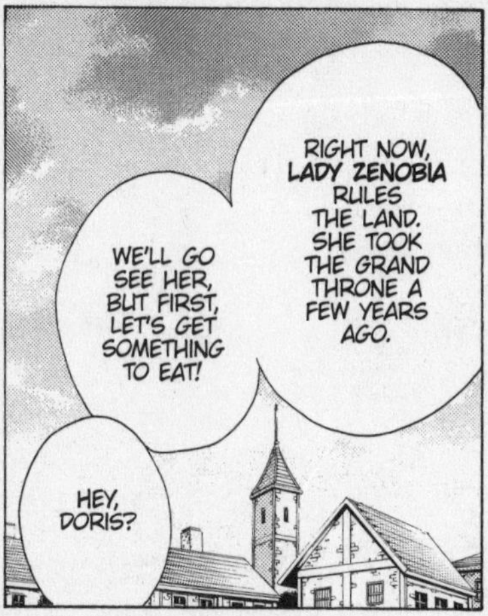
RIGHT NOW, **LADY ZENOBIA** RULES THE LAND. SHE TOOK THE GRAND THRONE A FEW YEARS AGO.
WE'LL GO SEE HER, BUT FIRST, LET'S GET SOMETHING TO EAT!
HEY, DORIS?

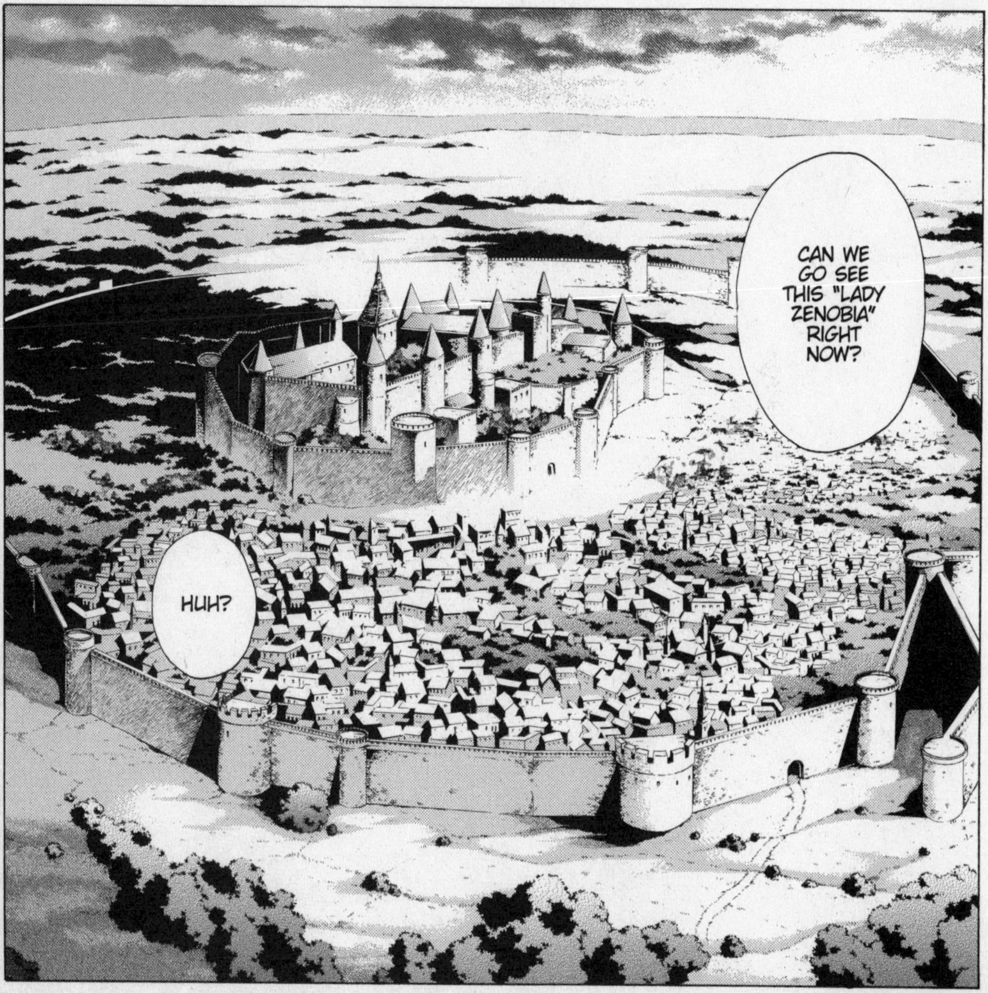
CAN WE GO SEE THIS "LADY ZENOBIA" RIGHT NOW?
HUH?

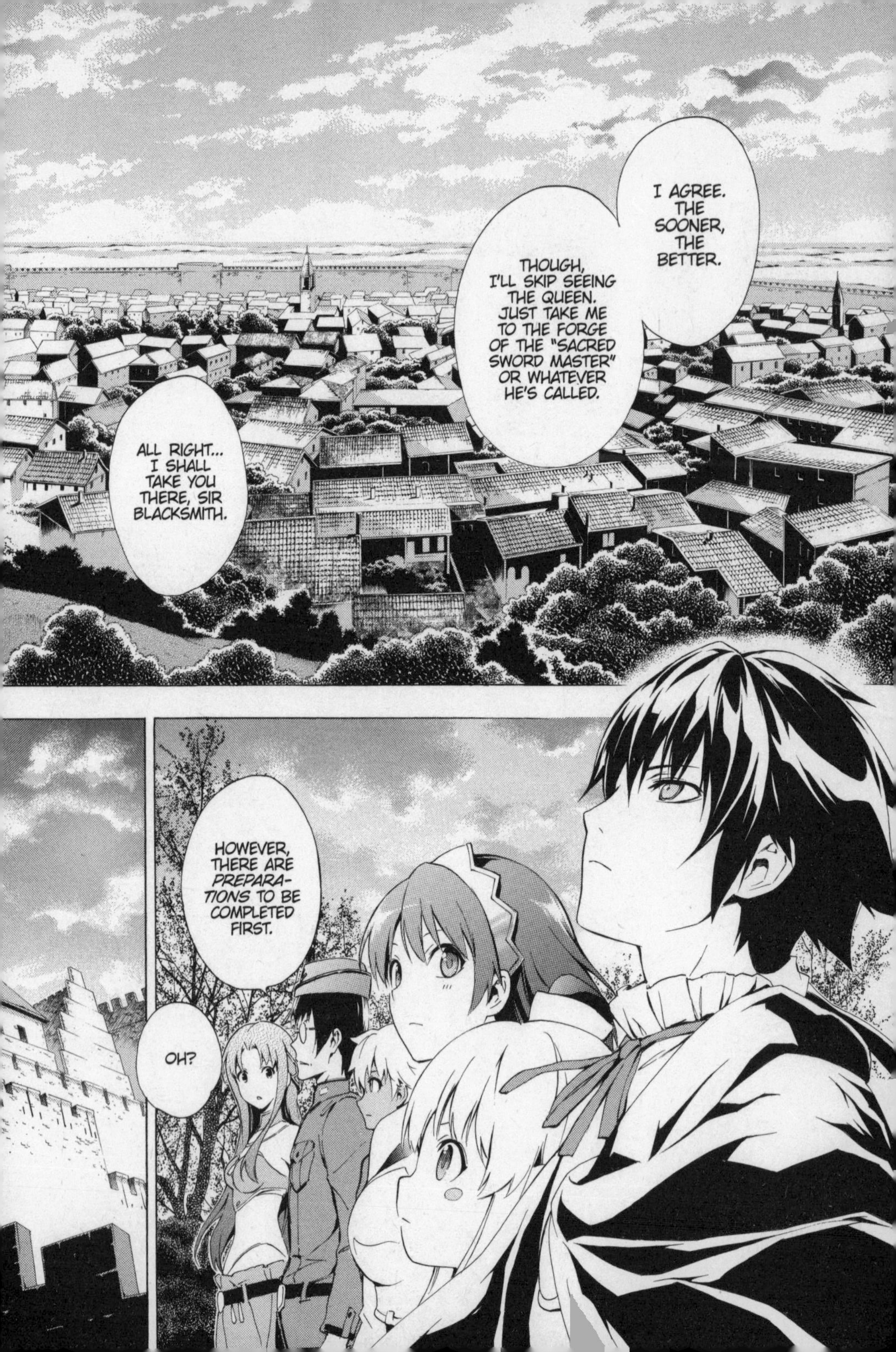
I AGREE. THE SOONER, THE BETTER.
THOUGH, I'LL SKIP SEEING THE QUEEN. JUST TAKE ME TO THE FORGE OF THE "SACRED SWORD MASTER" OR WHATEVER HE'S CALLED.
ALL RIGHT... I SHALL TAKE YOU THERE, SIR BLACKSMITH.
HOWEVER, THERE ARE *PREPARATIONS* TO BE COMPLETED FIRST.
OH?

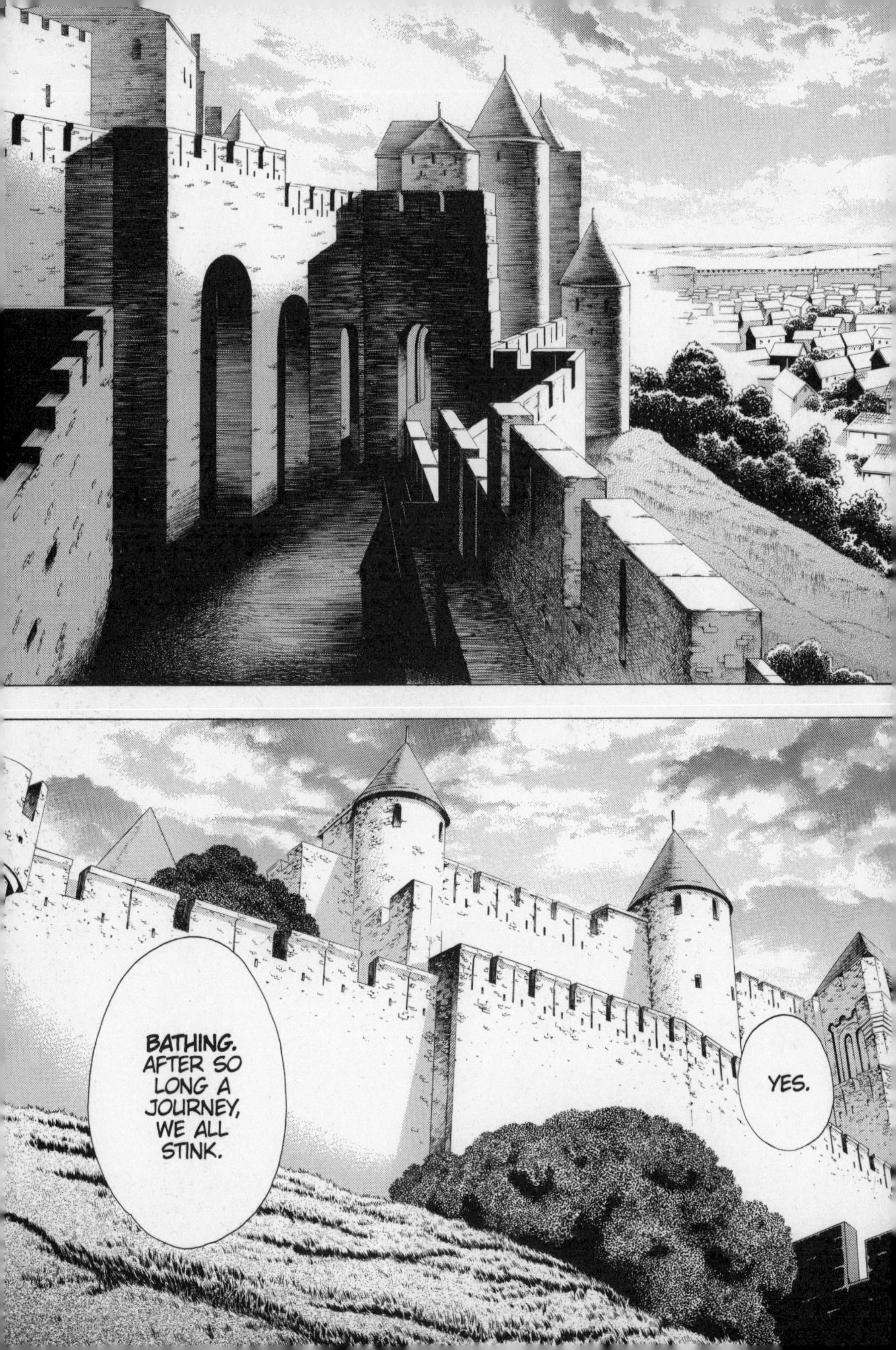
YES.
BATHING. AFTER SO LONG A JOURNEY, WE ALL STINK.

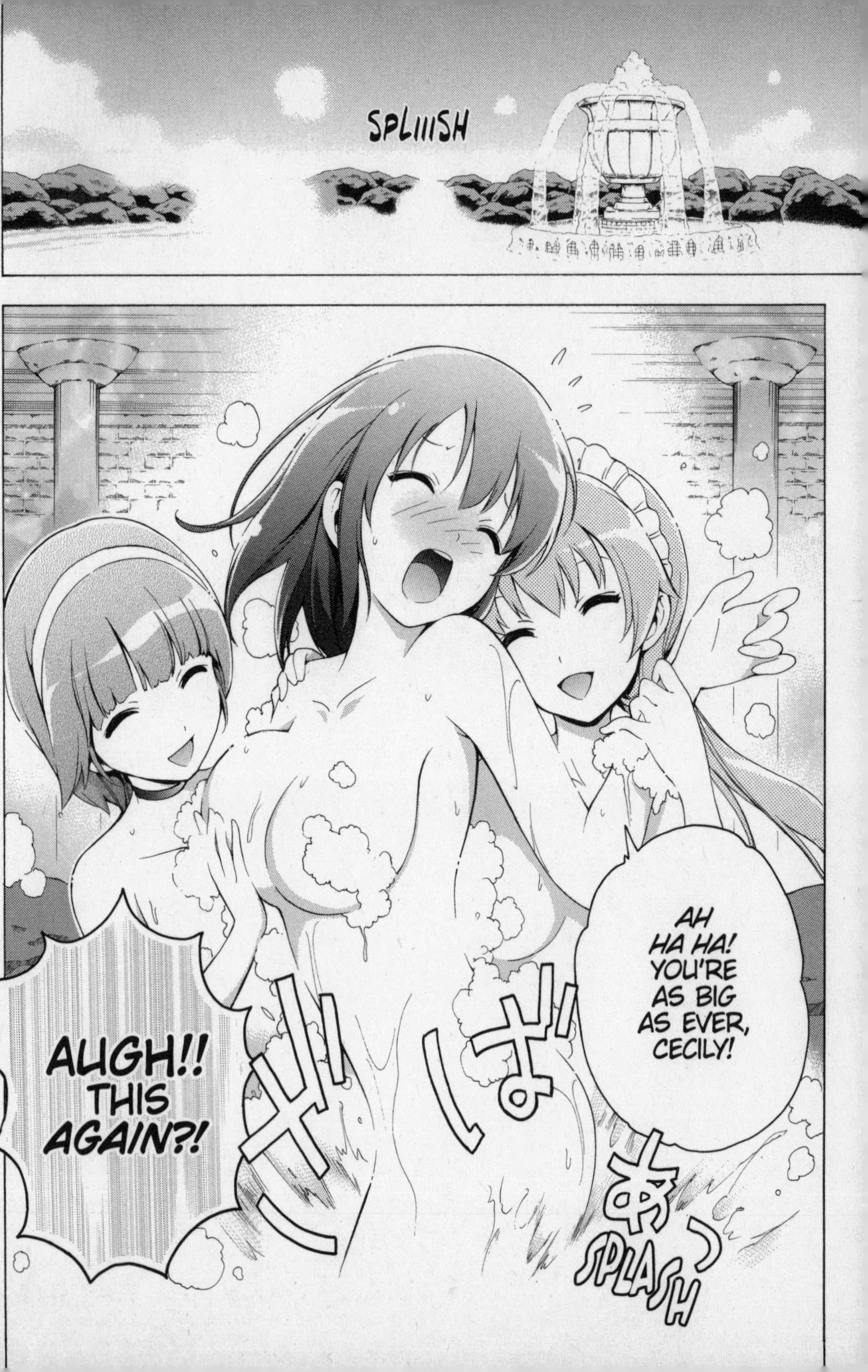
SPLIIISH
AH HA HA! YOU'RE AS BIG AS EVER, CECILY!
ざばあっ
SPLASH
AUGH!! THIS AGAIN?!

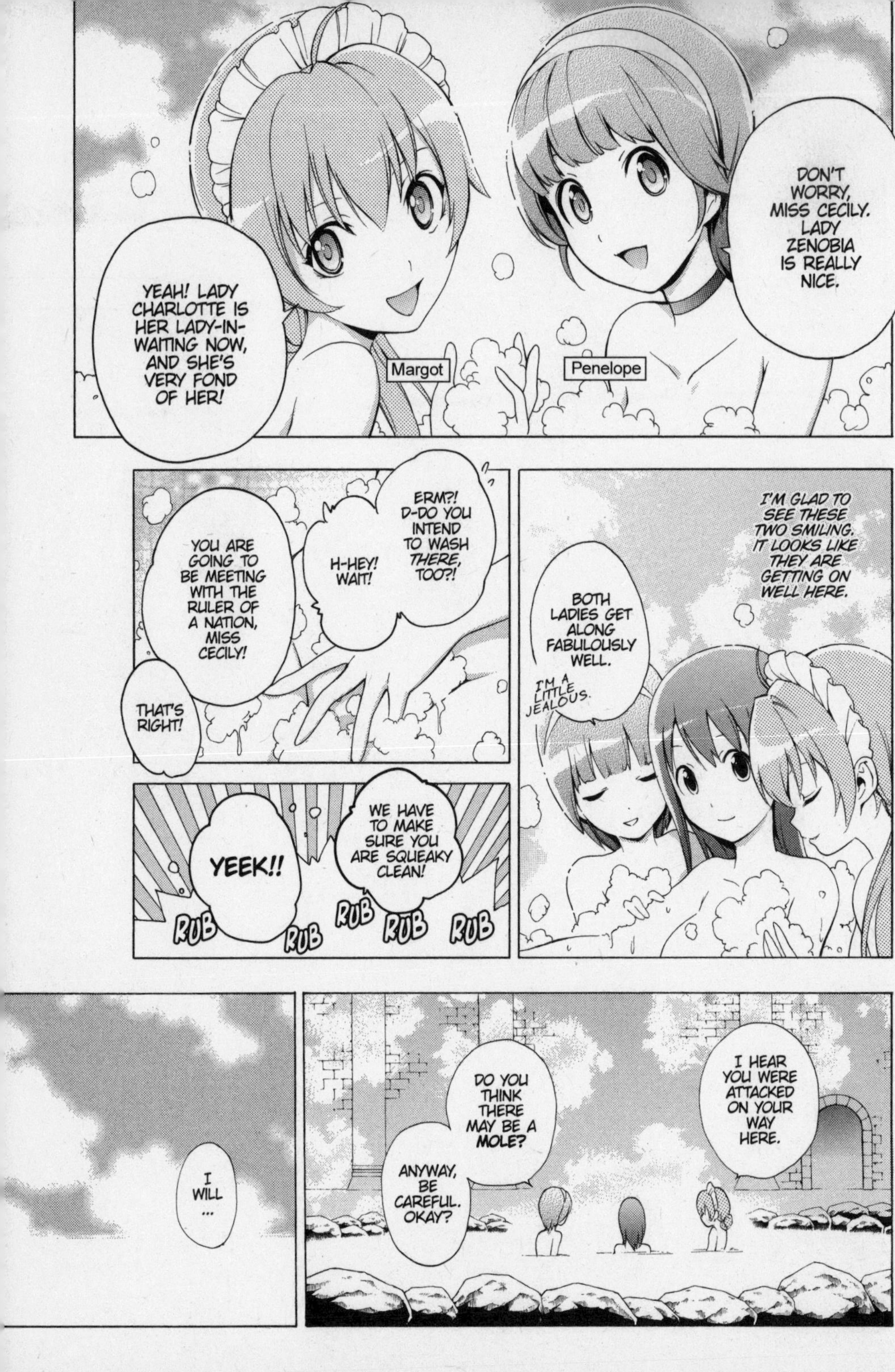
DON'T WORRY, MISS CECILY. LADY ZENOBIA IS REALLY NICE.
YEAH! LADY CHARLOTTE IS HER LADY-IN-WAITING NOW, AND SHE'S VERY FOND OF HER!
Penelope
Margot
I'M GLAD TO SEE THESE TWO SMILING. IT LOOKS LIKE THEY ARE GETTING ON WELL HERE.
BOTH LADIES GET ALONG FABULOUSLY WELL.
I'M A LITTLE JEALOUS.
ERM?! D-DO YOU INTEND TO WASH THERE, TOO?!
H-HEY! WAIT!
YOU ARE GOING TO BE MEETING WITH THE RULER OF A NATION, MISS CECILY!
THAT'S RIGHT!
WE HAVE TO MAKE SURE YOU ARE SQUEAKY CLEAN!
YEEK!!
RUB
RUB
RUB
RUB
RUB
I HEAR YOU WERE ATTACKED ON YOUR WAY HERE.
DO YOU THINK THERE MAY BE A MOLE?
ANYWAY, BE CAREFUL. OKAY?
I WILL ...

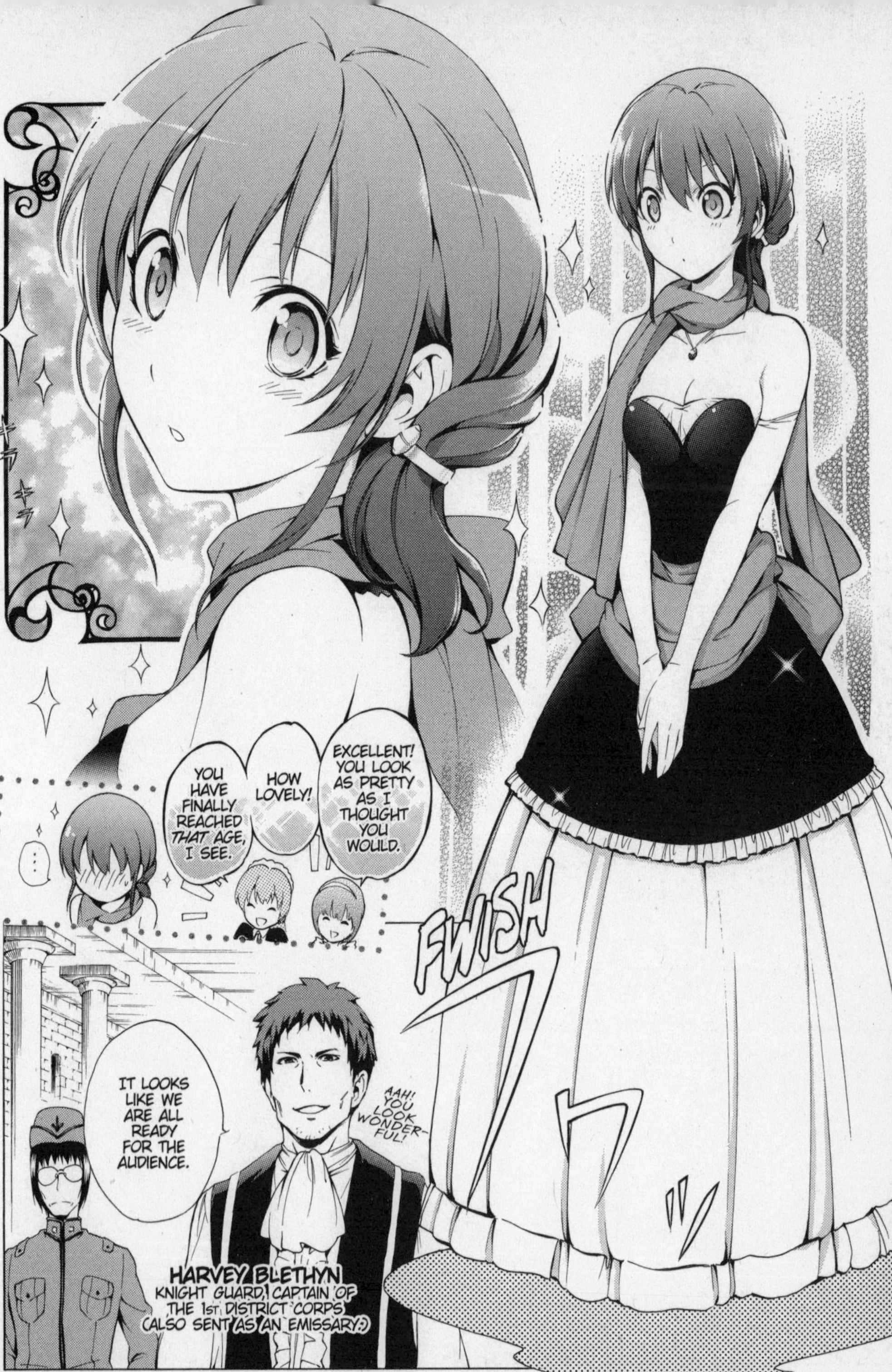
キラ キラ
EXCELLENT! YOU LOOK AS PRETTY AS I THOUGHT YOU WOULD.
HOW LOVELY!
YOU HAVE FINALLY REACHED *THAT* AGE, I SEE.
...
FWISH
AAH! YOU LOOK WONDERFUL!
IT LOOKS LIKE WE ARE ALL READY FOR THE AUDIENCE.
HARVEY BLETHYN
KNIGHT GUARD, CAPTAIN OF THE 1st DISTRICT CORPS (ALSO SENT AS AN EMISSARY.)

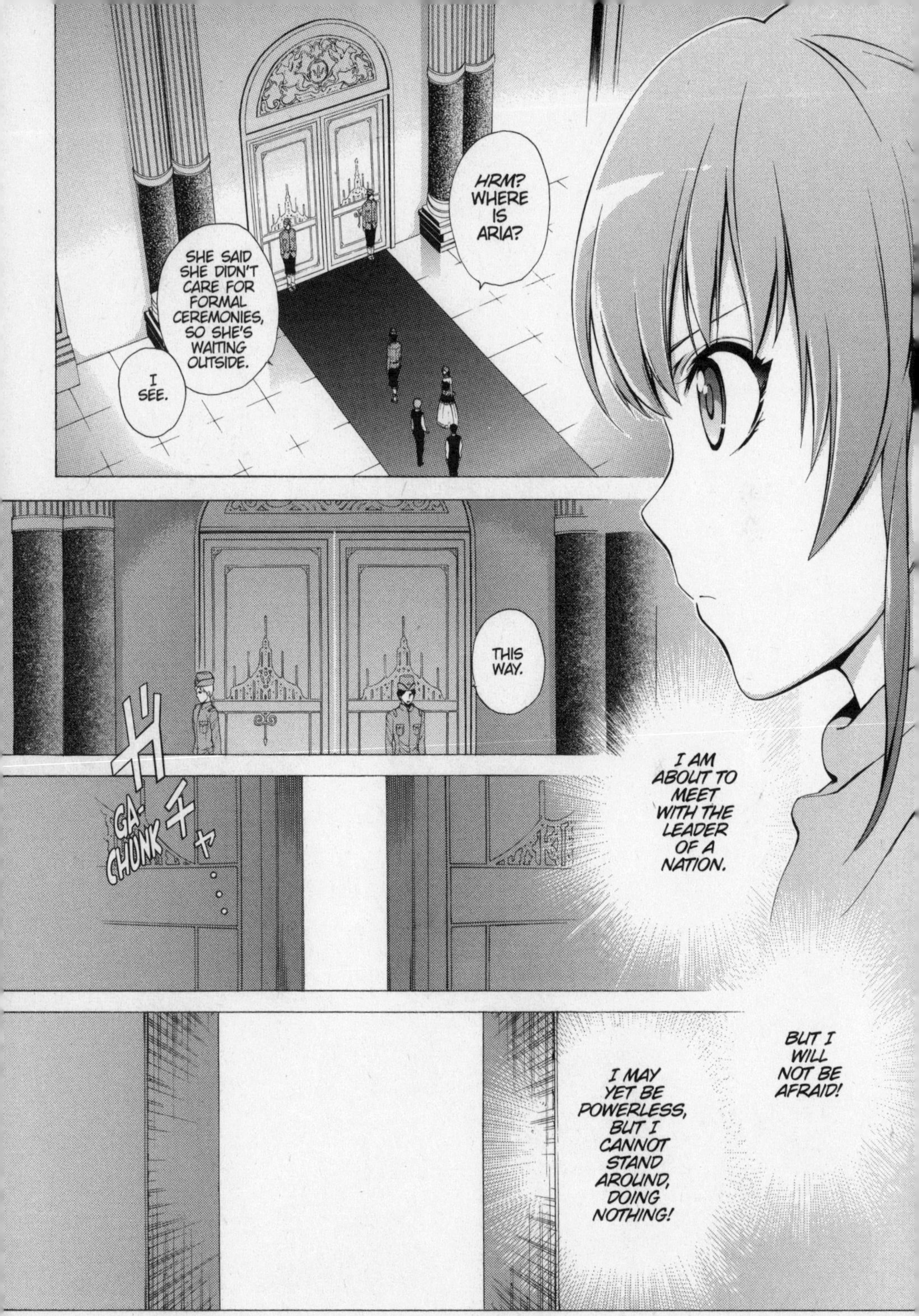
HRM? WHERE IS ARIA?
SHE SAID SHE DIDN'T CARE FOR FORMAL CEREMONIES, SO SHE'S WAITING OUTSIDE.
I SEE.
THIS WAY.
GA-CHUNK
I AM ABOUT TO MEET WITH THE LEADER OF A NATION.
BUT I WILL NOT BE AFRAID!
I MAY YET BE POWERLESS, BUT I CANNOT STAND AROUND, DOING NOTHING!

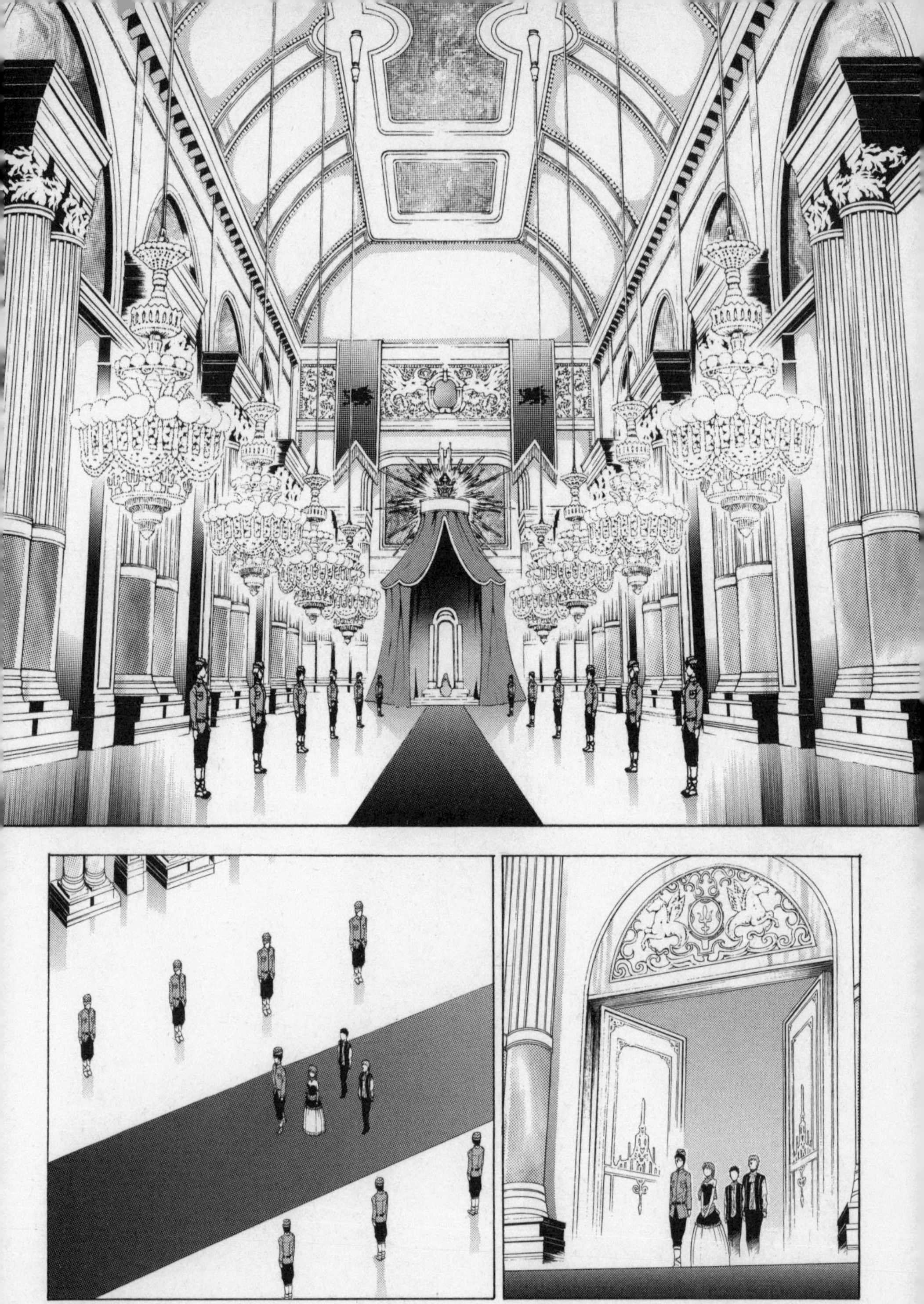

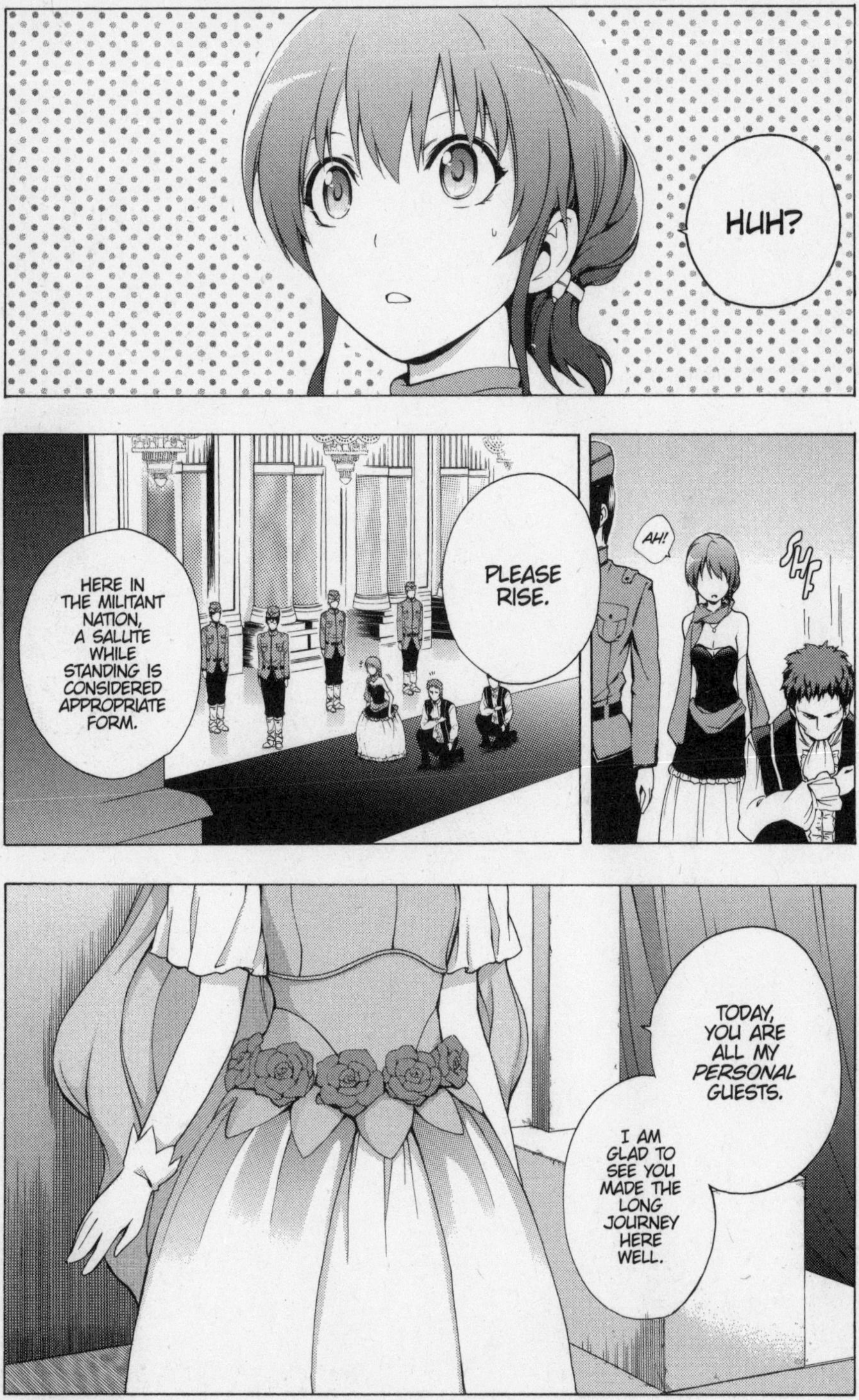
HUH?
AH!
SHF
PLEASE RISE.
HERE IN THE MILITANT NATION, A SALUTE WHILE STANDING IS CONSIDERED APPROPRIATE FORM.
TODAY, YOU ARE ALL MY PERSONAL GUESTS.
I AM GLAD TO SEE YOU MADE THE LONG JOURNEY HERE WELL.

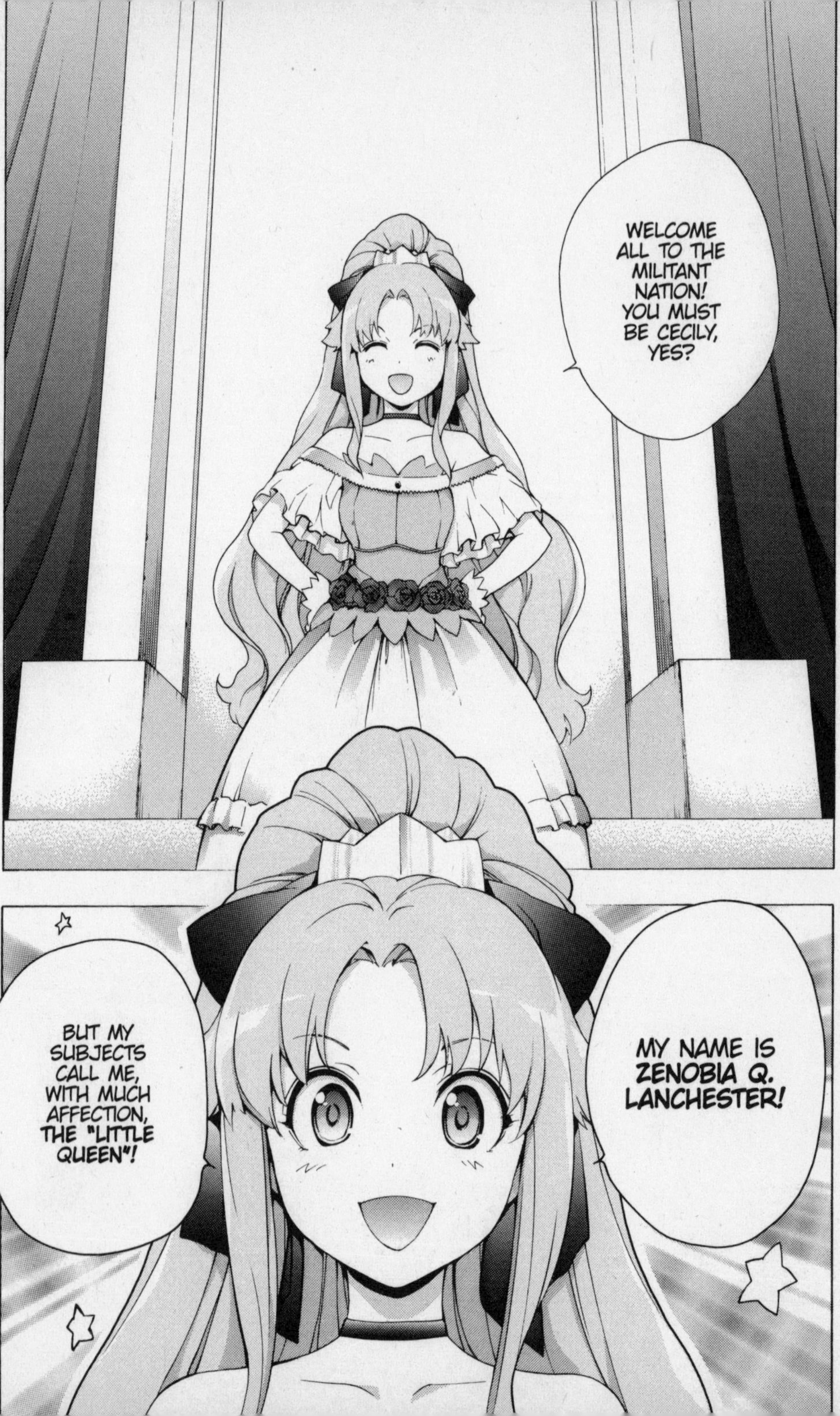
WELCOME ALL TO THE MILITANT NATION! YOU MUST BE CECILY, YES?
MY NAME IS ZENOBIA Q. LANCHESTER!
BUT MY SUBJECTS CALL ME, WITH MUCH AFFECTION, THE "LITTLE QUEEN"!

The Sacred Blacksmith

聖剣の刀鍛治

アトリエ 工房リーザ atelier Liza BRANCH OFFICE I

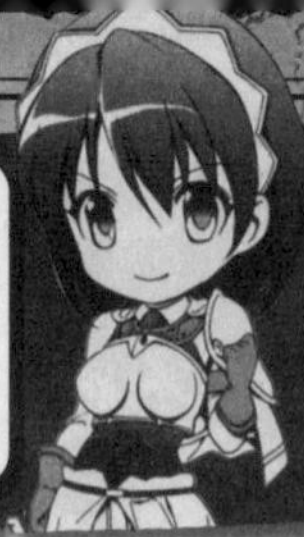
Time to open the Atelier Liza Branch Office, now a staple of the series! I love seeing what you all think!

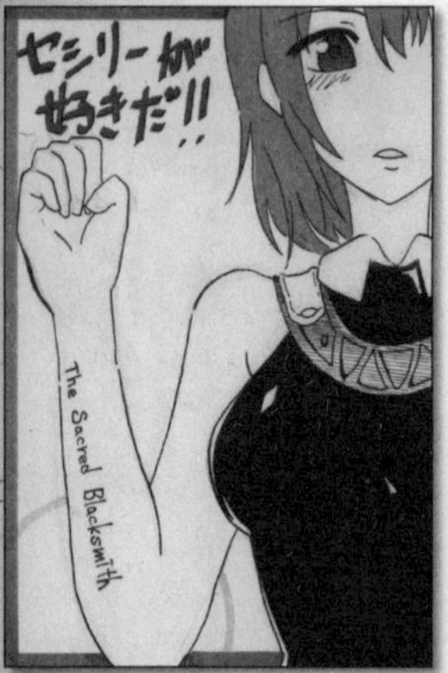
セシリーが好きだ!!
The Sacred Blacksmith

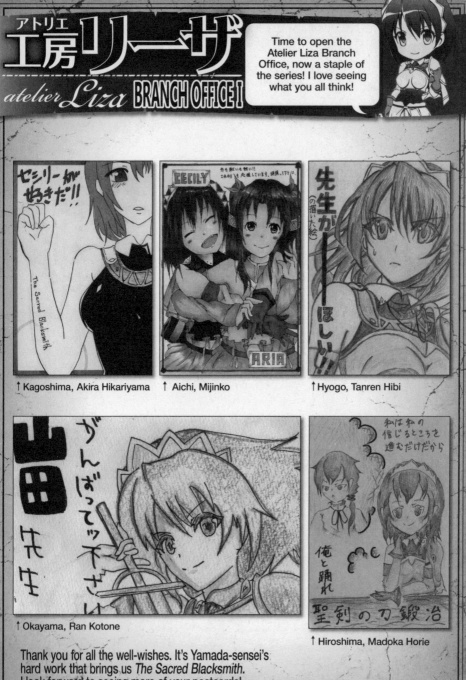

↑ Kagoshima, Akira Hikariyama

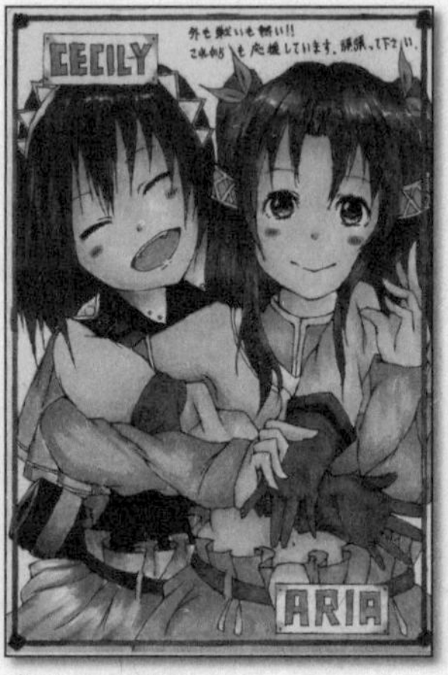
CECILY
これからも応援しています。頑張って下さい。
ARIA

↑ Aichi, Mijinko

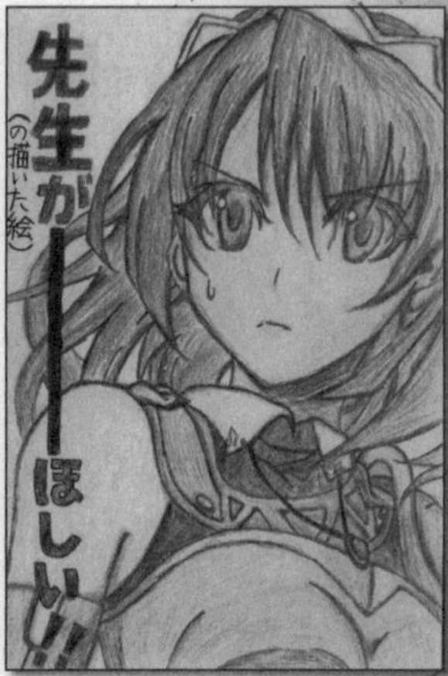
先生が（の描いた絵）ほしい!!

↑ Hyogo, Tanren Hibi

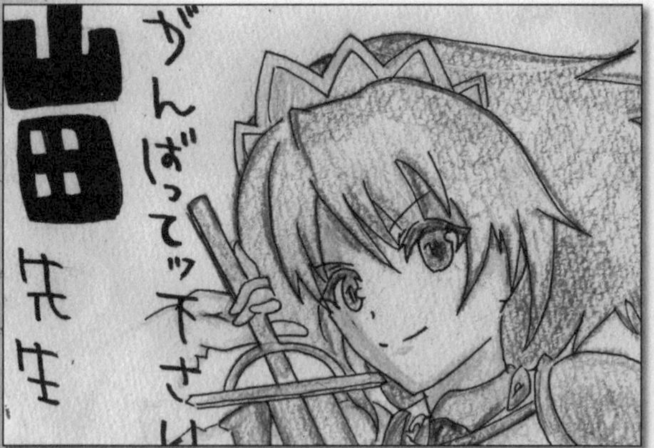
がんばってッ下さ
山田先生

↑ Okayama, Ran Kotone

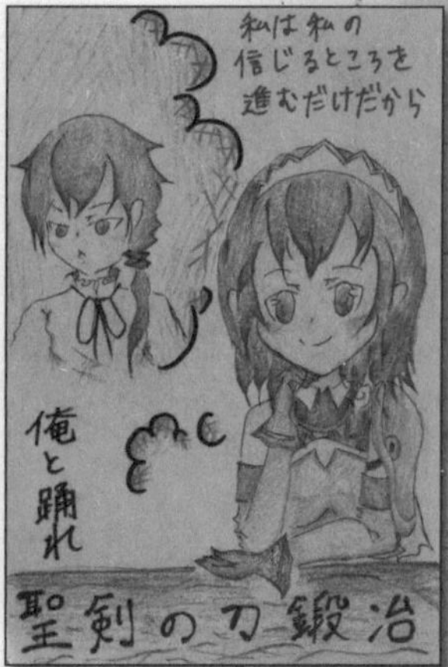
私は私の信じるところを進むだけだから
俺と踊れ
聖剣の刀鍛冶

↑ Hiroshima, Madoka Horie

Thank you for all the well-wishes. It's Yamada-sensei's hard work that brings us *The Sacred Blacksmith*. I look forward to seeing more of your postcards!

The Sacred Blacksmith

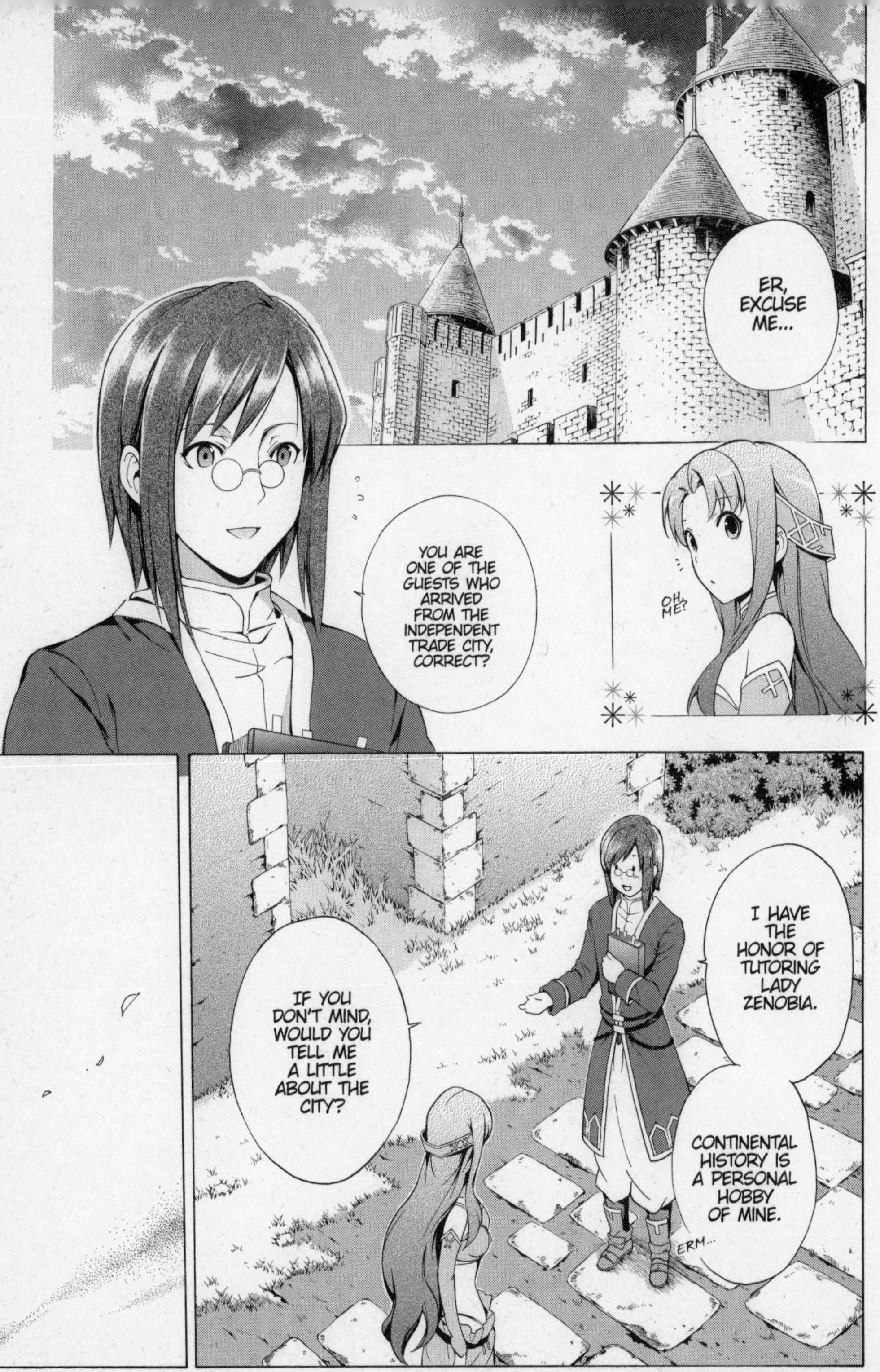
ER, EXCUSE ME...
OH, ME?
YOU ARE ONE OF THE GUESTS WHO ARRIVED FROM THE INDEPENDENT TRADE CITY, CORRECT?
I HAVE THE HONOR OF TUTORING LADY ZENOBIA.
CONTINENTAL HISTORY IS A PERSONAL HOBBY OF MINE.
IF YOU DON'T MIND, WOULD YOU TELL ME A LITTLE ABOUT THE CITY?
ERM...

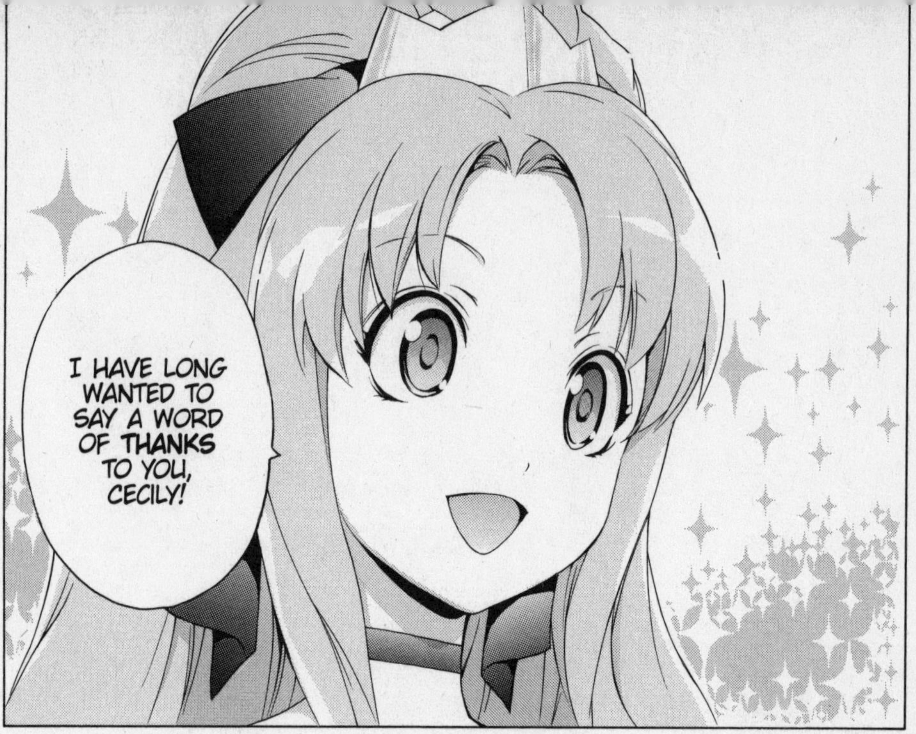
I HAVE LONG WANTED TO SAY A WORD OF THANKS TO YOU, CECILY!

Chapter 27 Patriot&Queen (Part 4)

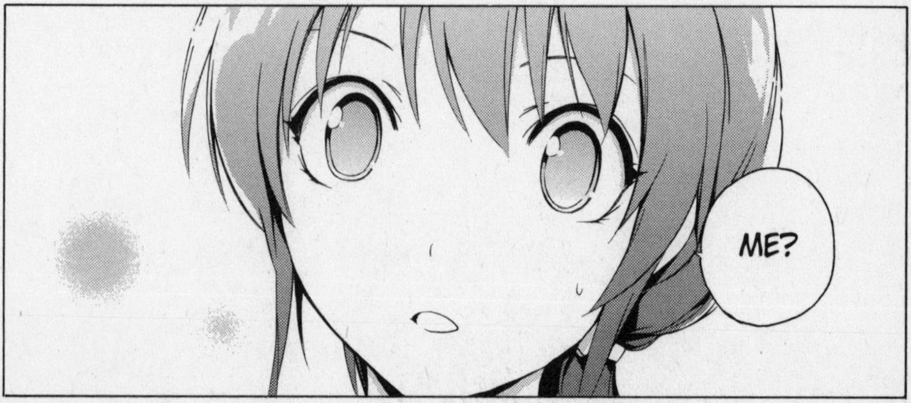
ME?

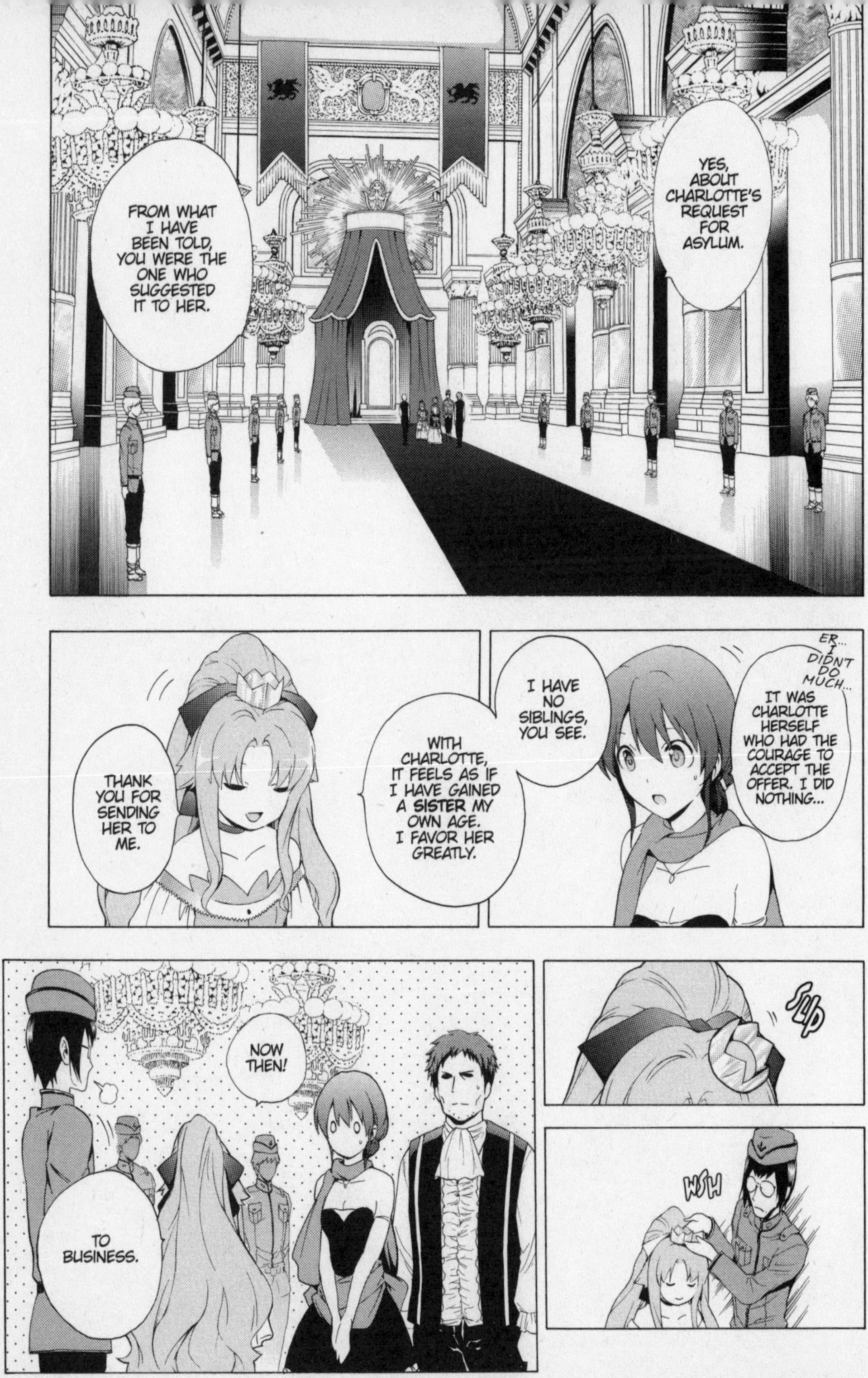
YES, ABOUT CHARLOTTE'S REQUEST FOR ASYLUM.
FROM WHAT I HAVE BEEN TOLD, YOU WERE THE ONE WHO SUGGESTED IT TO HER.
IT WAS CHARLOTTE HERSELF WHO HAD THE COURAGE TO ACCEPT THE OFFER. I DID NOTHING...
ER... I DIDN'T DO MUCH...
I HAVE NO SIBLINGS, YOU SEE.
WITH CHARLOTTE, IT FEELS AS IF I HAVE GAINED A **SISTER** MY OWN AGE. I FAVOR HER GREATLY.
THANK YOU FOR SENDING HER TO ME.
SLIP
WSH
NOW THEN!
TO BUSINESS.

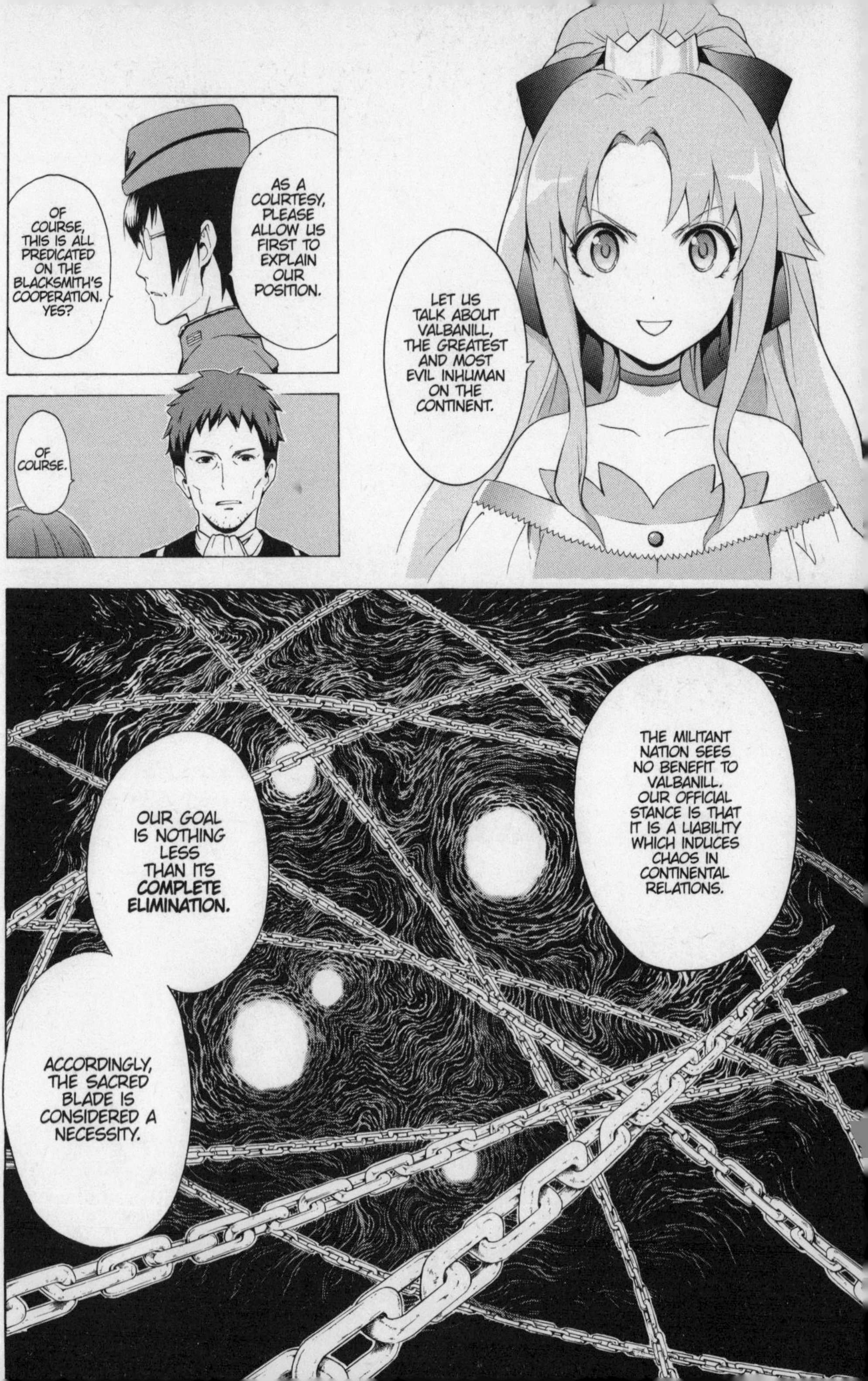
LET US TALK ABOUT VALBANILL, THE GREATEST AND MOST EVIL INHUMAN ON THE CONTINENT.
AS A COURTESY, PLEASE ALLOW US FIRST TO EXPLAIN OUR POSITION.
OF COURSE, THIS IS ALL PREDICATED ON THE BLACKSMITH'S COOPERATION. YES?
OF COURSE.
THE MILITANT NATION SEES NO BENEFIT TO VALBANILL. OUR OFFICIAL STANCE IS THAT IT IS A LIABILITY WHICH INDUCES CHAOS IN CONTINENTAL RELATIONS.
OUR GOAL IS NOTHING LESS THAN ITS **COMPLETE ELIMINATION.**
ACCORDINGLY, THE SACRED BLADE IS CONSIDERED A NECESSITY.

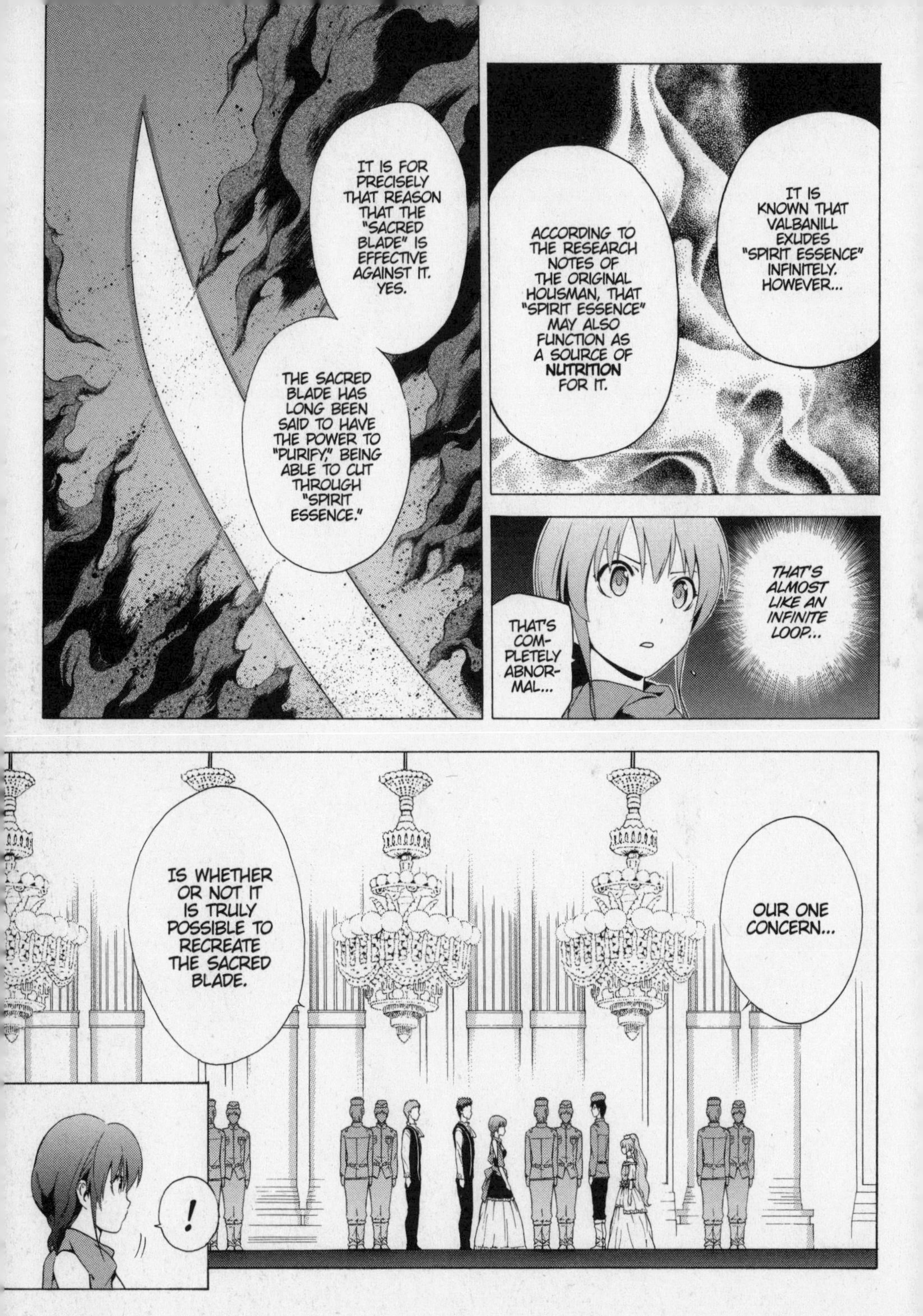
IT IS KNOWN THAT VALBANILL EXUDES "SPIRIT ESSENCE" INFINITELY. HOWEVER...
ACCORDING TO THE RESEARCH NOTES OF THE ORIGINAL HOUSMAN, THAT "SPIRIT ESSENCE" MAY ALSO FUNCTION AS A SOURCE OF **NUTRITION** FOR IT.
THAT'S ALMOST LIKE AN INFINITE LOOP...
THAT'S COM-PLETELY ABNOR-MAL...
IT IS FOR PRECISELY THAT REASON THAT THE "SACRED BLADE" IS EFFECTIVE AGAINST IT. YES.
THE SACRED BLADE HAS LONG BEEN SAID TO HAVE THE POWER TO "PURIFY," BEING ABLE TO CUT THROUGH "SPIRIT ESSENCE."
OUR ONE CONCERN...
IS WHETHER OR NOT IT IS TRULY POSSIBLE TO RECREATE THE SACRED BLADE.
!

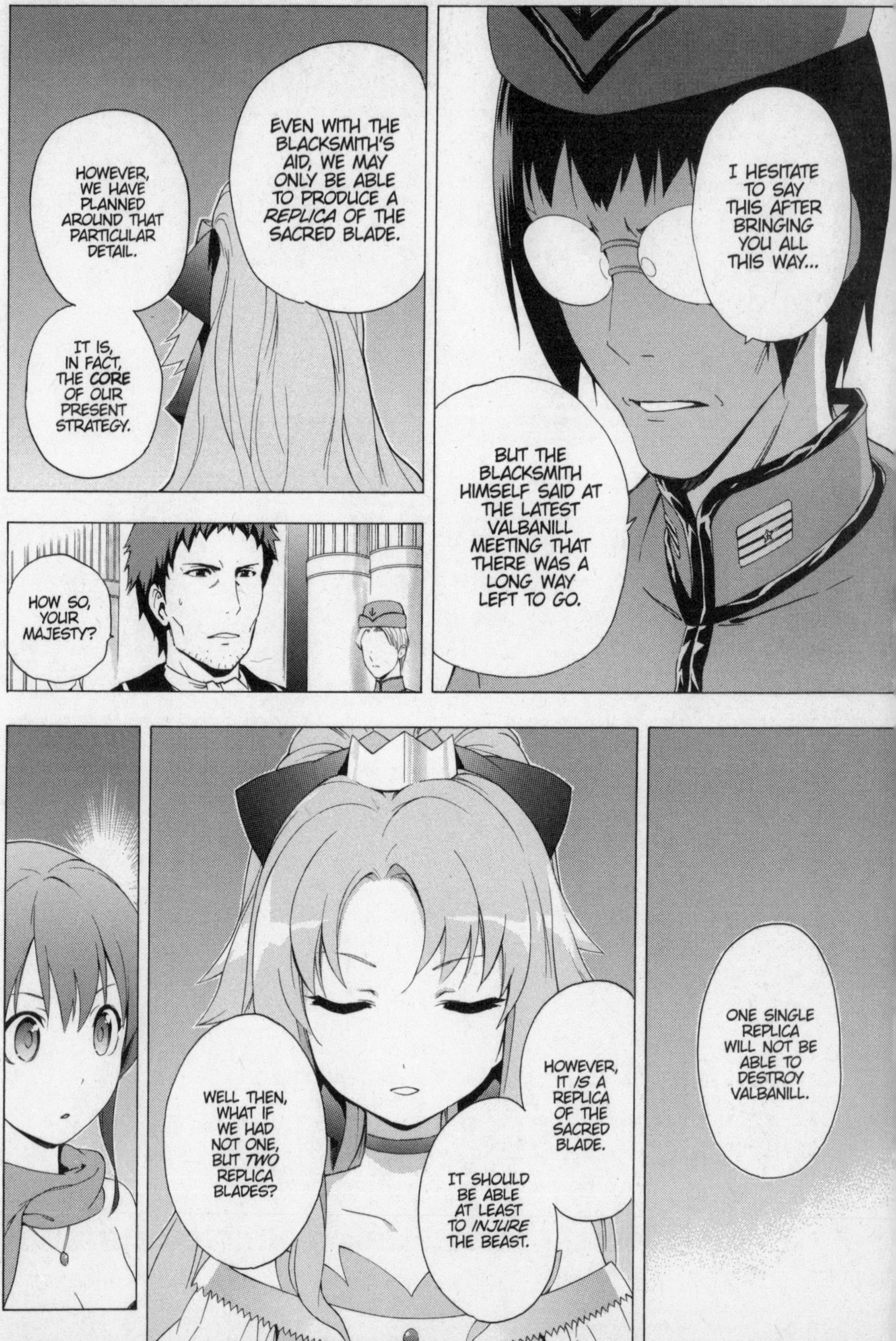
I HESITATE TO SAY THIS AFTER BRINGING YOU ALL THIS WAY...
BUT THE BLACKSMITH HIMSELF SAID AT THE LATEST VALBANILL MEETING THAT THERE WAS A LONG WAY LEFT TO GO.
EVEN WITH THE BLACKSMITH'S AID, WE MAY ONLY BE ABLE TO PRODUCE A *REPLICA* OF THE SACRED BLADE.
HOWEVER, WE HAVE PLANNED AROUND THAT PARTICULAR DETAIL.
IT IS, IN FACT, THE **CORE** OF OUR PRESENT STRATEGY.
HOW SO, YOUR MAJESTY?
ONE SINGLE REPLICA WILL NOT BE ABLE TO DESTROY VALBANILL.
HOWEVER, IT *IS* A REPLICA OF THE SACRED BLADE.
IT SHOULD BE ABLE AT LEAST TO *INJURE* THE BEAST.
WELL THEN, WHAT IF WE HAD NOT ONE, BUT *TWO* REPLICA BLADES?

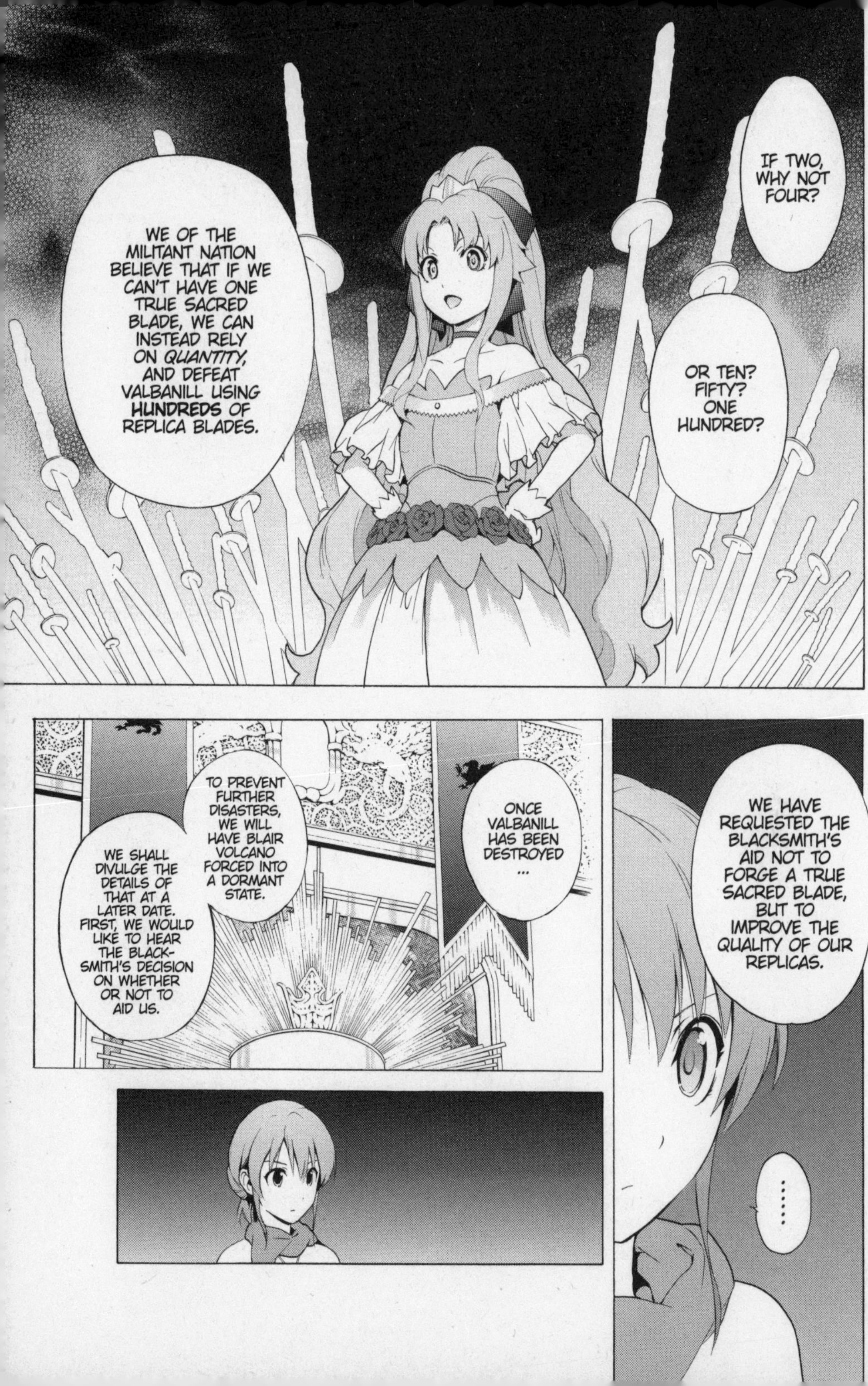
IF TWO, WHY NOT FOUR?
OR TEN? FIFTY? ONE HUNDRED?
WE OF THE MILITANT NATION BELIEVE THAT IF WE CAN'T HAVE ONE TRUE SACRED BLADE, WE CAN INSTEAD RELY ON *QUANTITY*, AND DEFEAT VALBANILL USING **HUNDREDS** OF REPLICA BLADES.
WE HAVE REQUESTED THE BLACKSMITH'S AID NOT TO FORGE A TRUE SACRED BLADE, BUT TO IMPROVE THE QUALITY OF OUR REPLICAS.
......
ONCE VALBANILL HAS BEEN DESTROYED ...
TO PREVENT FURTHER DISASTERS, WE WILL HAVE BLAIR VOLCANO FORCED INTO A DORMANT STATE.
WE SHALL DIVULGE THE DETAILS OF THAT AT A LATER DATE. FIRST, WE WOULD LIKE TO HEAR THE BLACK-SMITH'S DECISION ON WHETHER OR NOT TO AID US.

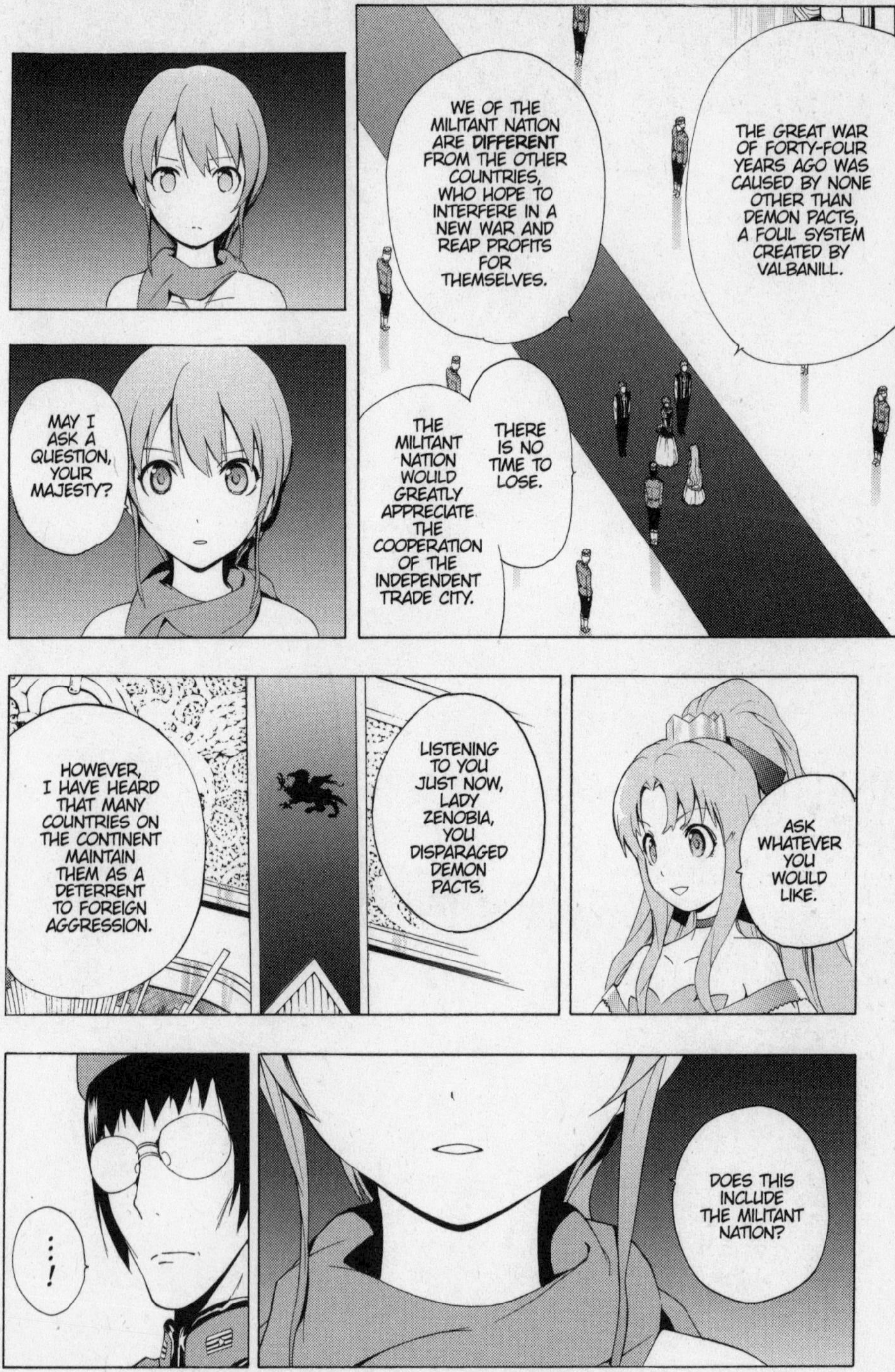
THE GREAT WAR OF FORTY-FOUR YEARS AGO WAS CAUSED BY NONE OTHER THAN DEMON PACTS, A FOUL SYSTEM CREATED BY VALBANILL.
WE OF THE MILITANT NATION ARE **DIFFERENT** FROM THE OTHER COUNTRIES, WHO HOPE TO INTERFERE IN A NEW WAR AND REAP PROFITS FOR THEMSELVES.
THERE IS NO TIME TO LOSE.
THE MILITANT NATION WOULD GREATLY APPRECIATE THE COOPERATION OF THE INDEPENDENT TRADE CITY.
MAY I ASK A QUESTION, YOUR MAJESTY?
ASK WHATEVER YOU WOULD LIKE.
LISTENING TO YOU JUST NOW, LADY ZENOBIA, YOU DISPARAGED DEMON PACTS.
HOWEVER, I HAVE HEARD THAT MANY COUNTRIES ON THE CONTINENT MAINTAIN THEM AS A DETERRENT TO FOREIGN AGGRESSION.
DOES THIS INCLUDE THE MILITANT NATION?
...!

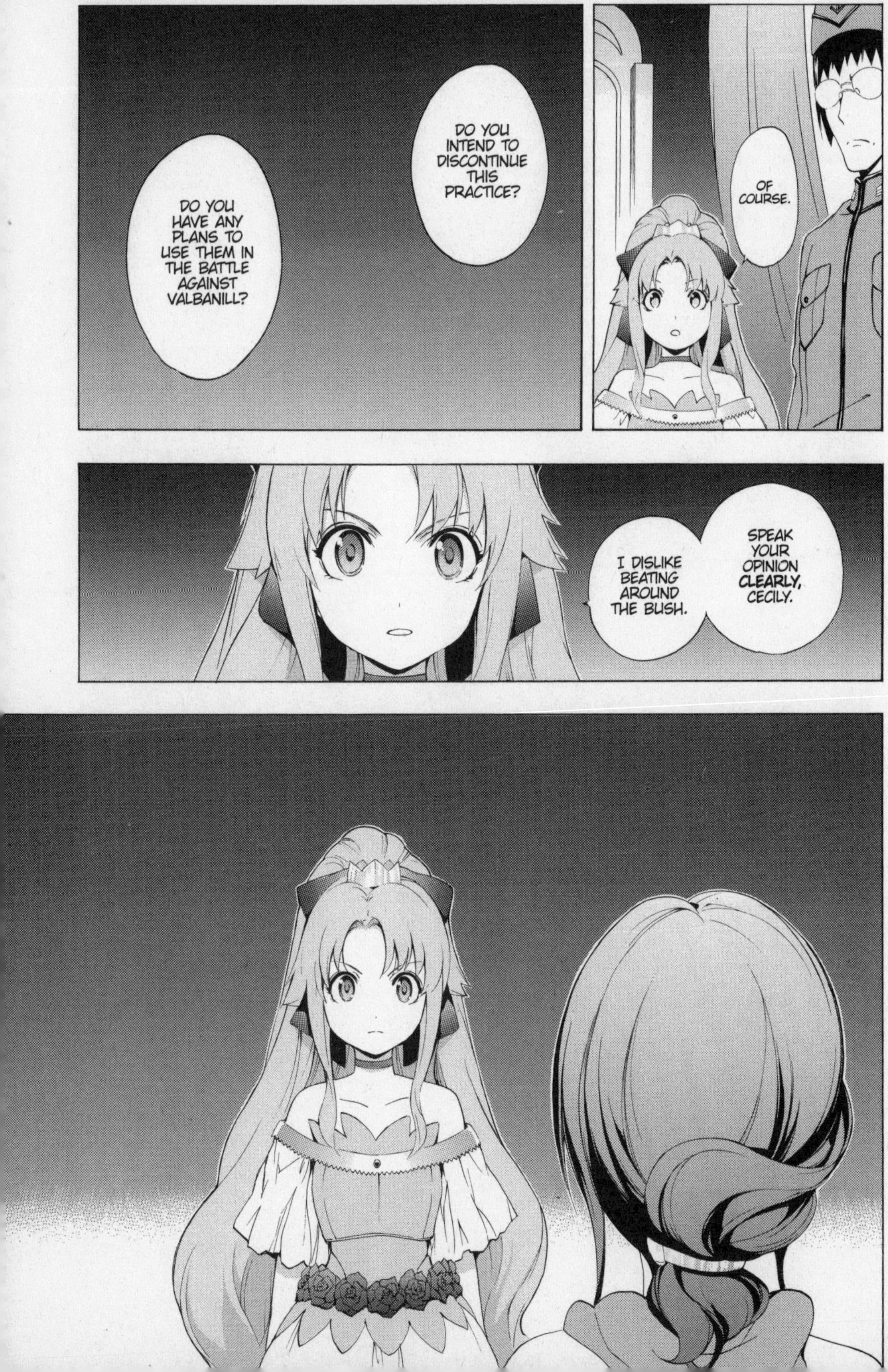
OF COURSE.
DO YOU INTEND TO DISCONTINUE THIS PRACTICE?
DO YOU HAVE ANY PLANS TO USE THEM IN THE BATTLE AGAINST VALBANILL?
SPEAK YOUR OPINION **CLEARLY,** CECILY.
I DISLIKE BEATING AROUND THE BUSH.

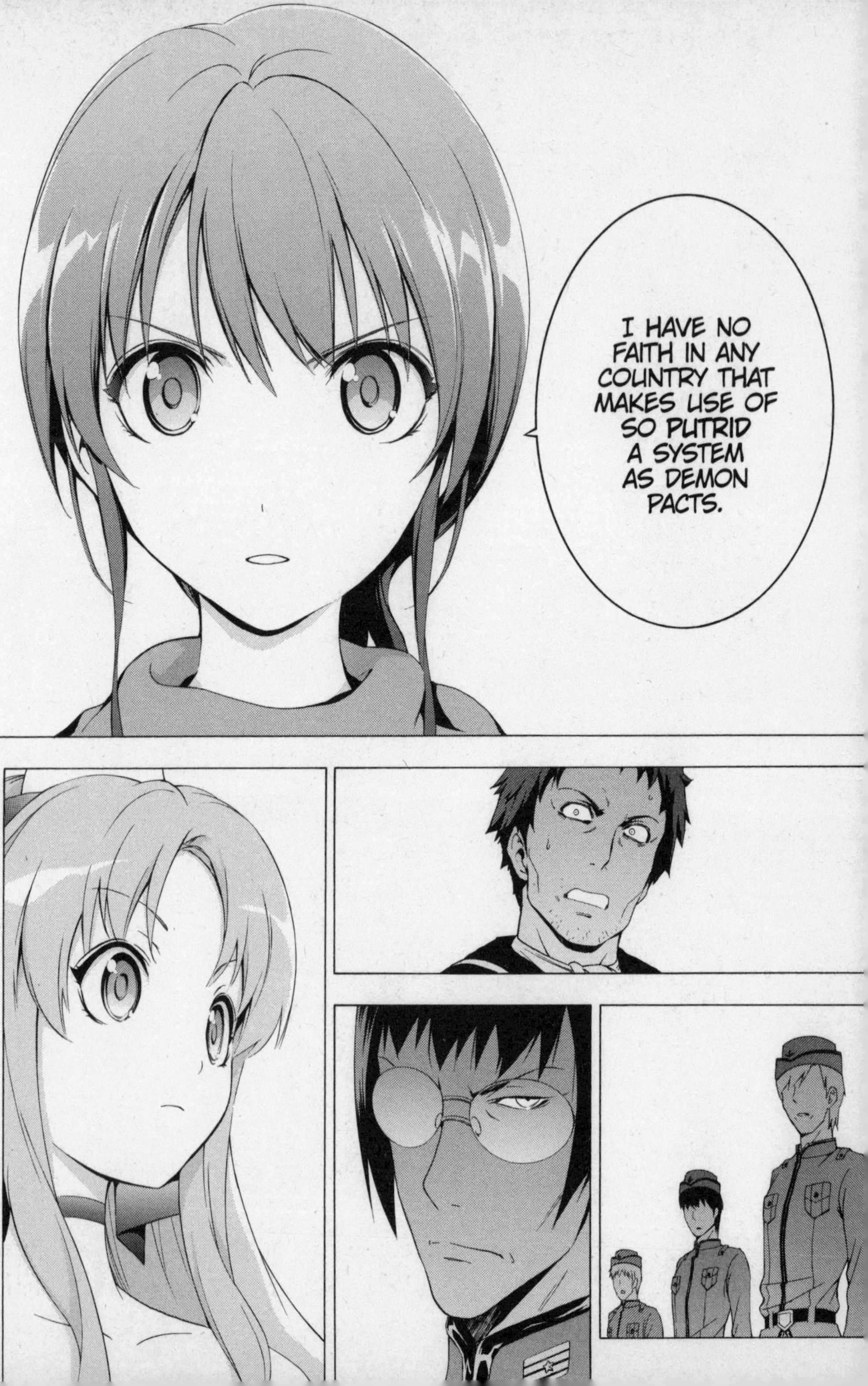
I HAVE NO FAITH IN ANY COUNTRY THAT MAKES USE OF SO PUTRID A SYSTEM AS DEMON PACTS.

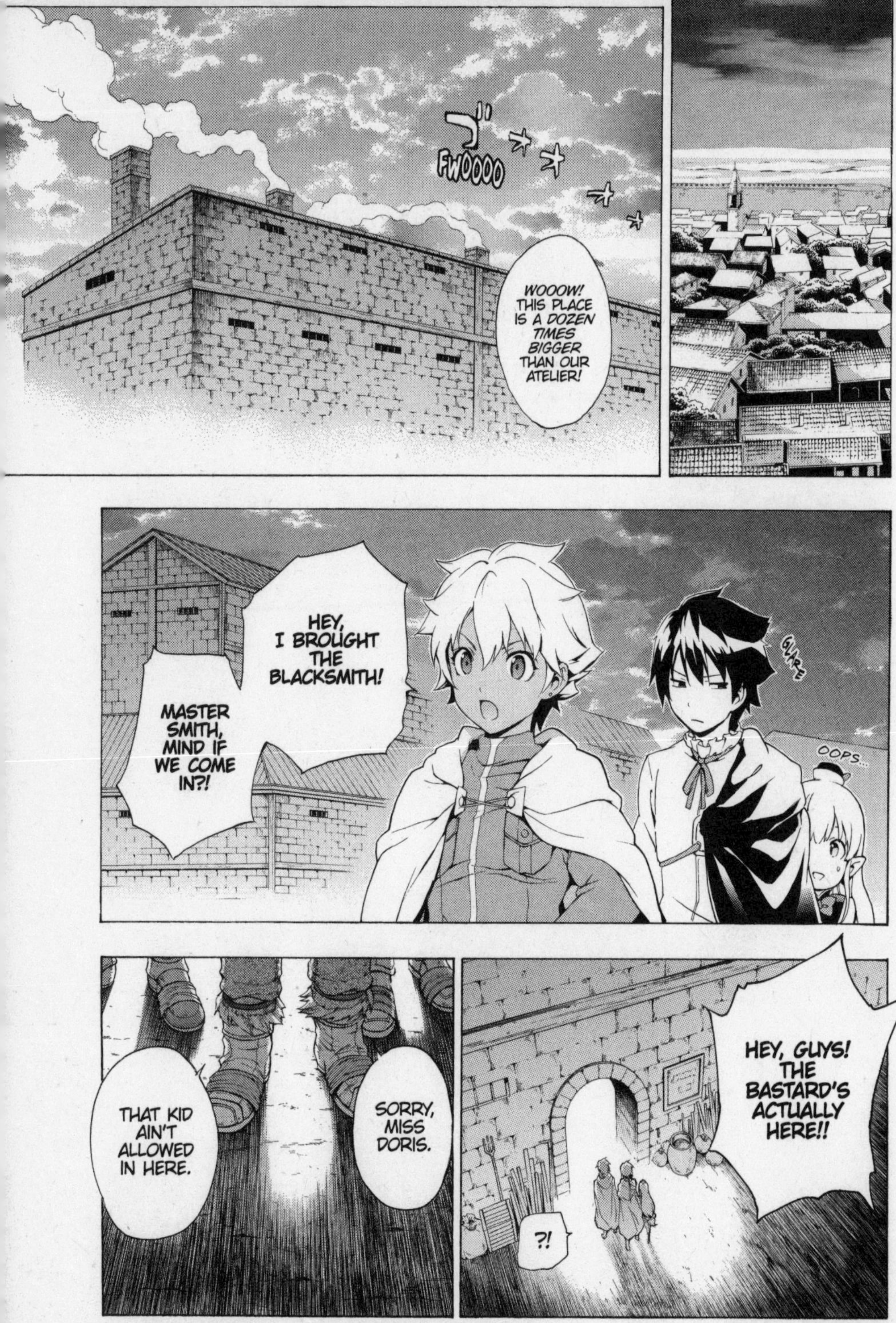
ゴォォォ
FWOOOO
WOOOW! THIS PLACE IS A DOZEN TIMES BIGGER THAN OUR ATELIER!
GLARE
OOPS...
HEY, I BROUGHT THE BLACKSMITH!
MASTER SMITH, MIND IF WE COME IN?!
HEY, GUYS! THE BASTARD'S ACTUALLY HERE!!
?!
SORRY, MISS DORIS.
THAT KID AIN'T ALLOWED IN HERE.

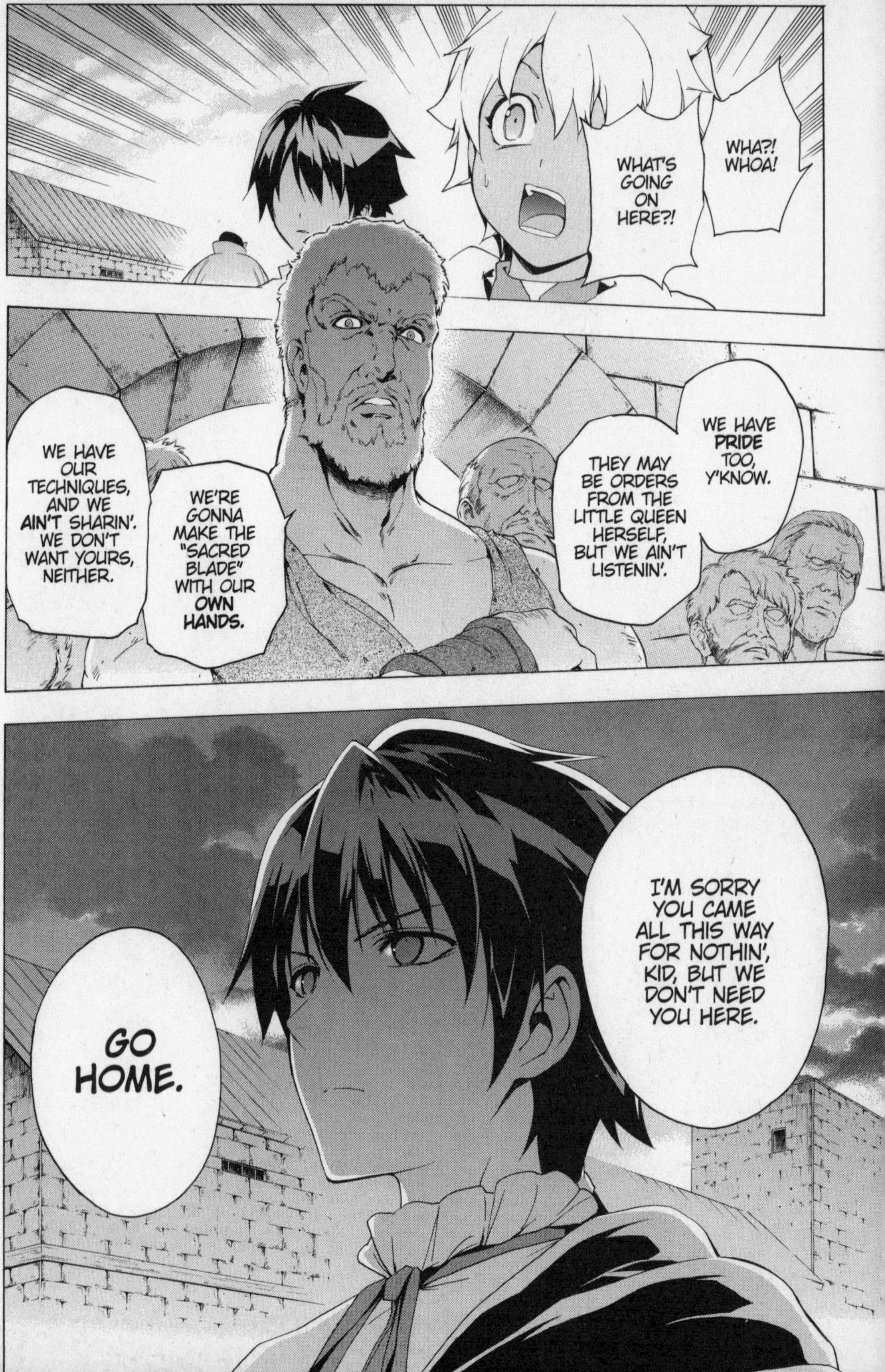
WHA?! WHOA!
WHAT'S GOING ON HERE?!
WE HAVE PRIDE TOO, Y'KNOW.
THEY MAY BE ORDERS FROM THE LITTLE QUEEN HERSELF, BUT WE AIN'T LISTENIN'.
WE'RE GONNA MAKE THE "SACRED BLADE" WITH OUR OWN HANDS.
WE HAVE OUR TECHNIQUES, AND WE AIN'T SHARIN'. WE DON'T WANT YOURS, NEITHER.
I'M SORRY YOU CAME ALL THIS WAY FOR NOTHIN', KID, BUT WE DON'T NEED YOU HERE.
GO HOME.

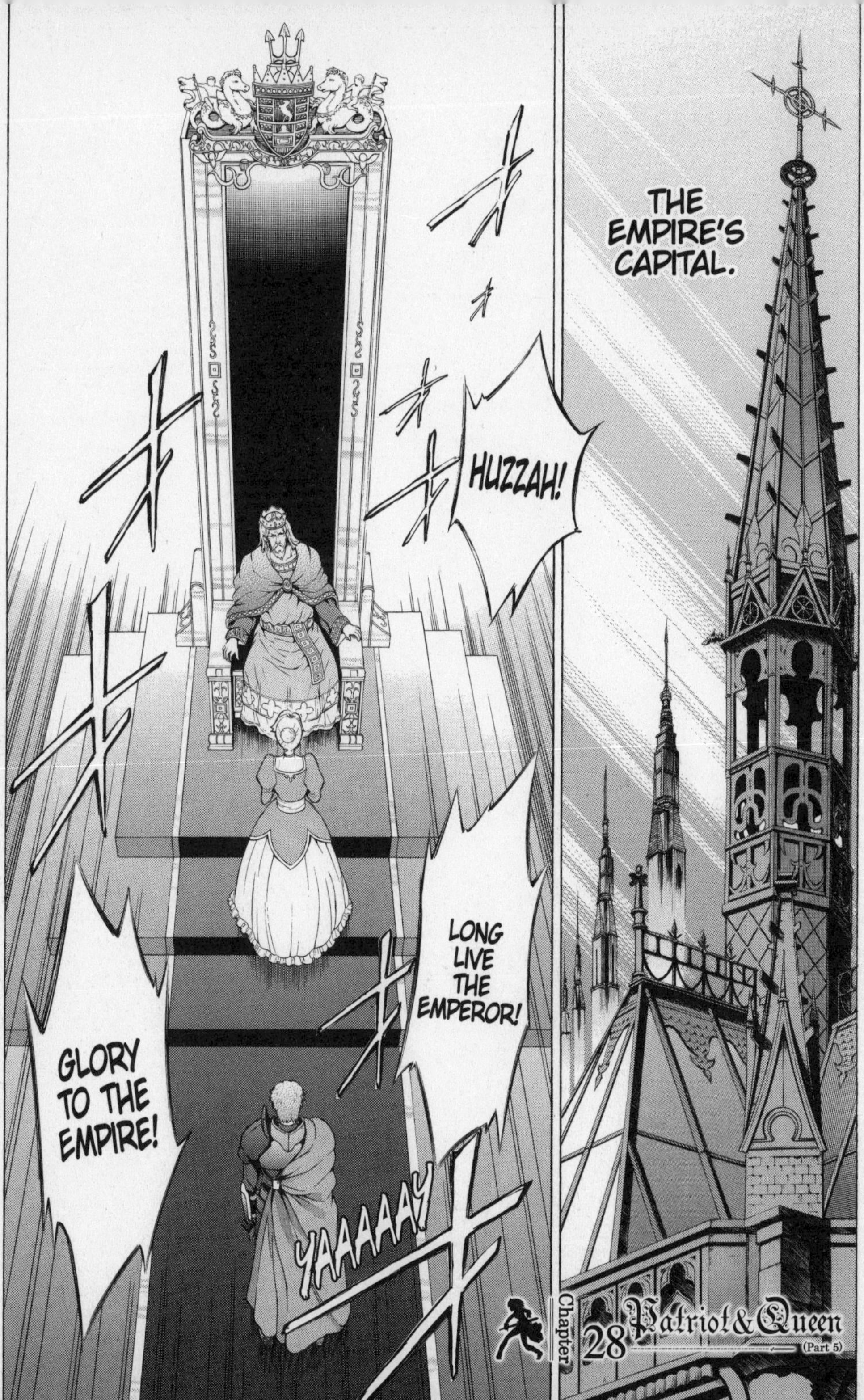
THE EMPIRE'S CAPITAL.
Chapter 28 Patriot & Queen
(Part 5)
HUZZAH!
LONG LIVE THE EMPEROR!
GLORY TO THE EMPIRE!
YAAAAAY

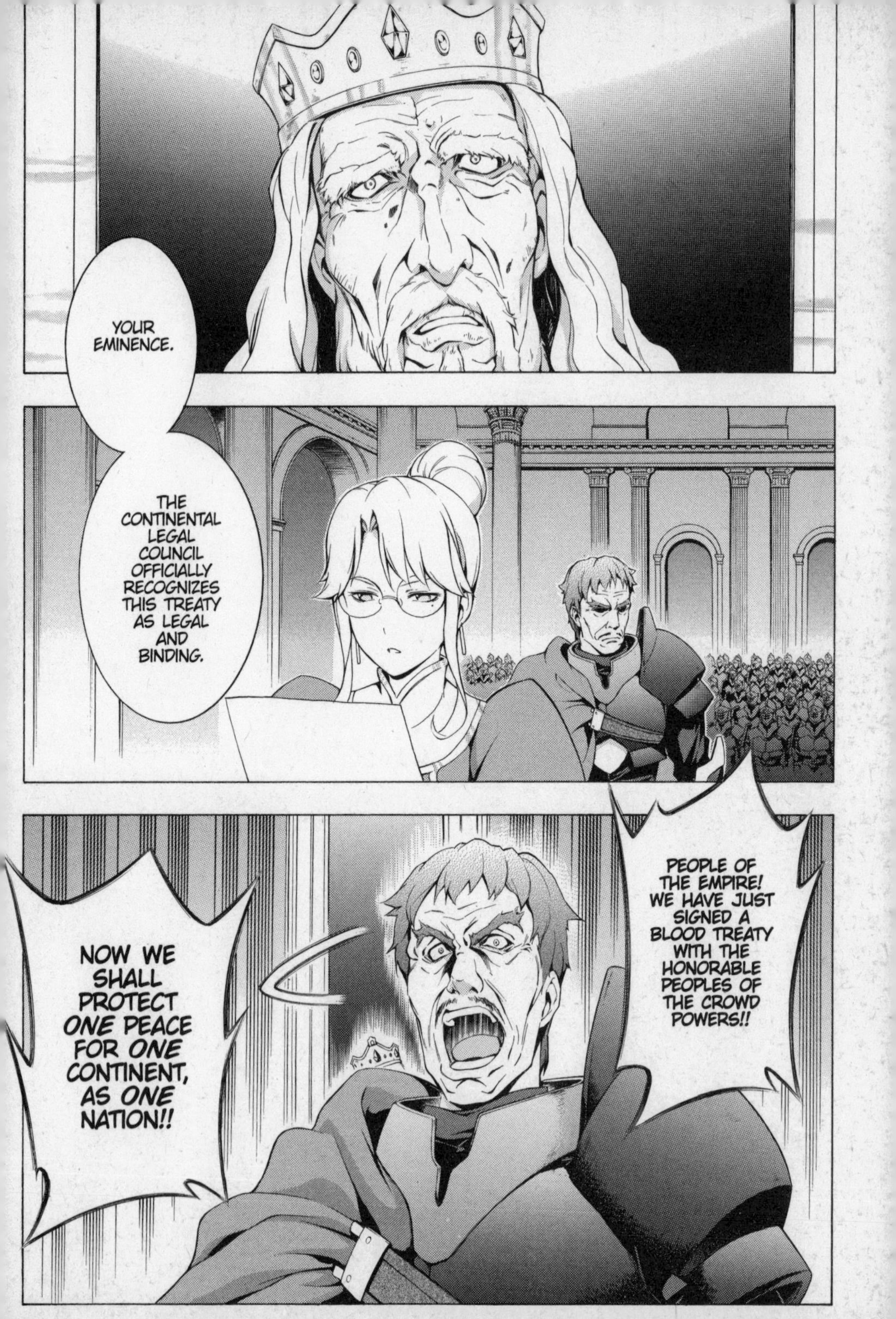
YOUR EMINENCE.
THE CONTINENTAL LEGAL COUNCIL OFFICIALLY RECOGNIZES THIS TREATY AS LEGAL AND BINDING.
PEOPLE OF THE EMPIRE! WE HAVE JUST SIGNED A BLOOD TREATY WITH THE HONORABLE PEOPLES OF THE CROWD POWERS!!
NOW WE SHALL PROTECT *ONE* PEACE FOR *ONE* CONTINENT, AS *ONE* NATION!!

WE HEREBY DECLARE THE BIRTH OF THE IMPERIAL CROWD POWER!!
HOORAAAAAY

Chapter 28 Patriot & Queen (Part 5)

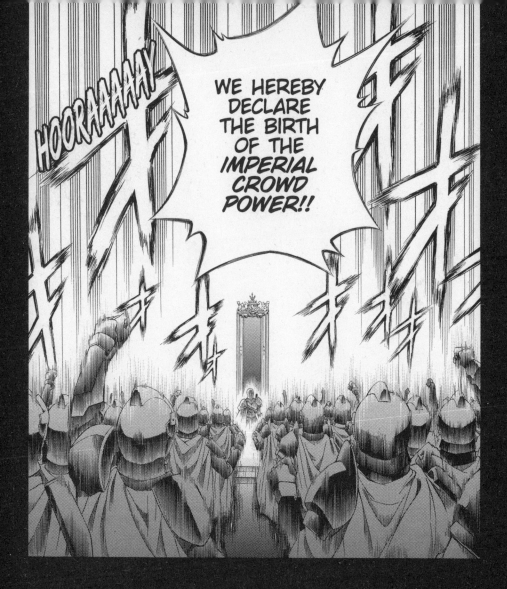

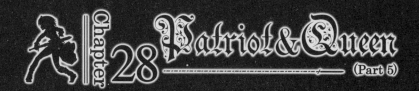

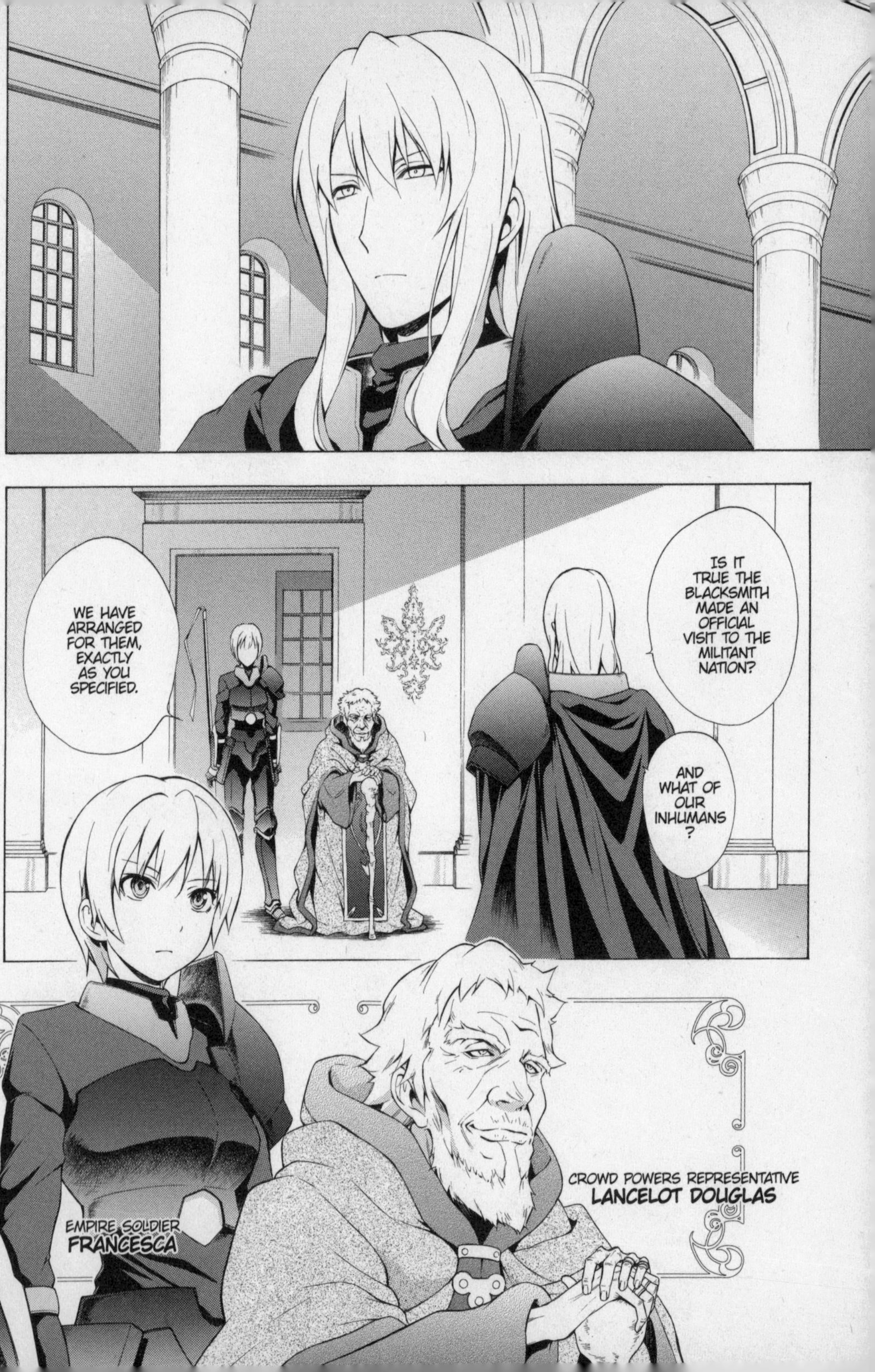
IS IT TRUE THE BLACKSMITH MADE AN OFFICIAL VISIT TO THE MILITANT NATION?
AND WHAT OF OUR INHUMANS?
WE HAVE ARRANGED FOR THEM, EXACTLY AS YOU SPECIFIED.
CROWD POWERS REPRESENTATIVE
LANCELOT DOUGLAS
EMPIRE SOLDIER
FRANCESCA

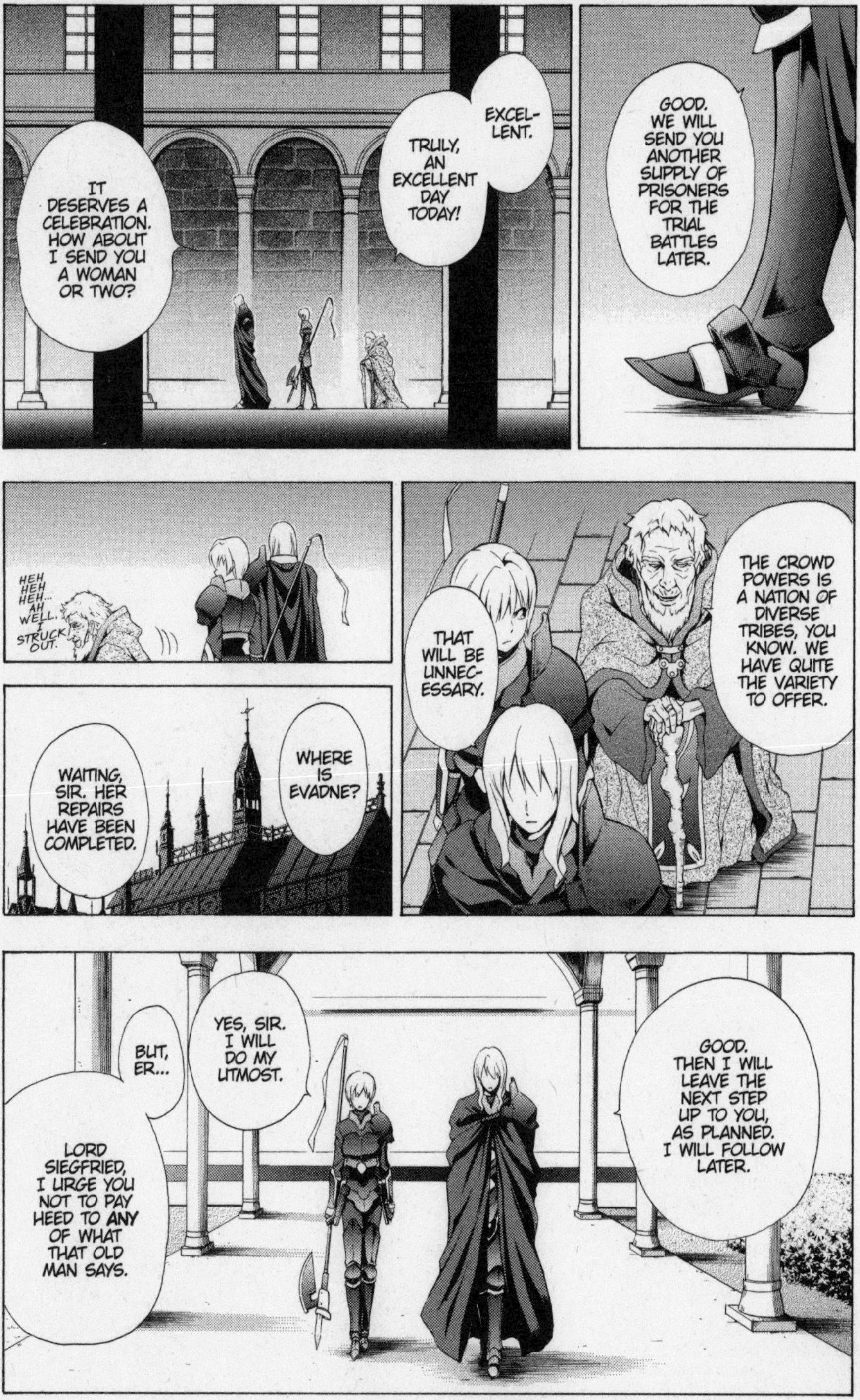
GOOD. WE WILL SEND YOU ANOTHER SUPPLY OF PRISONERS FOR THE TRIAL BATTLES LATER.
EXCEL-LENT.
TRULY, AN EXCELLENT DAY TODAY!
IT DESERVES A CELEBRATION. HOW ABOUT I SEND YOU A WOMAN OR TWO?
THE CROWD POWERS IS A NATION OF DIVERSE TRIBES, YOU KNOW. WE HAVE QUITE THE VARIETY TO OFFER.
THAT WILL BE UNNEC-ESSARY.
HEH HEH HEH... AH WELL. I STRUCK OUT.
WHERE IS EVADNE?
WAITING, SIR. HER REPAIRS HAVE BEEN COMPLETED.
GOOD. THEN I WILL LEAVE THE NEXT STEP UP TO YOU, AS PLANNED. I WILL FOLLOW LATER.
YES, SIR. I WILL DO MY UTMOST.
BUT, ER...
LORD SIEGFRIED, I URGE YOU NOT TO PAY HEED TO ANY OF WHAT THAT OLD MAN SAYS.

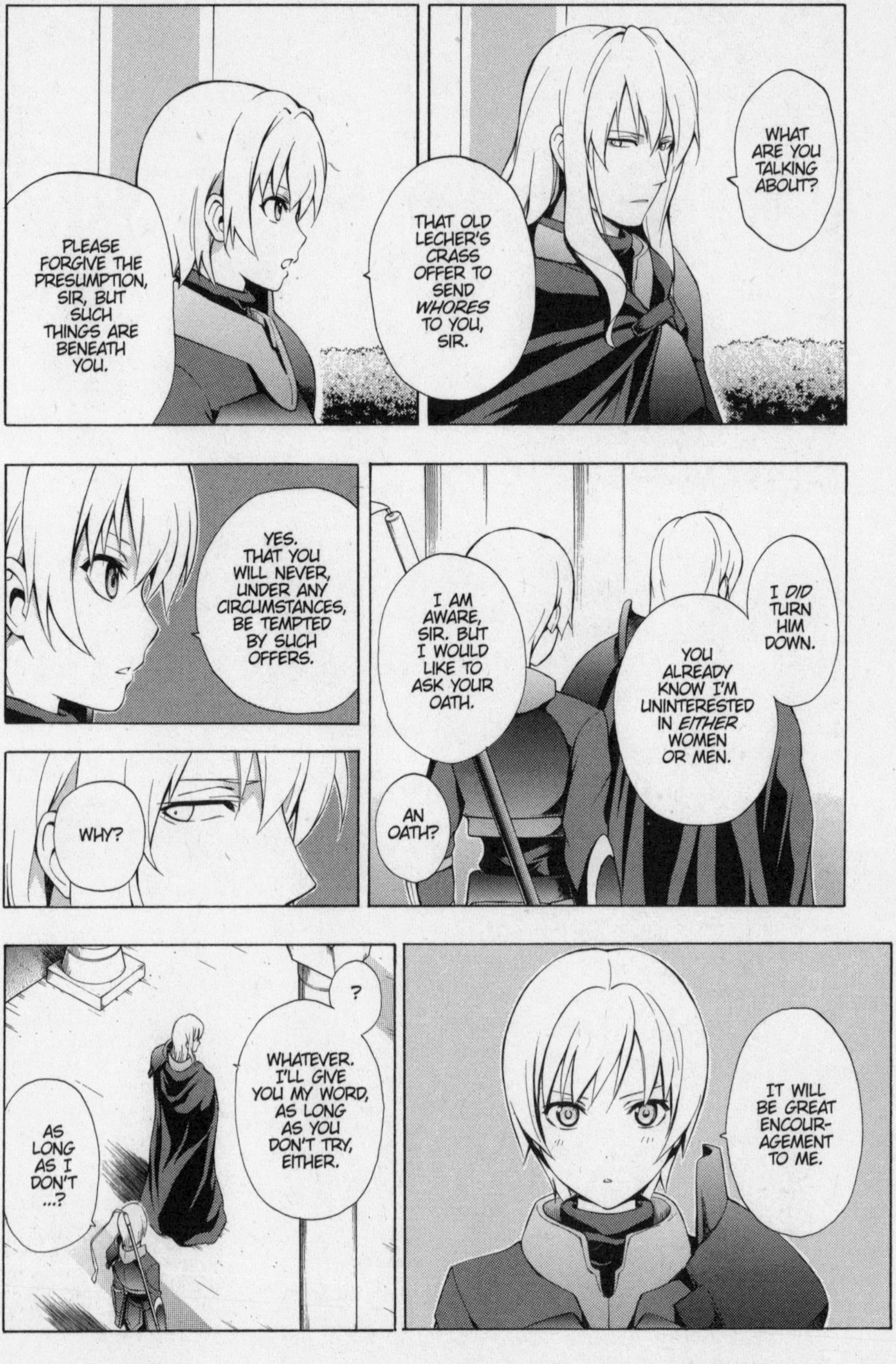
WHAT ARE YOU TALKING ABOUT?
THAT OLD LECHER'S CRASS OFFER TO SEND *WHORES* TO YOU, SIR.
PLEASE FORGIVE THE PRESUMPTION, SIR, BUT SUCH THINGS ARE BENEATH YOU.
I *DID* TURN HIM DOWN.
YOU ALREADY KNOW I'M UNINTERESTED IN *EITHER* WOMEN OR MEN.
I AM AWARE, SIR. BUT I WOULD LIKE TO ASK YOUR OATH.
AN OATH?
YES. THAT YOU WILL NEVER, UNDER ANY CIRCUMSTANCES, BE TEMPTED BY SUCH OFFERS.
WHY?
IT WILL BE GREAT ENCOUR-AGEMENT TO ME.
?
WHATEVER. I'LL GIVE YOU MY WORD, AS LONG AS YOU DON'T TRY, EITHER.
AS LONG AS I DON'T ...?

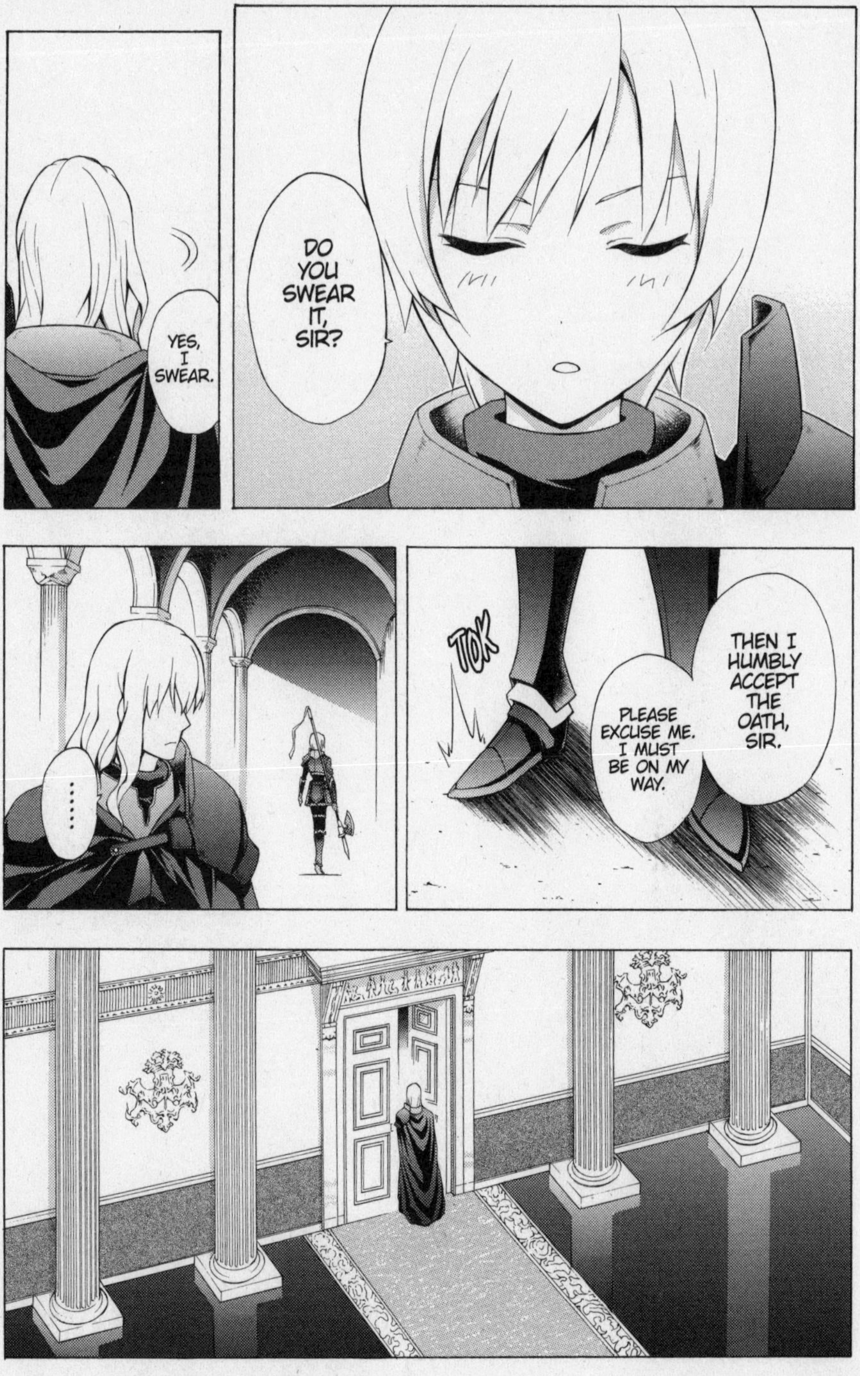
DO YOU SWEAR IT, SIR?
YES, I SWEAR.
THEN I HUMBLY ACCEPT THE OATH, SIR.
PLEASE EXCUSE ME. I MUST BE ON MY WAY.
TOK
......

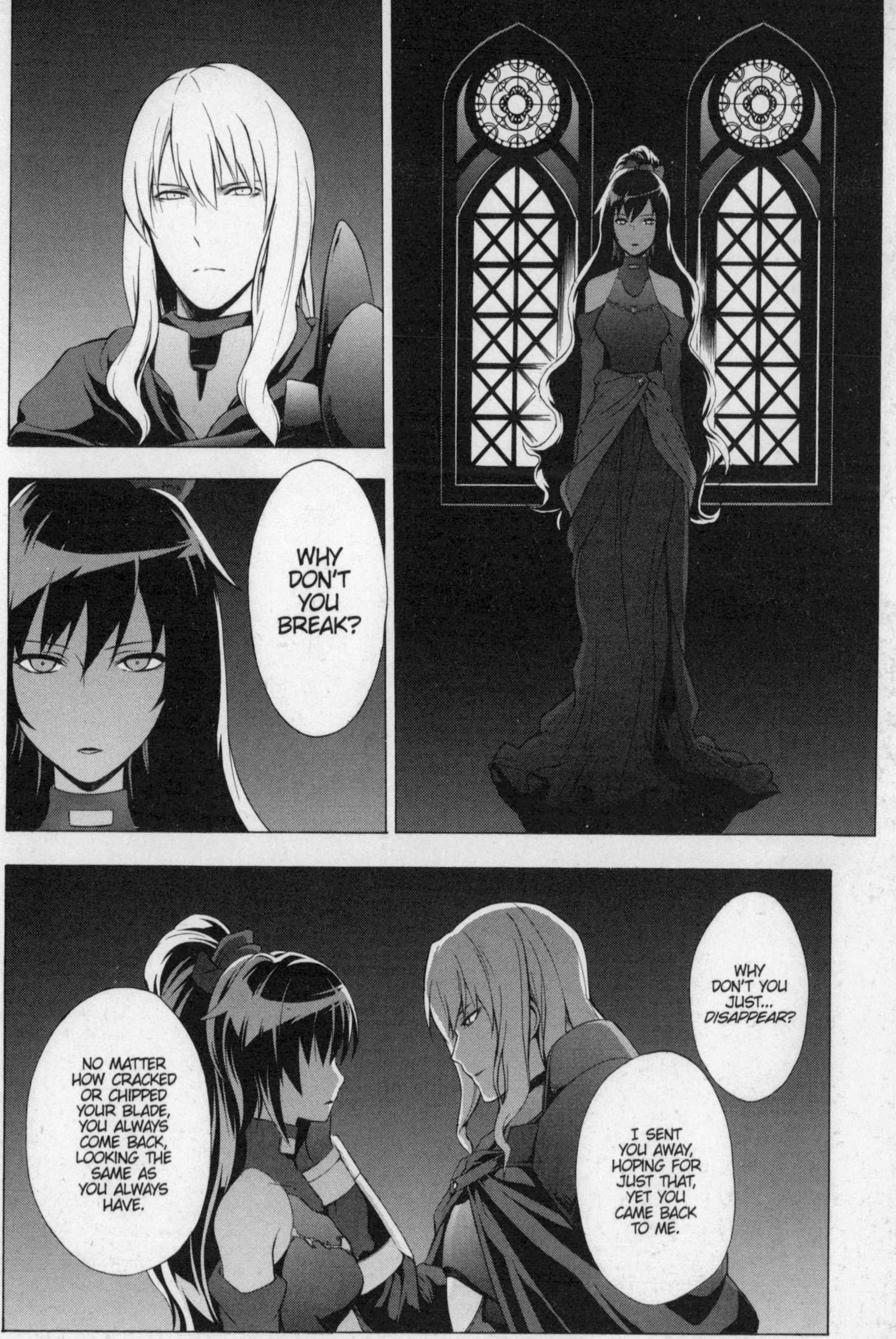
WHY DON'T YOU BREAK?
WHY DON'T YOU JUST... *DISAPPEAR?*
I SENT YOU AWAY, HOPING FOR JUST THAT, YET YOU CAME BACK TO ME.
NO MATTER HOW CRACKED OR CHIPPED YOUR BLADE, YOU ALWAYS COME BACK, LOOKING THE SAME AS YOU ALWAYS HAVE.

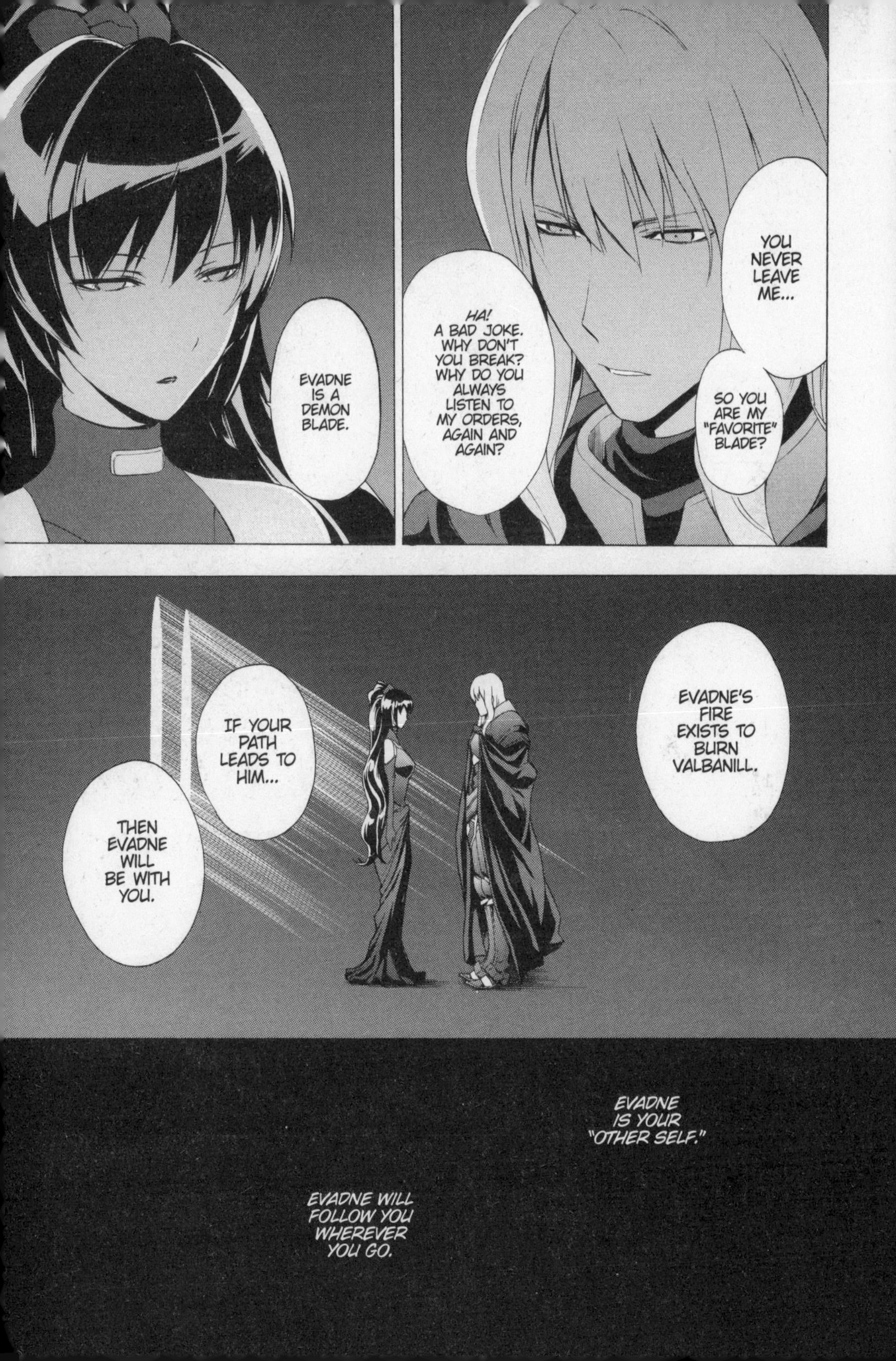
YOU NEVER LEAVE ME...
SO YOU ARE MY "FAVORITE" BLADE?
HA! A BAD JOKE. WHY DON'T YOU BREAK? WHY DO YOU ALWAYS LISTEN TO MY ORDERS, AGAIN AND AGAIN?
EVADNE IS A DEMON BLADE.
EVADNE'S FIRE EXISTS TO BURN VALBANILL.
IF YOUR PATH LEADS TO HIM...
THEN EVADNE WILL BE WITH YOU.
EVADNE IS YOUR "OTHER SELF."
EVADNE WILL FOLLOW YOU WHEREVER YOU GO.

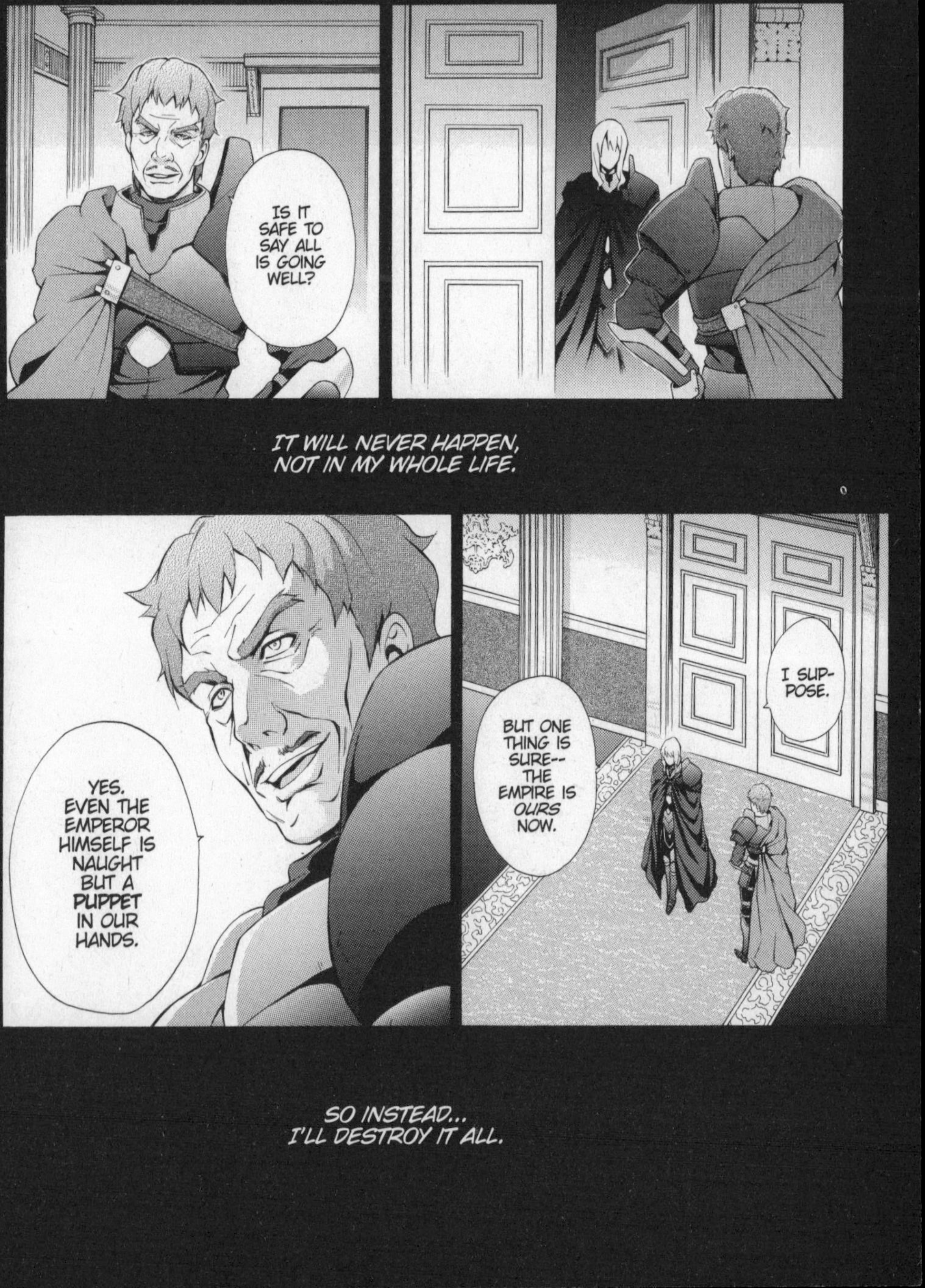
IS IT SAFE TO SAY ALL IS GOING WELL?
IT WILL NEVER HAPPEN, NOT IN MY WHOLE LIFE.
I SUP-POSE.
BUT ONE THING IS SURE-- THE EMPIRE IS OURS NOW.
YES. EVEN THE EMPEROR HIMSELF IS NAUGHT BUT A PUPPET IN OUR HANDS.
SO INSTEAD... I'LL DESTROY IT ALL.

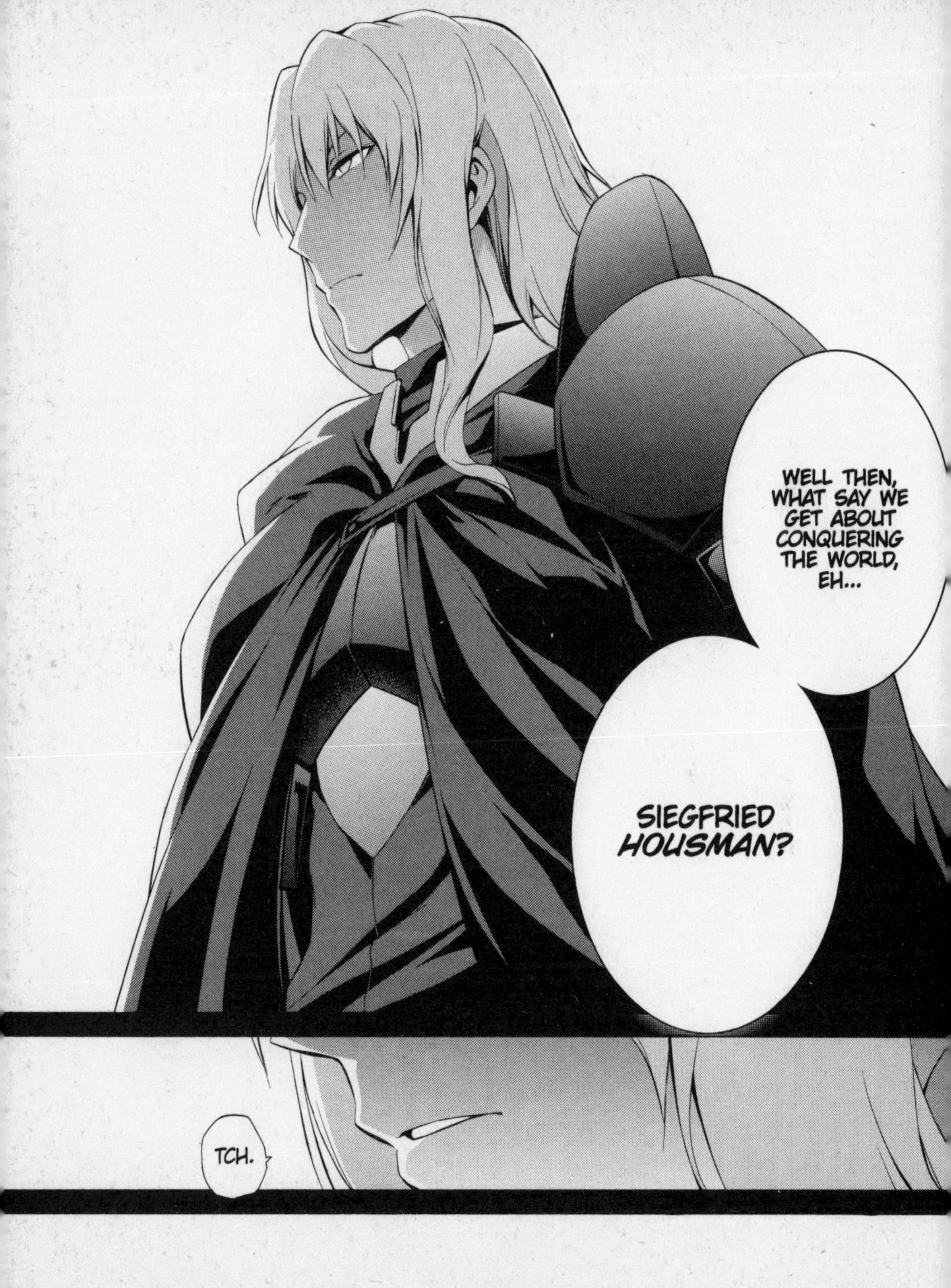
WELL THEN, WHAT SAY WE GET ABOUT CONQUERING THE WORLD, EH...
SIEGFRIED HOUSMAN?
TCH.

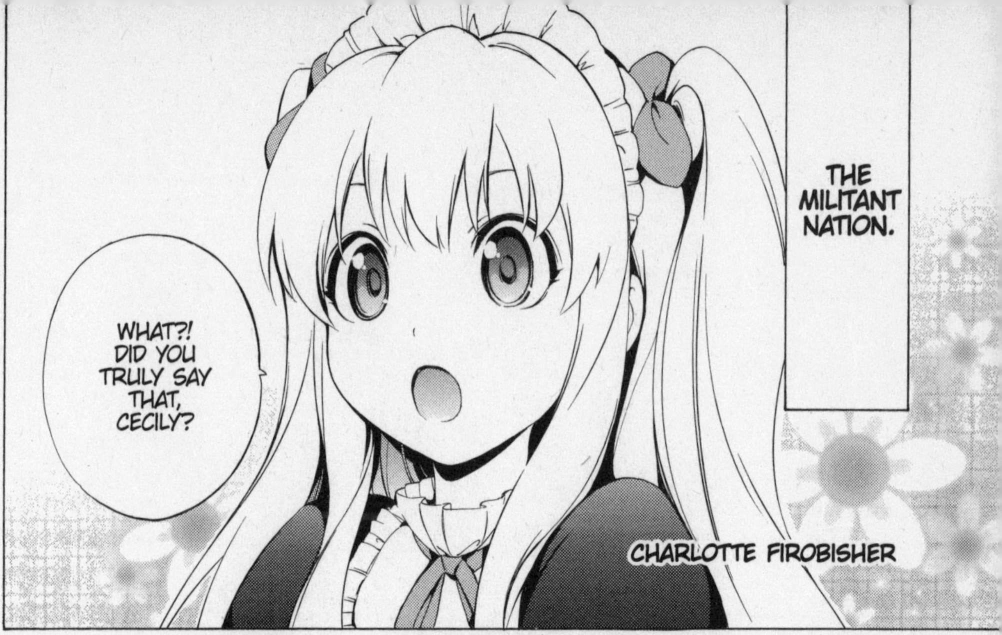
THE MILITANT NATION.
WHAT?! DID YOU TRULY SAY THAT, CECILY?
CHARLOTTE FIROBISHER

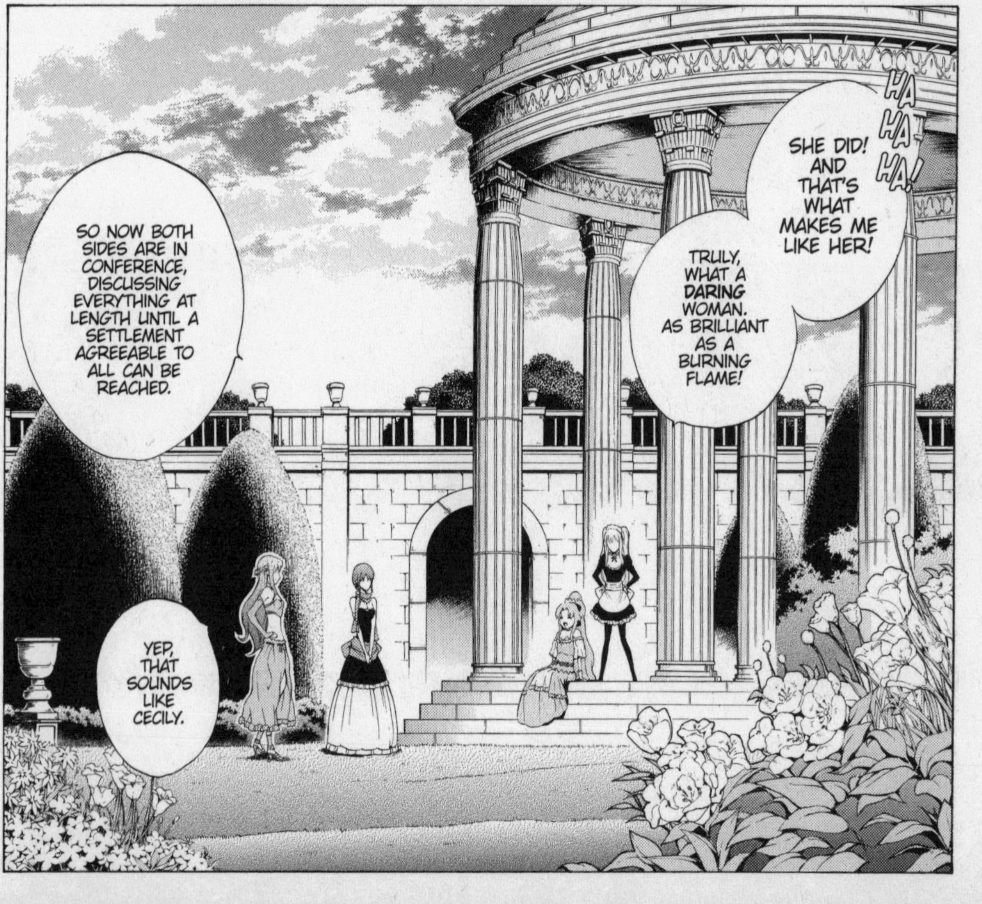
HA HA HA!
SHE DID! AND THAT'S WHAT MAKES ME LIKE HER!
TRULY, WHAT A DARING WOMAN. AS BRILLIANT AS A BURNING FLAME!
SO NOW BOTH SIDES ARE IN CONFERENCE, DISCUSSING EVERYTHING AT LENGTH UNTIL A SETTLEMENT AGREEABLE TO ALL CAN BE REACHED.
YEP, THAT SOUNDS LIKE CECILY.

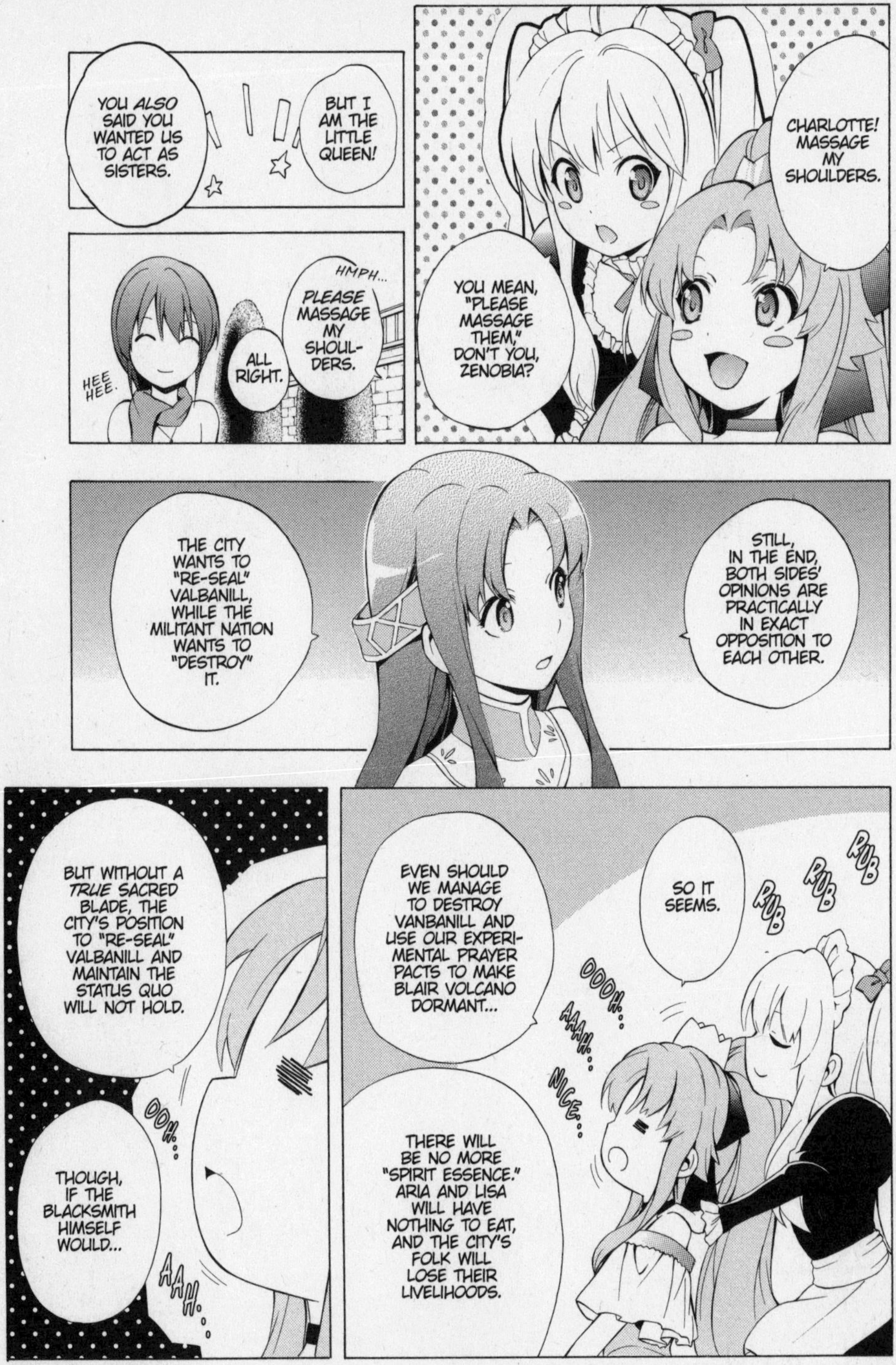
CHARLOTTE! MASSAGE MY SHOULDERS.
YOU MEAN, "PLEASE MASSAGE THEM," DON'T YOU, ZENOBIA?
BUT I AM THE LITTLE QUEEN!
YOU *ALSO* SAID YOU WANTED US TO ACT AS SISTERS.
HMPH...
PLEASE MASSAGE MY SHOULDERS.
ALL RIGHT.
HEE HEE.
STILL, IN THE END, BOTH SIDES' OPINIONS ARE PRACTICALLY IN EXACT OPPOSITION TO EACH OTHER.
THE CITY WANTS TO "RE-SEAL" VALBANILL, WHILE THE MILITANT NATION WANTS TO "DESTROY" IT.
SO IT SEEMS.
RUB
RUB
RUB
EVEN SHOULD WE MANAGE TO DESTROY VANBANILL AND USE OUR EXPERIMENTAL PRAYER PACTS TO MAKE BLAIR VOLCANO DORMANT...
OOOH...
AAAH...
NICE...
THERE WILL BE NO MORE "SPIRIT ESSENCE." ARIA AND LISA WILL HAVE NOTHING TO EAT, AND THE CITY'S FOLK WILL LOSE THEIR LIVELIHOODS.
BUT WITHOUT A *TRUE* SACRED BLADE, THE CITY'S POSITION TO "RE-SEAL" VALBANILL AND MAINTAIN THE STATUS QUO WILL NOT HOLD.
OOH...
THOUGH, IF THE BLACKSMITH HIMSELF WOULD...
AAH...

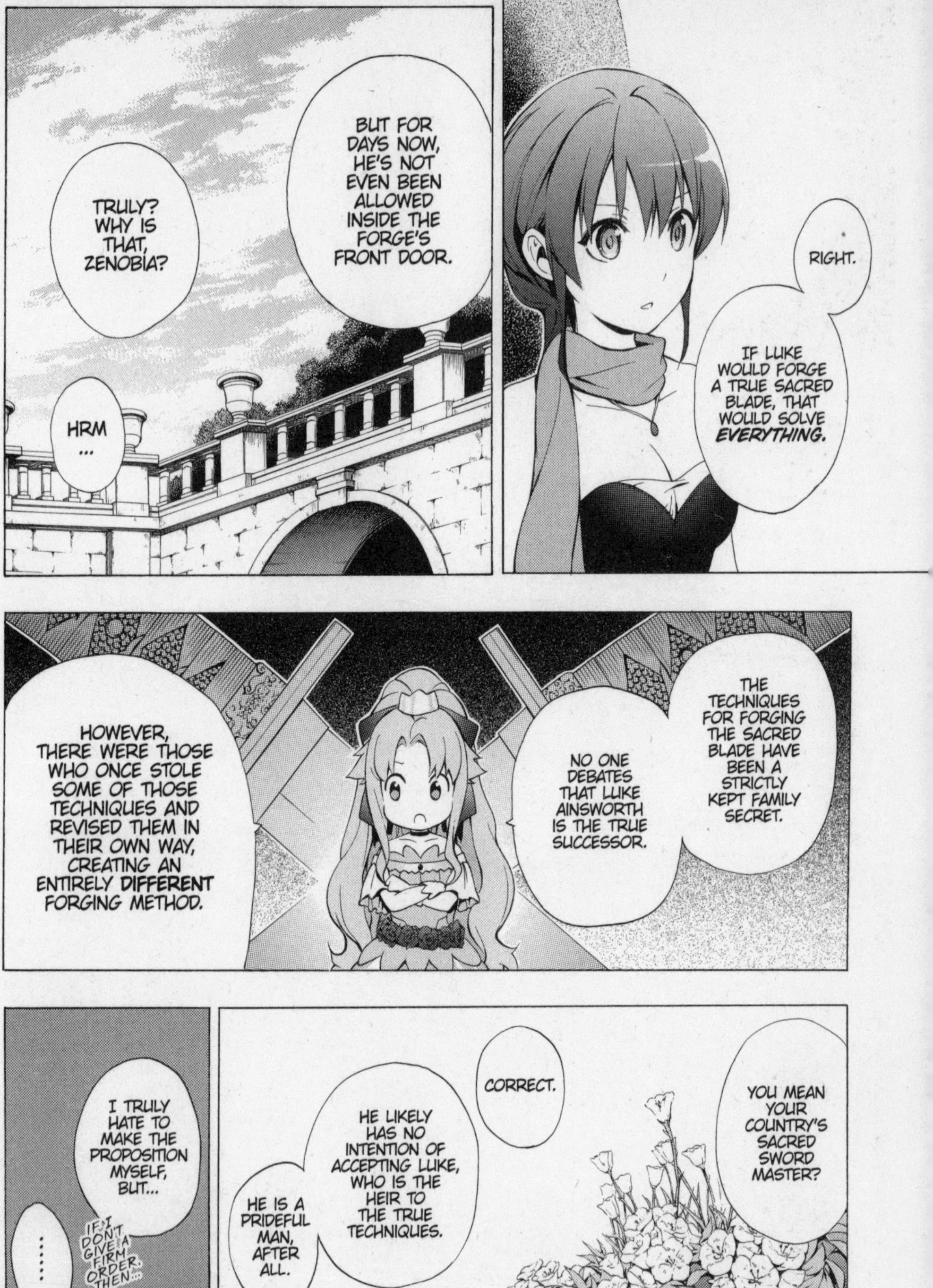
RIGHT.
IF LUKE WOULD FORGE A TRUE SACRED BLADE, THAT WOULD SOLVE EVERYTHING.
BUT FOR DAYS NOW, HE'S NOT EVEN BEEN ALLOWED INSIDE THE FORGE'S FRONT DOOR.
TRULY? WHY IS THAT, ZENOBIA?
HRM ...
THE TECHNIQUES FOR FORGING THE SACRED BLADE HAVE BEEN A STRICTLY KEPT FAMILY SECRET.
NO ONE DEBATES THAT LUKE AINSWORTH IS THE TRUE SUCCESSOR.
HOWEVER, THERE WERE THOSE WHO ONCE STOLE SOME OF THOSE TECHNIQUES AND REVISED THEM IN THEIR OWN WAY, CREATING AN ENTIRELY DIFFERENT FORGING METHOD.
YOU MEAN YOUR COUNTRY'S SACRED SWORD MASTER?
CORRECT.
HE LIKELY HAS NO INTENTION OF ACCEPTING LUKE, WHO IS THE HEIR TO THE TRUE TECHNIQUES.
HE IS A PRIDEFUL MAN, AFTER ALL.
I TRULY HATE TO MAKE THE PROPOSITION MYSELF, BUT...
IF I DON'T GIVE A FIRM ORDER, THEN...
......

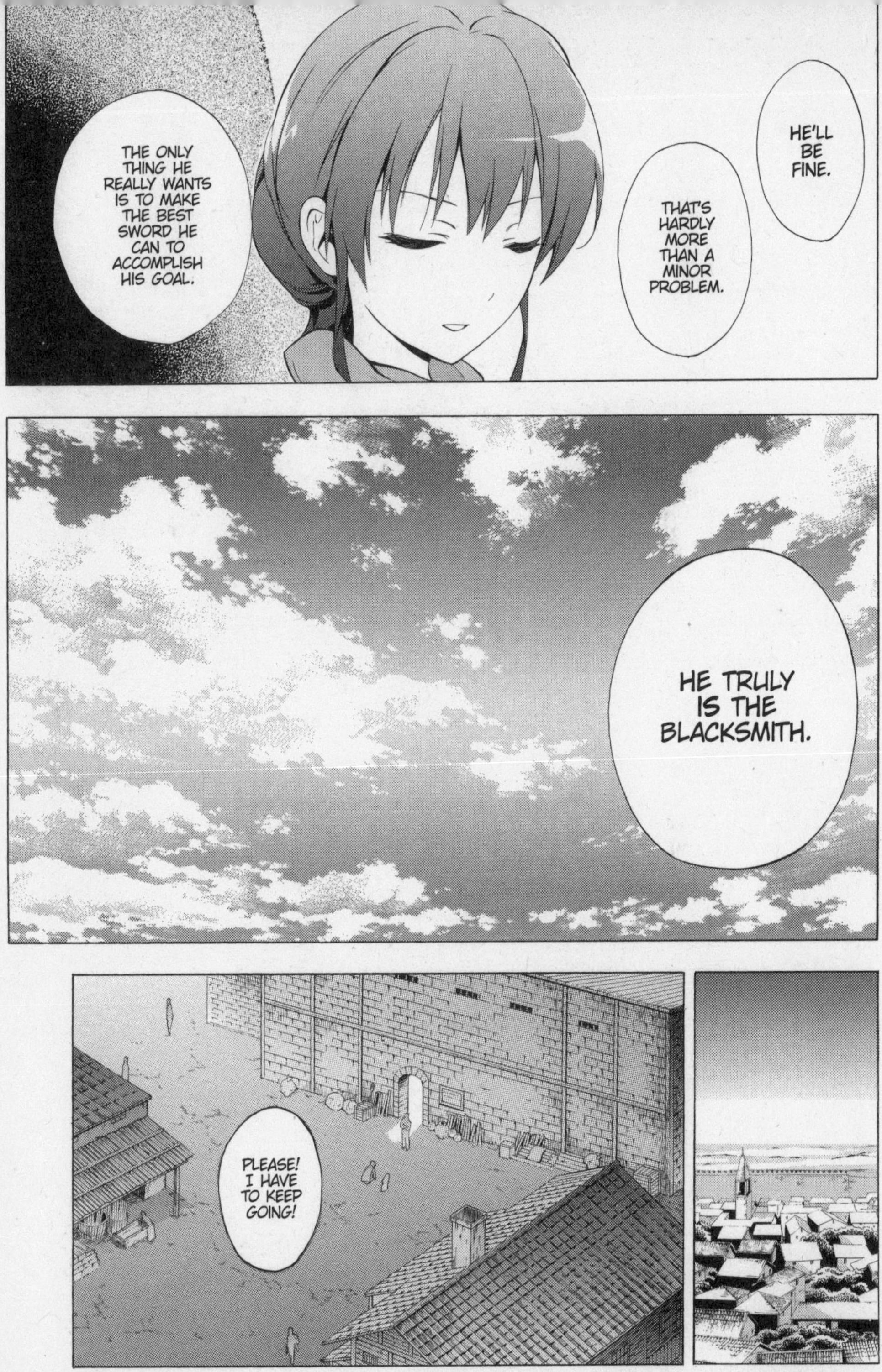
HE'LL BE FINE.
THAT'S HARDLY MORE THAN A MINOR PROBLEM.
THE ONLY THING HE REALLY WANTS IS TO MAKE THE BEST SWORD HE CAN TO ACCOMPLISH HIS GOAL.
HE TRULY IS THE BLACKSMITH.
PLEASE! I HAVE TO KEEP GOING!

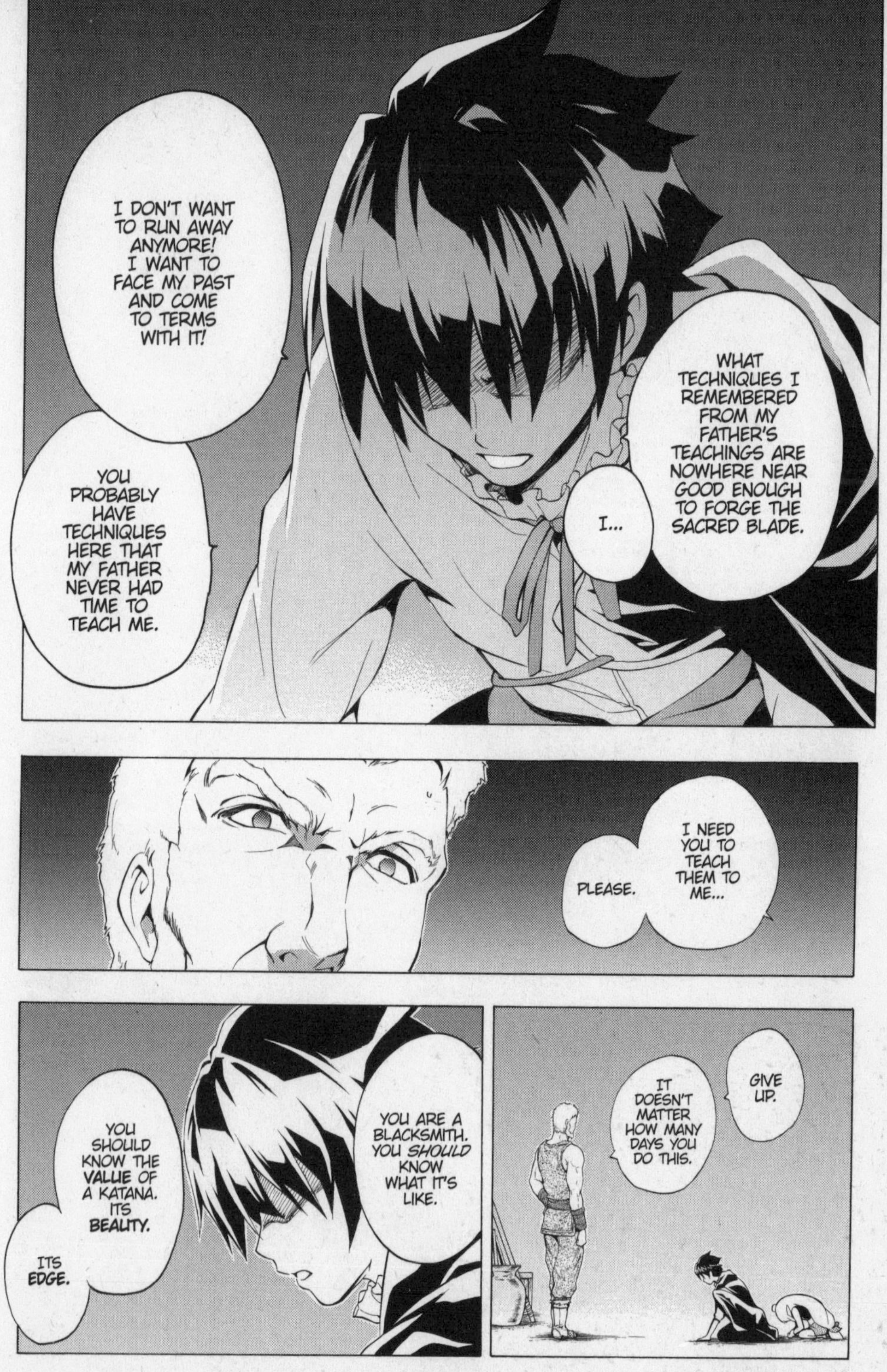
WHAT TECHNIQUES I REMEMBERED FROM MY FATHER'S TEACHINGS ARE NOWHERE NEAR GOOD ENOUGH TO FORGE THE SACRED BLADE.
I...
I DON'T WANT TO RUN AWAY ANYMORE! I WANT TO FACE MY PAST AND COME TO TERMS WITH IT!
YOU PROBABLY HAVE TECHNIQUES HERE THAT MY FATHER NEVER HAD TIME TO TEACH ME.
I NEED YOU TO TEACH THEM TO ME...
PLEASE.
GIVE UP.
IT DOESN'T MATTER HOW MANY DAYS YOU DO THIS.
YOU ARE A BLACKSMITH. YOU *SHOULD* KNOW WHAT IT'S LIKE.
YOU SHOULD KNOW THE **VALUE** OF A KATANA. ITS **BEAUTY**.
ITS **EDGE**.

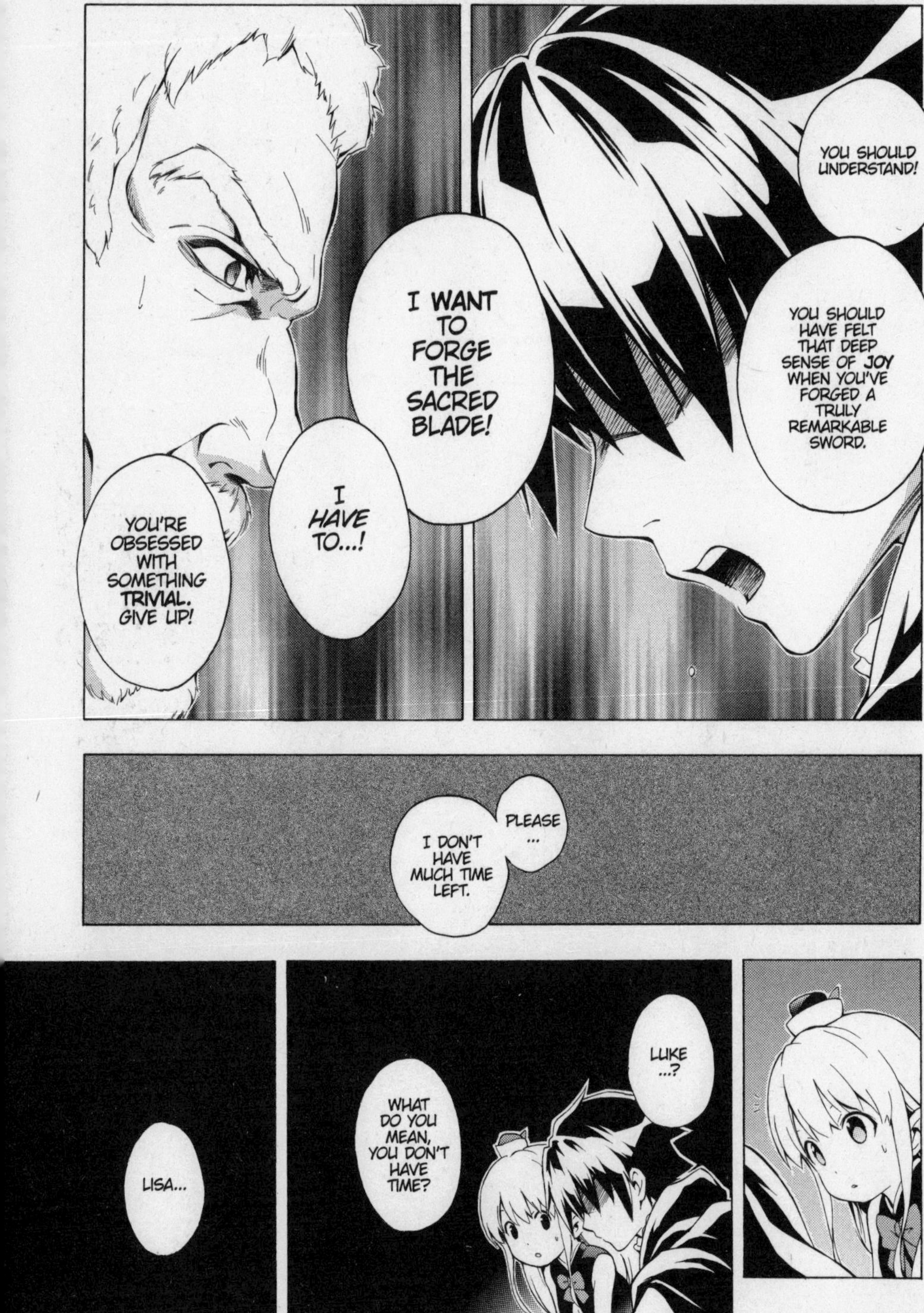
YOU SHOULD UNDERSTAND!
YOU SHOULD HAVE FELT THAT DEEP SENSE OF JOY WHEN YOU'VE FORGED A TRULY REMARKABLE SWORD.
I WANT TO FORGE THE SACRED BLADE!
I *HAVE* TO...!
YOU'RE OBSESSED WITH SOMETHING TRIVIAL. GIVE UP!
PLEASE...
I DON'T HAVE MUCH TIME LEFT.
LUKE...?
WHAT DO YOU MEAN, YOU DON'T HAVE TIME?
LISA...

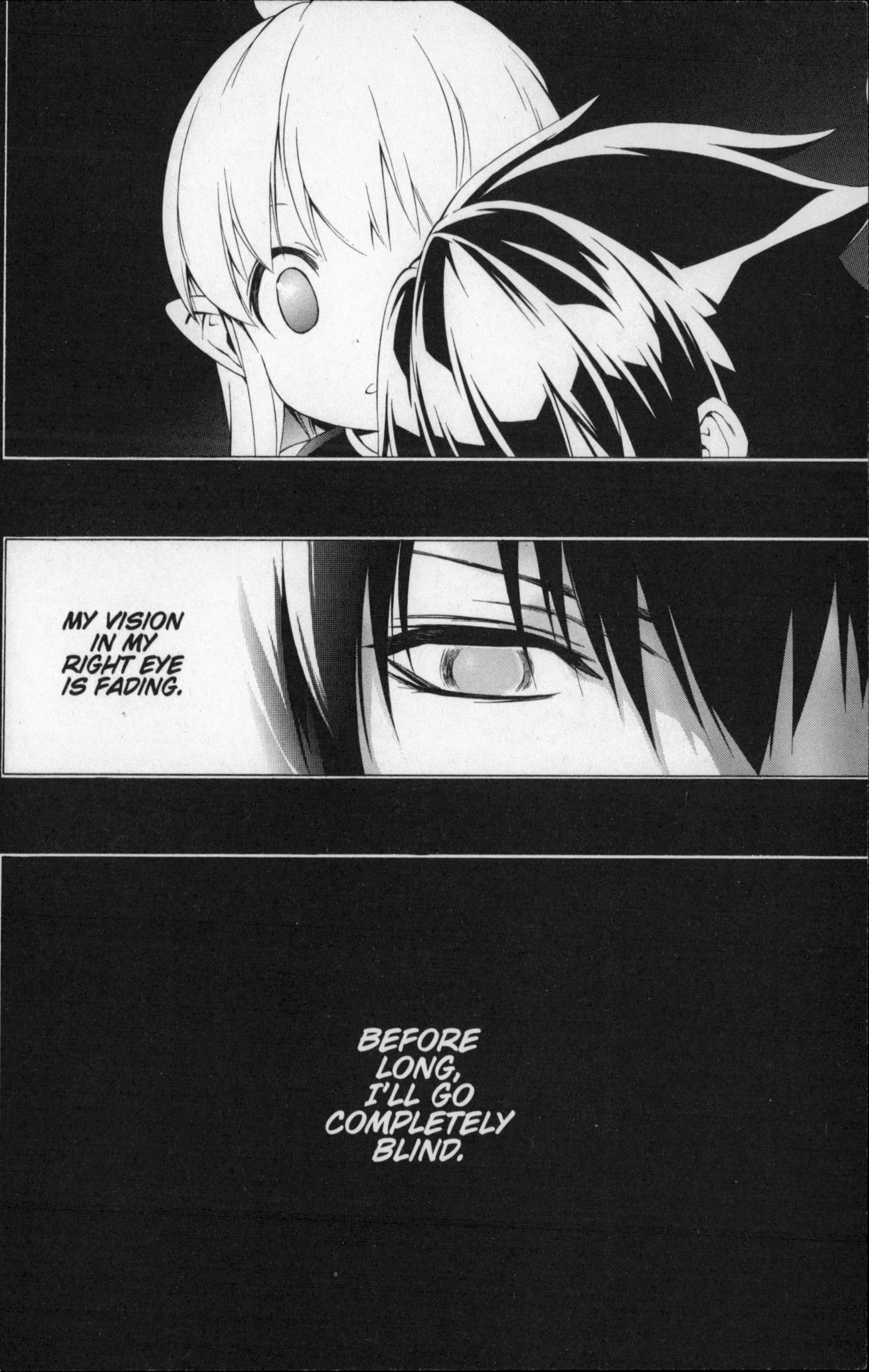
MY VISION IN MY RIGHT EYE IS FADING.
BEFORE LONG, I'LL GO COMPLETELY BLIND.

The Sacred Blacksmith

聖剣の刀鍛治

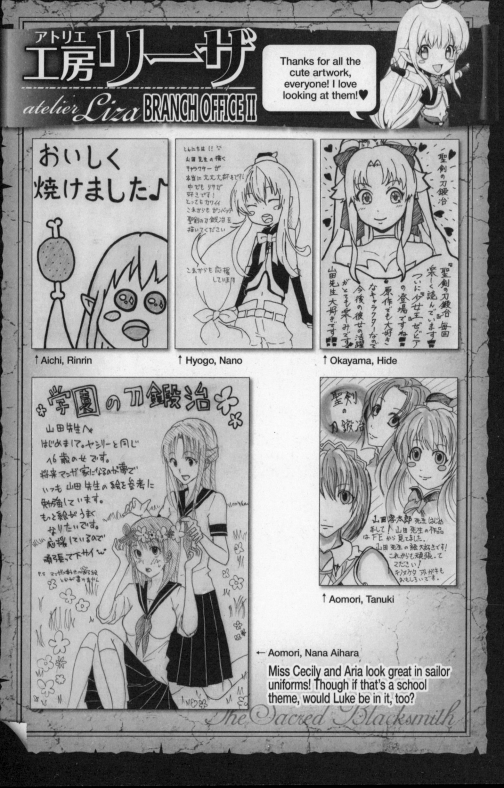

アトリエ 工房リーザ
atelier Liza BRANCH OFFICE II

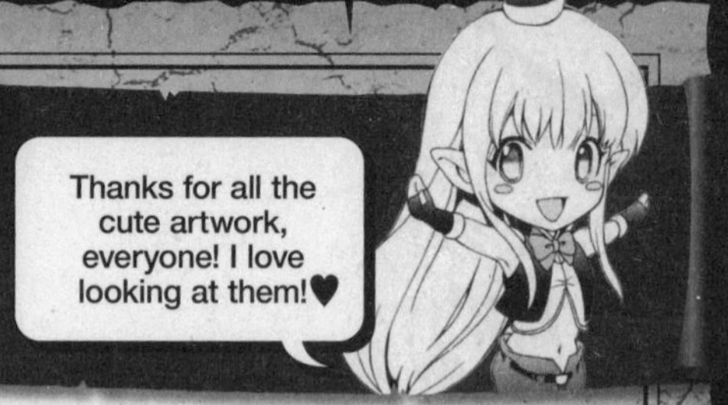
Thanks for all the cute artwork, everyone! I love looking at them!♥

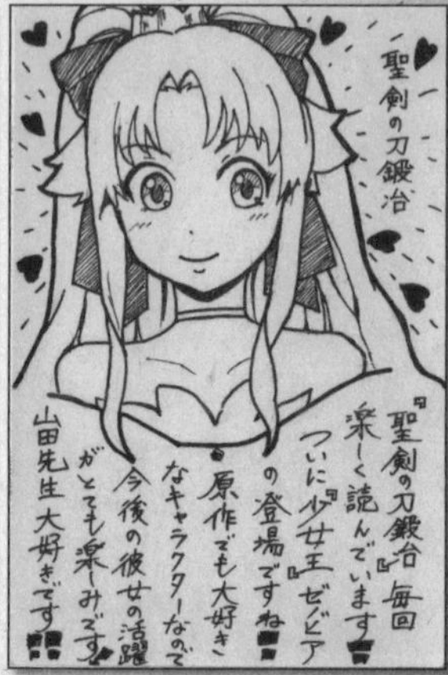
聖剣の刀鍛冶
『聖剣の刀鍛冶』毎回楽しく読んでいます
ついに少女王ゼノビアの登場ですね
原作でも大好きなキャラクターなので
今後の彼女の活躍がとても楽しみです
山田先生大好きです

↑ Okayama, Hide

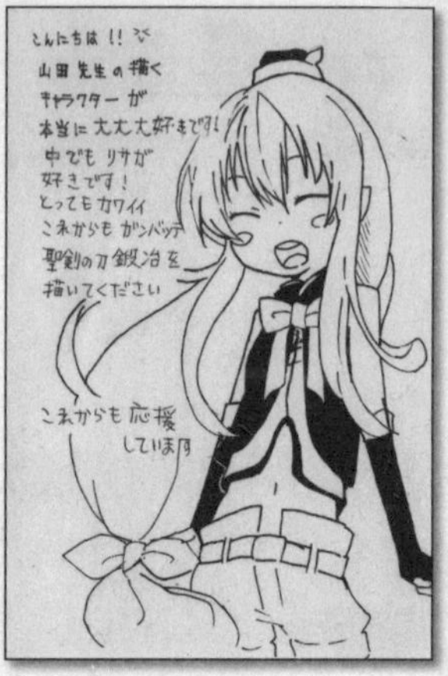
こんにちは!!
山田先生の描く
キャラクターが
本当に大大大好きです!
中でもリサが
好きです!
とってもカワイイ
これからもガンバッテ
聖剣の刀鍛冶を
描いてください
これからも応援
しています

↑ Hyogo, Nano

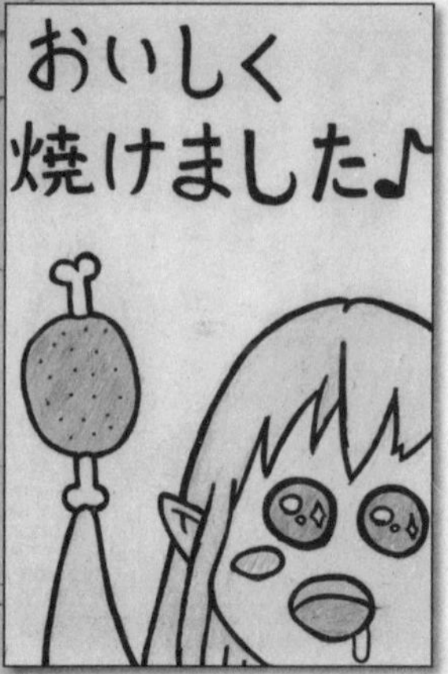
おいしく
焼けました♪

↑ Aichi, Rinrin

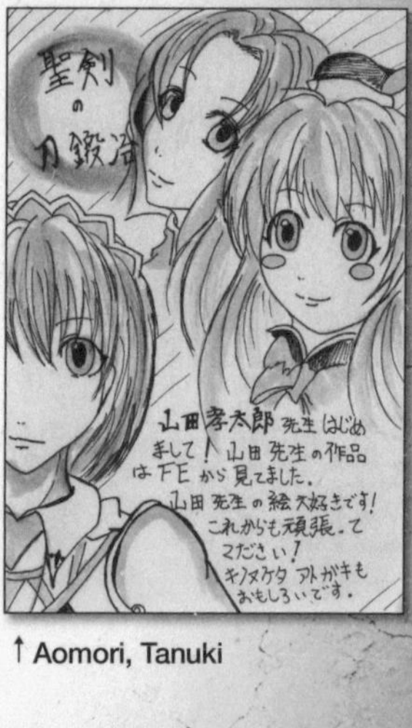
聖剣の刀鍛冶
山田孝太郎先生はじめまして!山田先生の作品はFEから見てました。
山田先生の絵大好きです!
これからも頑張ってください!
キノヌケタ アトガキも おもしろいです。

↑ Aomori, Tanuki

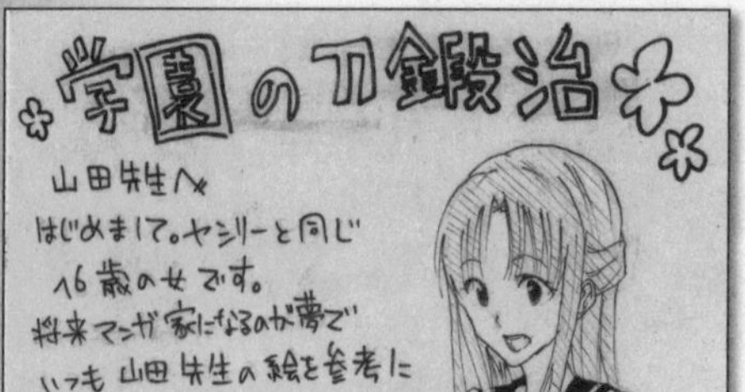
学園の刀鍛冶
山田先生へ
はじめまして。ヤシリーと同じ
16歳の女です。
将来マンガ家になるのが夢で
いつも山田先生の絵を参考に
勉強しています。
もっと絵がうまく
なりたいです。
応援しているので
頑張って下サイ

← Aomori, Nana Aihara

Miss Cecily and Aria look great in sailor uniforms! Though if that's a school theme, would Luke be in it, too?

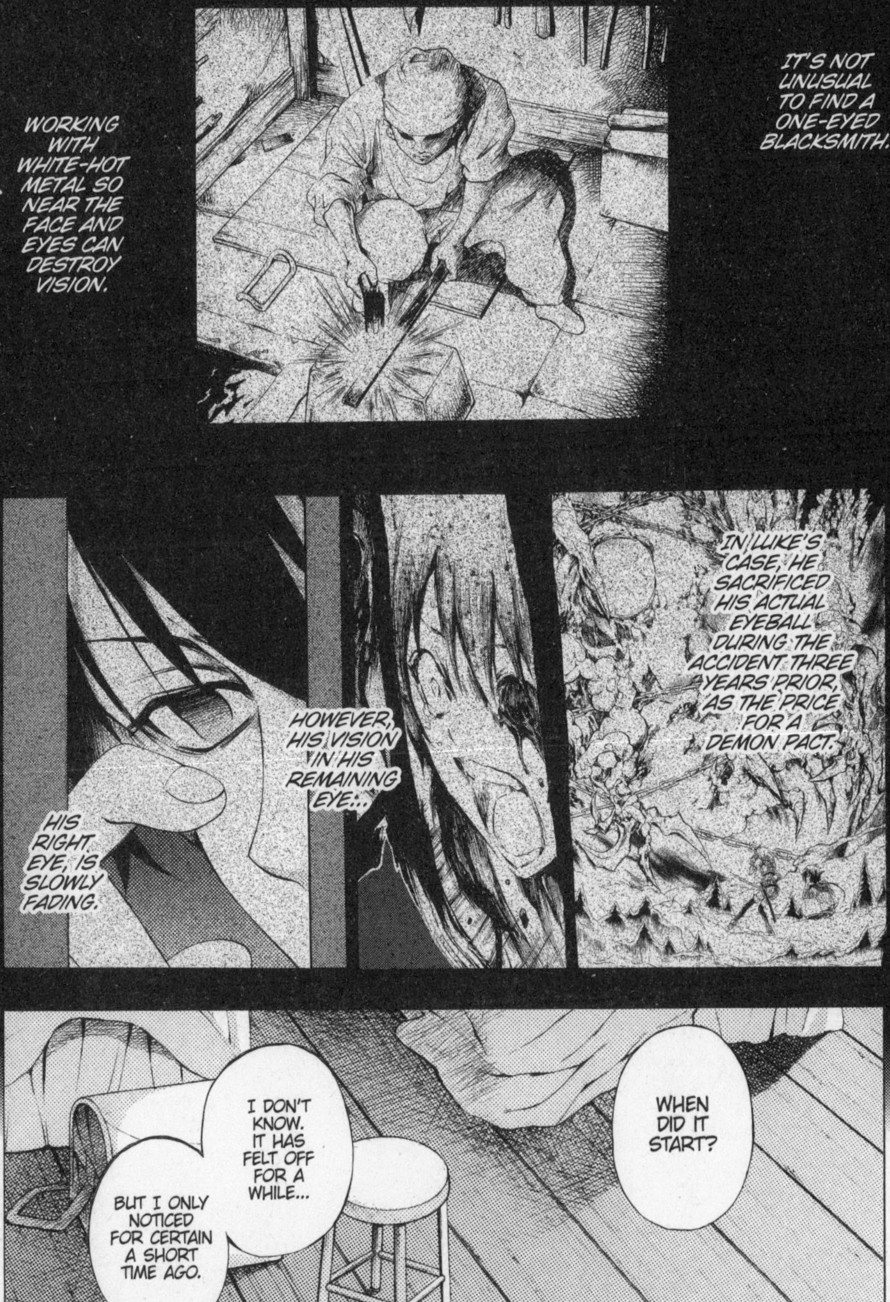
IT'S NOT UNUSUAL TO FIND A ONE-EYED BLACKSMITH.
WORKING WITH WHITE-HOT METAL SO NEAR THE FACE AND EYES CAN DESTROY VISION.
IN LUKE'S CASE, HE SACRIFICED HIS ACTUAL EYEBALL DURING THE ACCIDENT THREE YEARS PRIOR, AS THE PRICE FOR A DEMON PACT.
HOWEVER, HIS VISION IN HIS REMAINING EYE...
HIS RIGHT EYE, IS SLOWLY FADING.
WHEN DID IT START?
I DON'T KNOW. IT HAS FELT OFF FOR A WHILE...
BUT I ONLY NOTICED FOR CERTAIN A SHORT TIME AGO.

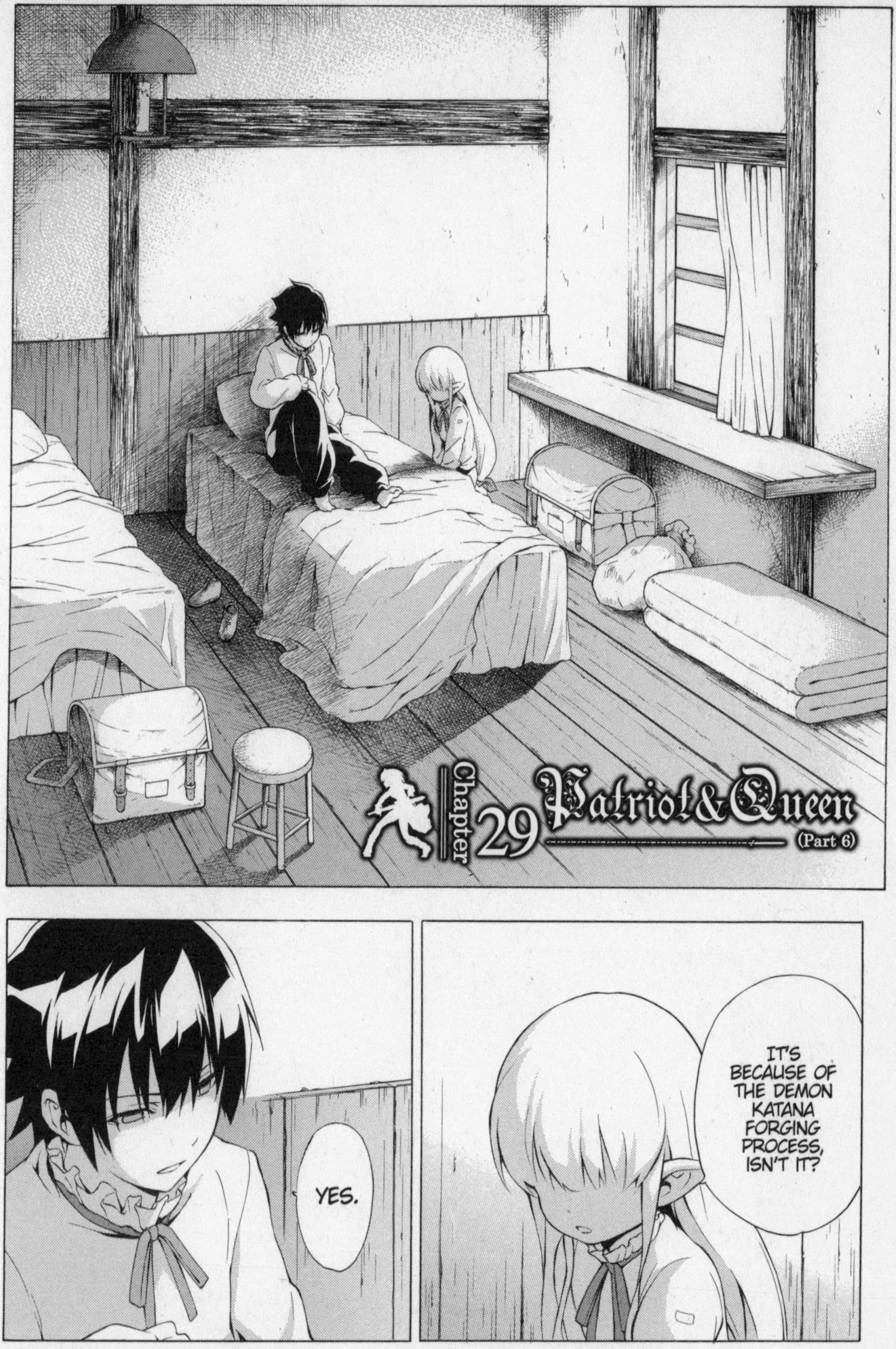
Chapter 29 Patriot&Queen (Part 6)
IT'S BECAUSE OF THE DEMON KATANA FORGING PROCESS, ISN'T IT?
YES.

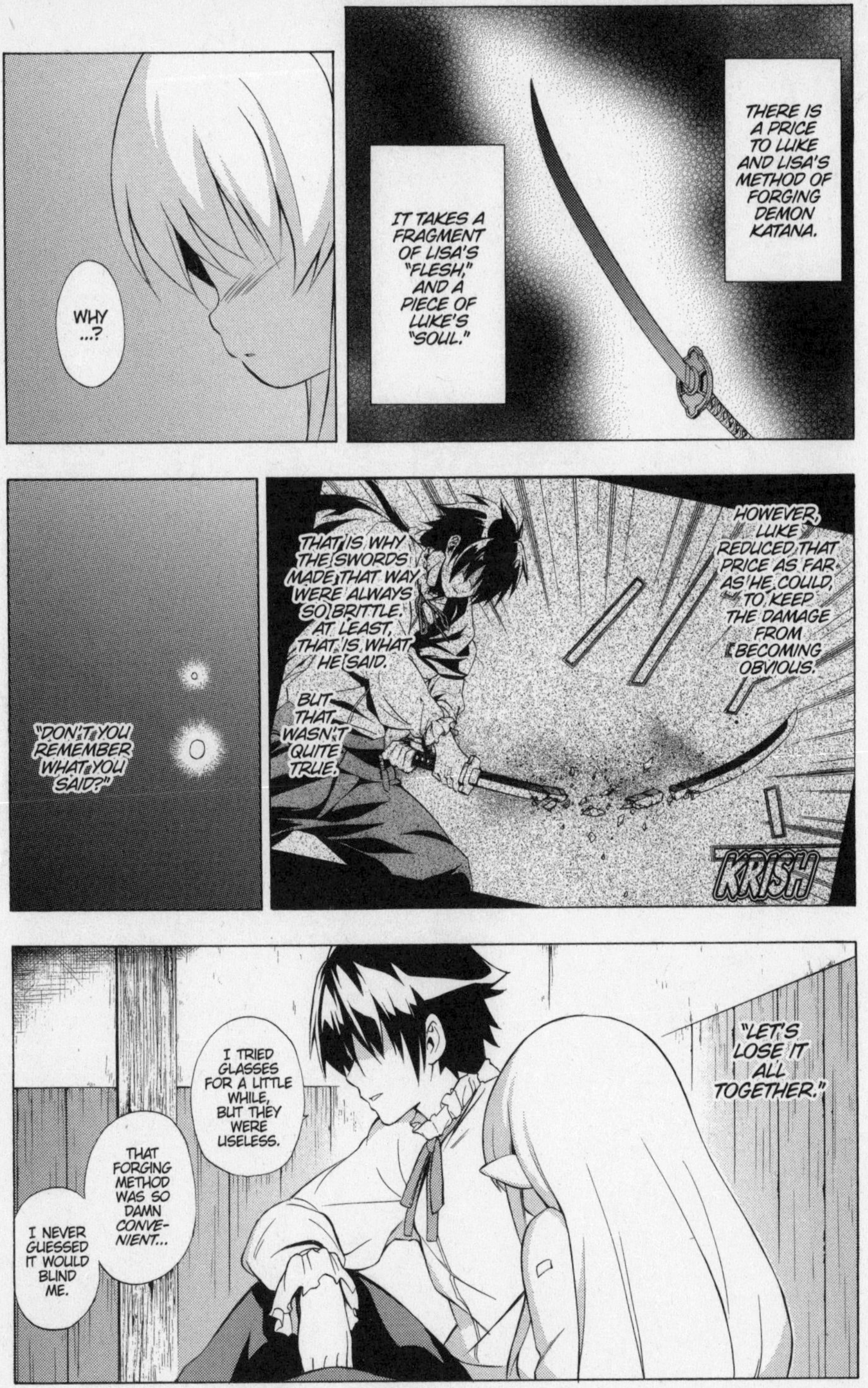
THERE IS A PRICE TO LUKE AND LISA'S METHOD OF FORGING DEMON KATANA.
IT TAKES A FRAGMENT OF LISA'S "FLESH," AND A PIECE OF LUKE'S "SOUL."
WHY ...?
HOWEVER, LUKE REDUCED THAT PRICE AS FAR AS HE COULD, TO KEEP THE DAMAGE FROM BECOMING OBVIOUS.
THAT IS WHY THE SWORDS MADE THAT WAY WERE ALWAYS SO BRITTLE. AT LEAST, THAT IS WHAT HE SAID.
BUT THAT WASN'T QUITE TRUE.
KRISH
"DON'T YOU REMEMBER WHAT YOU SAID?"
"LET'S LOSE IT ALL TOGETHER."
I TRIED GLASSES FOR A LITTLE WHILE, BUT THEY WERE USELESS.
THAT FORGING METHOD WAS SO DAMN CONVE-NIENT...
I NEVER GUESSED IT WOULD BLIND ME.

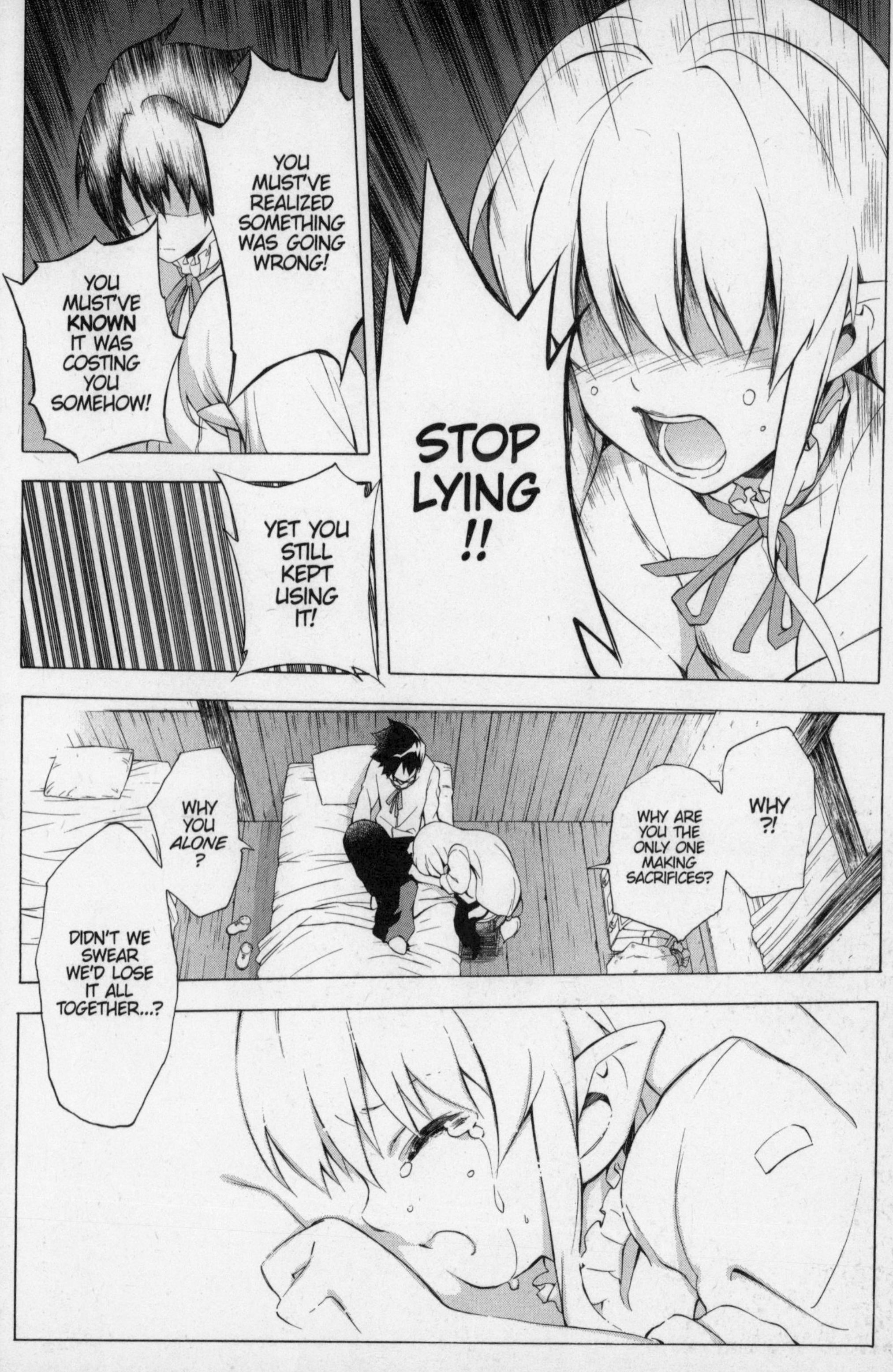
STOP LYING!!
YOU MUST'VE REALIZED SOMETHING WAS GOING WRONG!
YOU MUST'VE **KNOWN** IT WAS COSTING YOU SOMEHOW!
YET YOU STILL KEPT USING IT!
WHY?!
WHY ARE YOU THE ONLY ONE MAKING SACRIFICES?
WHY YOU *ALONE*?
DIDN'T WE SWEAR WE'D LOSE IT ALL TOGETHER...?

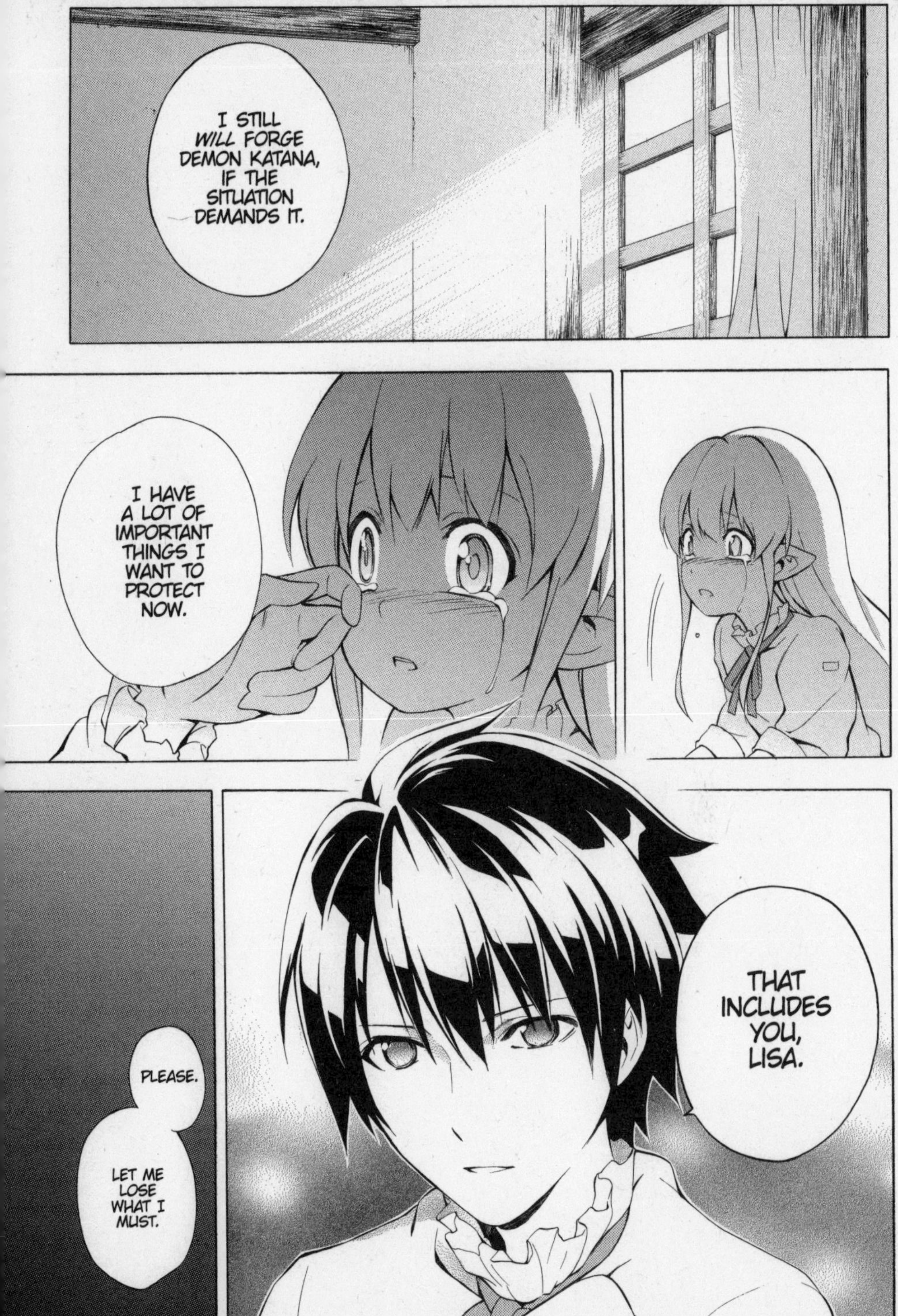
I STILL *WILL* FORGE DEMON KATANA, IF THE SITUATION DEMANDS IT.
I HAVE A LOT OF IMPORTANT THINGS I WANT TO PROTECT NOW.
THAT INCLUDES YOU, LISA.
PLEASE.
LET ME LOSE WHAT I MUST.

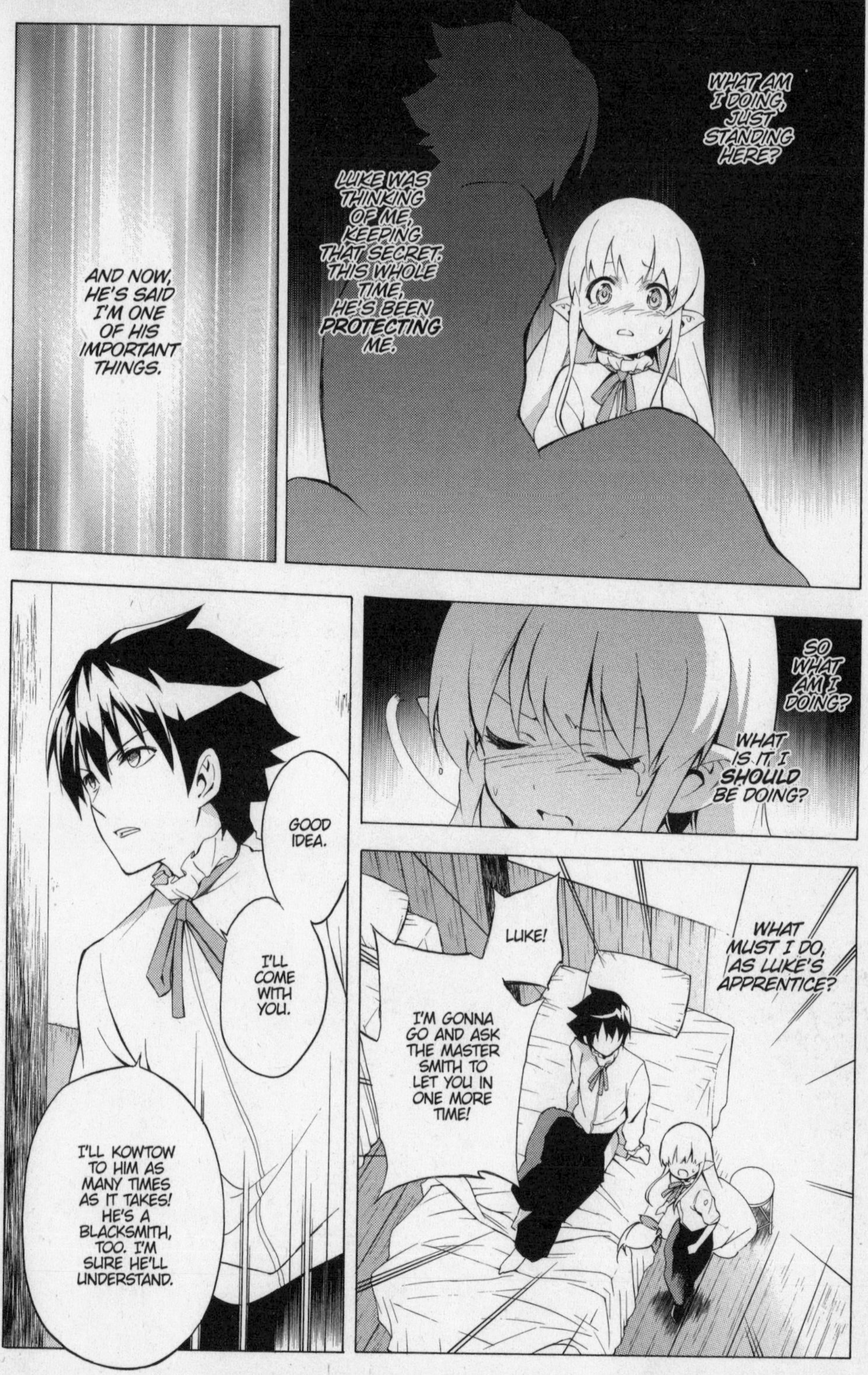
WHAT AM I DOING, JUST STANDING HERE?
LUKE WAS THINKING OF ME, KEEPING THAT SECRET. THIS WHOLE TIME, HE'S BEEN PROTECTING ME.
AND NOW, HE'S SAID I'M ONE OF HIS IMPORTANT THINGS.
SO WHAT AM I DOING?
WHAT IS IT I SHOULD BE DOING?
WHAT MUST I DO, AS LUKE'S APPRENTICE?
LUKE!
I'M GONNA GO AND ASK THE MASTER SMITH TO LET YOU IN ONE MORE TIME!
GOOD IDEA.
I'LL COME WITH YOU.
I'LL KOWTOW TO HIM AS MANY TIMES AS IT TAKES! HE'S A BLACKSMITH, TOO. I'M SURE HE'LL UNDERSTAND.

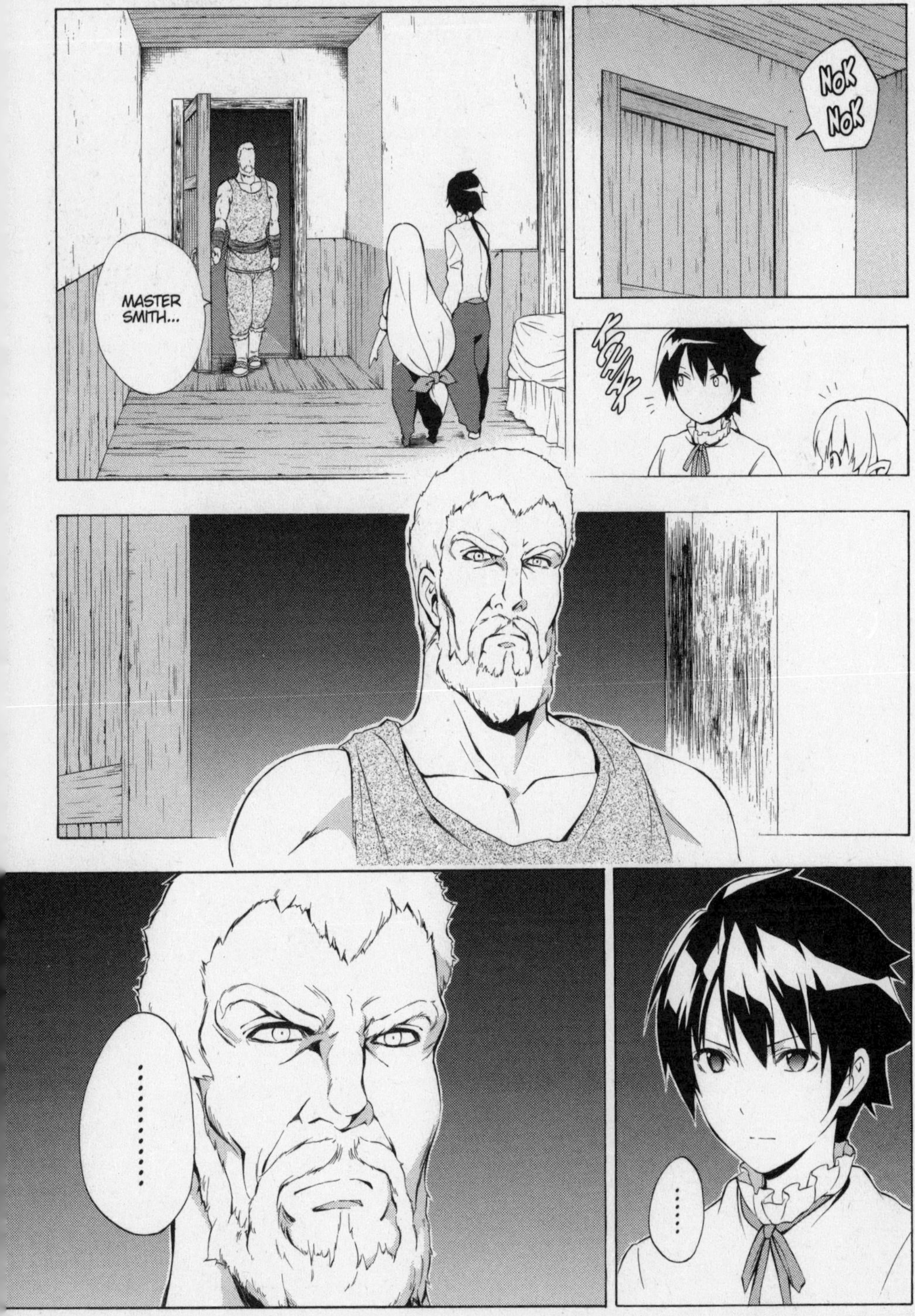
NOK NOK
KCHAK
MASTER SMITH...
......
....

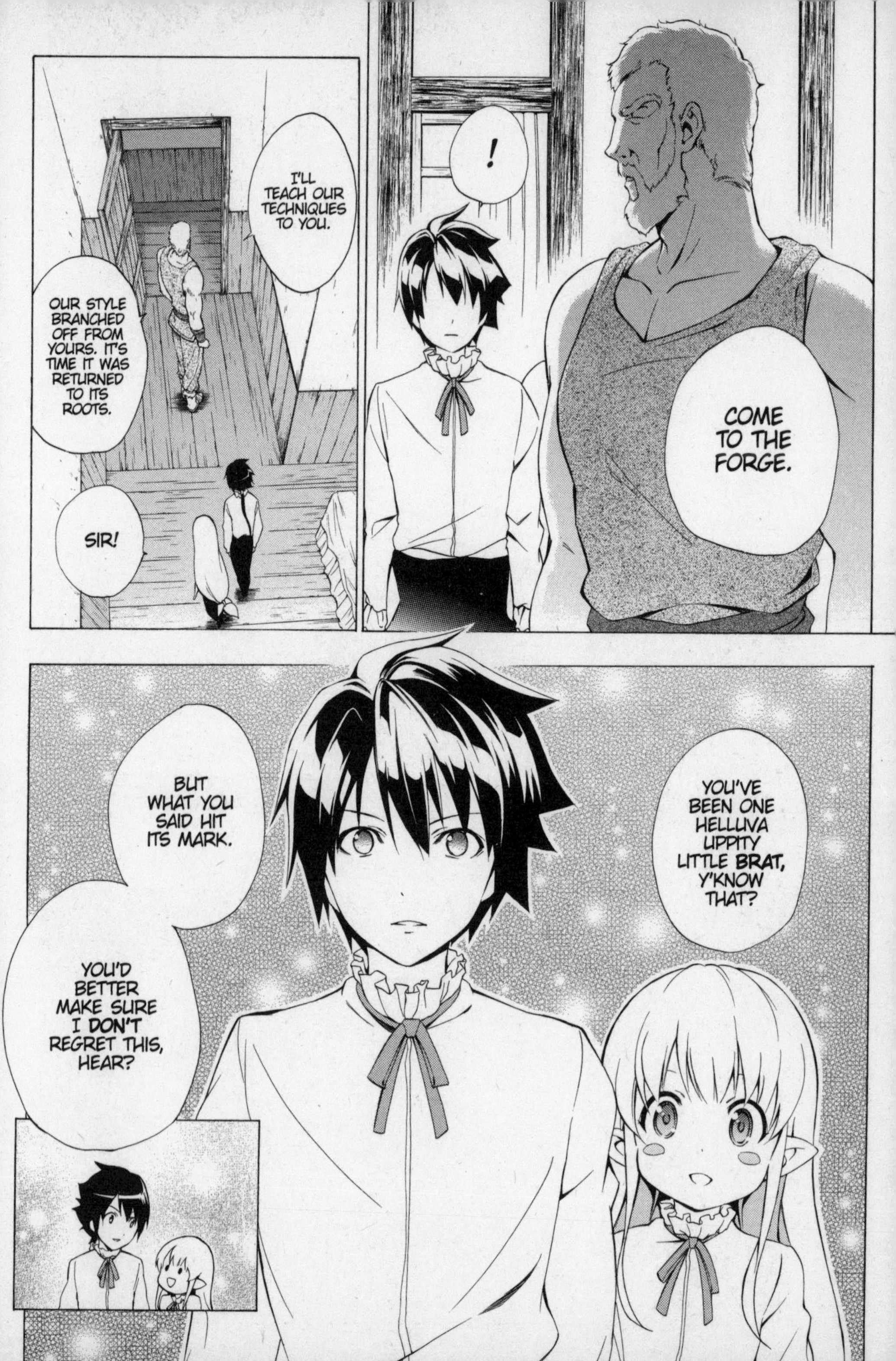
COME TO THE FORGE.
!
I'LL TEACH OUR TECHNIQUES TO YOU.
OUR STYLE BRANCHED OFF FROM YOURS. IT'S TIME IT WAS RETURNED TO ITS ROOTS.
SIR!
YOU'VE BEEN ONE HELLUVA UPPITY LITTLE BRAT, Y'KNOW THAT?
BUT WHAT YOU SAID HIT ITS MARK.
YOU'D BETTER MAKE SURE I DON'T REGRET THIS, HEAR?

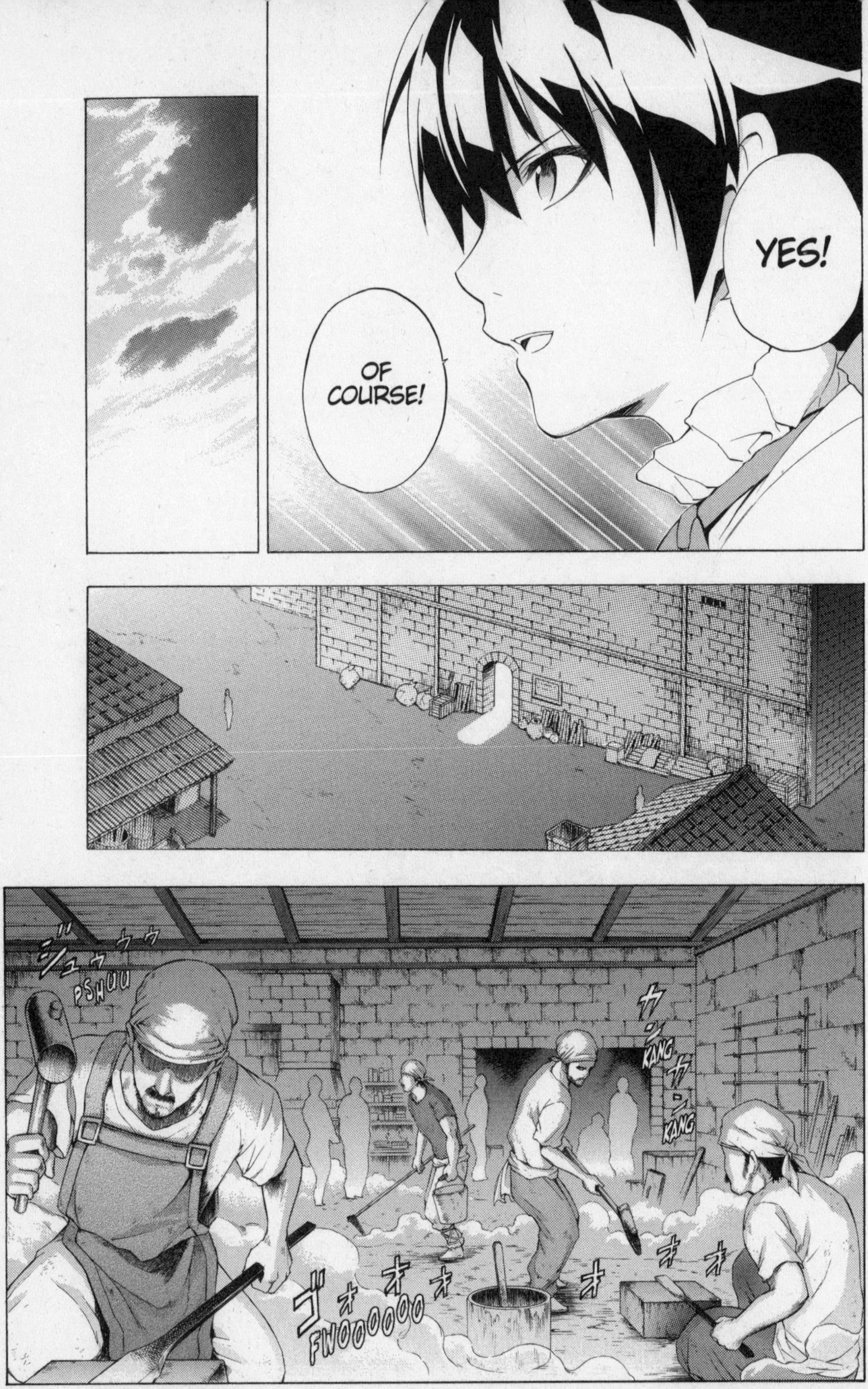
YES!
OF COURSE!
カンカン
KANG
KANG
ジュウウウ
PSHUU
ゴオオオオオオ
FWOOOOOO

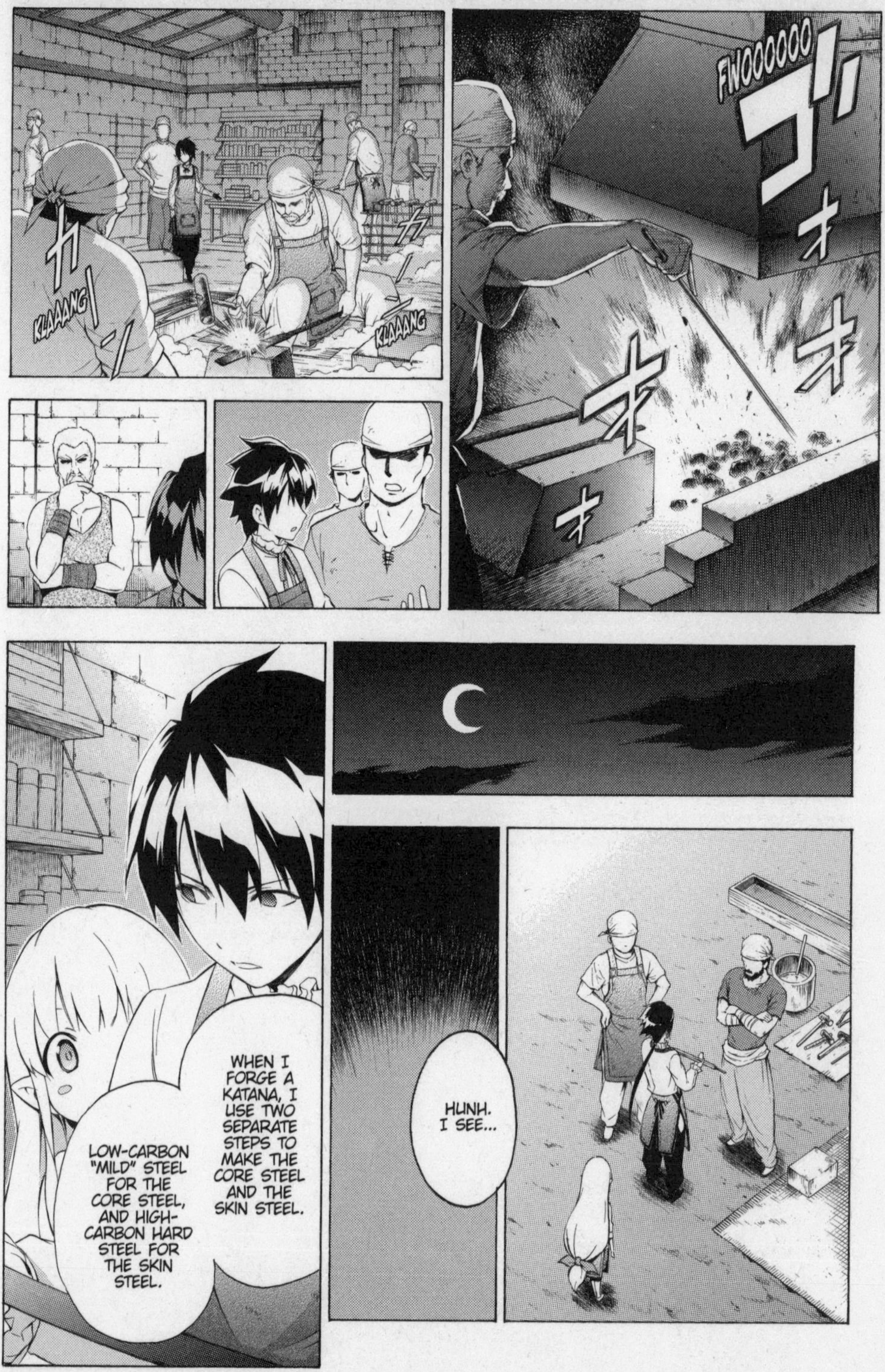

FWOOOOOO
ゴォォォォ
KLAAANG
カーン
KLAAANG
カーン
HUNH. I SEE...
WHEN I FORGE A KATANA, I USE TWO SEPARATE STEPS TO MAKE THE CORE STEEL AND THE SKIN STEEL.
LOW-CARBON "MILD" STEEL FOR THE CORE STEEL, AND HIGH-CARBON HARD STEEL FOR THE SKIN STEEL.

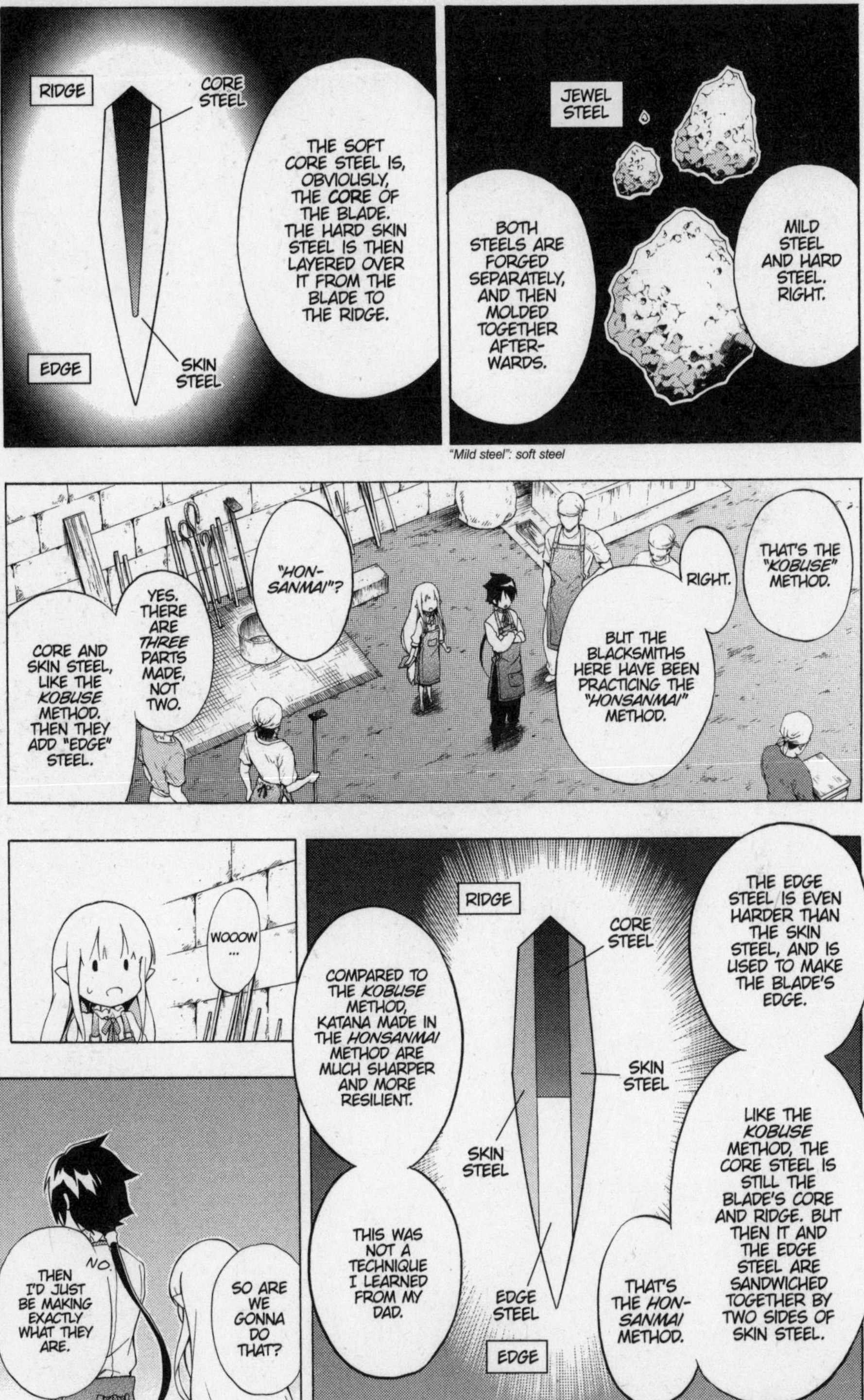
JEWEL STEEL
MILD STEEL AND HARD STEEL. RIGHT.
BOTH STEELS ARE FORGED SEPARATELY, AND THEN MOLDED TOGETHER AFTER-WARDS.
THE SOFT CORE STEEL IS, OBVIOUSLY, THE CORE OF THE BLADE. THE HARD SKIN STEEL IS THEN LAYERED OVER IT FROM THE BLADE TO THE RIDGE.
RIDGE
CORE STEEL
SKIN STEEL
EDGE
"Mild steel": soft steel
THAT'S THE "KOBUSE" METHOD.
RIGHT.
BUT THE BLACKSMITHS HERE HAVE BEEN PRACTICING THE "HONSANMAI" METHOD.
"HON-SANMAI"?
YES. THERE ARE THREE PARTS MADE, NOT TWO.
CORE AND SKIN STEEL, LIKE THE KOBUSE METHOD. THEN THEY ADD "EDGE" STEEL.
THE EDGE STEEL IS EVEN HARDER THAN THE SKIN STEEL, AND IS USED TO MAKE THE BLADE'S EDGE.
LIKE THE KOBUSE METHOD, THE CORE STEEL IS STILL THE BLADE'S CORE AND RIDGE. BUT THEN IT AND THE EDGE STEEL ARE SANDWICHED TOGETHER BY TWO SIDES OF SKIN STEEL.
THAT'S THE HON-SANMAI METHOD.
RIDGE
CORE STEEL
SKIN STEEL
SKIN STEEL
EDGE STEEL
EDGE
COMPARED TO THE KOBUSE METHOD, KATANA MADE IN THE HONSANMAI METHOD ARE MUCH SHARPER AND MORE RESILIENT.
THIS WAS NOT A TECHNIQUE I LEARNED FROM MY DAD.
WOOOW ...
SO ARE WE GONNA DO THAT?
NO.
THEN I'D JUST BE MAKING EXACTLY WHAT THEY ARE.

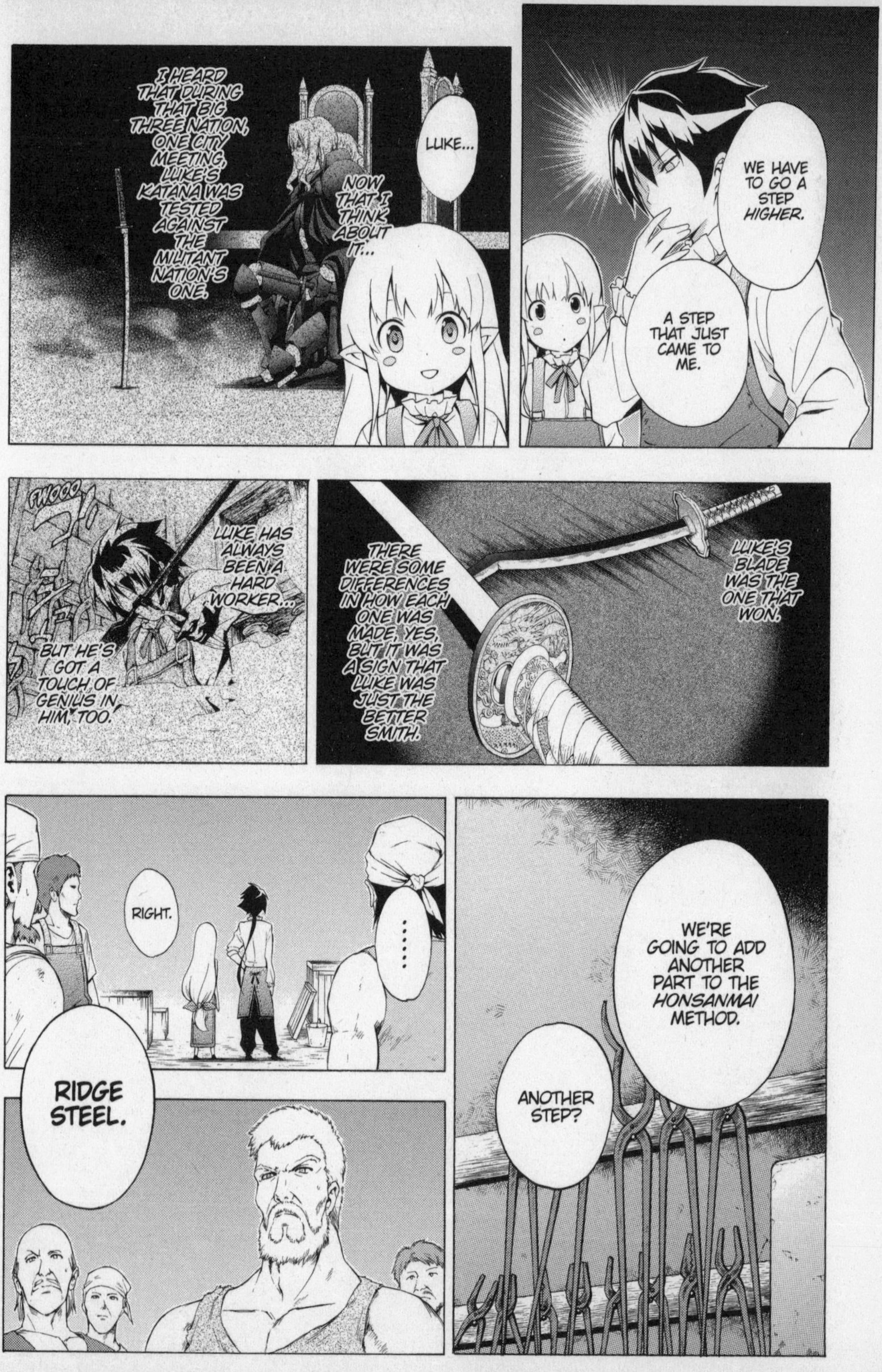
WE HAVE TO GO A STEP HIGHER.
A STEP THAT JUST CAME TO ME.
LUKE...
NOW THAT I THINK ABOUT IT...
I HEARD THAT DURING THAT BIG THREE NATION, ONE CITY MEETING, LUKE'S KATANA WAS TESTED AGAINST THE MILITANT NATION'S ONE.
LUKE'S BLADE WAS THE ONE THAT WON.
THERE WERE SOME DIFFERENCES IN HOW EACH ONE WAS MADE, YES, BUT IT WAS A SIGN THAT LUKE WAS JUST THE BETTER SMITH.
FWOOO
LUKE HAS ALWAYS BEEN A HARD WORKER...
BUT HE'S GOT A TOUCH OF GENIUS IN HIM, TOO.
WE'RE GOING TO ADD ANOTHER PART TO THE *HONSANMAI* METHOD.
ANOTHER STEP?
......
RIGHT.
RIDGE STEEL.

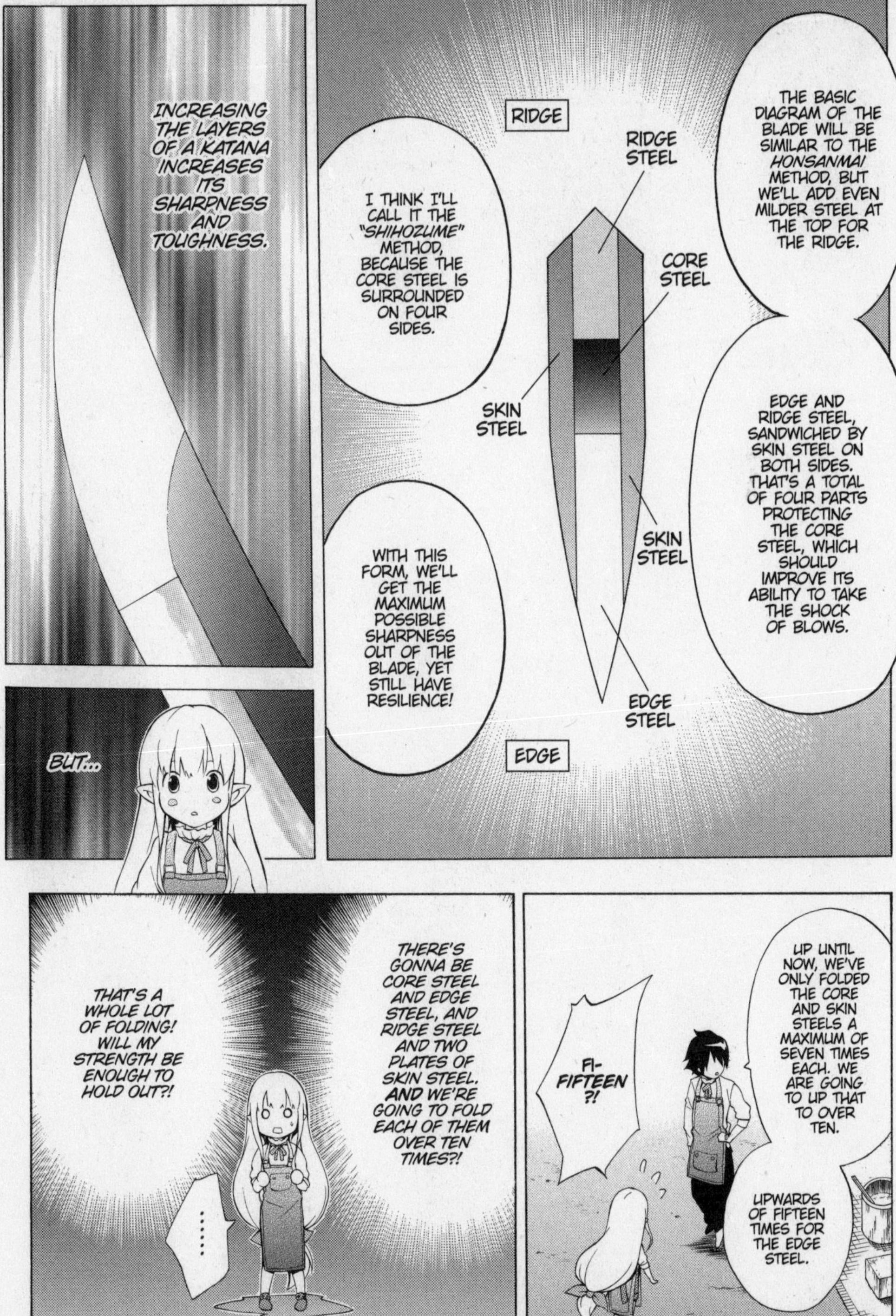
THE BASIC DIAGRAM OF THE BLADE WILL BE SIMILAR TO THE *HONSANMAI* METHOD, BUT WE'LL ADD EVEN MILDER STEEL AT THE TOP FOR THE RIDGE.
EDGE AND RIDGE STEEL, SANDWICHED BY SKIN STEEL ON BOTH SIDES. THAT'S A TOTAL OF FOUR PARTS PROTECTING THE CORE STEEL, WHICH SHOULD IMPROVE ITS ABILITY TO TAKE THE SHOCK OF BLOWS.
RIDGE
RIDGE STEEL
CORE STEEL
SKIN STEEL
SKIN STEEL
EDGE STEEL
EDGE
I THINK I'LL CALL IT THE "*SHIHOZUME*" METHOD, BECAUSE THE CORE STEEL IS SURROUNDED ON FOUR SIDES.
WITH THIS FORM, WE'LL GET THE MAXIMUM POSSIBLE SHARPNESS OUT OF THE BLADE, YET STILL HAVE RESILIENCE!
INCREASING THE LAYERS OF A KATANA INCREASES ITS SHARPNESS AND TOUGHNESS.
BUT...
UP UNTIL NOW, WE'VE ONLY FOLDED THE CORE AND SKIN STEELS A MAXIMUM OF SEVEN TIMES EACH. WE ARE GOING TO UP THAT TO OVER TEN.
UPWARDS OF FIFTEEN TIMES FOR THE EDGE STEEL.
FI-FIFTEEN?!
THERE'S GONNA BE CORE STEEL AND EDGE STEEL, AND RIDGE STEEL AND TWO PLATES OF SKIN STEEL. **AND** WE'RE GOING TO FOLD EACH OF THEM OVER TEN TIMES?!
THAT'S A WHOLE LOT OF FOLDING! WILL MY STRENGTH BE ENOUGH TO HOLD OUT?!
......

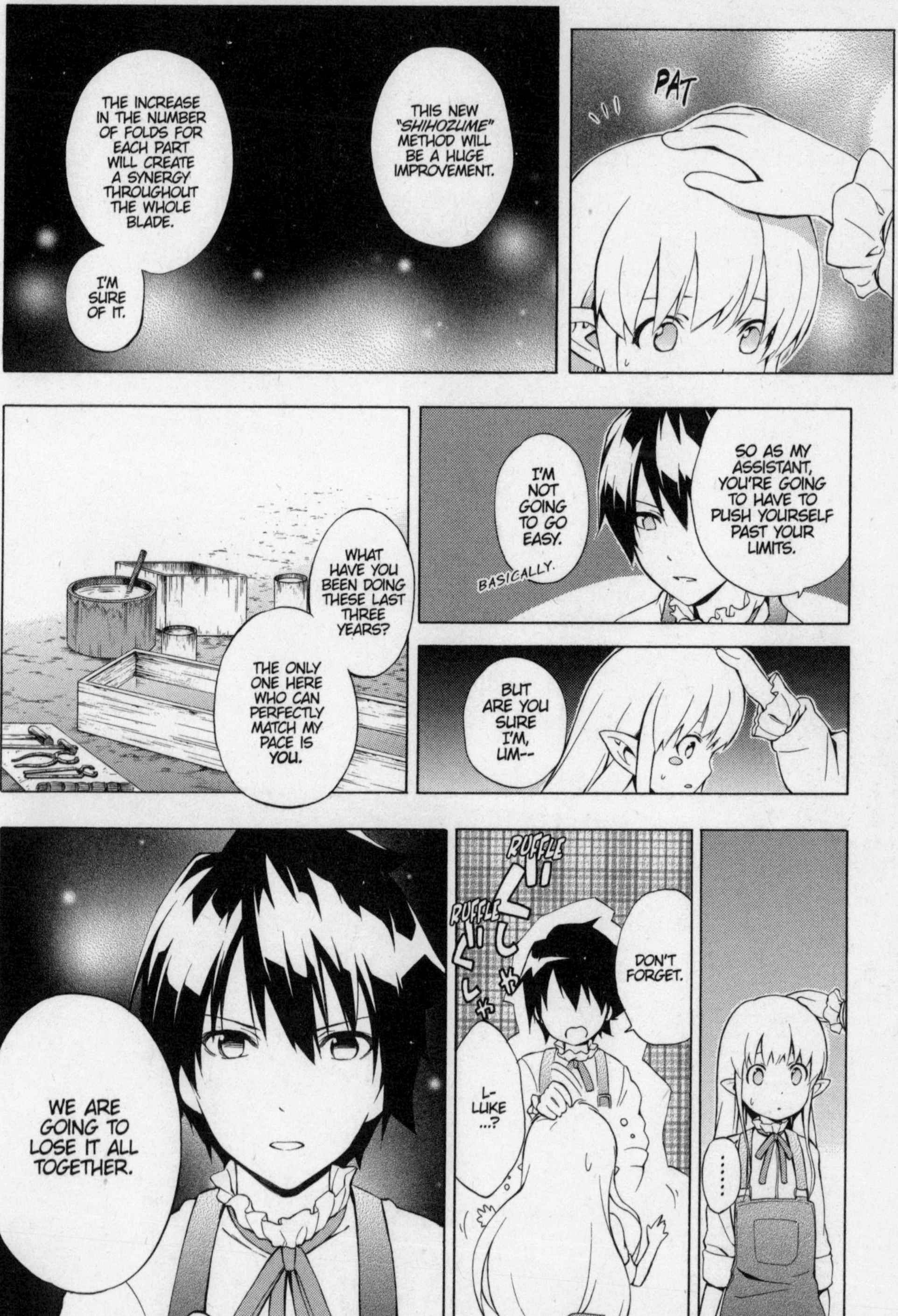
PAT
THIS NEW "SHIHOZUME" METHOD WILL BE A HUGE IMPROVEMENT.
THE INCREASE IN THE NUMBER OF FOLDS FOR EACH PART WILL CREATE A SYNERGY THROUGHOUT THE WHOLE BLADE.
I'M SURE OF IT.
SO AS MY ASSISTANT, YOU'RE GOING TO HAVE TO PUSH YOURSELF PAST YOUR LIMITS.
I'M NOT GOING TO GO EASY.
BASICALLY.
BUT ARE YOU SURE I'M, UM--
WHAT HAVE YOU BEEN DOING THESE LAST THREE YEARS?
THE ONLY ONE HERE WHO CAN PERFECTLY MATCH MY PACE IS YOU.
......
DON'T FORGET.
RUFFLE
RUFFLE
L-LUKE ...?
WE ARE GOING TO LOSE IT ALL TOGETHER.

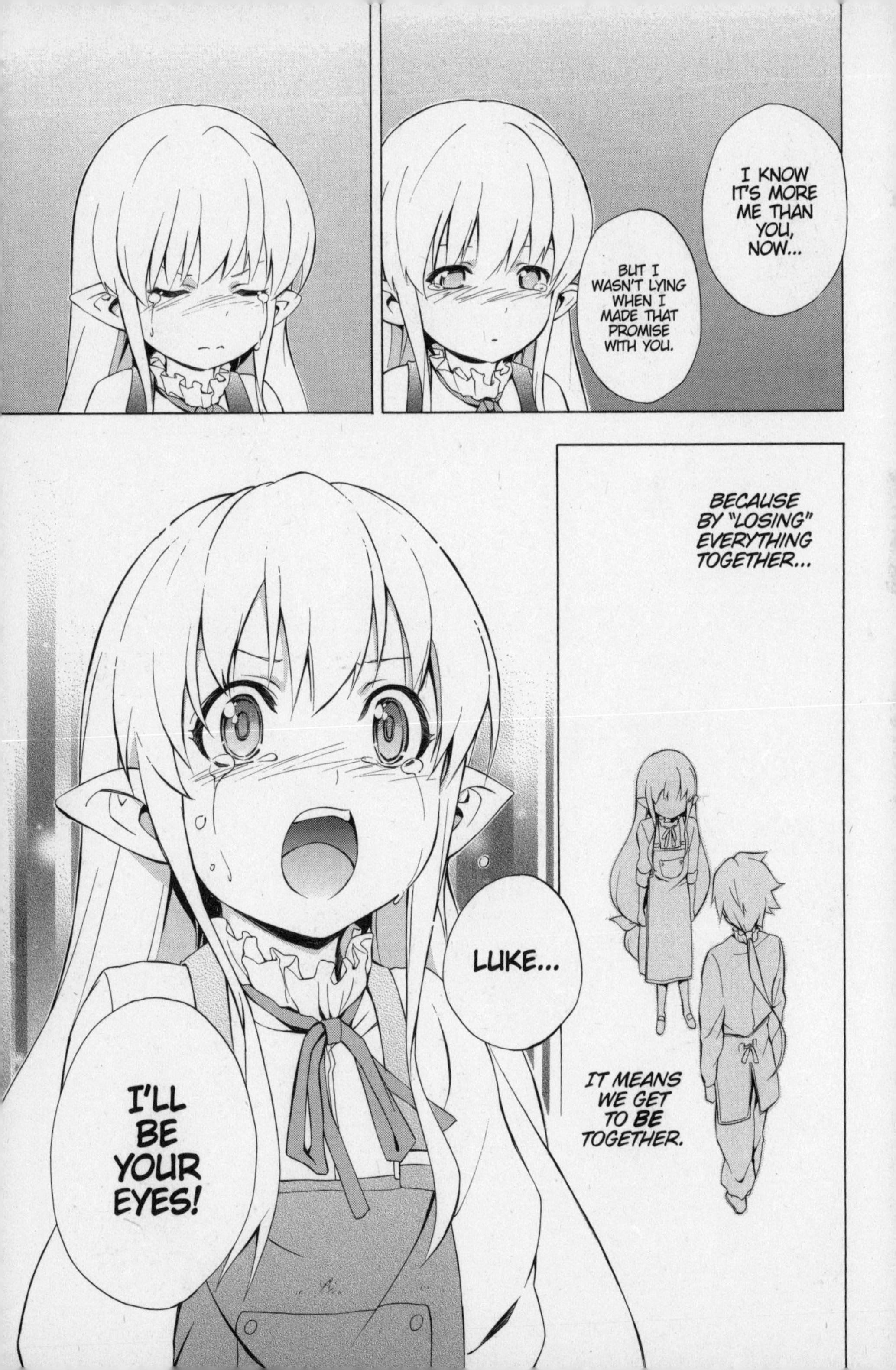
I KNOW IT'S MORE ME THAN YOU, NOW...
BUT I WASN'T LYING WHEN I MADE THAT PROMISE WITH YOU.
BECAUSE BY "LOSING" EVERYTHING TOGETHER...
IT MEANS WE GET TO BE TOGETHER.
LUKE...
I'LL BE YOUR EYES!

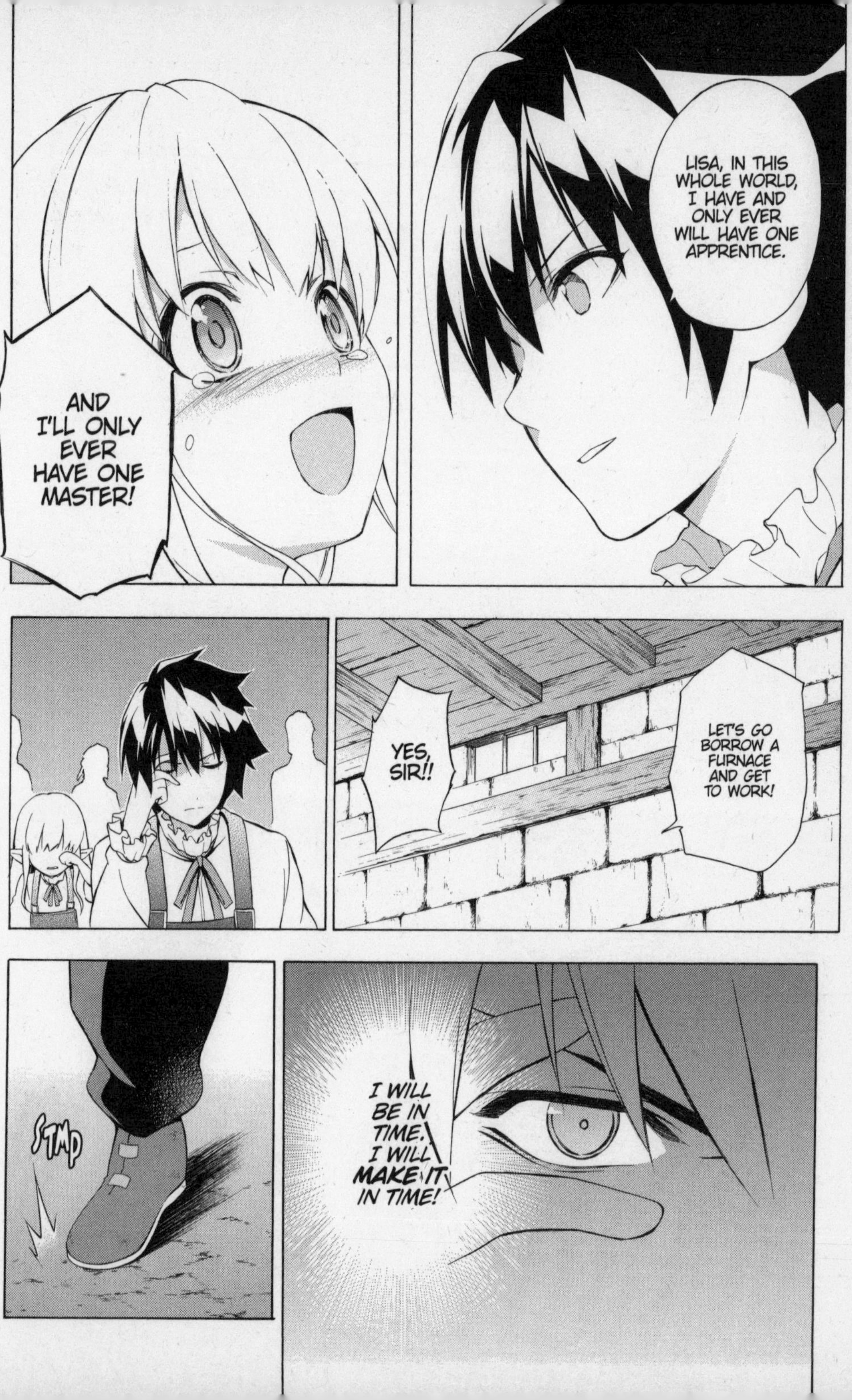
LISA, IN THIS WHOLE WORLD, I HAVE AND ONLY EVER WILL HAVE ONE APPRENTICE.
AND I'LL ONLY EVER HAVE ONE MASTER!
LET'S GO BORROW A FURNACE AND GET TO WORK!
YES, SIR!!
I WILL BE IN TIME. I WILL MAKE IT IN TIME!
STMP

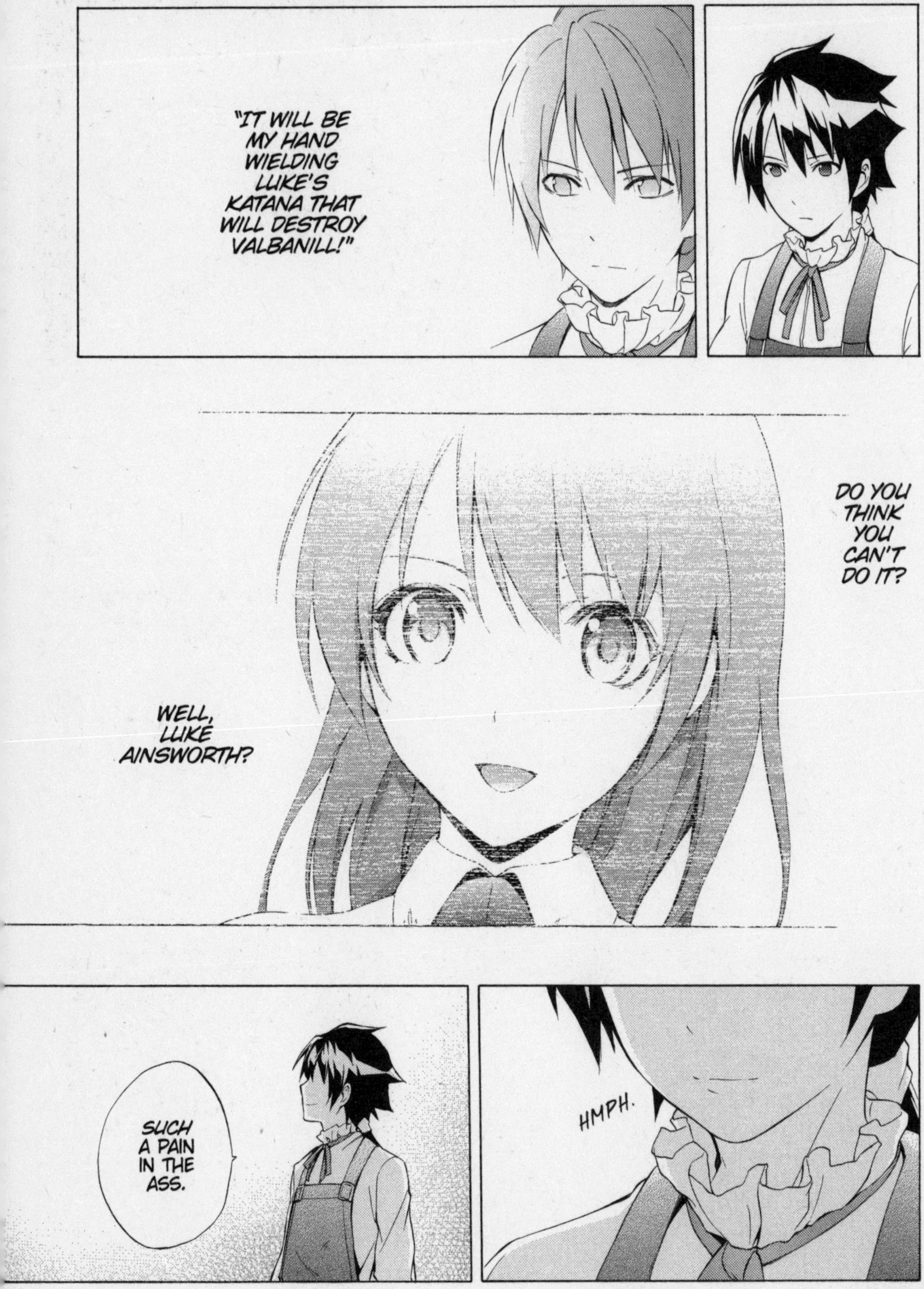
"IT WILL BE MY HAND WIELDING LUKE'S KATANA THAT WILL DESTROY VALBANILL!"
DO YOU THINK YOU CAN'T DO IT?
WELL, LUKE AINSWORTH?
HMPH.
SUCH A PAIN IN THE ASS.

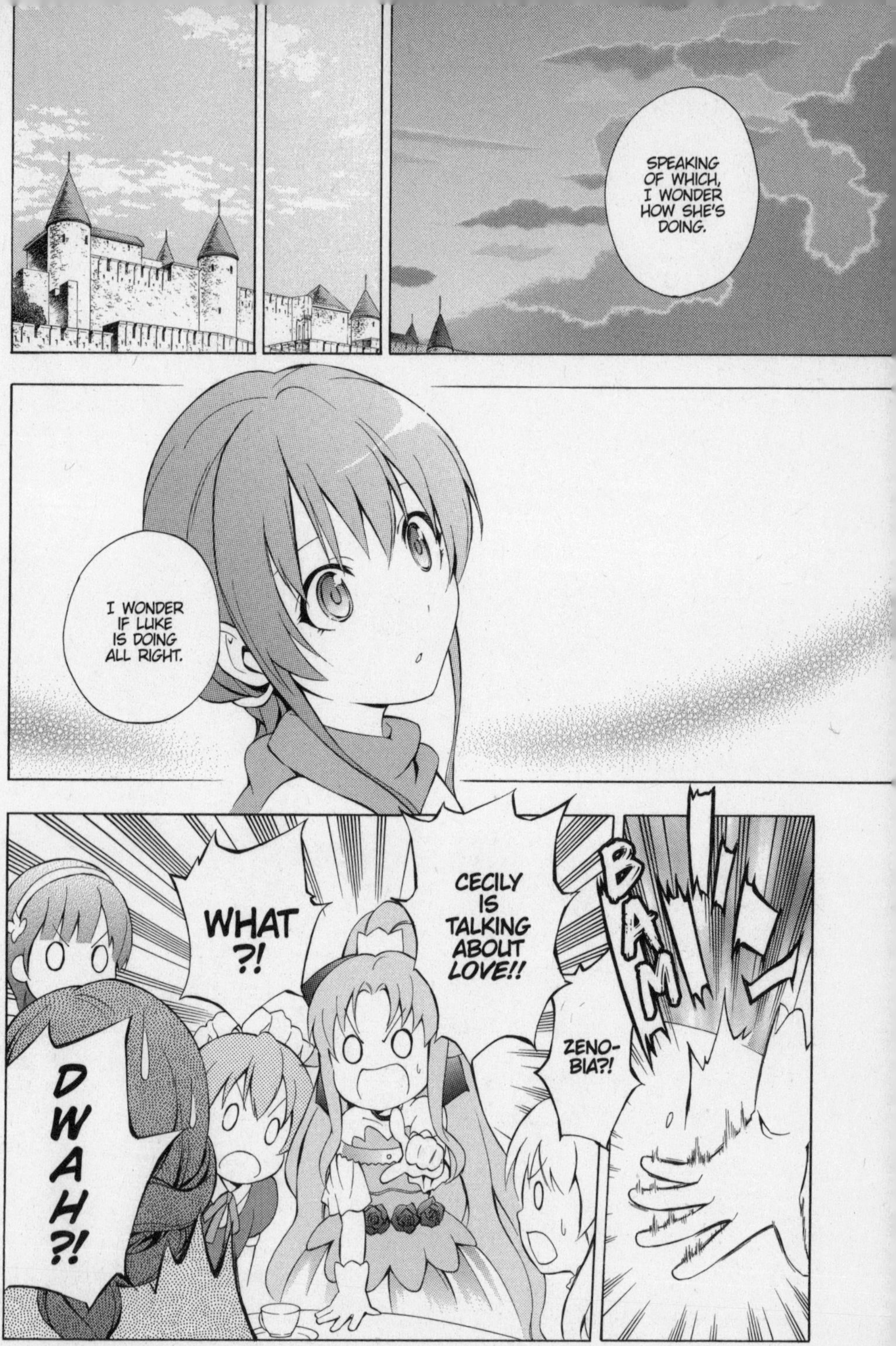
SPEAKING OF WHICH, I WONDER HOW SHE'S DOING.
I WONDER IF LUKE IS DOING ALL RIGHT.
BAM
ZENO-BIA?!
CECILY IS TALKING ABOUT LOVE!!
WHAT?!
DWAH?!

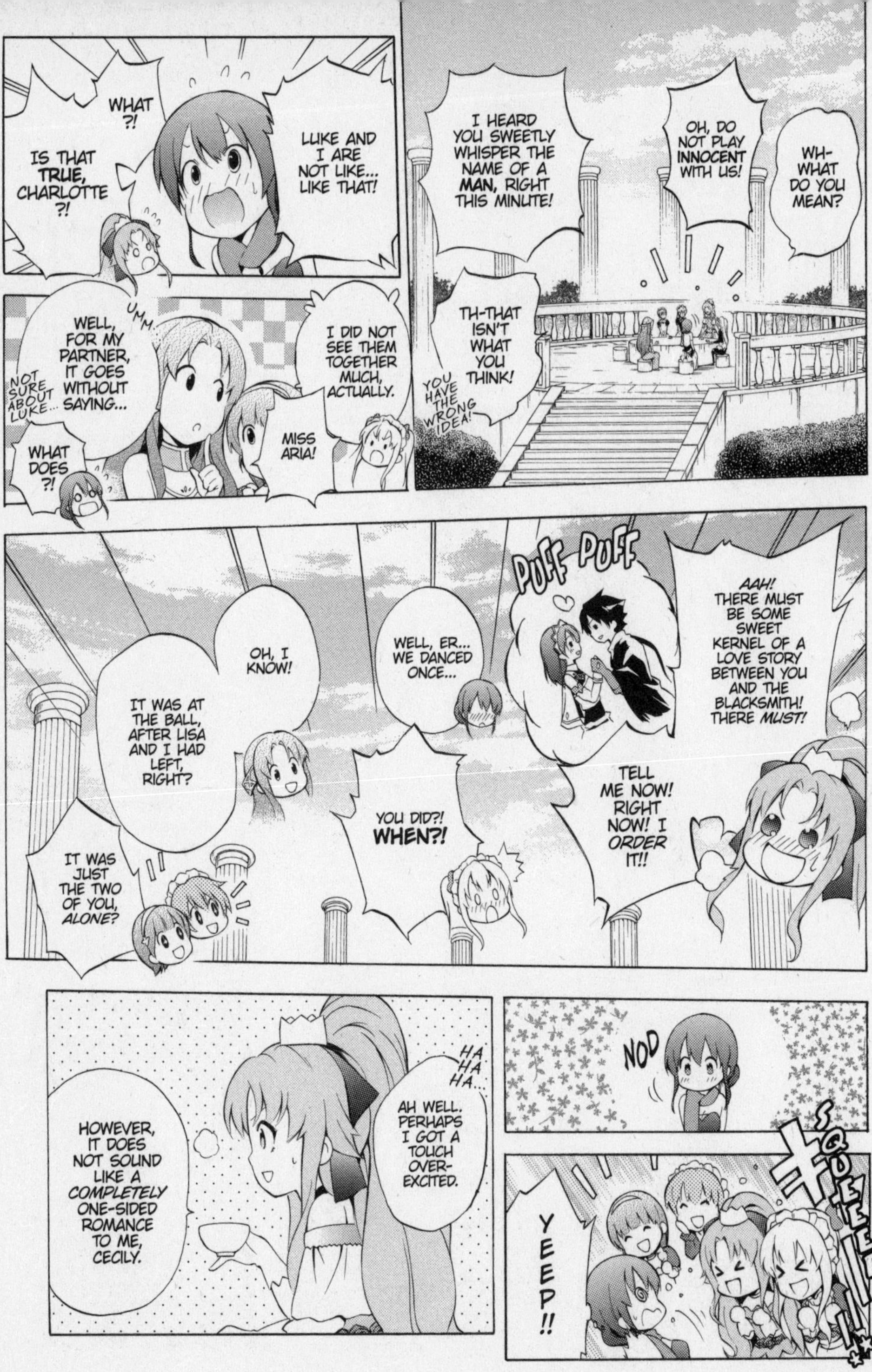
WH-WHAT DO YOU MEAN?
OH, DO NOT PLAY INNOCENT WITH US!
I HEARD YOU SWEETLY WHISPER THE NAME OF A MAN, RIGHT THIS MINUTE!
TH-THAT ISN'T WHAT YOU THINK!
YOU HAVE THE WRONG IDEA!
LUKE AND I ARE NOT LIKE... LIKE THAT!
WHAT ?!
IS THAT TRUE, CHARLOTTE ?!
I DID NOT SEE THEM TOGETHER MUCH, ACTUALLY.
MISS ARIA!
UMM...
WELL, FOR MY PARTNER, IT GOES WITHOUT SAYING...
NOT SURE ABOUT LUKE...
WHAT DOES ?!
AAH! THERE MUST BE SOME SWEET KERNEL OF A LOVE STORY BETWEEN YOU AND THE BLACKSMITH! THERE MUST!
PUFF PUFF
TELL ME NOW! RIGHT NOW! I ORDER IT!!
WELL, ER... WE DANCED ONCE...
YOU DID?! WHEN?!
OH, I KNOW!
IT WAS AT THE BALL, AFTER LISA AND I HAD LEFT, RIGHT?
IT WAS JUST THE TWO OF YOU, ALONE?
NOD
SQUEEEE!!
YEEP!!
HA HA HA...
AH WELL. PERHAPS I GOT A TOUCH OVER-EXCITED.
HOWEVER, IT DOES NOT SOUND LIKE A COMPLETELY ONE-SIDED ROMANCE TO ME, CECILY.

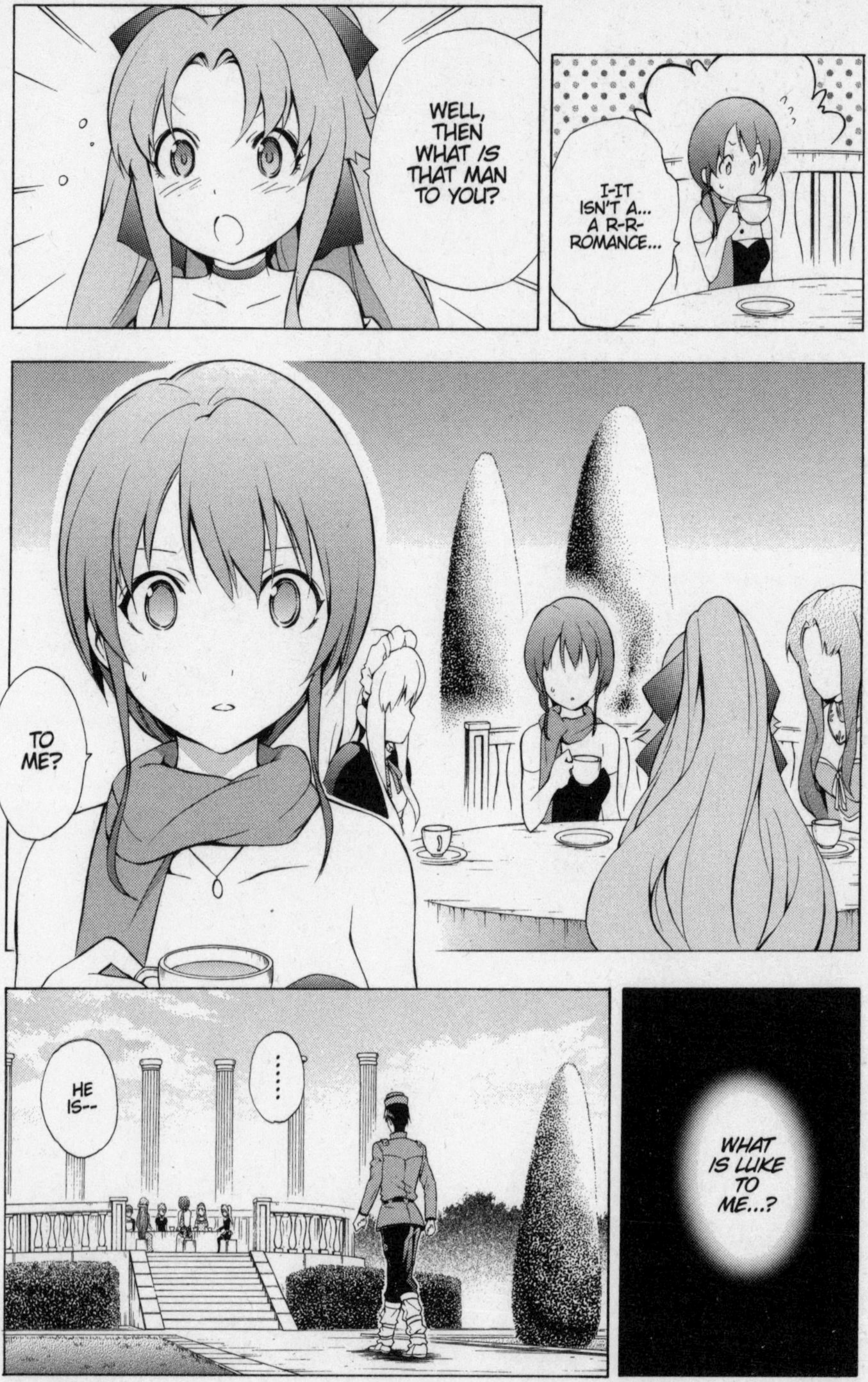
I-IT ISN'T A... A R-R-ROMANCE...
WELL, THEN WHAT IS THAT MAN TO YOU?
TO ME?
WHAT IS LUKE TO ME...?
......
HE IS--

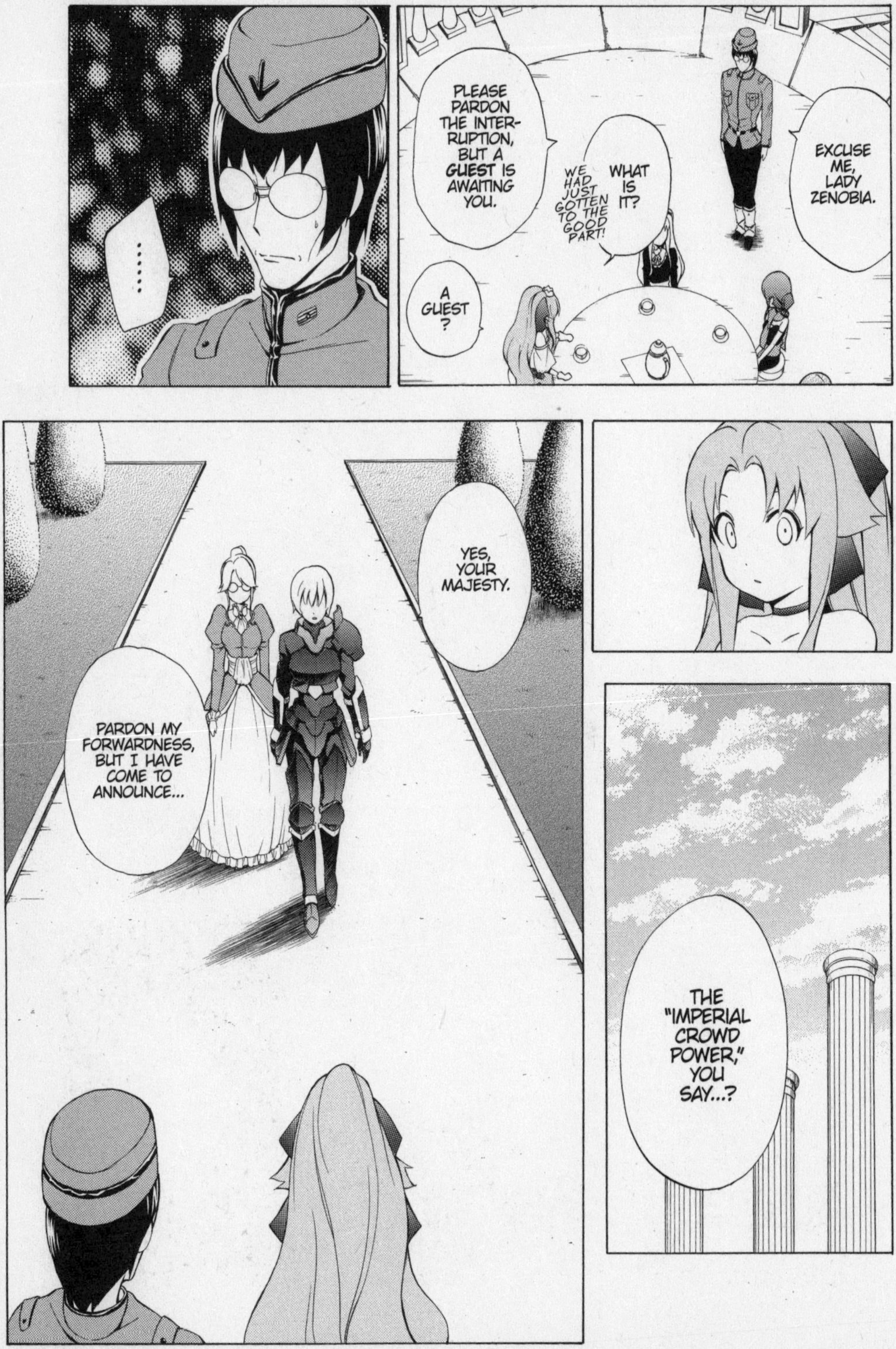
EXCUSE ME, LADY ZENOBIA.
WHAT IS IT?
WE HAD JUST GOTTEN TO THE GOOD PART!
PLEASE PARDON THE INTER-RUPTION, BUT A GUEST IS AWAITING YOU.
A GUEST?
......
THE "IMPERIAL CROWD POWER," YOU SAY...?
YES, YOUR MAJESTY.
PARDON MY FORWARDNESS, BUT I HAVE COME TO ANNOUNCE...

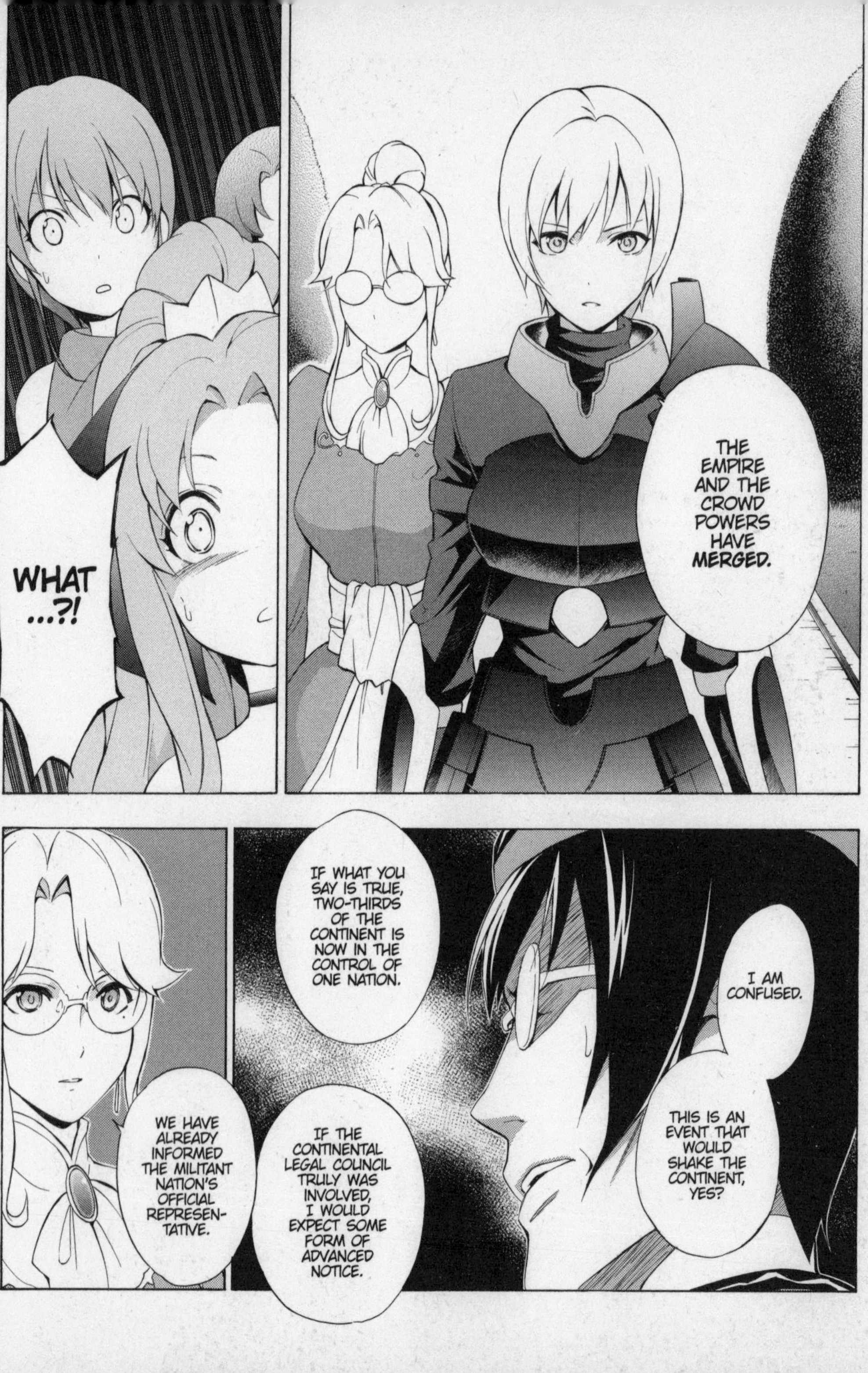
THE EMPIRE AND THE CROWD POWERS HAVE MERGED.
WHAT ...?!
I AM CONFUSED.
IF WHAT YOU SAY IS TRUE, TWO-THIRDS OF THE CONTINENT IS NOW IN THE CONTROL OF ONE NATION.
THIS IS AN EVENT THAT WOULD SHAKE THE CONTINENT, YES?
IF THE CONTINENTAL LEGAL COUNCIL TRULY WAS INVOLVED, I WOULD EXPECT SOME FORM OF ADVANCED NOTICE.
WE HAVE ALREADY INFORMED THE MILITANT NATION'S OFFICIAL REPRESEN-TATIVE.

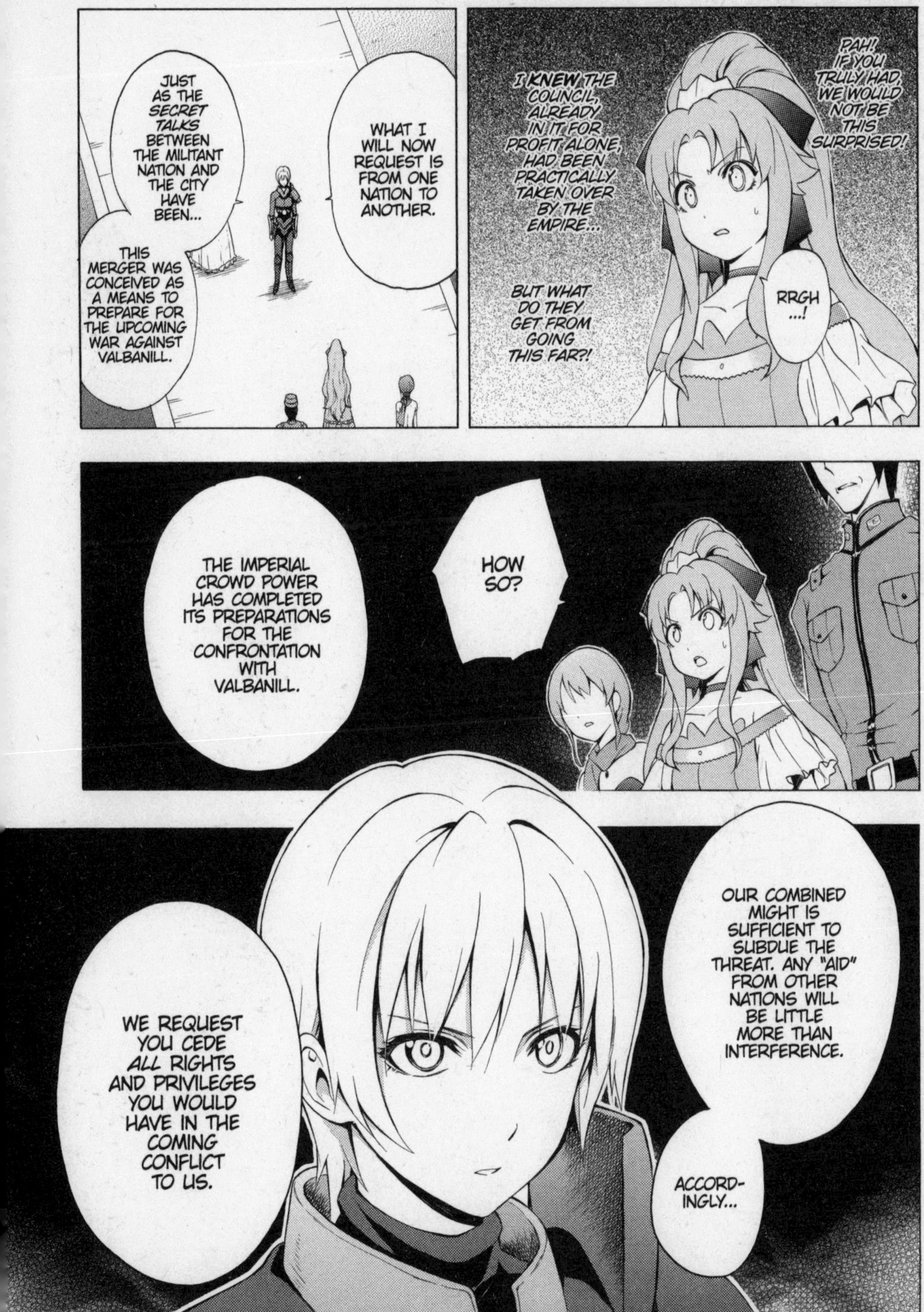

PAH! IF YOU TRULY HAD, WE WOULD NOT BE THIS SURPRISED!
I KNEW THE COUNCIL, ALREADY IN IT FOR PROFIT ALONE, HAD BEEN PRACTICALLY TAKEN OVER BY THE EMPIRE...
RRGH ...!
BUT WHAT DO THEY GET FROM GOING THIS FAR?!
WHAT I WILL NOW REQUEST IS FROM ONE NATION TO ANOTHER.
JUST AS THE SECRET TALKS BETWEEN THE MILITANT NATION AND THE CITY HAVE BEEN...
THIS MERGER WAS CONCEIVED AS A MEANS TO PREPARE FOR THE UPCOMING WAR AGAINST VALBANILL.
HOW SO?
THE IMPERIAL CROWD POWER HAS COMPLETED ITS PREPARATIONS FOR THE CONFRONTATION WITH VALBANILL.
OUR COMBINED MIGHT IS SUFFICIENT TO SUBDUE THE THREAT. ANY "AID" FROM OTHER NATIONS WILL BE LITTLE MORE THAN INTERFERENCE.
ACCORD-INGLY...
WE REQUEST YOU CEDE ALL RIGHTS AND PRIVILEGES YOU WOULD HAVE IN THE COMING CONFLICT TO US.

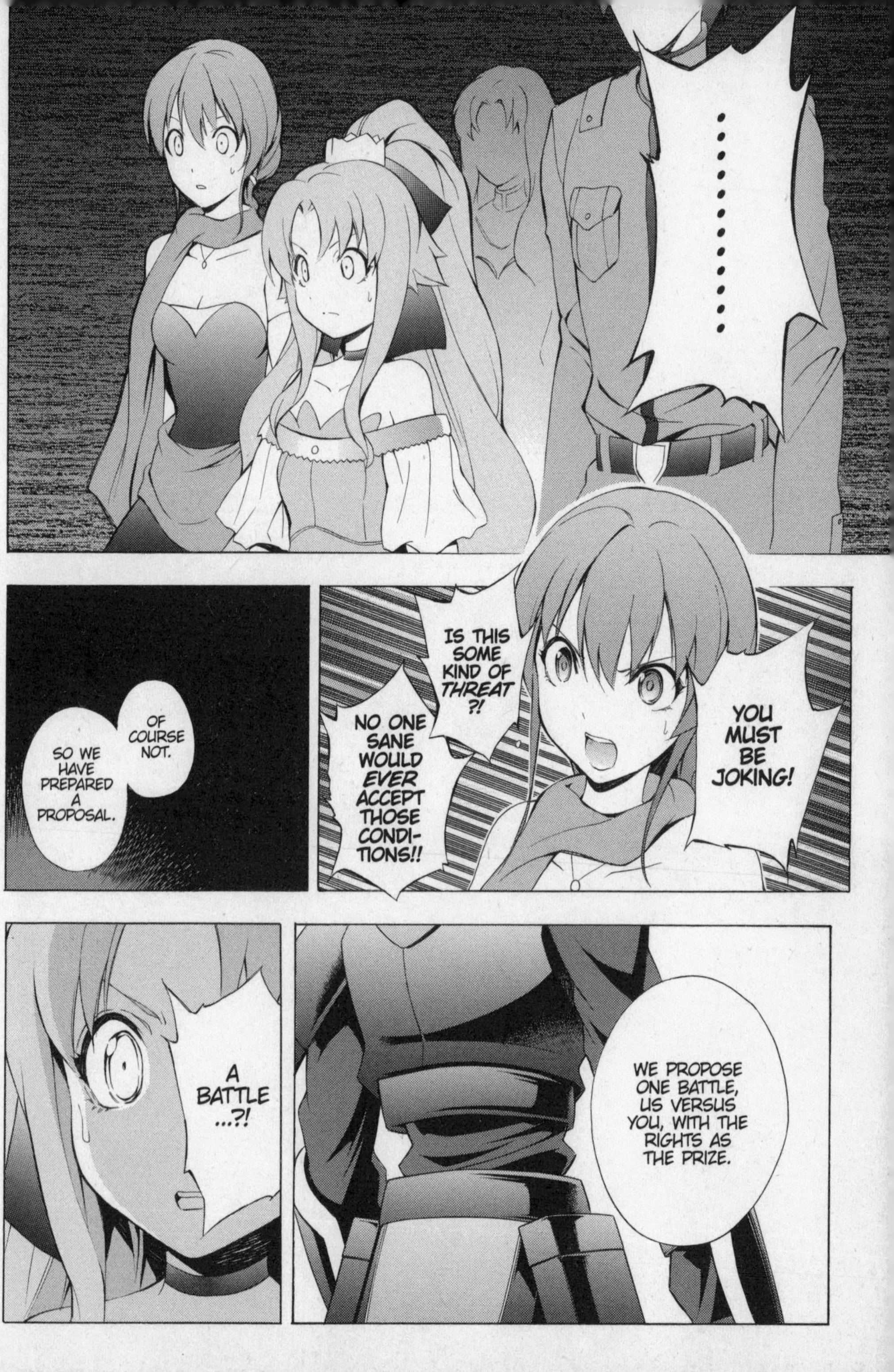
......
YOU MUST BE JOKING!
IS THIS SOME KIND OF THREAT ?!
NO ONE SANE WOULD EVER ACCEPT THOSE CONDITIONS!!
OF COURSE NOT.
SO WE HAVE PREPARED A PROPOSAL.
WE PROPOSE ONE BATTLE, US VERSUS YOU, WITH THE RIGHTS AS THE PRIZE.
A BATTLE ...?!

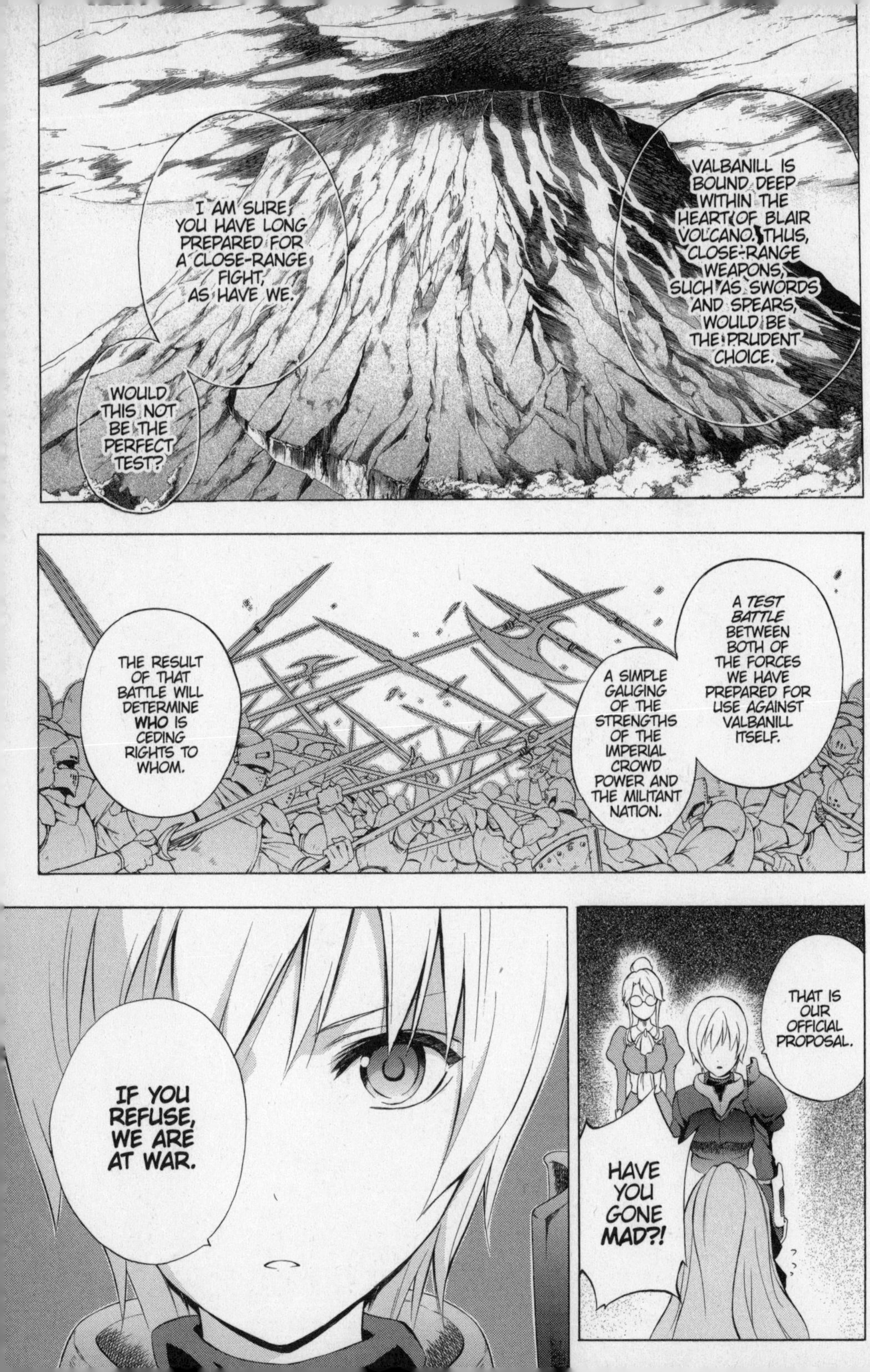
VALBANILL IS BOUND DEEP WITHIN THE HEART OF BLAIR VOLCANO. THUS, CLOSE-RANGE WEAPONS, SUCH AS SWORDS AND SPEARS, WOULD BE THE PRUDENT CHOICE.
I AM SURE YOU HAVE LONG PREPARED FOR A CLOSE-RANGE FIGHT, AS HAVE WE.
WOULD THIS NOT BE THE PERFECT TEST?
A *TEST BATTLE* BETWEEN BOTH OF THE FORCES WE HAVE PREPARED FOR USE AGAINST VALBANILL ITSELF.
A SIMPLE GAUGING OF THE STRENGTHS OF THE IMPERIAL CROWD POWER AND THE MILITANT NATION.
THE RESULT OF THAT BATTLE WILL DETERMINE WHO IS CEDING RIGHTS TO WHOM.
THAT IS OUR OFFICIAL PROPOSAL.
HAVE YOU GONE MAD?!
IF YOU REFUSE, WE ARE AT WAR.

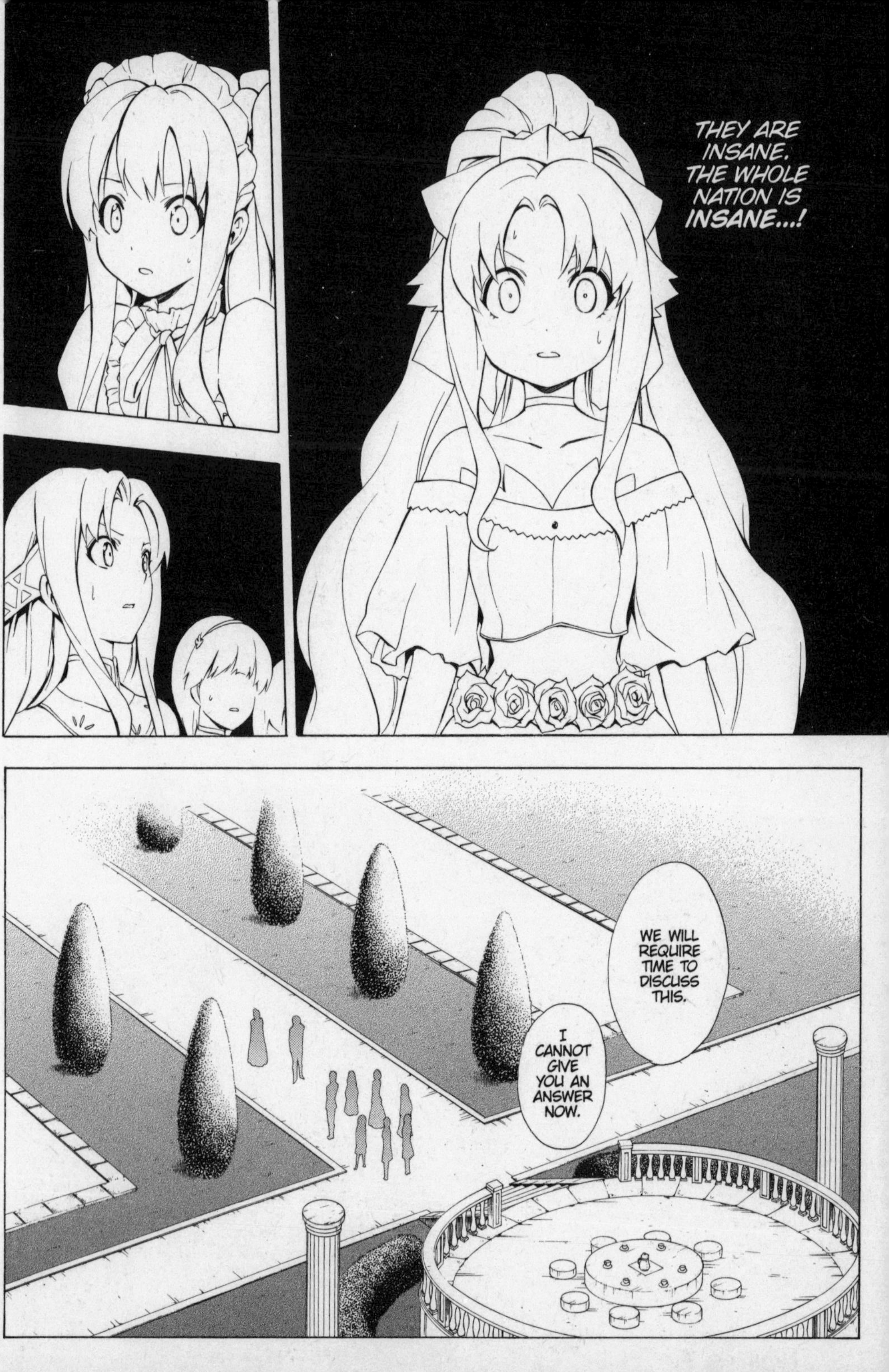
THEY ARE INSANE. THE WHOLE NATION IS INSANE...!
WE WILL REQUIRE TIME TO DISCUSS THIS.
I CANNOT GIVE YOU AN ANSWER NOW.

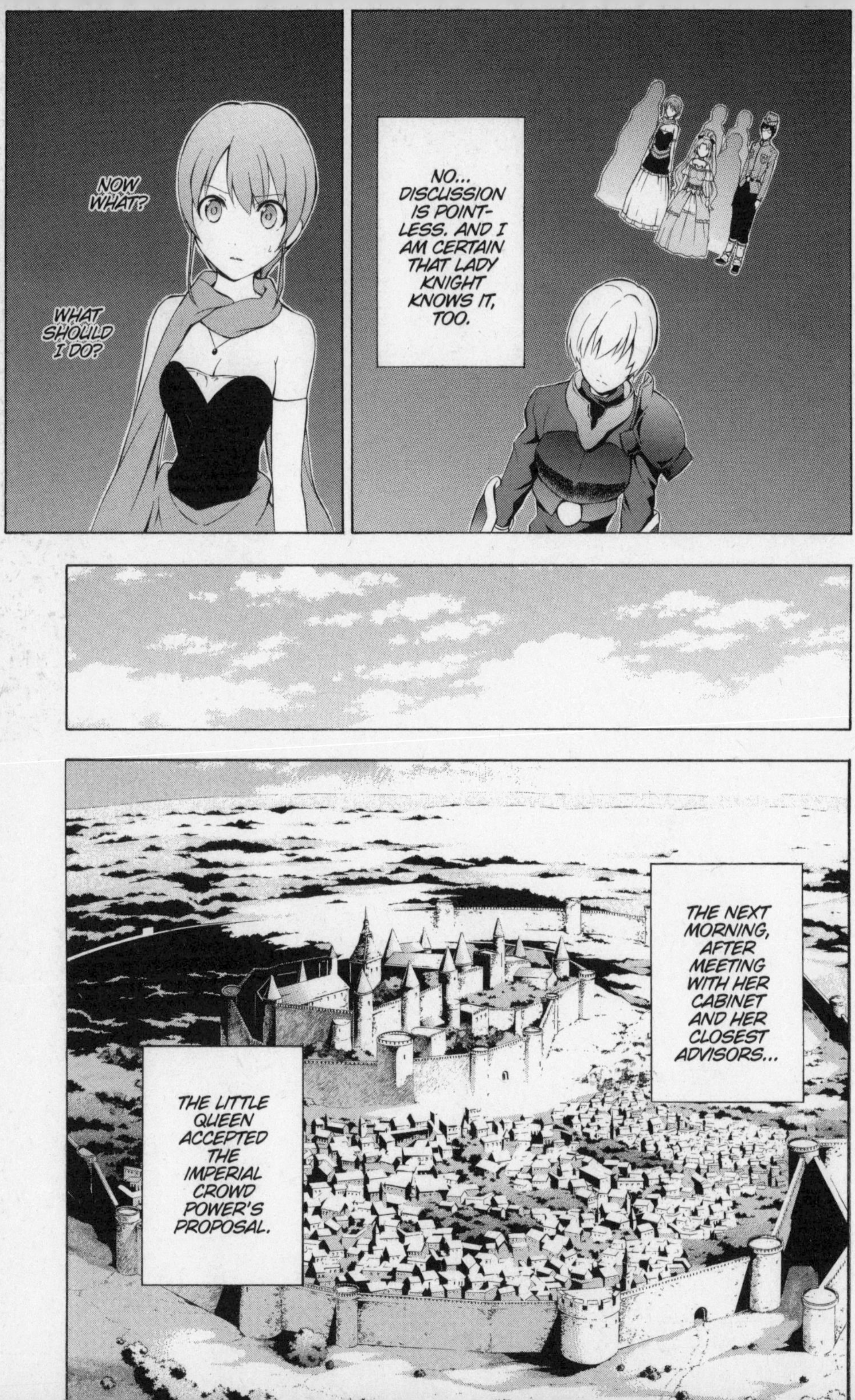
NO... DISCUSSION IS POINTLESS. AND I AM CERTAIN THAT LADY KNIGHT KNOWS IT, TOO.
NOW WHAT?
WHAT SHOULD I DO?
THE NEXT MORNING, AFTER MEETING WITH HER CABINET AND HER CLOSEST ADVISORS...
THE LITTLE QUEEN ACCEPTED THE IMPERIAL CROWD POWER'S PROPOSAL.

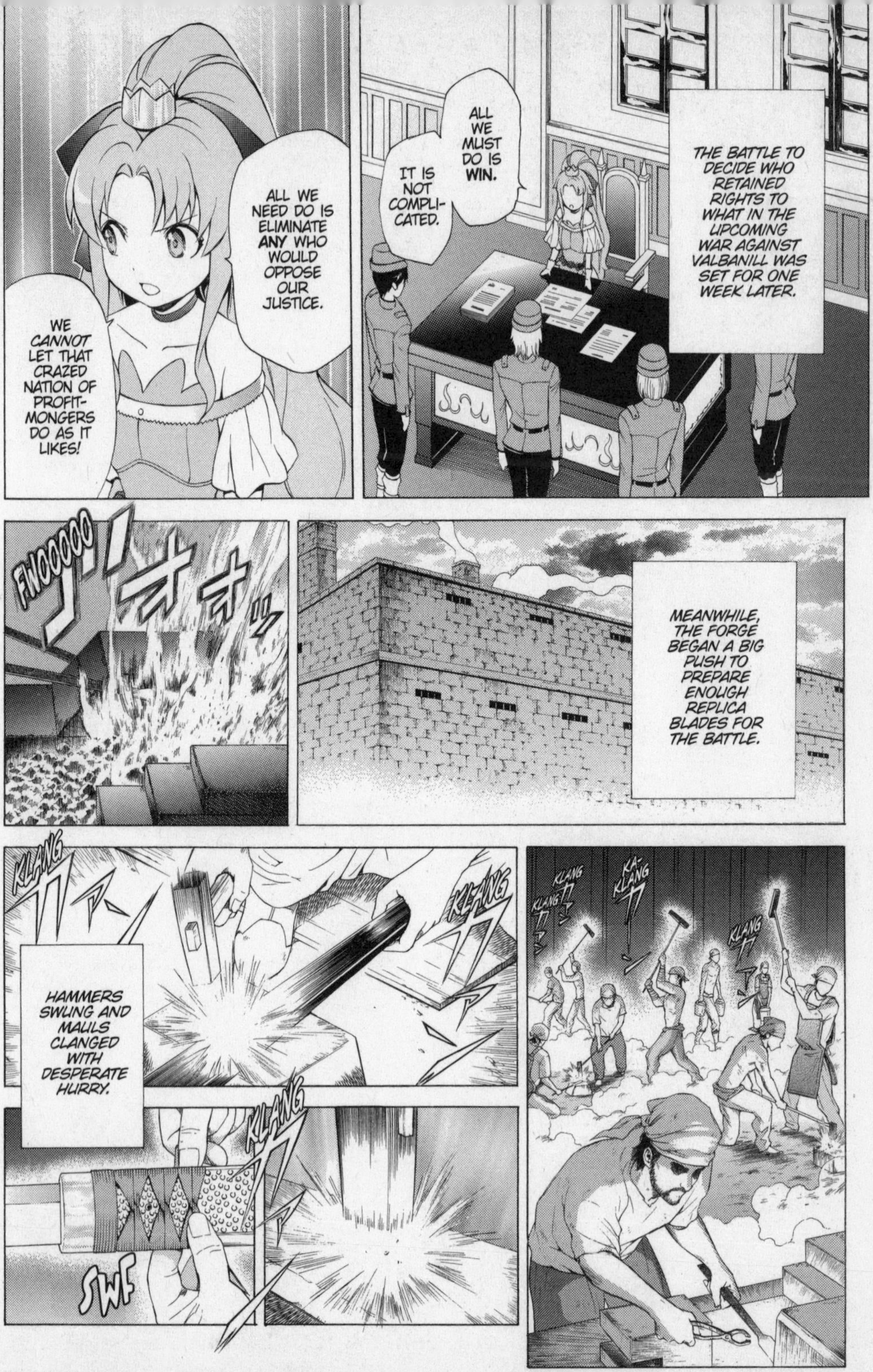
THE BATTLE TO DECIDE WHO RETAINED RIGHTS TO WHAT IN THE UPCOMING WAR AGAINST VALBANILL WAS SET FOR ONE WEEK LATER.
ALL WE MUST DO IS WIN.
IT IS NOT COMPLICATED.
ALL WE NEED DO IS ELIMINATE ANY WHO WOULD OPPOSE OUR JUSTICE.
WE CANNOT LET THAT CRAZED NATION OF PROFIT-MONGERS DO AS IT LIKES!
MEANWHILE, THE FORGE BEGAN A BIG PUSH TO PREPARE ENOUGH REPLICA BLADES FOR THE BATTLE.
FWOOOOO
KA-KLANG
KLANG
KLANG
KLANG
KLANG
KLANG
HAMMERS SWUNG AND MAULS CLANGED WITH DESPERATE HURRY.
KLANG
SWF

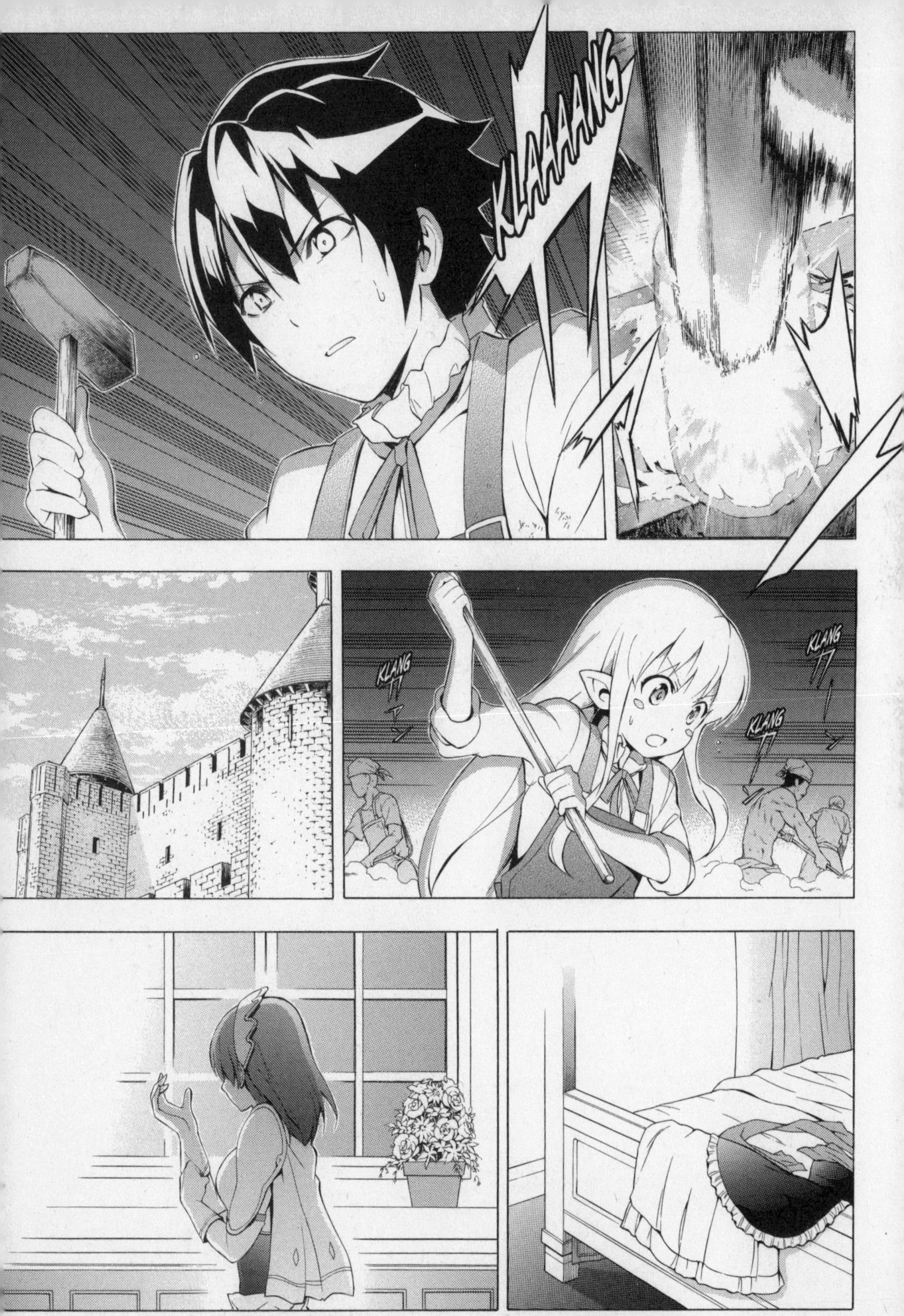
KLAAAANG
KLANG
KLANG
KLANG

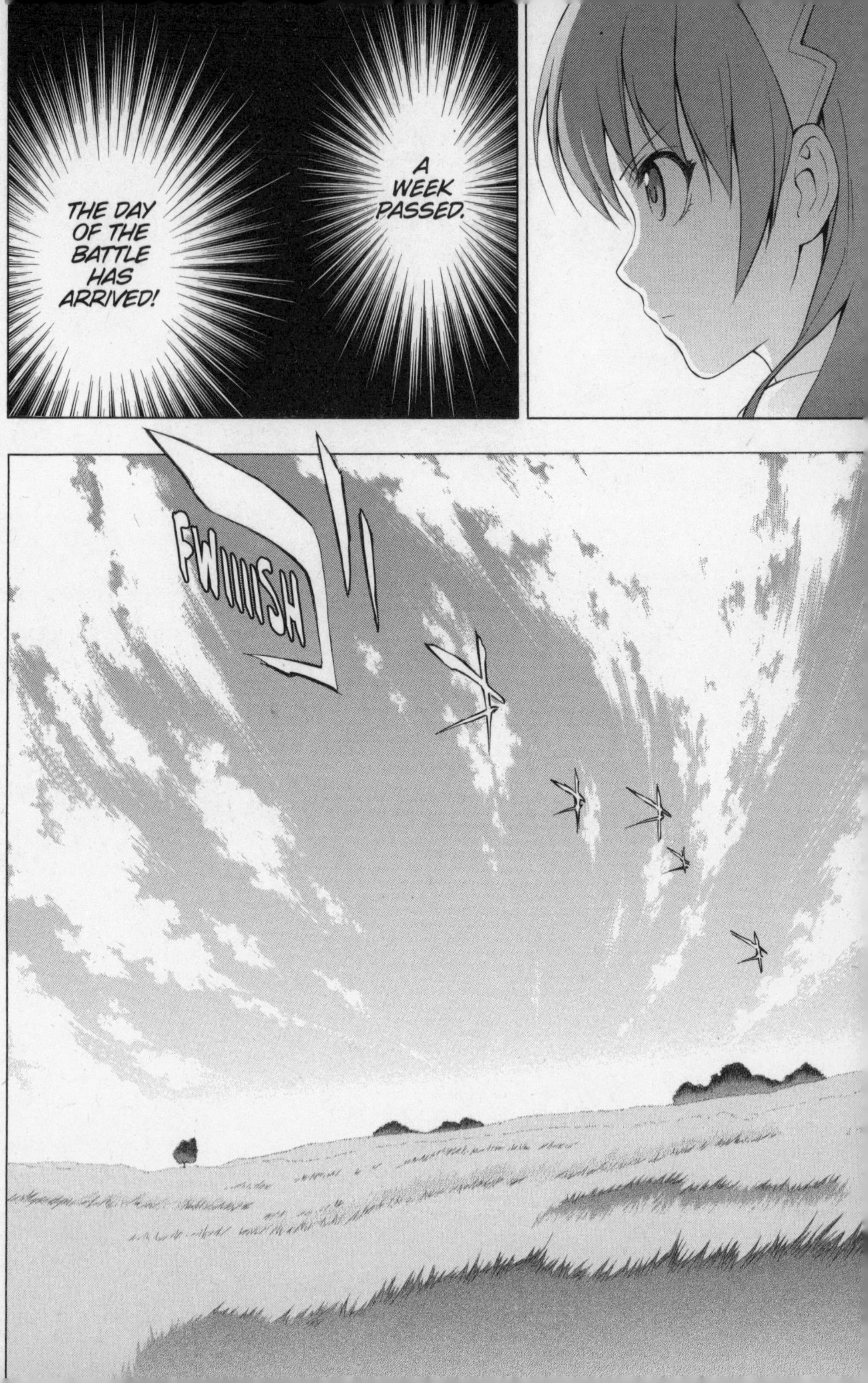
A WEEK PASSED.
THE DAY OF THE BATTLE HAS ARRIVED!
FWIIIISH

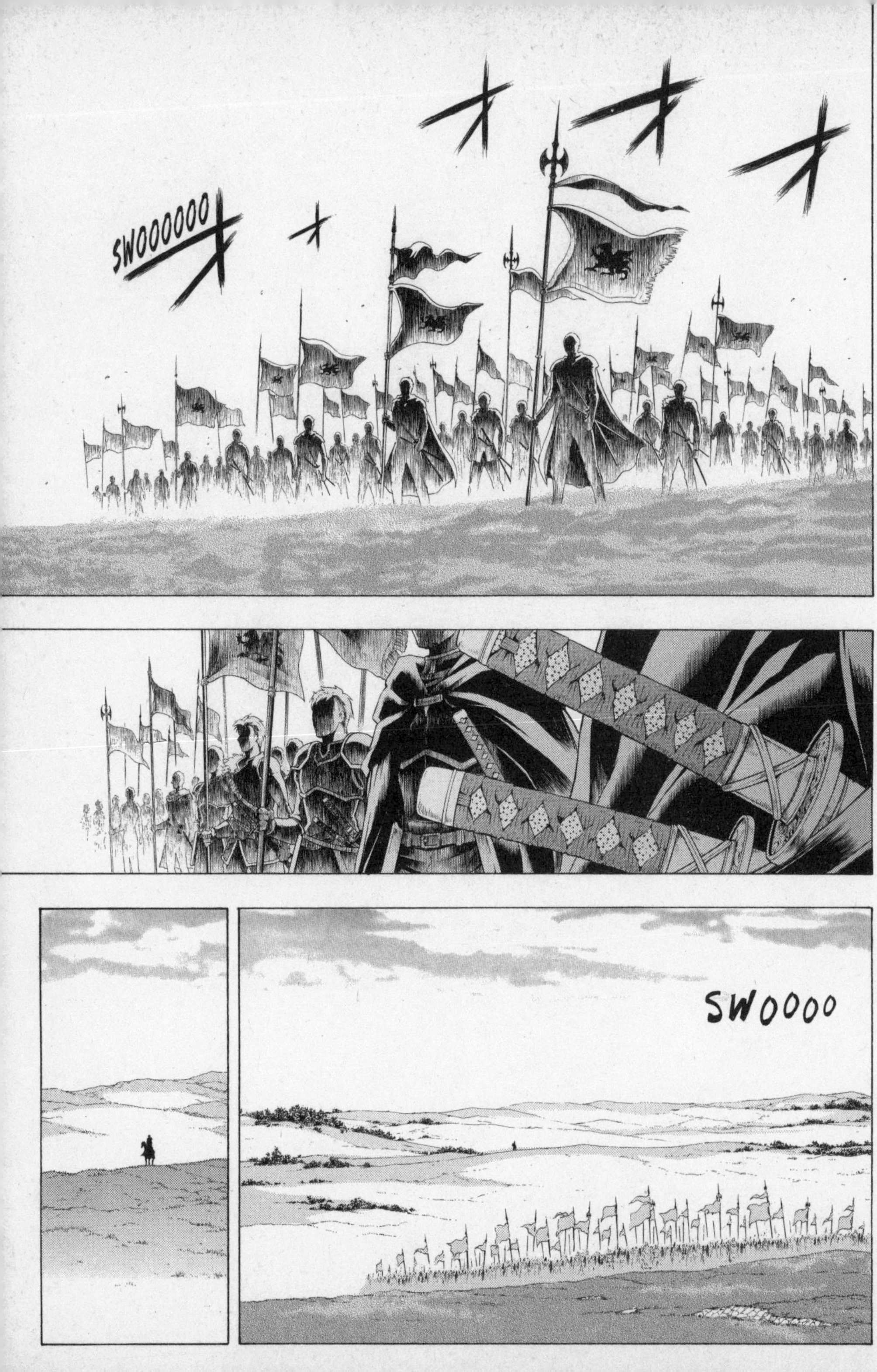
オ オ オ オ
SWOOOOOO
SWOOOO

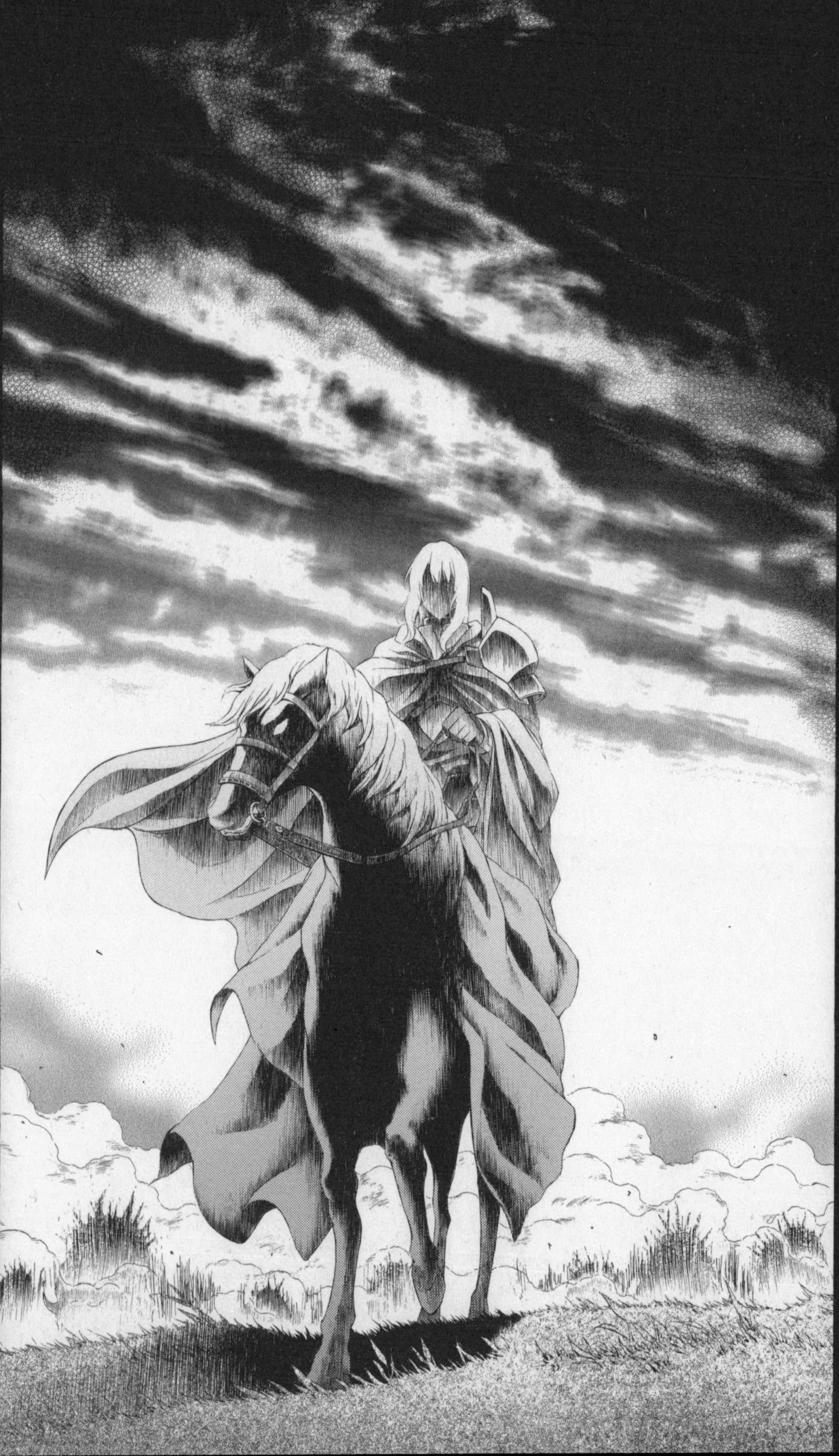

The Sacred Blacksmith

聖剣の刀鍛冶

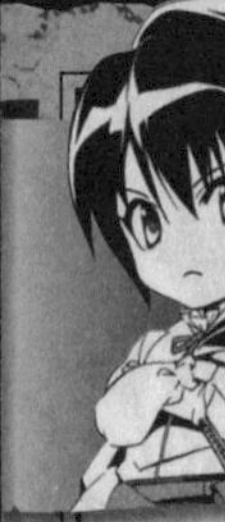

Everyone's skill is improving day by day. I'm impressed.

アトリエ 工房リーザ

atelier Liza BRANCH OFFICE III

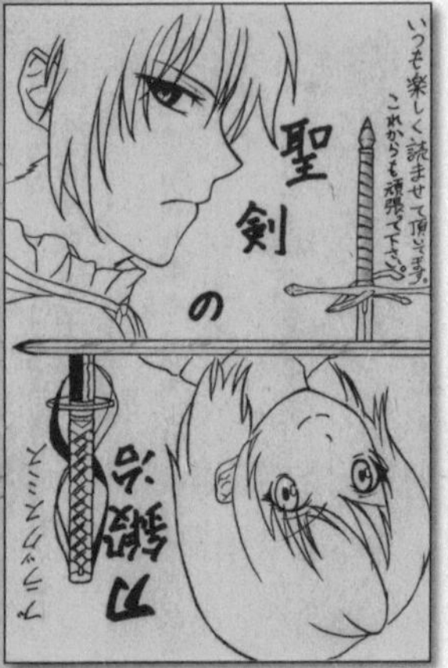
聖剣の

↑Yamagata, Natsumi Watarai

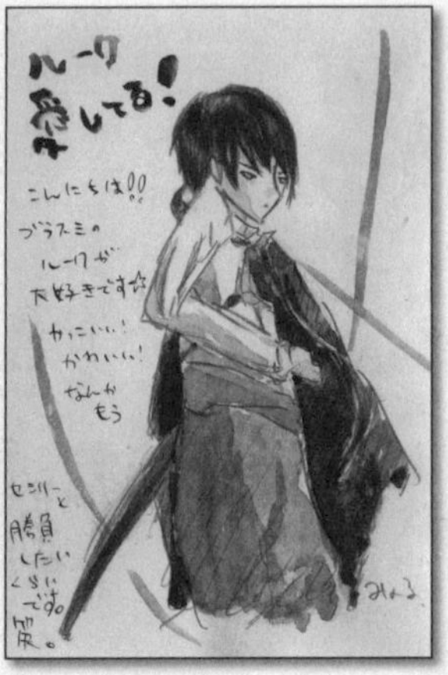
ルーク愛してる!
こんにちは!!

↑Gifu, Minoru

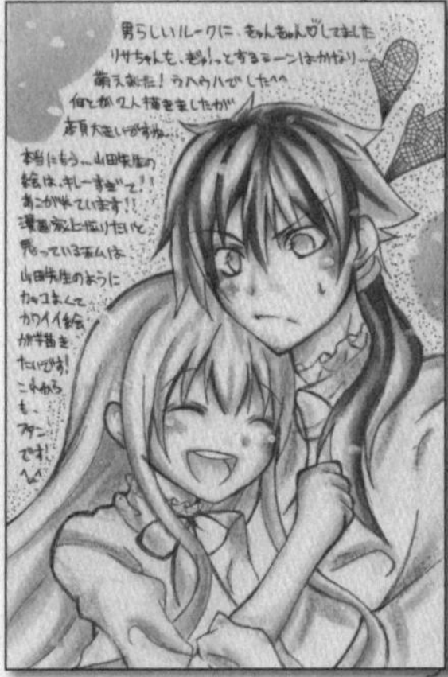

↑Chiba, Shuya Himezora

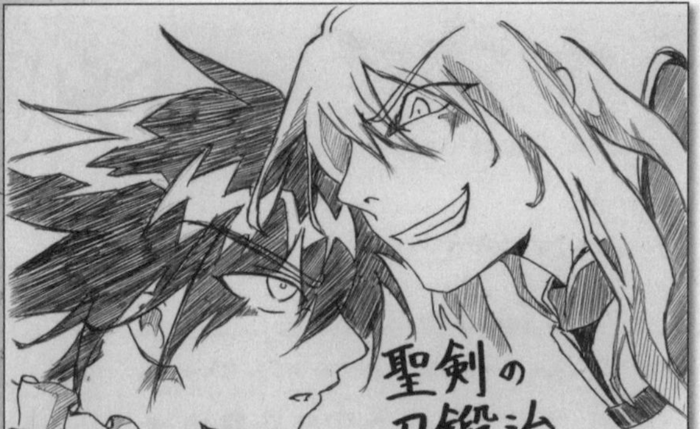
聖剣の
刀鍛治

↑Hyogo, Sakura

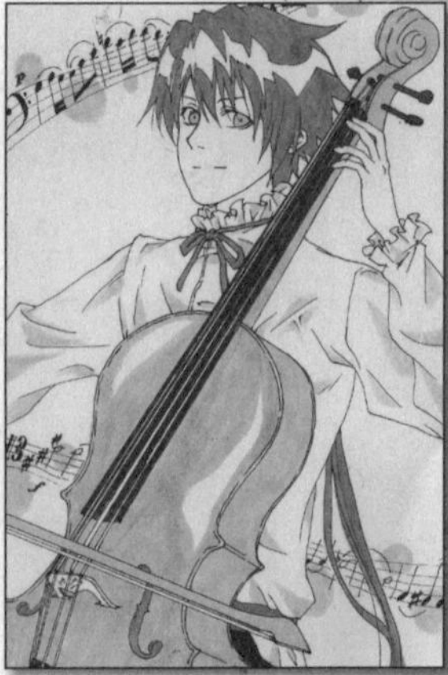

↑Kanagawa, Gu Xiang

An excellent depiction of the battle between Siegfried and myself. One day, I will finish him with my own hands.

The Sacred Blacksmith

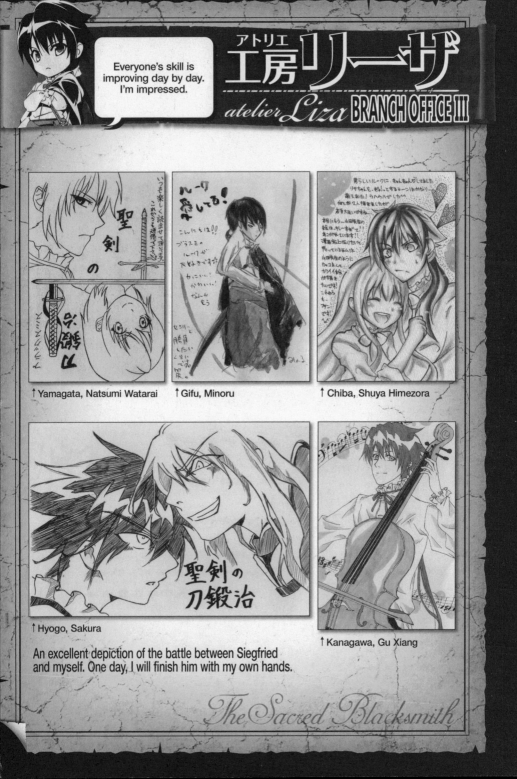

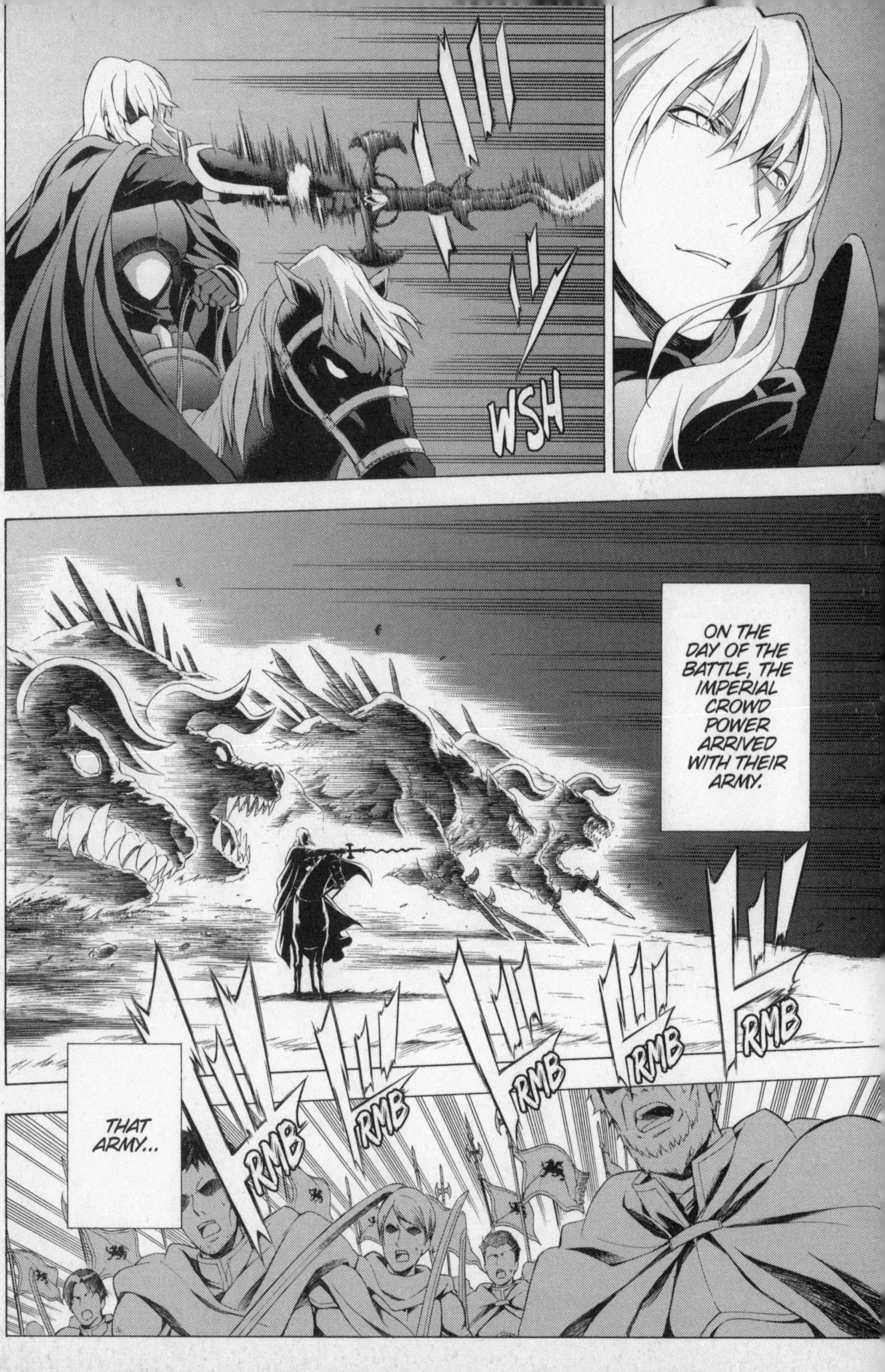

WSH
ON THE DAY OF THE BATTLE, THE IMPERIAL CROWD POWER ARRIVED WITH THEIR ARMY.
RMB
RMB
RMB
RMB
RMB
THAT ARMY...

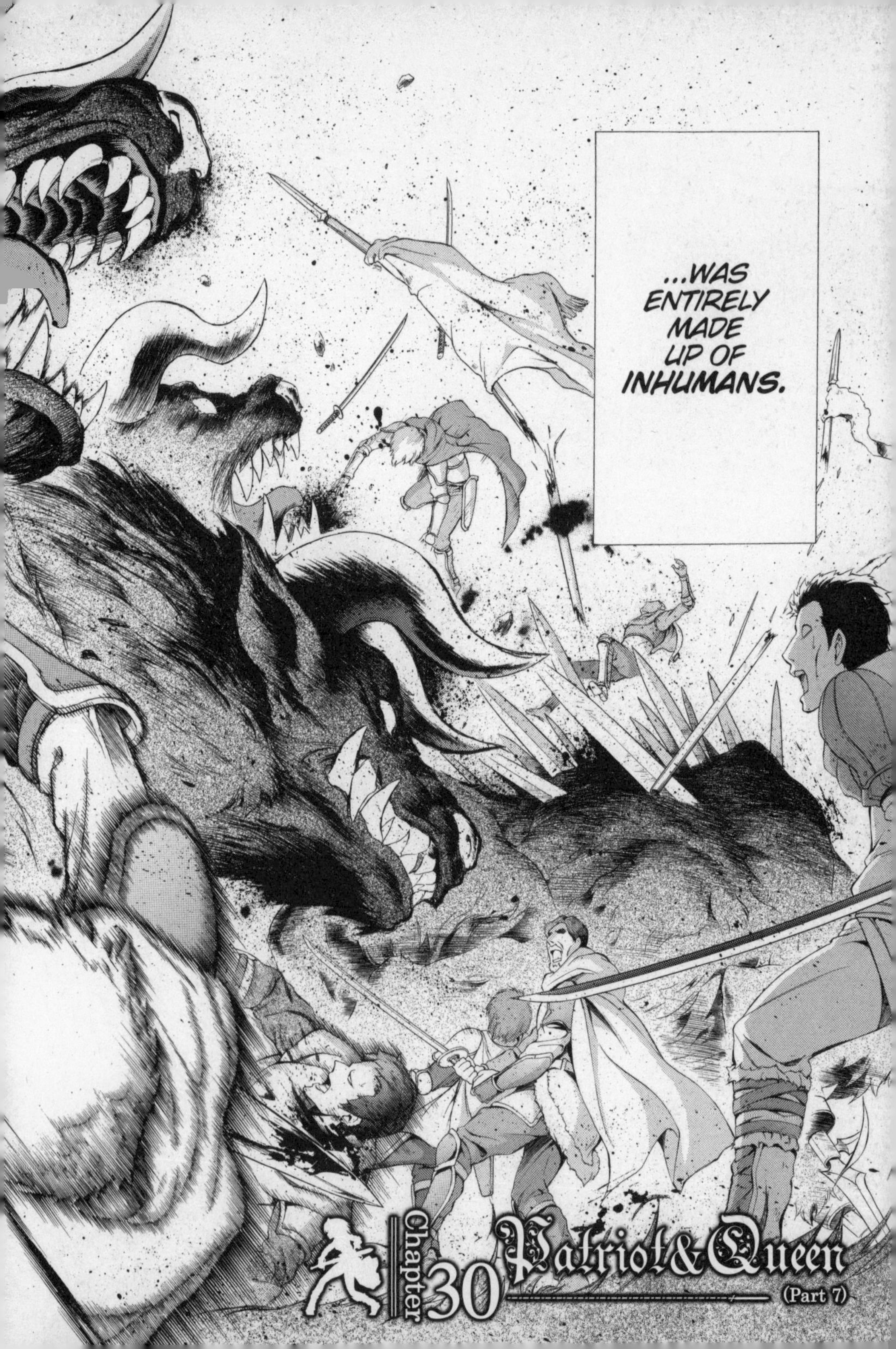
...WAS ENTIRELY MADE UP OF INHUMANS.
Chapter 30
Patriot & Queen
(Part 7)

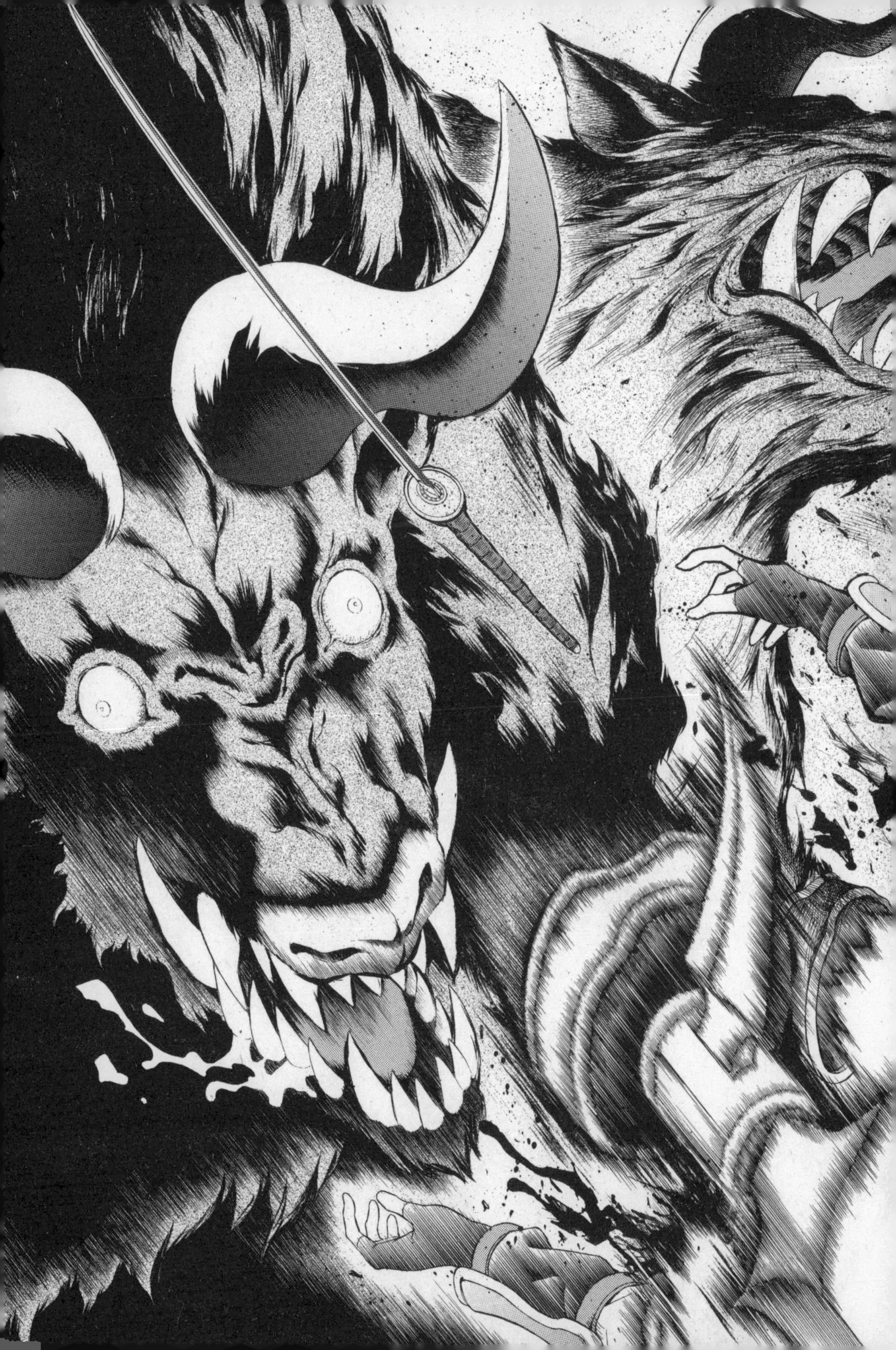

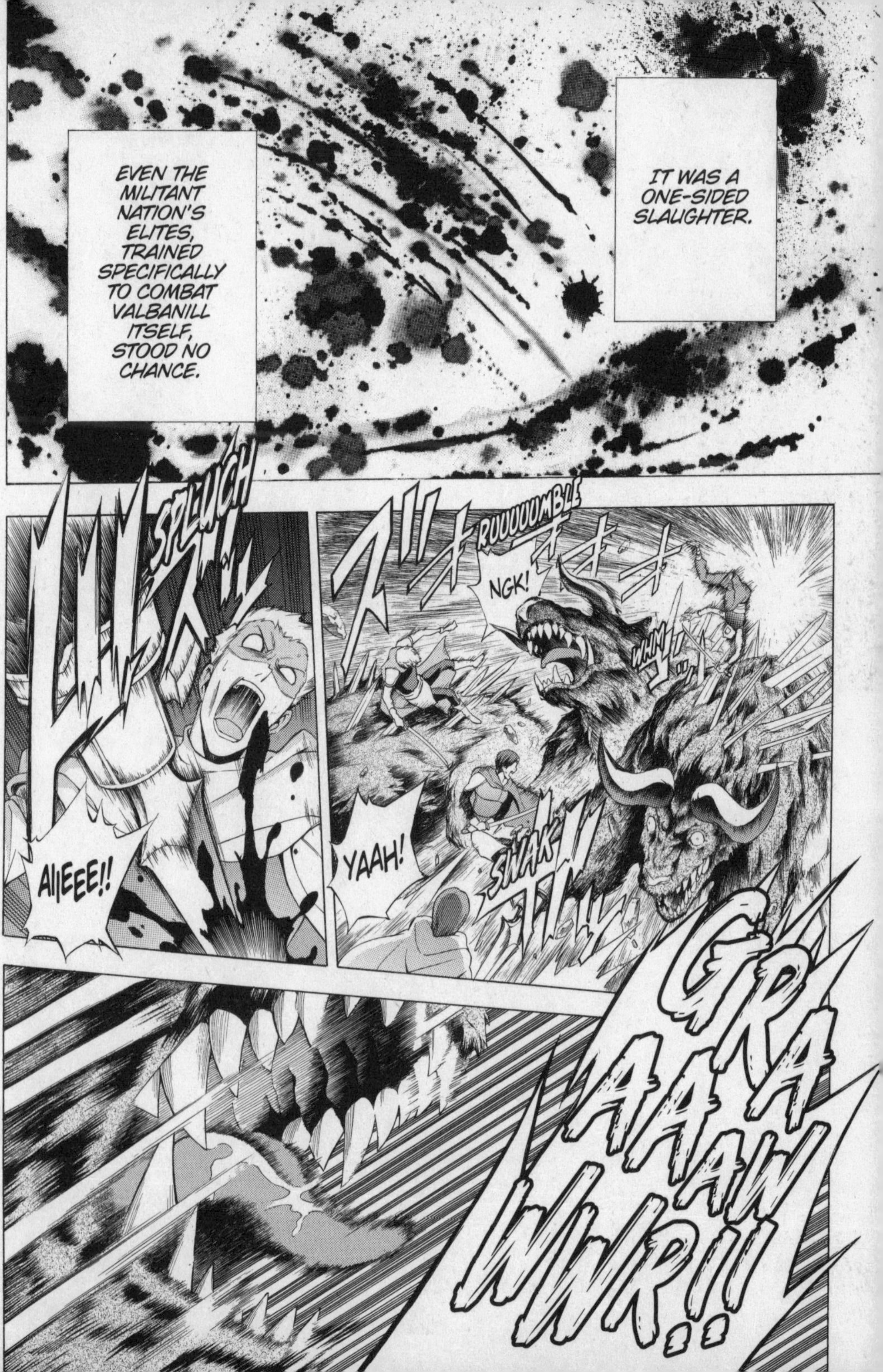
IT WAS A ONE-SIDED SLAUGHTER.
EVEN THE MILITANT NATION'S ELITES, TRAINED SPECIFICALLY TO COMBAT VALBANILL ITSELF, STOOD NO CHANCE.
RUUUUUMBLE
NGK!
SWAK
YAAH!
SPLUCH
AIIEEE!!
GRAAAAAWWR!!

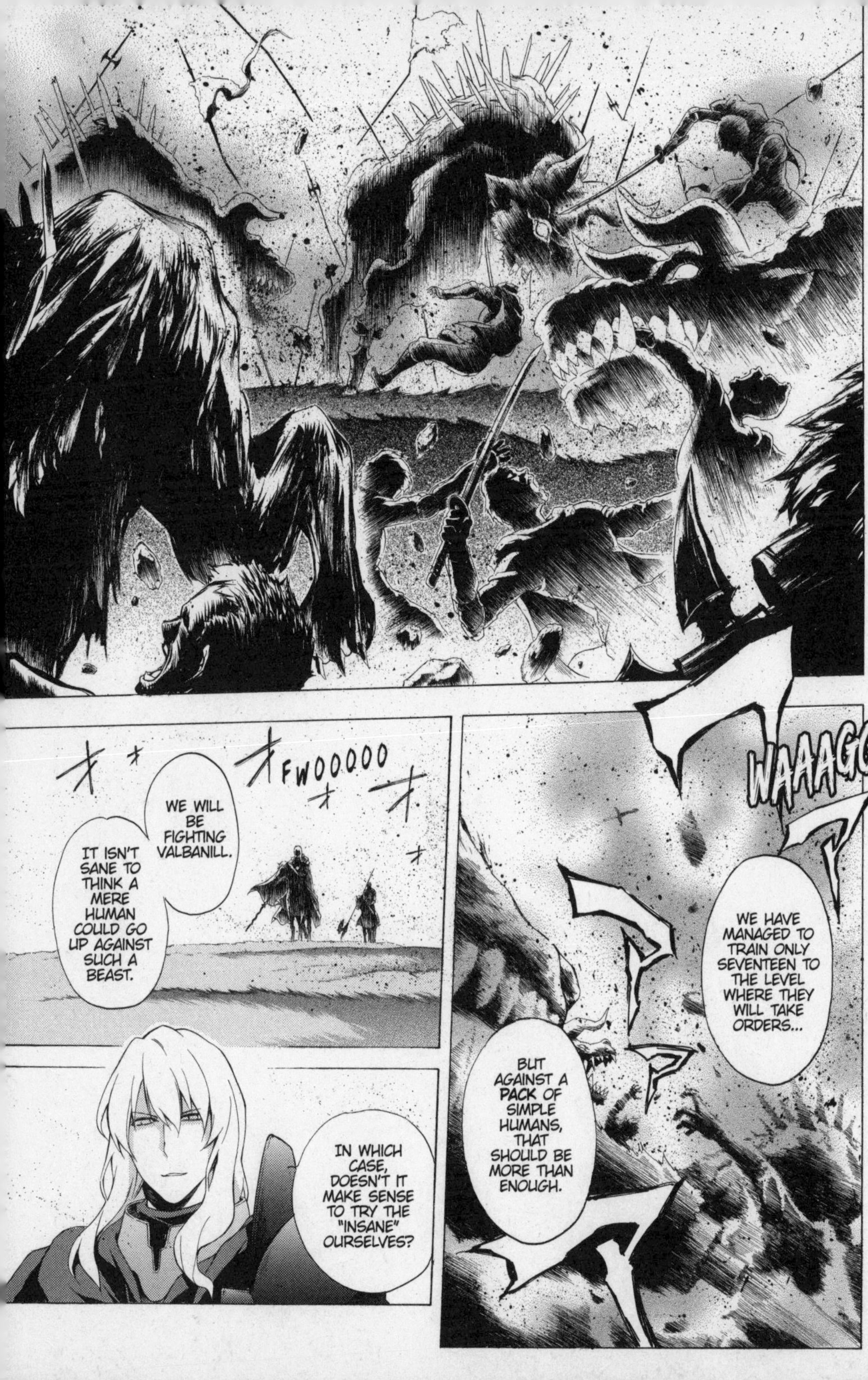
WAAAGGH
WE HAVE MANAGED TO TRAIN ONLY SEVENTEEN TO THE LEVEL WHERE THEY WILL TAKE ORDERS...
BUT AGAINST A PACK OF SIMPLE HUMANS, THAT SHOULD BE MORE THAN ENOUGH.
FWOOOOO
WE WILL BE FIGHTING VALBANILL.
IT ISN'T SANE TO THINK A MERE HUMAN COULD GO UP AGAINST SUCH A BEAST.
IN WHICH CASE, DOESN'T IT MAKE SENSE TO TRY THE "INSANE" OURSELVES?

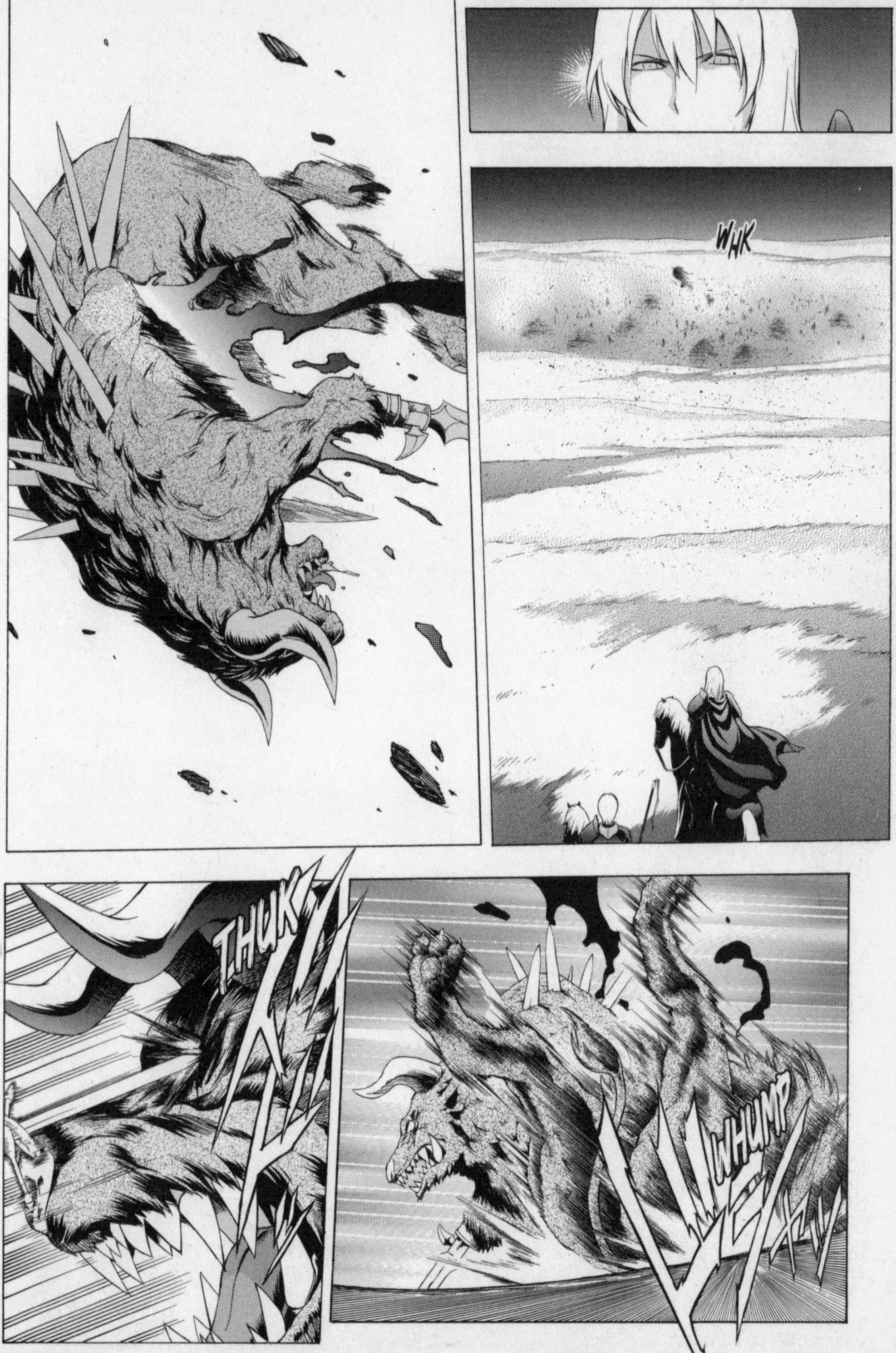
WHK
WHUMP
THUK

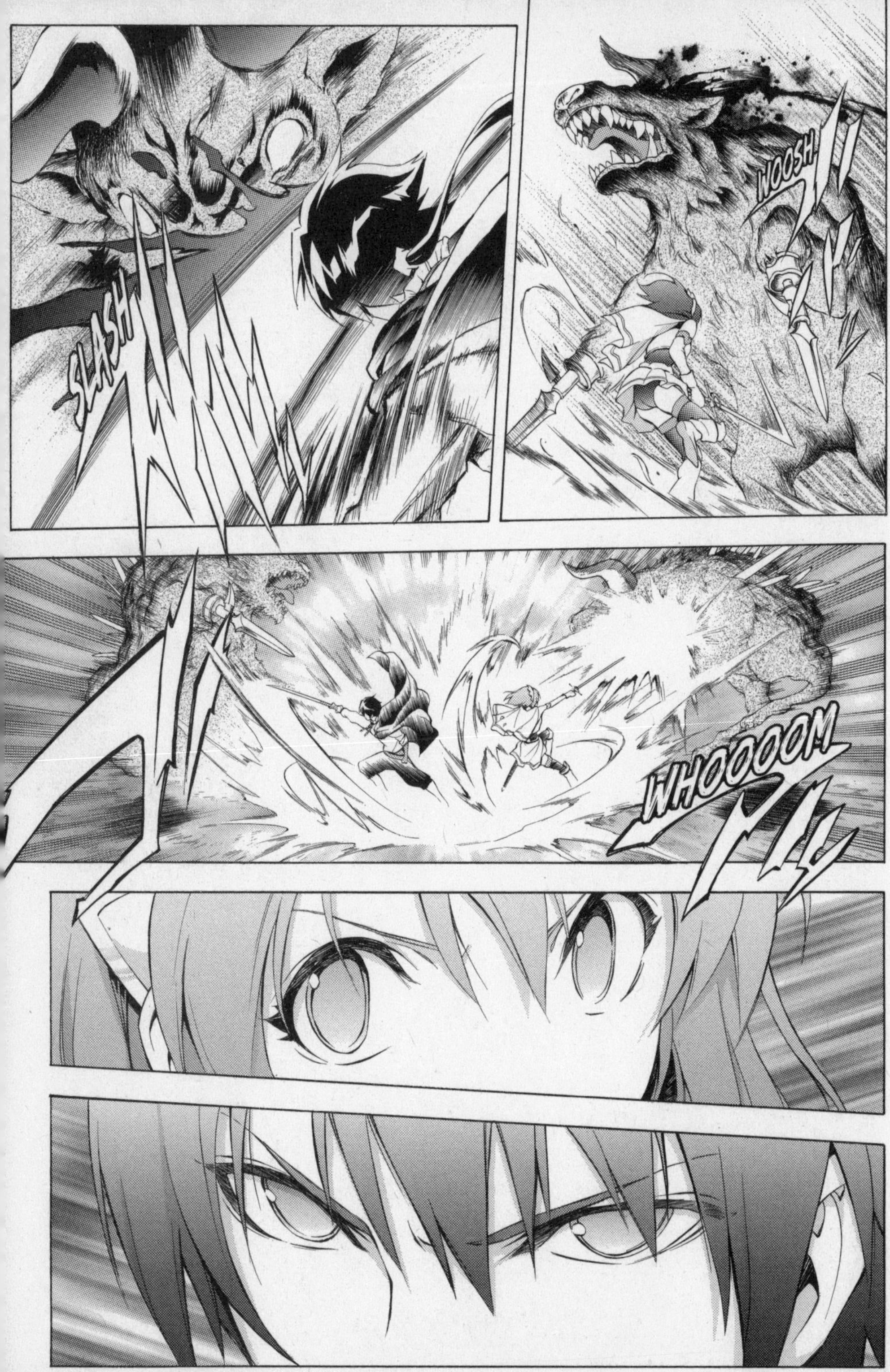
WOOSH
SLASH
WHOOOOM

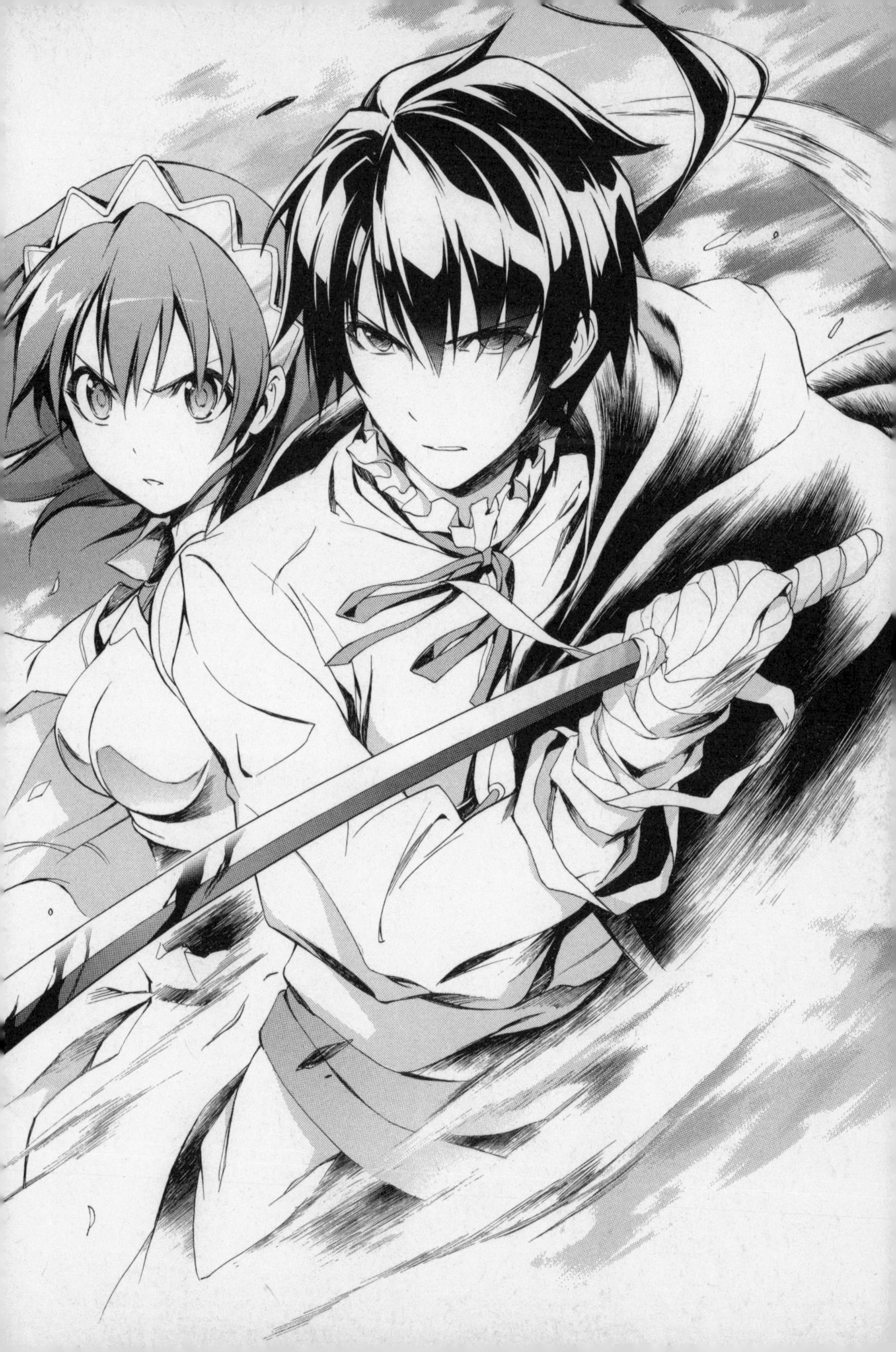

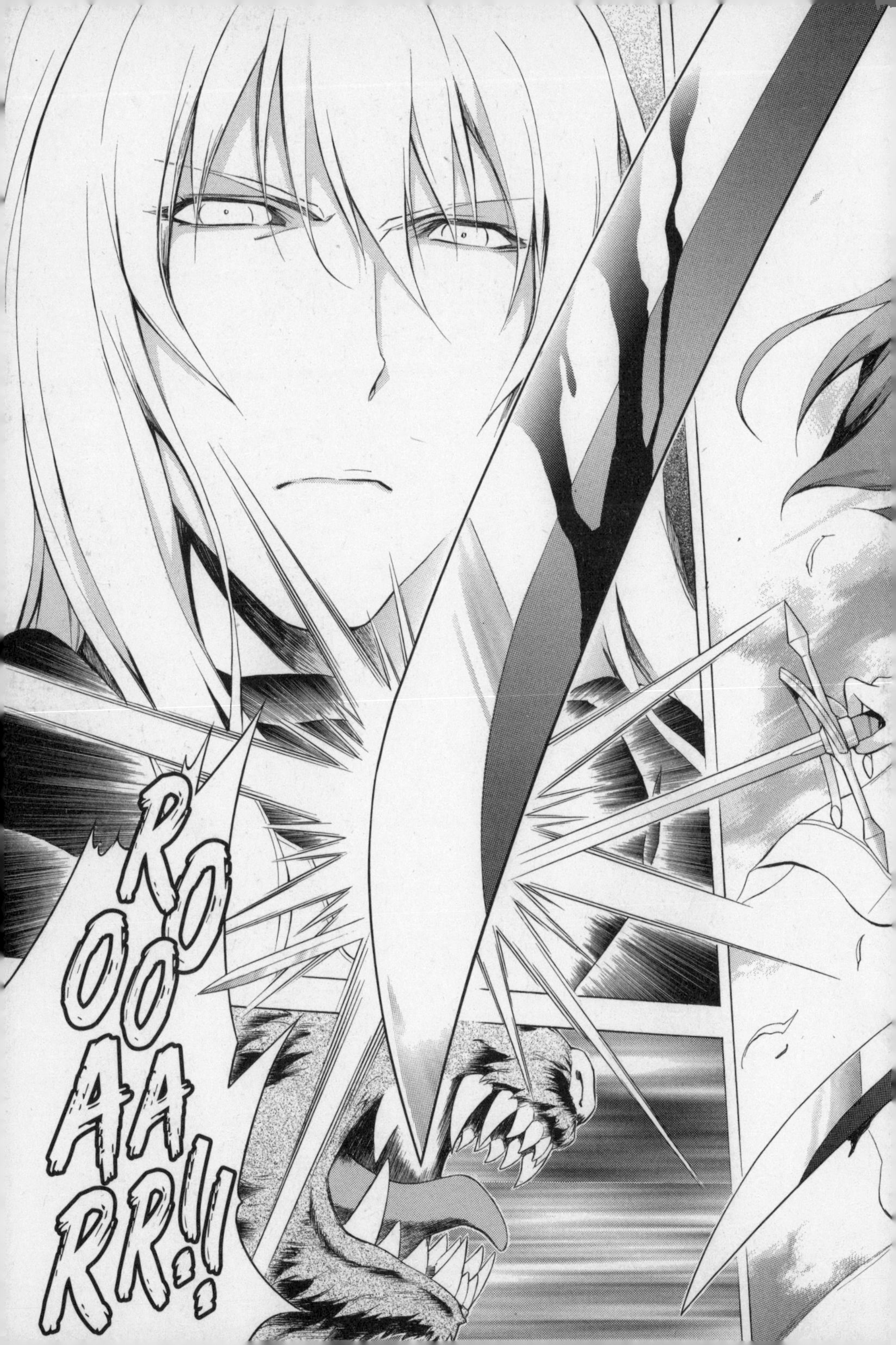
ROOOOAARR!!

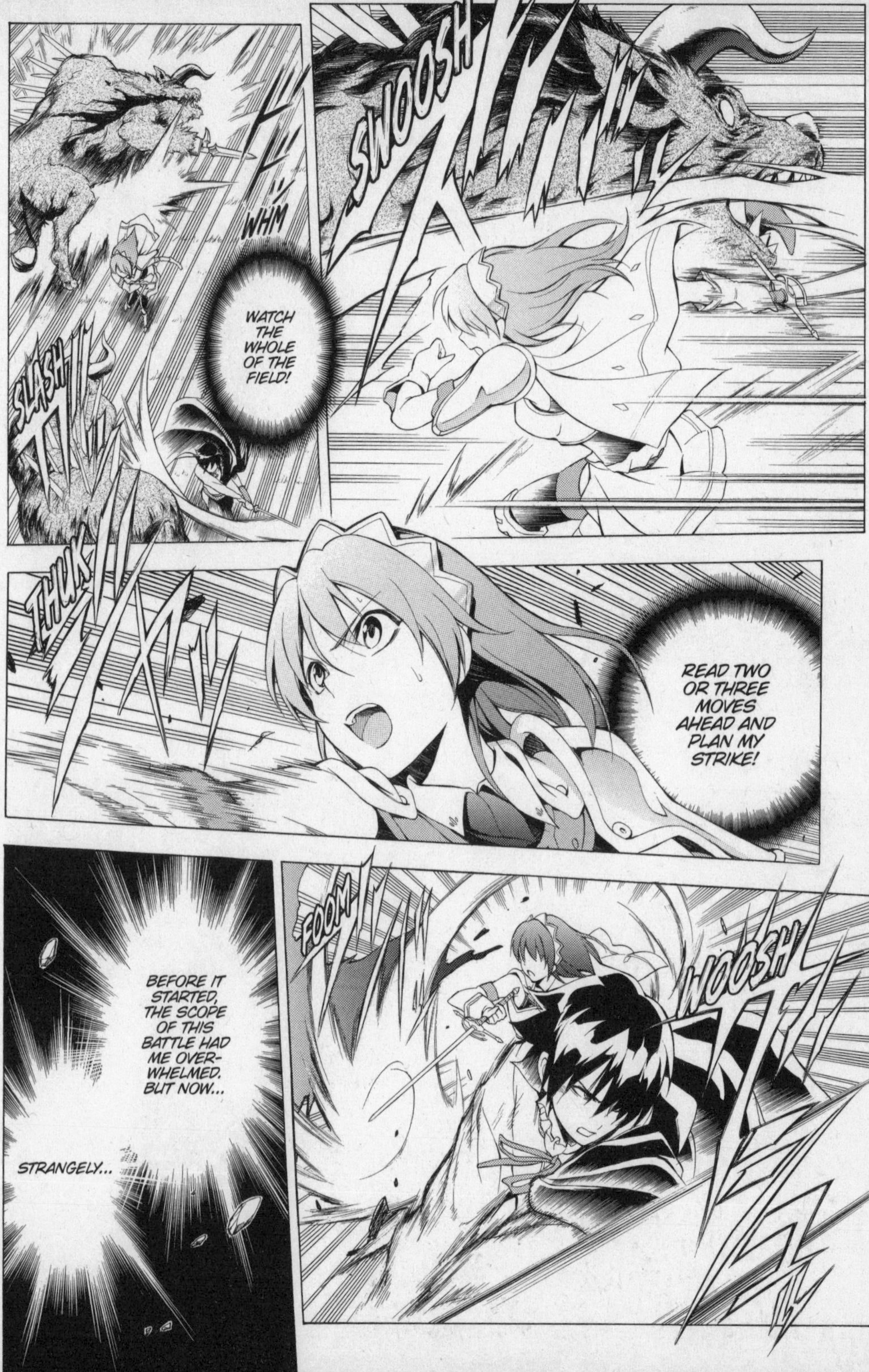
SWOOSH
WHM
WATCH THE WHOLE OF THE FIELD!
SLASH
READ TWO OR THREE MOVES AHEAD AND PLAN MY STRIKE!
THUK
WOOSH
FOOM
BEFORE IT STARTED, THE SCOPE OF THIS BATTLE HAD ME OVER-WHELMED. BUT NOW...
STRANGELY...

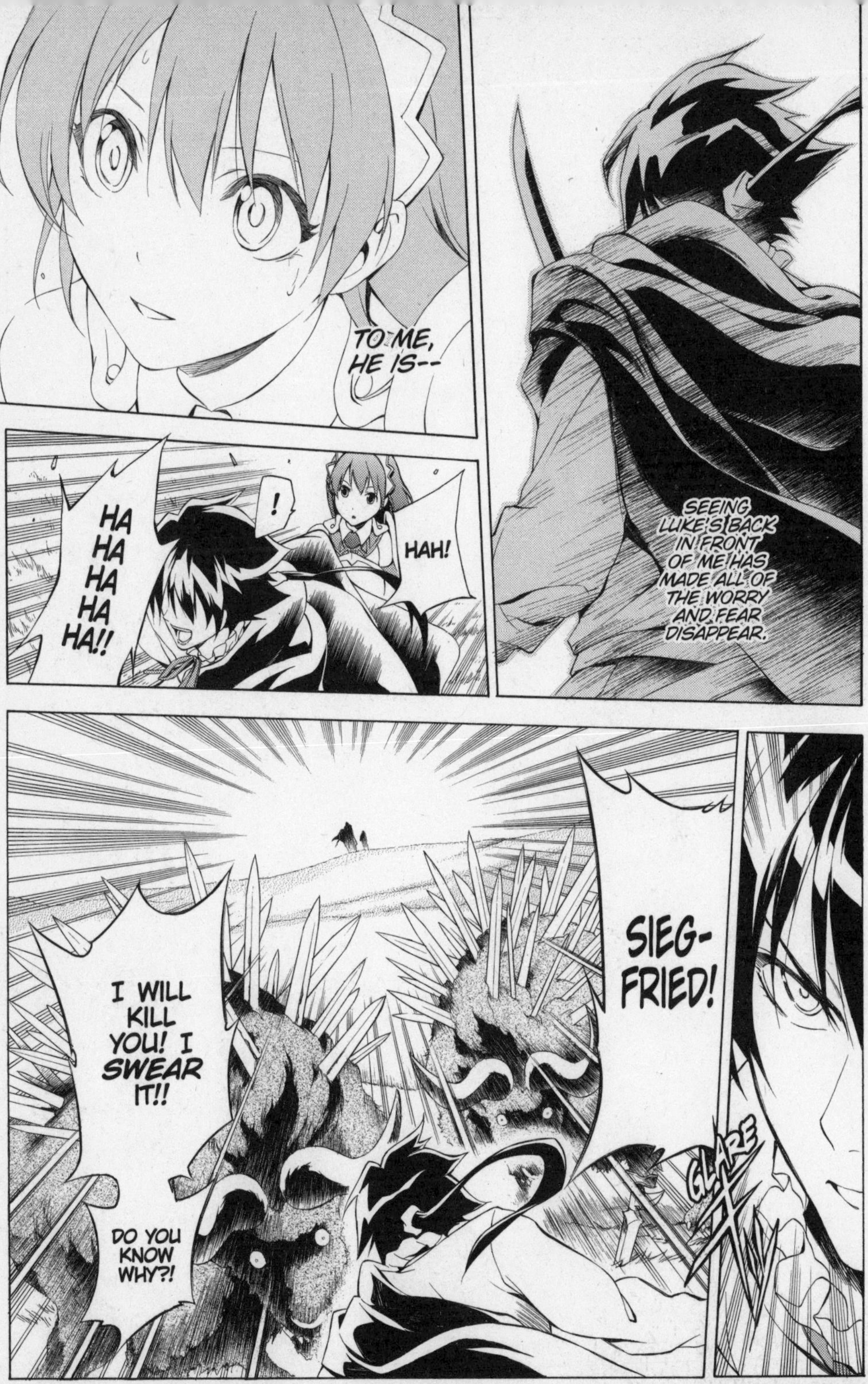
SEEING LUKE'S BACK IN FRONT OF ME HAS MADE ALL OF THE WORRY AND FEAR DISAPPEAR.
TO ME, HE IS--
!
HAH!
HA HA HA HA HA!!
GLARE
SIEG-FRIED!
I WILL KILL YOU! I SWEAR IT!!
DO YOU KNOW WHY?!

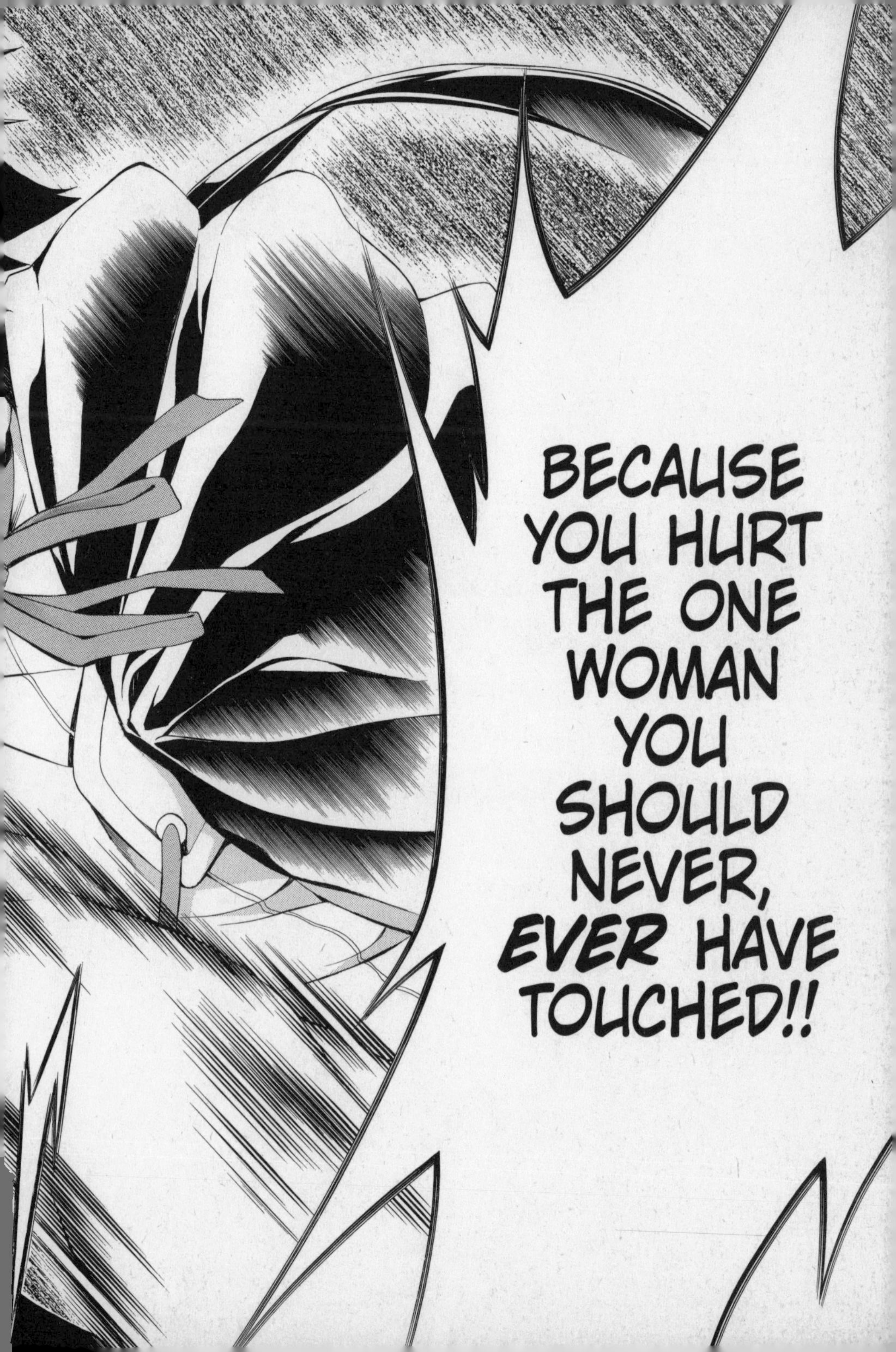
BECAUSE YOU HURT THE ONE WOMAN YOU SHOULD NEVER, EVER HAVE TOUCHED!!

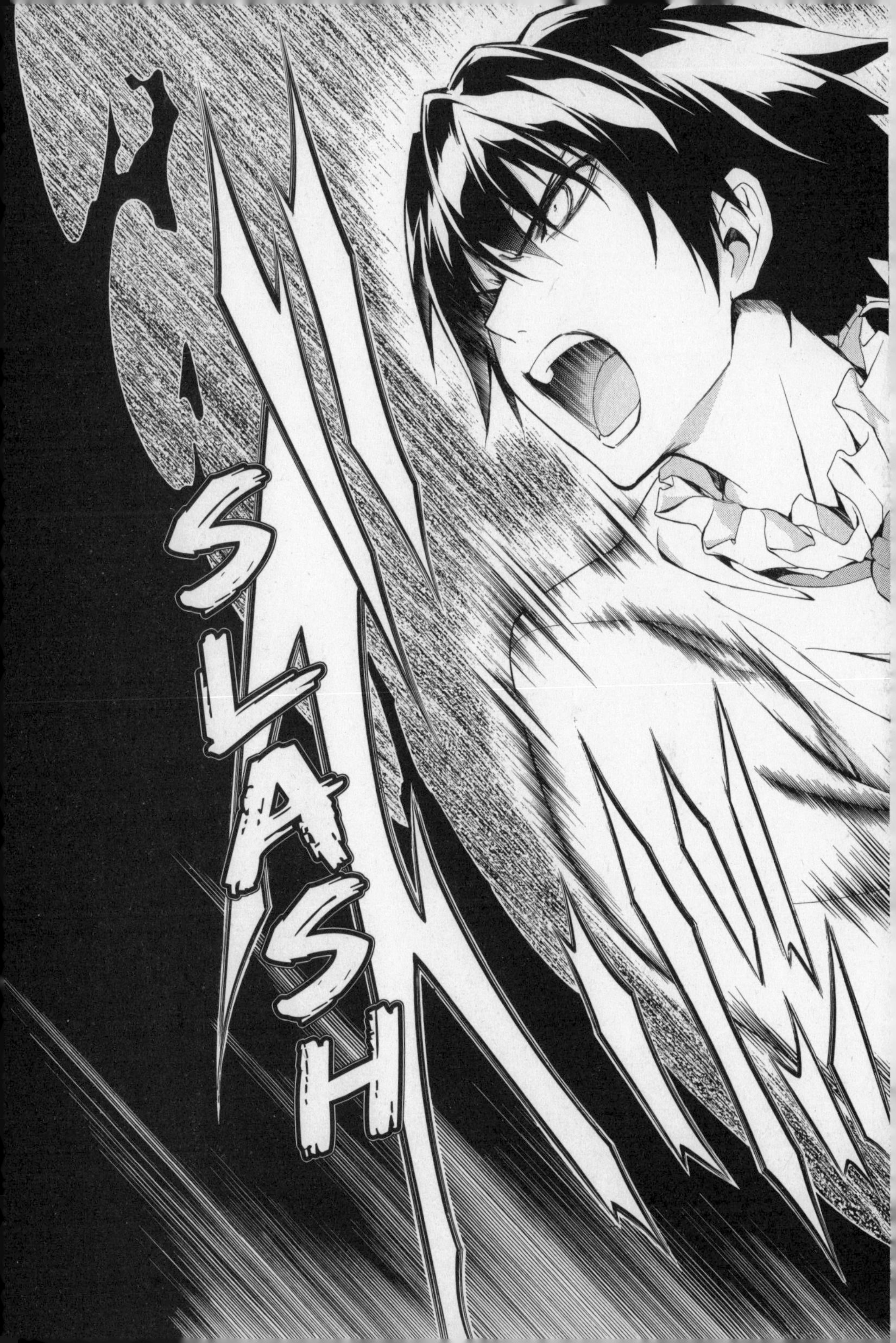
SLASH

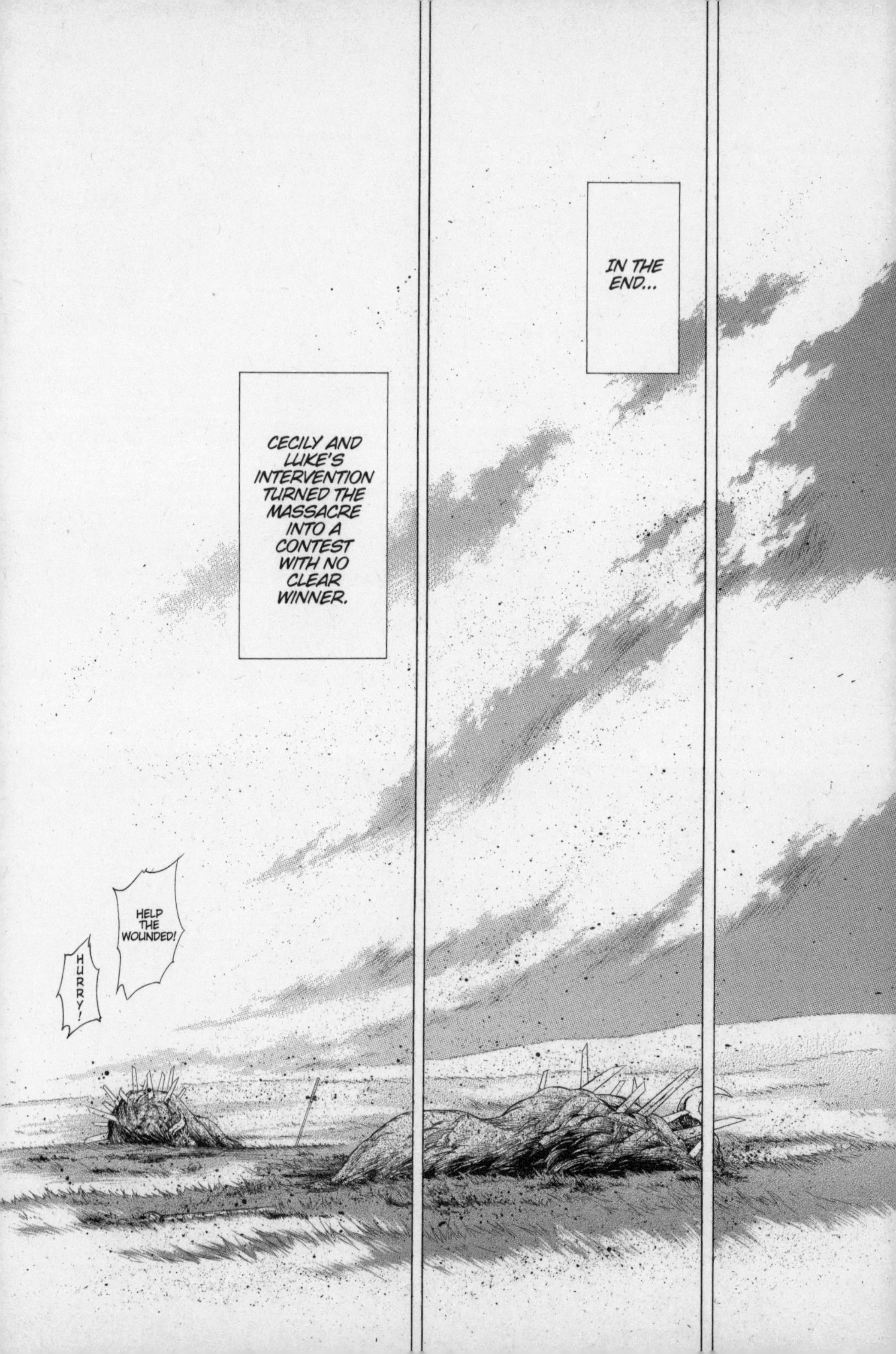
IN THE END...
CECILY AND LUKE'S INTERVENTION TURNED THE MASSACRE INTO A CONTEST WITH NO CLEAR WINNER.
HELP THE WOUNDED!
HURRY!

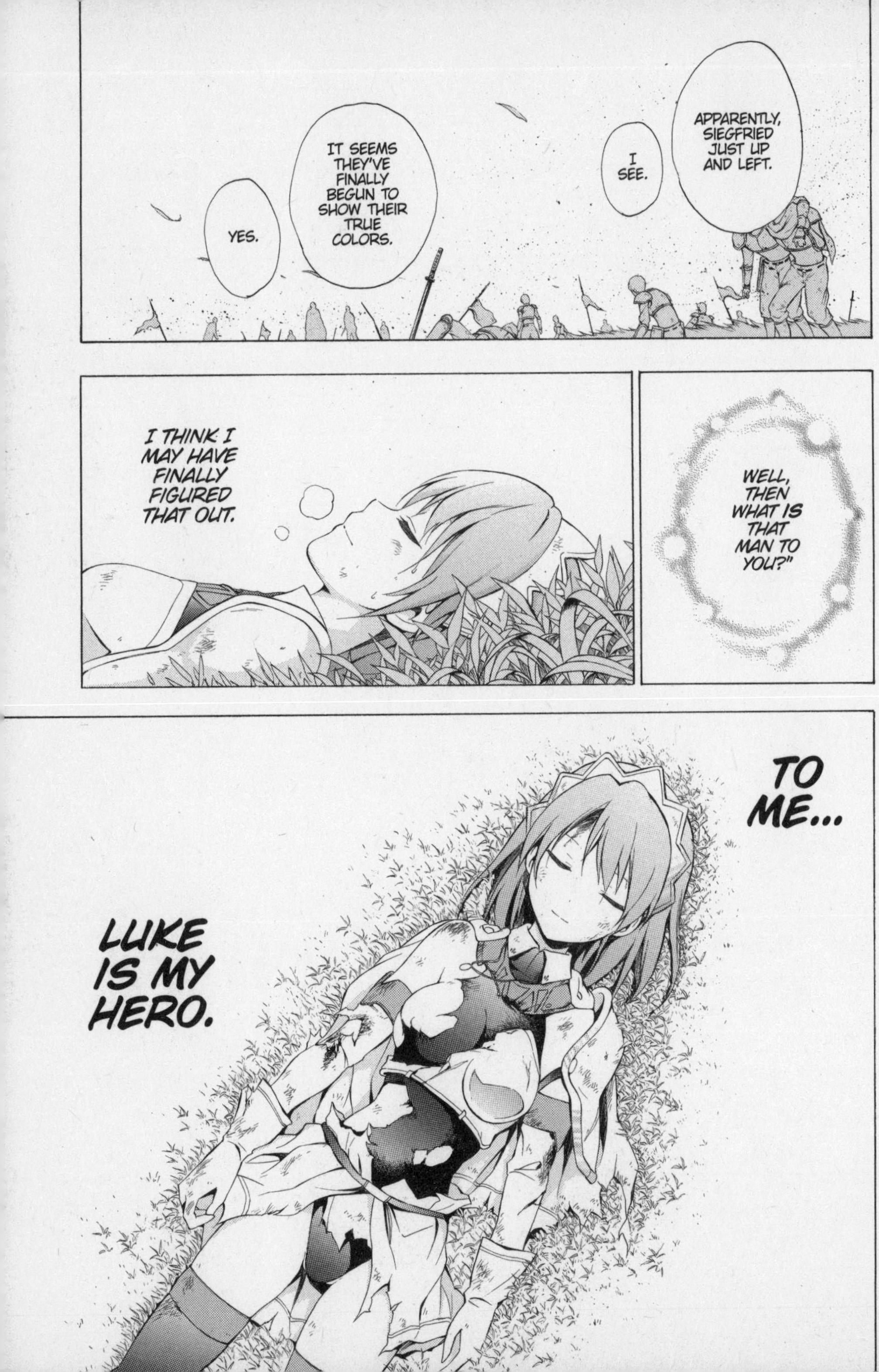
APPARENTLY, SIEGFRIED JUST UP AND LEFT.
I SEE.
IT SEEMS THEY'VE FINALLY BEGUN TO SHOW THEIR TRUE COLORS.
YES.
WELL, THEN WHAT IS THAT MAN TO YOU?"
I THINK I MAY HAVE FINALLY FIGURED THAT OUT.
TO ME...
LUKE IS MY HERO.

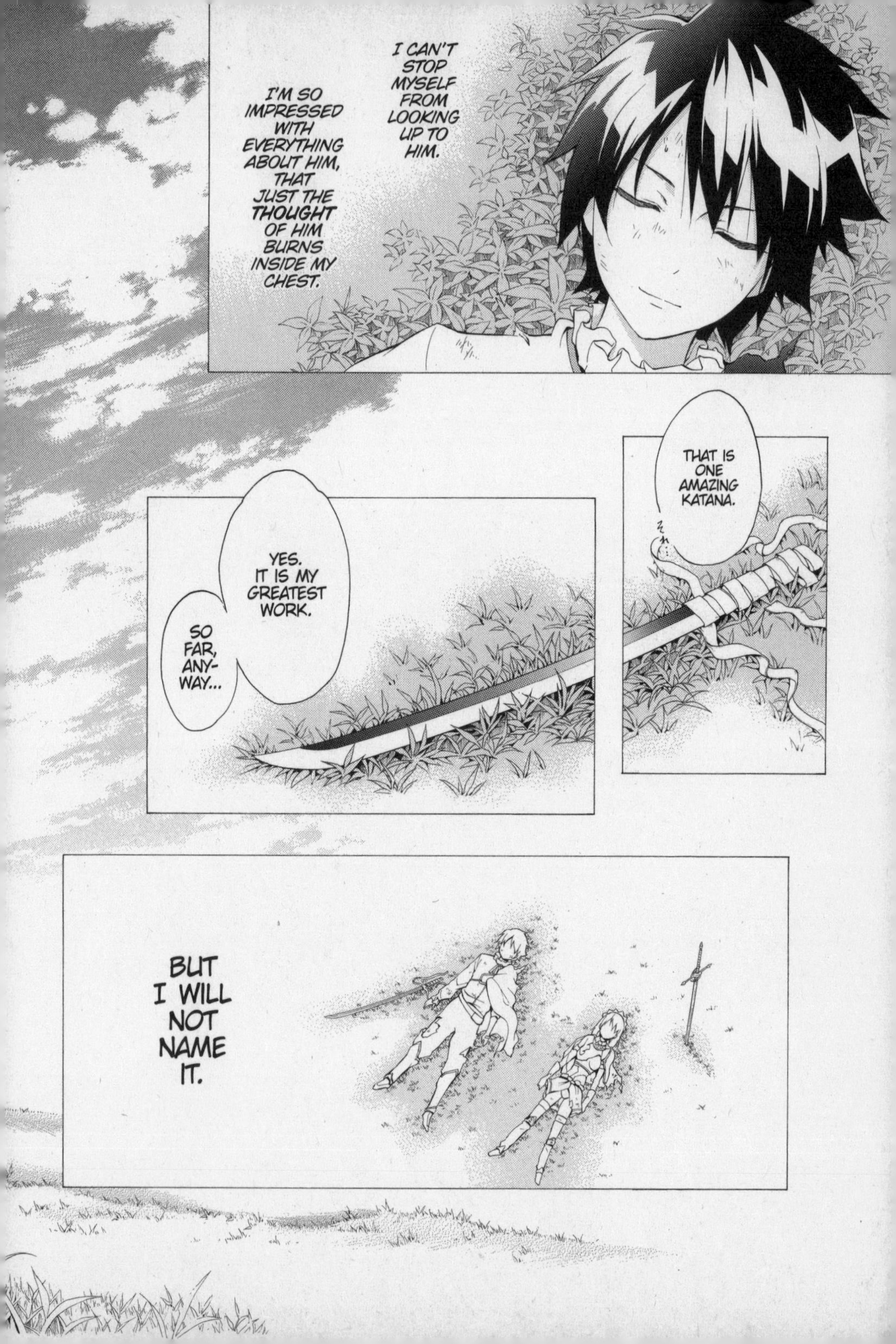
I CAN'T STOP MYSELF FROM LOOKING UP TO HIM.
I'M SO IMPRESSED WITH EVERYTHING ABOUT HIM, THAT JUST THE THOUGHT OF HIM BURNS INSIDE MY CHEST.
THAT IS ONE AMAZING KATANA.
YES. IT IS MY GREATEST WORK.
SO FAR, ANY-WAY...
BUT I WILL NOT NAME IT.

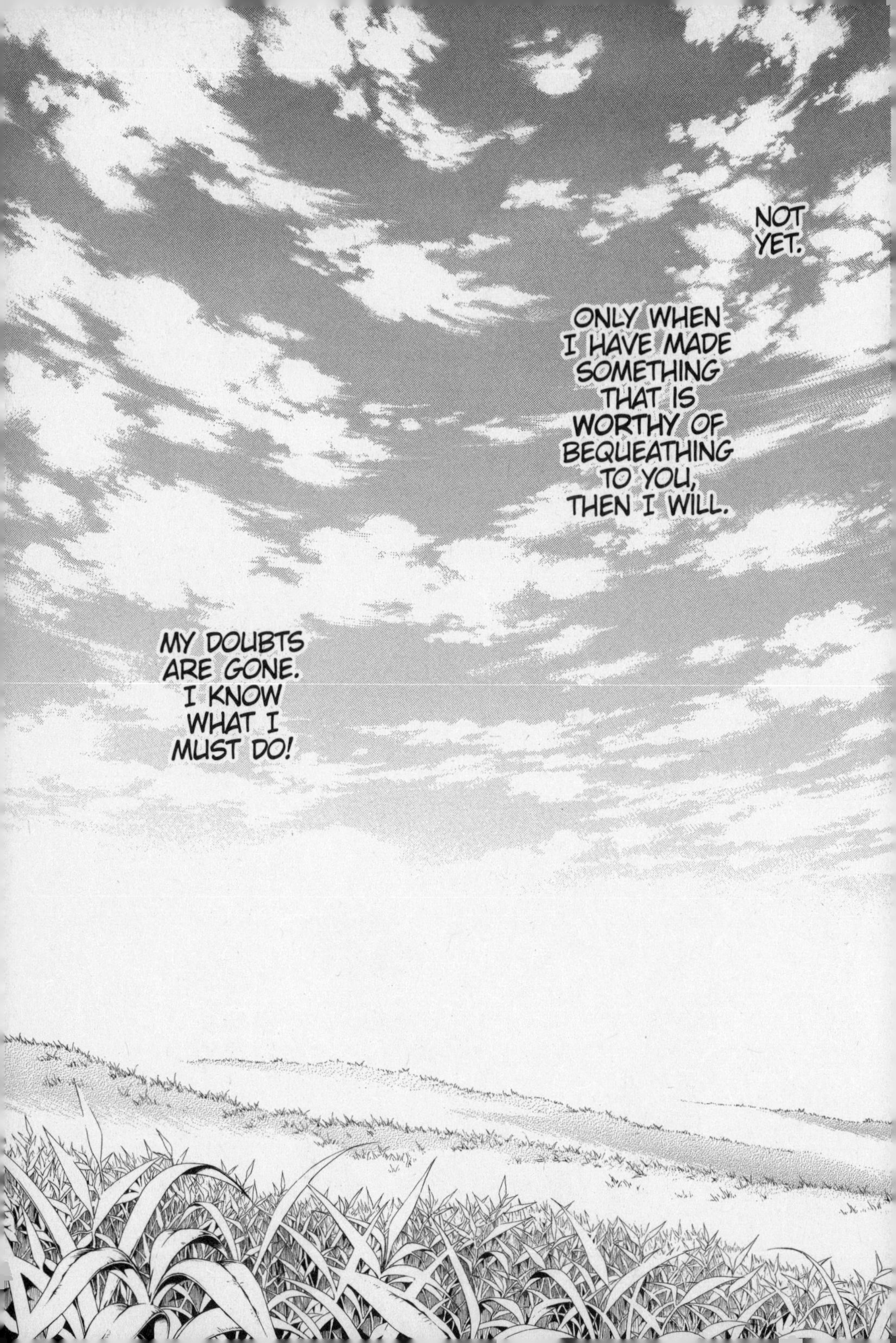
NOT YET.
ONLY WHEN I HAVE MADE SOMETHING THAT IS WORTHY OF BEQUEATHING TO YOU, THEN I WILL.
MY DOUBTS ARE GONE. I KNOW WHAT I MUST DO!

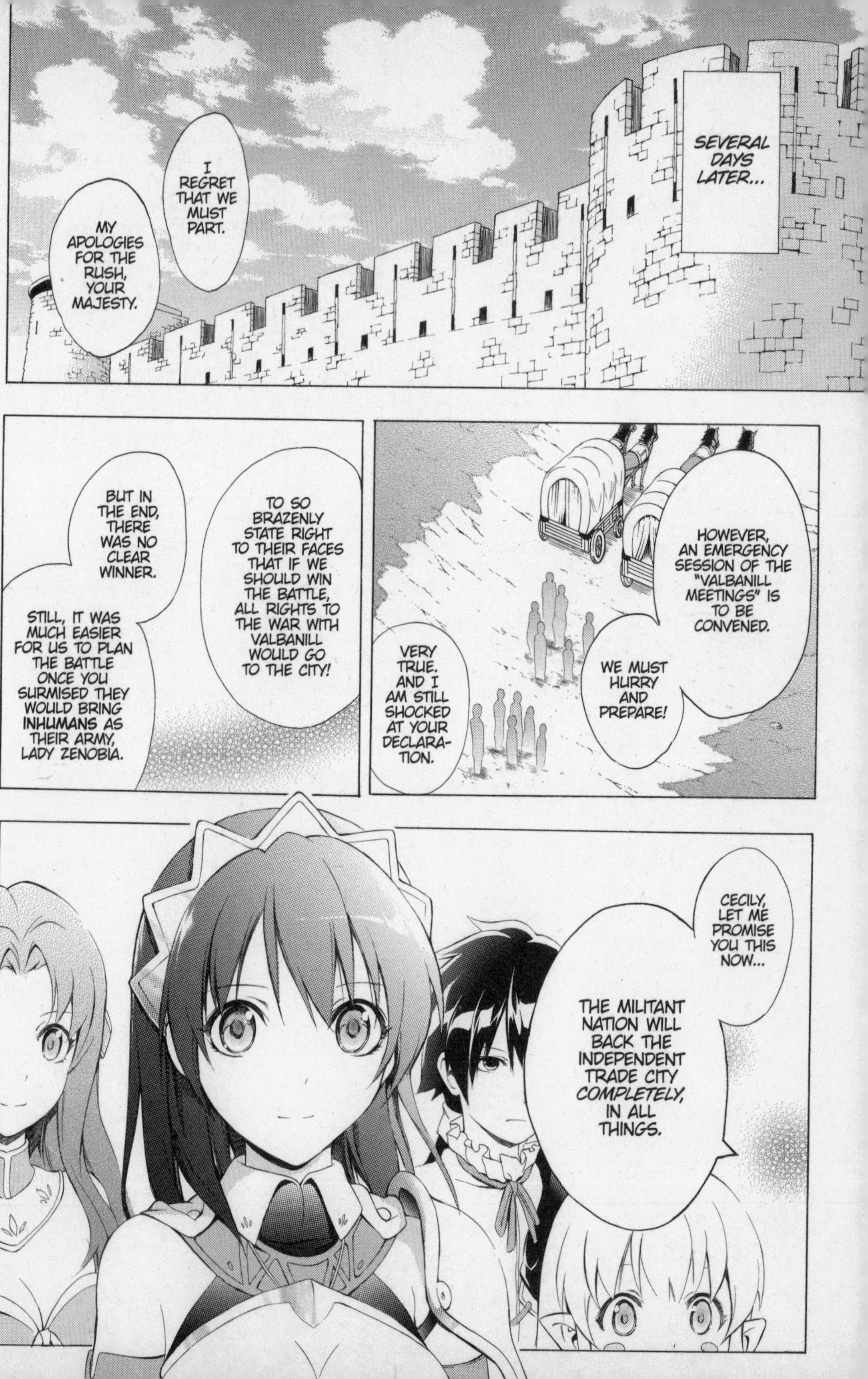
SEVERAL DAYS LATER...
I REGRET THAT WE MUST PART.
MY APOLOGIES FOR THE RUSH, YOUR MAJESTY.
HOWEVER, AN EMERGENCY SESSION OF THE "VALBANILL MEETINGS" IS TO BE CONVENED.
WE MUST HURRY AND PREPARE!
VERY TRUE. AND I AM STILL SHOCKED AT YOUR DECLARATION.
TO SO BRAZENLY STATE RIGHT TO THEIR FACES THAT IF WE SHOULD WIN THE BATTLE, ALL RIGHTS TO THE WAR WITH VALBANILL WOULD GO TO THE CITY!
BUT IN THE END, THERE WAS NO CLEAR WINNER.
STILL, IT WAS MUCH EASIER FOR US TO PLAN THE BATTLE ONCE YOU SURMISED THEY WOULD BRING INHUMANS AS THEIR ARMY, LADY ZENOBIA.
CECILY, LET ME PROMISE YOU THIS NOW...
THE MILITANT NATION WILL BACK THE INDEPENDENT TRADE CITY *COMPLETELY*, IN ALL THINGS.

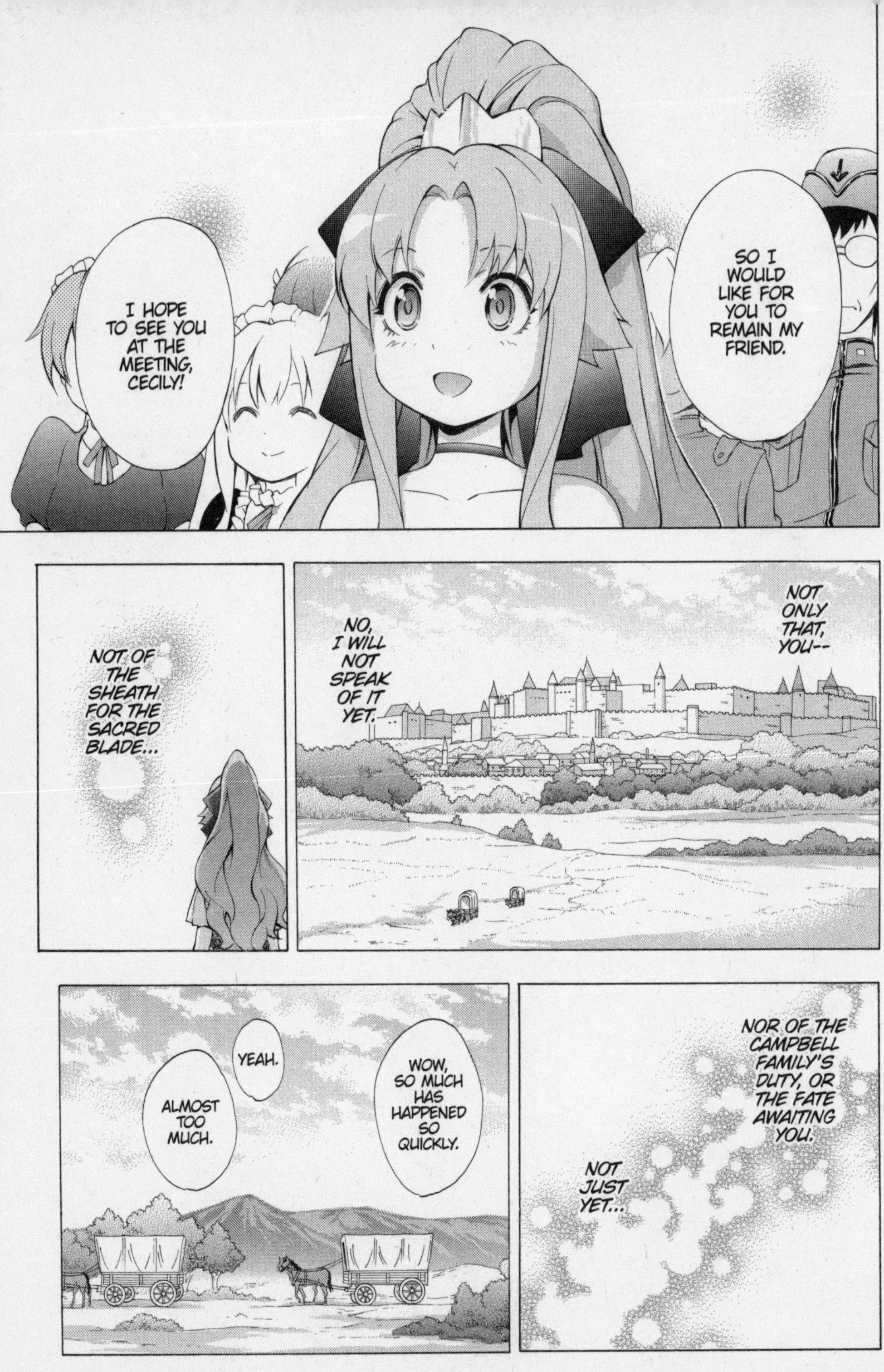
SO I WOULD LIKE FOR YOU TO REMAIN MY FRIEND.
I HOPE TO SEE YOU AT THE MEETING, CECILY!
NOT ONLY THAT, YOU--
NO, I WILL NOT SPEAK OF IT YET.
NOT OF THE SHEATH FOR THE SACRED BLADE...
NOR OF THE CAMPBELL FAMILY'S DUTY, OR THE FATE AWAITING YOU.
NOT JUST YET...
WOW, SO MUCH HAS HAPPENED SO QUICKLY.
YEAH.
ALMOST TOO MUCH.

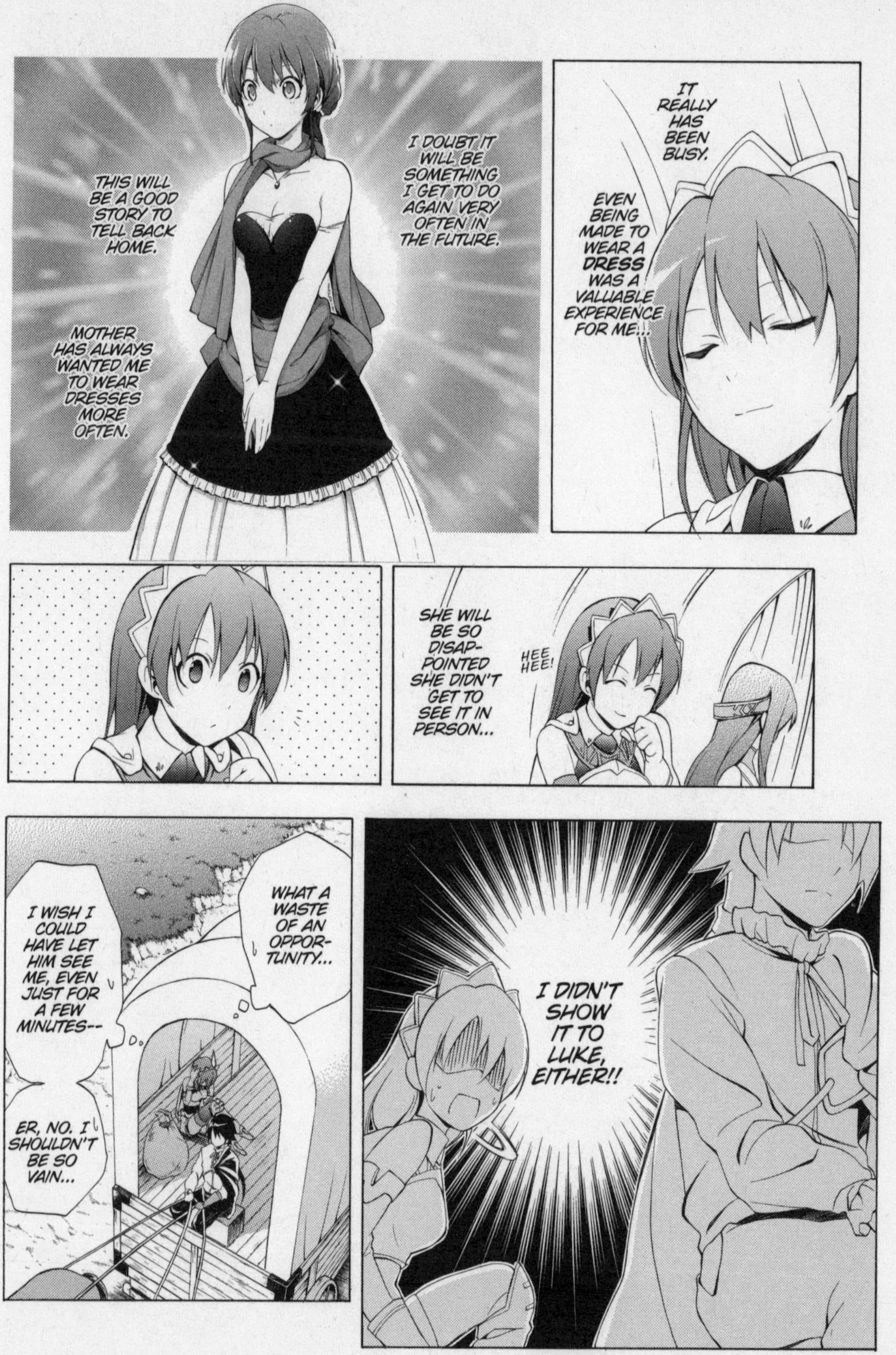
IT REALLY HAS BEEN BUSY.
EVEN BEING MADE TO WEAR A **DRESS** WAS A VALUABLE EXPERIENCE FOR ME...
I DOUBT IT WILL BE SOMETHING I GET TO DO AGAIN VERY OFTEN IN THE FUTURE.
THIS WILL BE A GOOD STORY TO TELL BACK HOME.
MOTHER HAS ALWAYS WANTED ME TO WEAR DRESSES MORE OFTEN.
SHE WILL BE SO DISAP-POINTED SHE DIDN'T GET TO SEE IT IN PERSON...
HEE HEE!
I DIDN'T SHOW IT TO LUKE, EITHER!!
WHAT A WASTE OF AN OPPOR-TUNITY...
I WISH I COULD HAVE LET HIM SEE ME, EVEN JUST FOR A FEW MINUTES--
ER, NO. I SHOULDN'T BE SO VAIN...

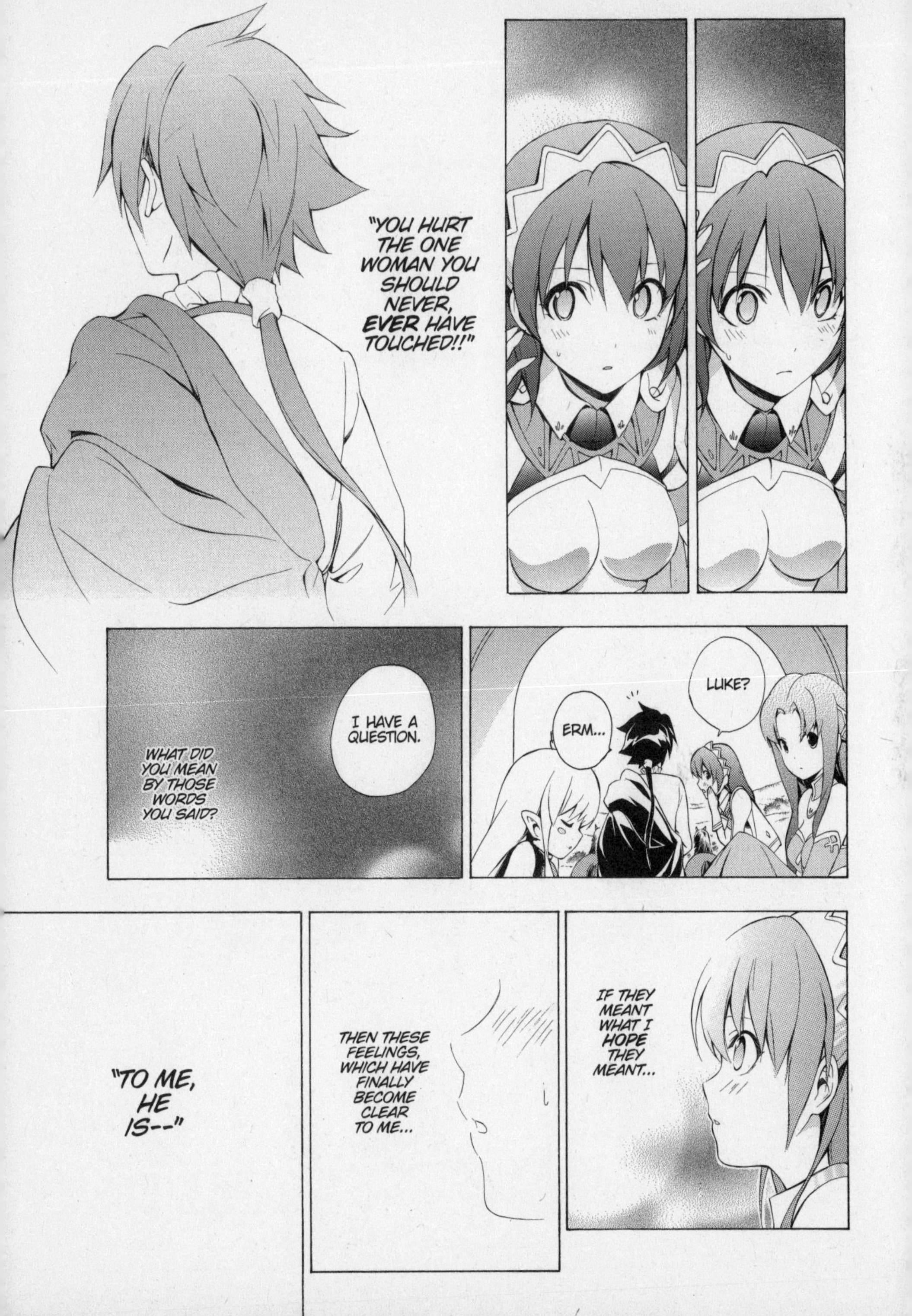
"YOU HURT THE ONE WOMAN YOU SHOULD NEVER, EVER HAVE TOUCHED!!"
LUKE?
ERM...
I HAVE A QUESTION.
WHAT DID YOU MEAN BY THOSE WORDS YOU SAID?
IF THEY MEANT WHAT I HOPE THEY MEANT...
THEN THESE FEELINGS, WHICH HAVE FINALLY BECOME CLEAR TO ME...
"TO ME, HE IS--"

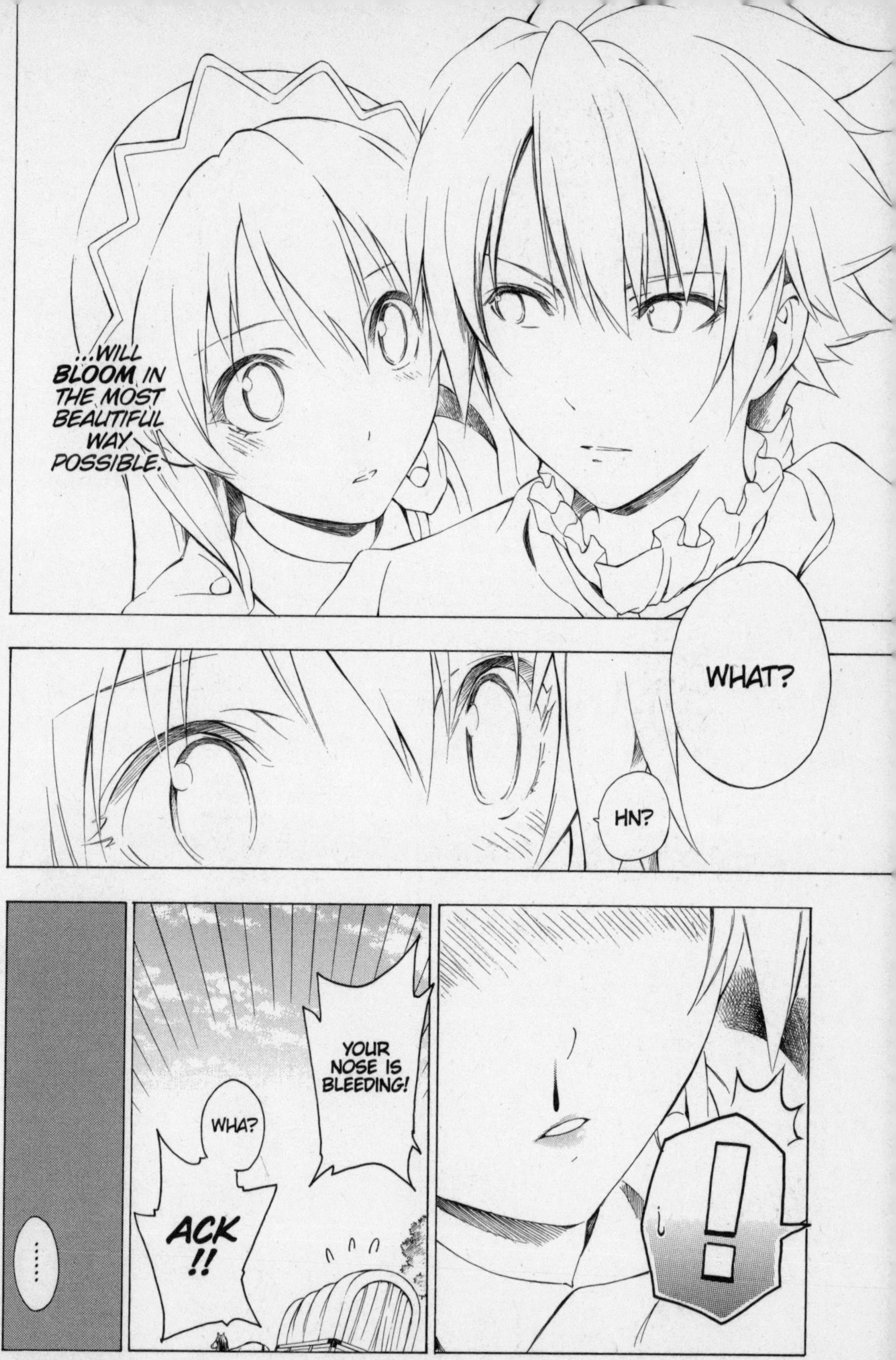
...WILL BLOOM IN THE MOST BEAUTIFUL WAY POSSIBLE.
WHAT?
HN?
!
YOUR NOSE IS BLEEDING!
WHA?
ACK!!
......

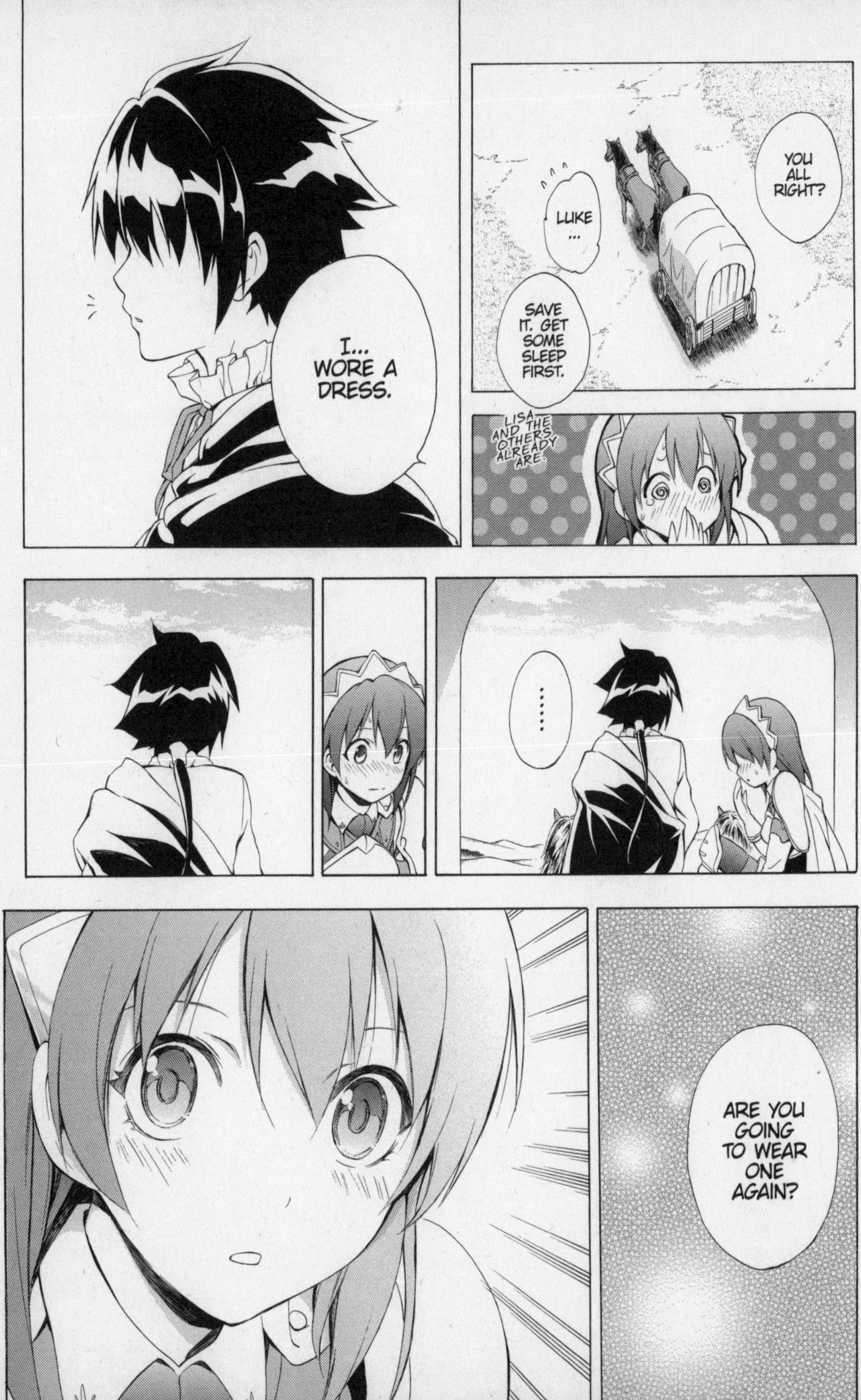
YOU ALL RIGHT?
LUKE ...
SAVE IT. GET SOME SLEEP FIRST.
LISA AND THE OTHERS ALREADY ARE.
I... WORE A DRESS.
......
ARE YOU GOING TO WEAR ONE AGAIN?

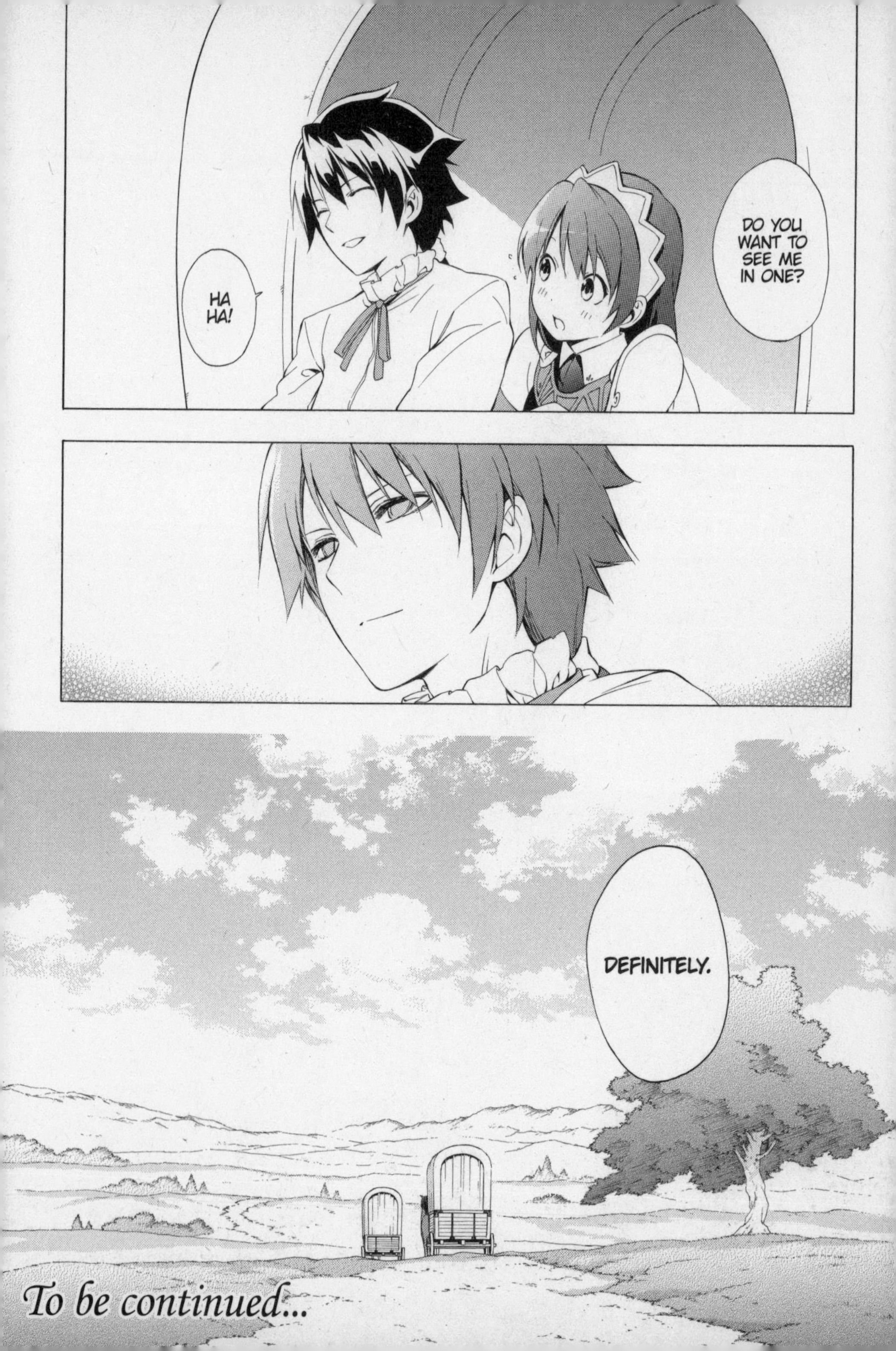
DO YOU WANT TO SEE ME IN ONE?
HA HA!
DEFINITELY.
To be continued...

The Sacred Blacksmith

聖剣の刀鍛冶

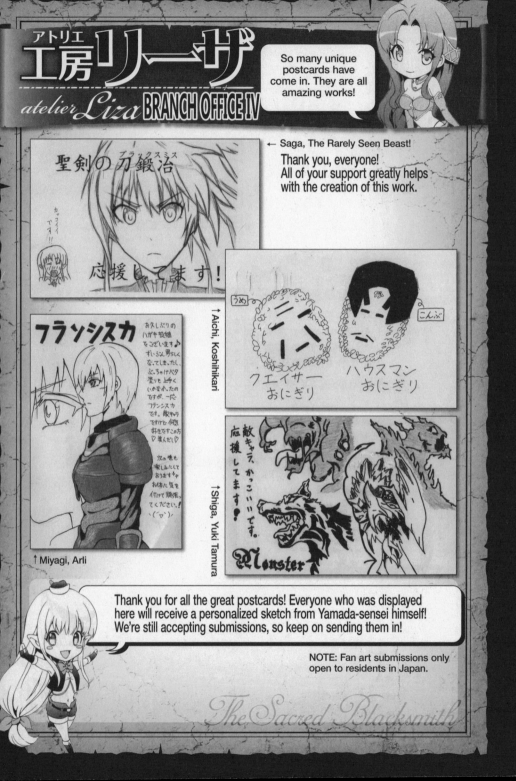

アトリエ 工房リーザ
atelier Liza BRANCH OFFICE IV

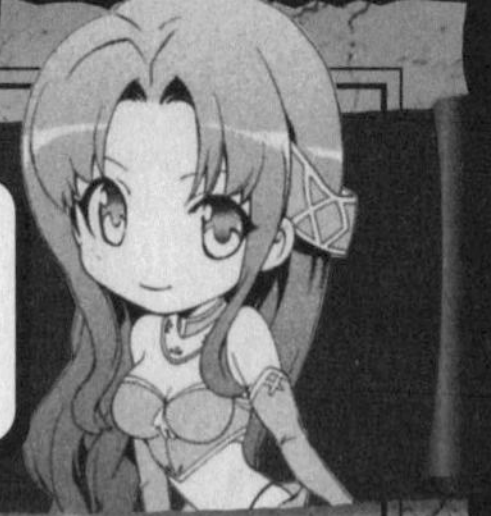

So many unique postcards have come in. They are all amazing works!

← Saga, The Rarely Seen Beast!

Thank you, everyone!
All of your support greatly helps with the creation of this work.

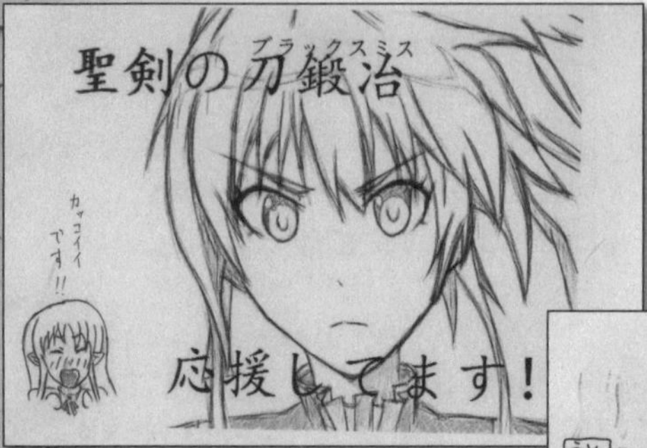

聖剣の刀鍛治
ブラックスミス
カッコイイです!!
応援してます!

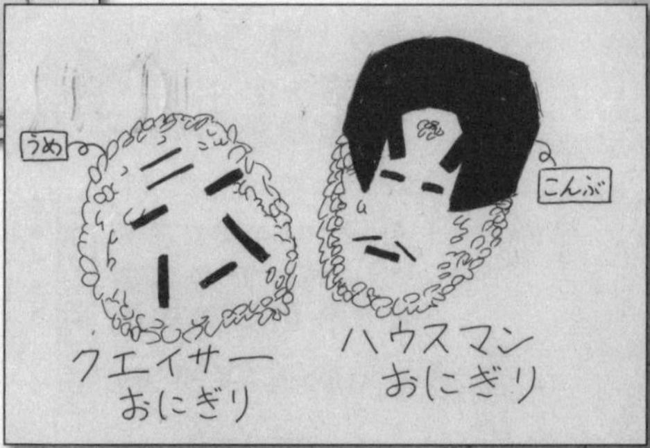

うめ
こんぶ
クエイサーおにぎり
ハウスマンおにぎり

↑Aichi, Koshihikari

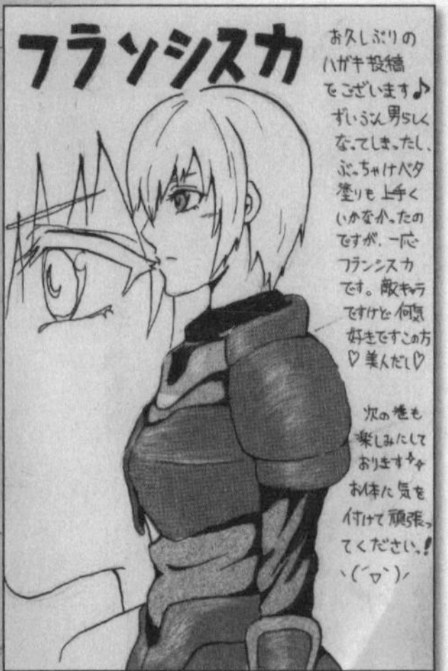

フランシスカ
お久しぶりのハガキ投稿でございます♪ ずいぶん男らしくなってしまいたし、ぶっちゃけベタ塗りも上手くいかなかったのですが、一応フランシスカです。敵キャラですけど何気好きですこの方♡美人だし♡
次の巻も楽しみにしております お体に気を付けて頑張ってください!

↑Miyagi, Arli

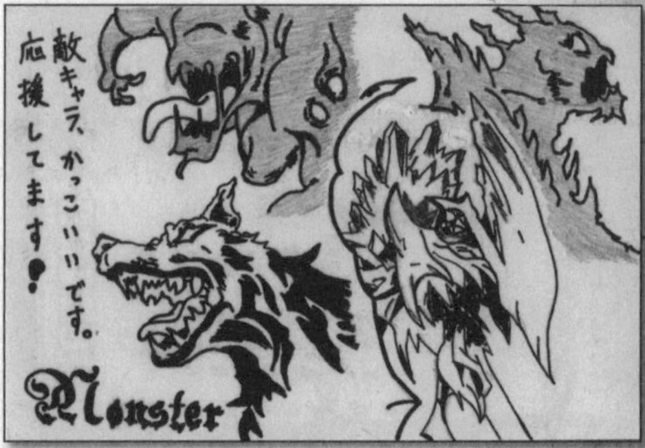

敵キャラ、かっこいいです。
応援してます!
Monster

↑Shiga, Yuki Tamura

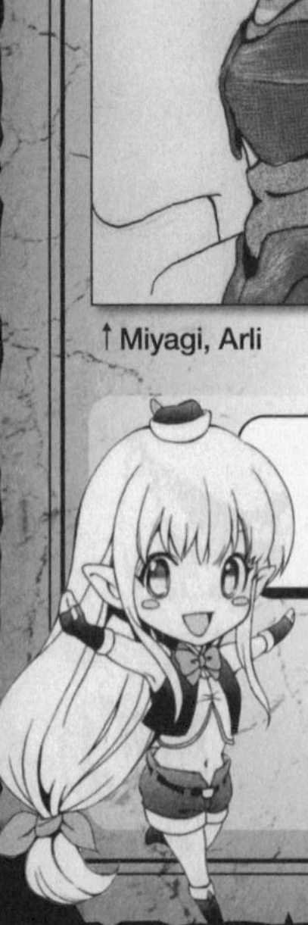

Thank you for all the great postcards! Everyone who was displayed here will receive a personalized sketch from Yamada-sensei himself! We're still accepting submissions, so keep on sending them in!

NOTE: Fan art submissions only open to residents in Japan.

The Sacred Blacksmith

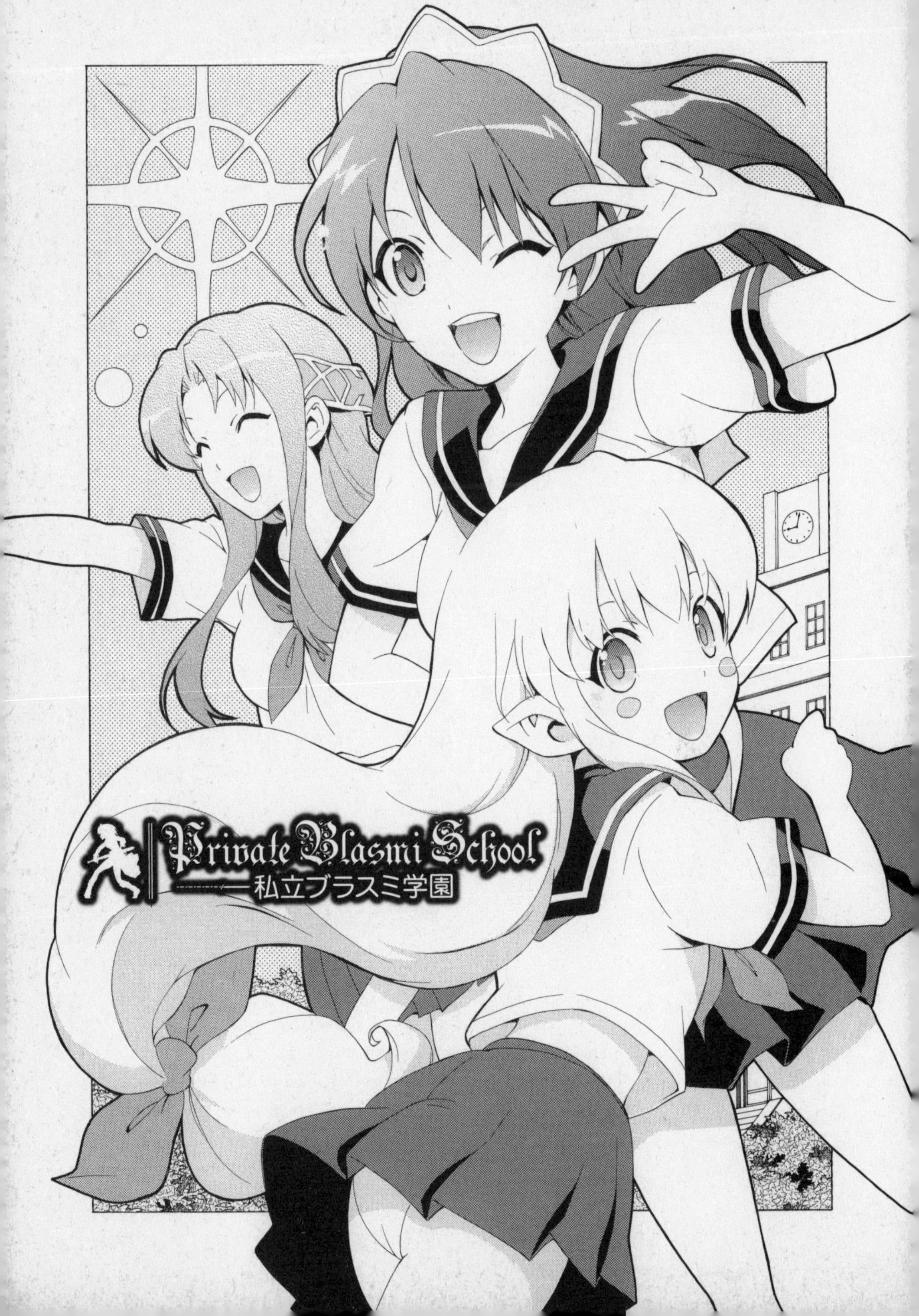
Private Blasmi School
私立ブラスミ学園

TESTS

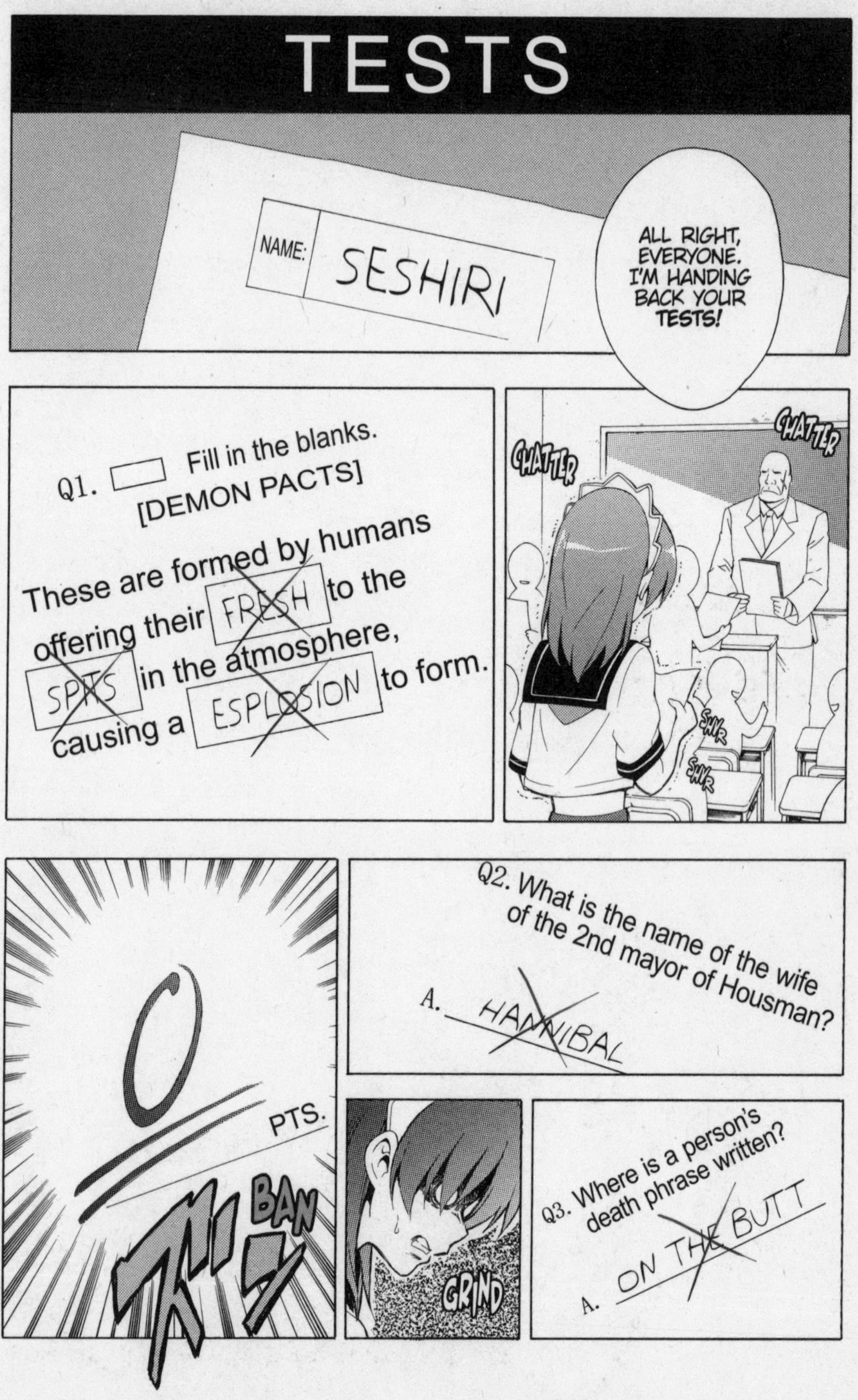
NAME:
SESHIRI
ALL RIGHT, EVERYONE. I'M HANDING BACK YOUR TESTS!
CHATTER
CHATTER
SHR
SHR
Q1. Fill in the blanks. [DEMON PACTS]
These are formed by humans offering their FRESH to the SPITS in the atmosphere, causing a ESPLOSION to form.
Q2. What is the name of the wife of the 2nd mayor of Housman?
A. HANNIBAL
Q3. Where is a person's death phrase written?
A. ON THE BUTT
GRIND
0
PTS.
BAN

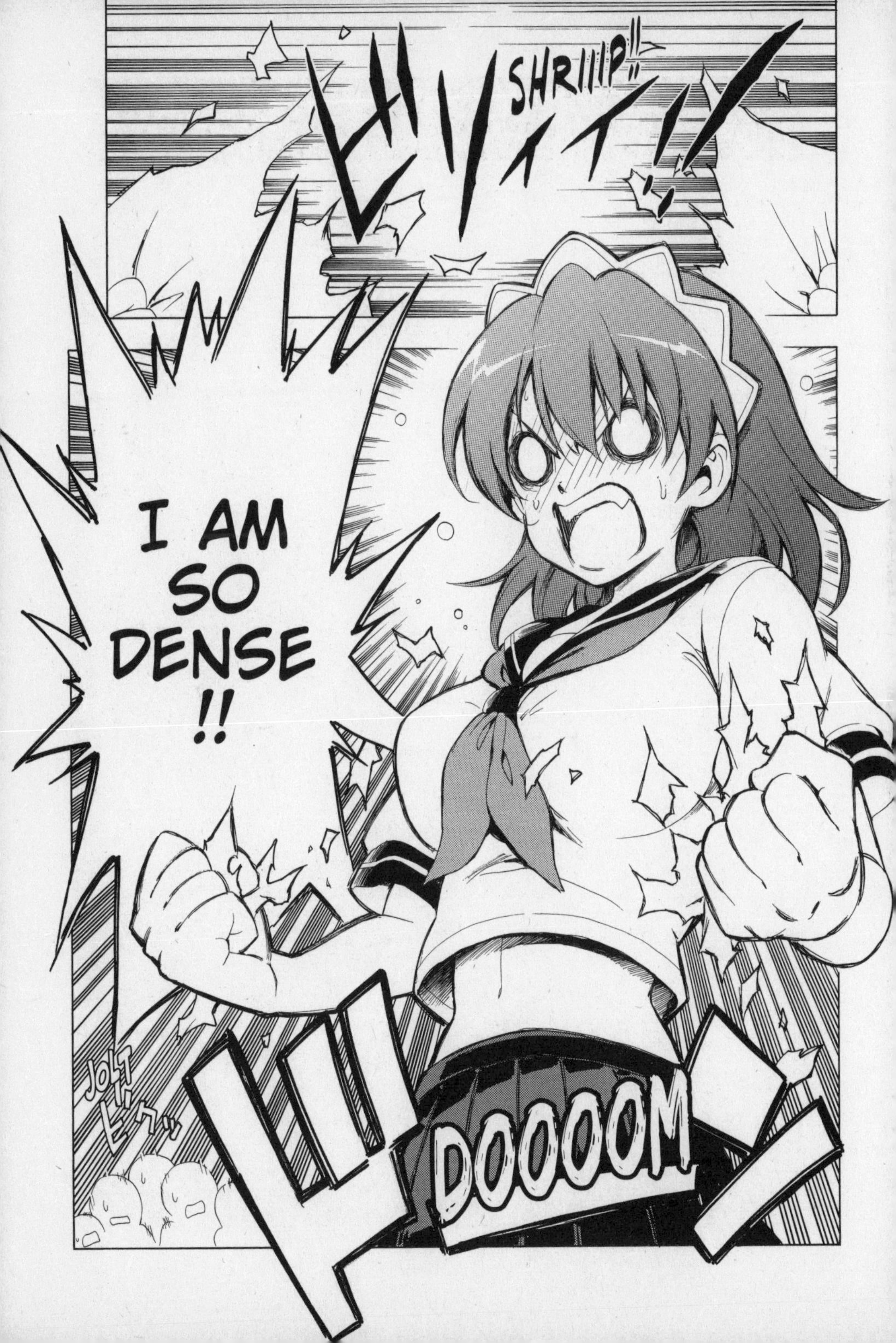
SHRIIIP!!
I AM SO DENSE!!
JOLT
DOOOOM

LOVE LETTER?

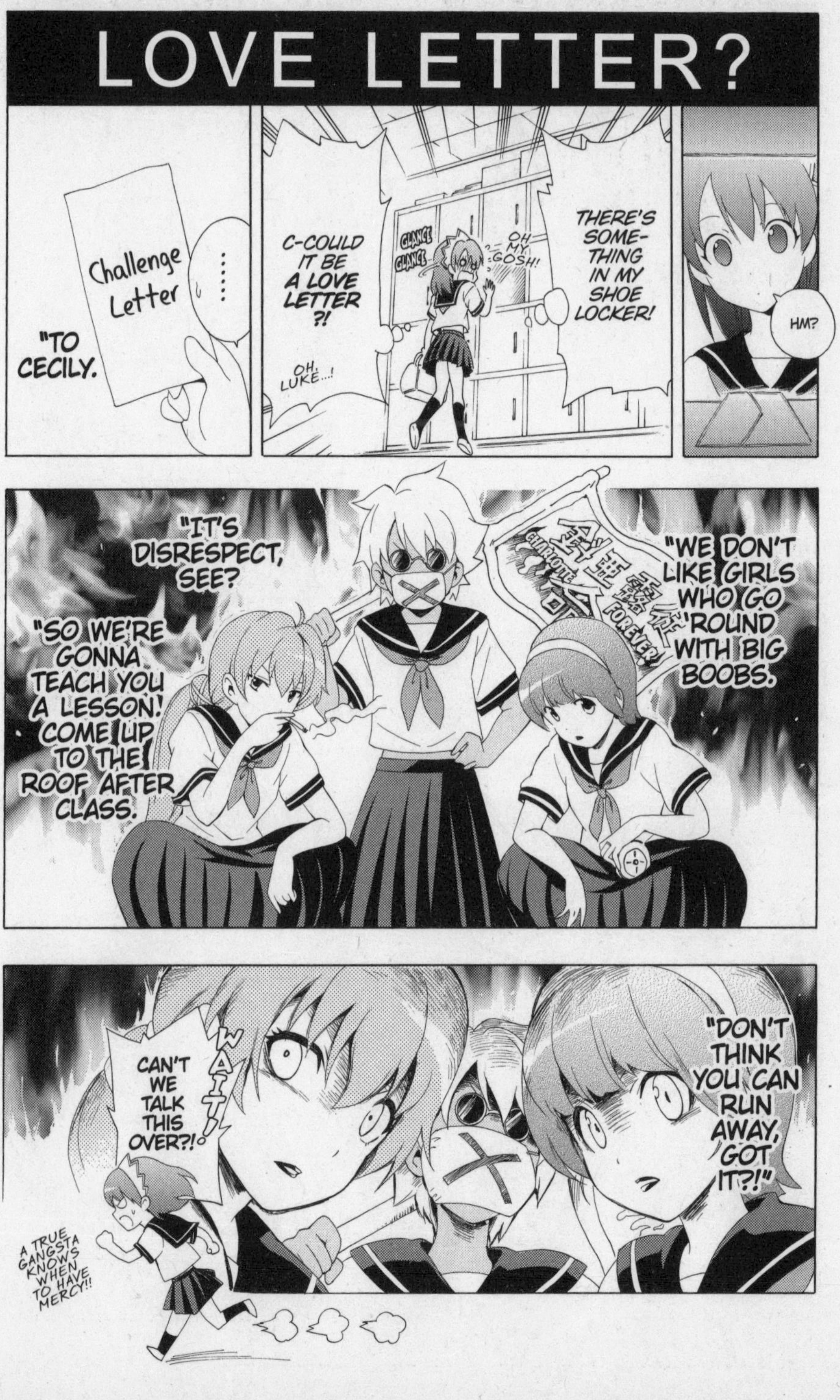
HM?
THERE'S SOME-THING IN MY SHOE LOCKER!
OH MY GOSH!
GLANCE GLANCE
C-COULD IT BE A LOVE LETTER?!
OH, LUKE...!
......
Challenge Letter
"TO CECILY.
"WE DON'T LIKE GIRLS WHO GO 'ROUND WITH BIG BOOBS.
CHARLOTTE
FOREVER!
"IT'S DISRESPECT, SEE?
"SO WE'RE GONNA TEACH YOU A LESSON! COME UP TO THE ROOF AFTER CLASS.
"DON'T THINK YOU CAN RUN AWAY, GOT IT?!"
WAIT!
CAN'T WE TALK THIS OVER?!
A TRUE GANGSTA KNOWS WHEN TO HAVE MERCY!!

AFTER SCHOOL

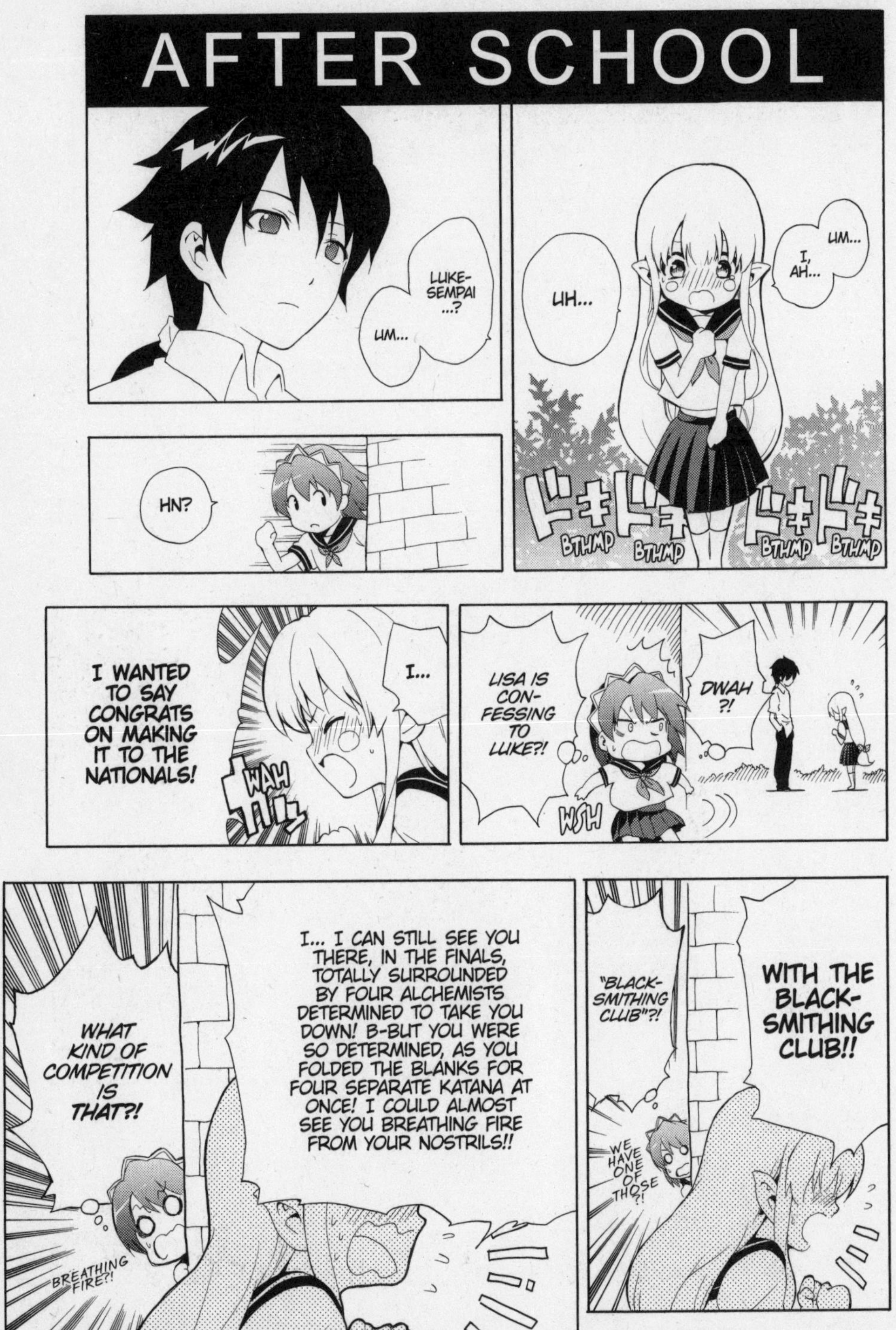
UM... I, AH...
UH...
BTHMP BTHMP BTHMP BTHMP
LUKE-SEMPAI ...?
UM...
HN?
DWAH ?!
LISA IS CON-FESSING TO LUKE?!
WSH
I...
I WANTED TO SAY CONGRATS ON MAKING IT TO THE NATIONALS!
WAH
WITH THE BLACK-SMITHING CLUB!!
"BLACK-SMITHING CLUB"?!
WE HAVE ONE OF THOSE?!
I... I CAN STILL SEE YOU THERE, IN THE FINALS, TOTALLY SURROUNDED BY FOUR ALCHEMISTS DETERMINED TO TAKE YOU DOWN! B-BUT YOU WERE SO DETERMINED, AS YOU FOLDED THE BLANKS FOR FOUR SEPARATE KATANA AT ONCE! I COULD ALMOST SEE YOU BREATHING FIRE FROM YOUR NOSTRILS!!
WHAT KIND OF COMPETITION IS THAT?!
BREATHING FIRE?!

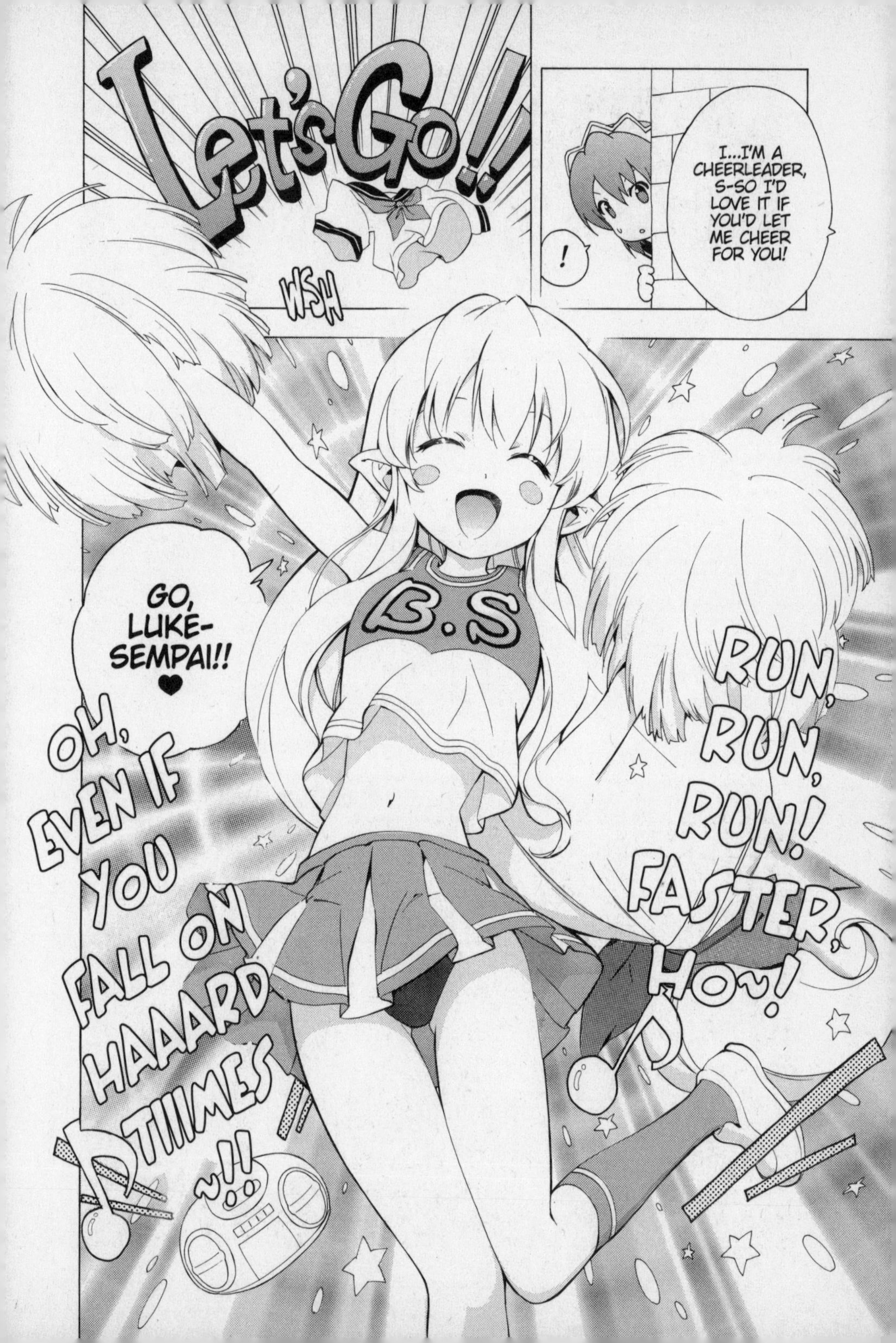
I...I'M A CHEERLEADER, S-SO I'D LOVE IT IF YOU'D LET ME CHEER FOR YOU!
!
LET'S GO!!
WSH
RUN, RUN, RUN! FASTER, HO~!
GO, LUKE-SEMPAI!! ♥
OH, EVEN IF YOU FALL ON HAAARD TIIIMES ~!!

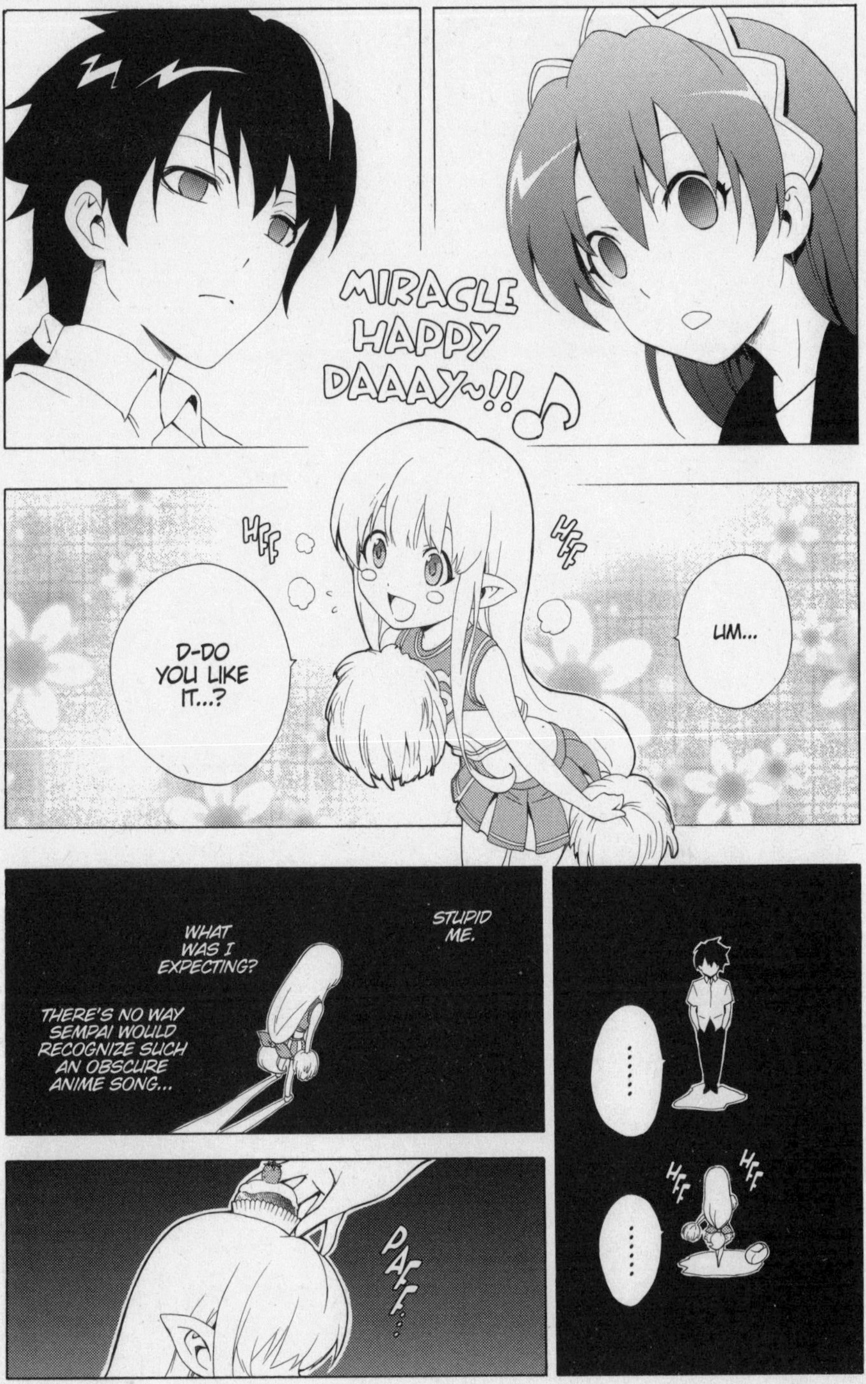
MIRACLE HAPPY DAAAY~!!
HFF
UM...
HFF
D-DO YOU LIKE IT...?
......
HFF
HFF
......
STUPID ME.
WHAT WAS I EXPECTING?
THERE'S NO WAY SEMPAI WOULD RECOGNIZE SUCH AN OBSCURE ANIME SONG...
PAFF..

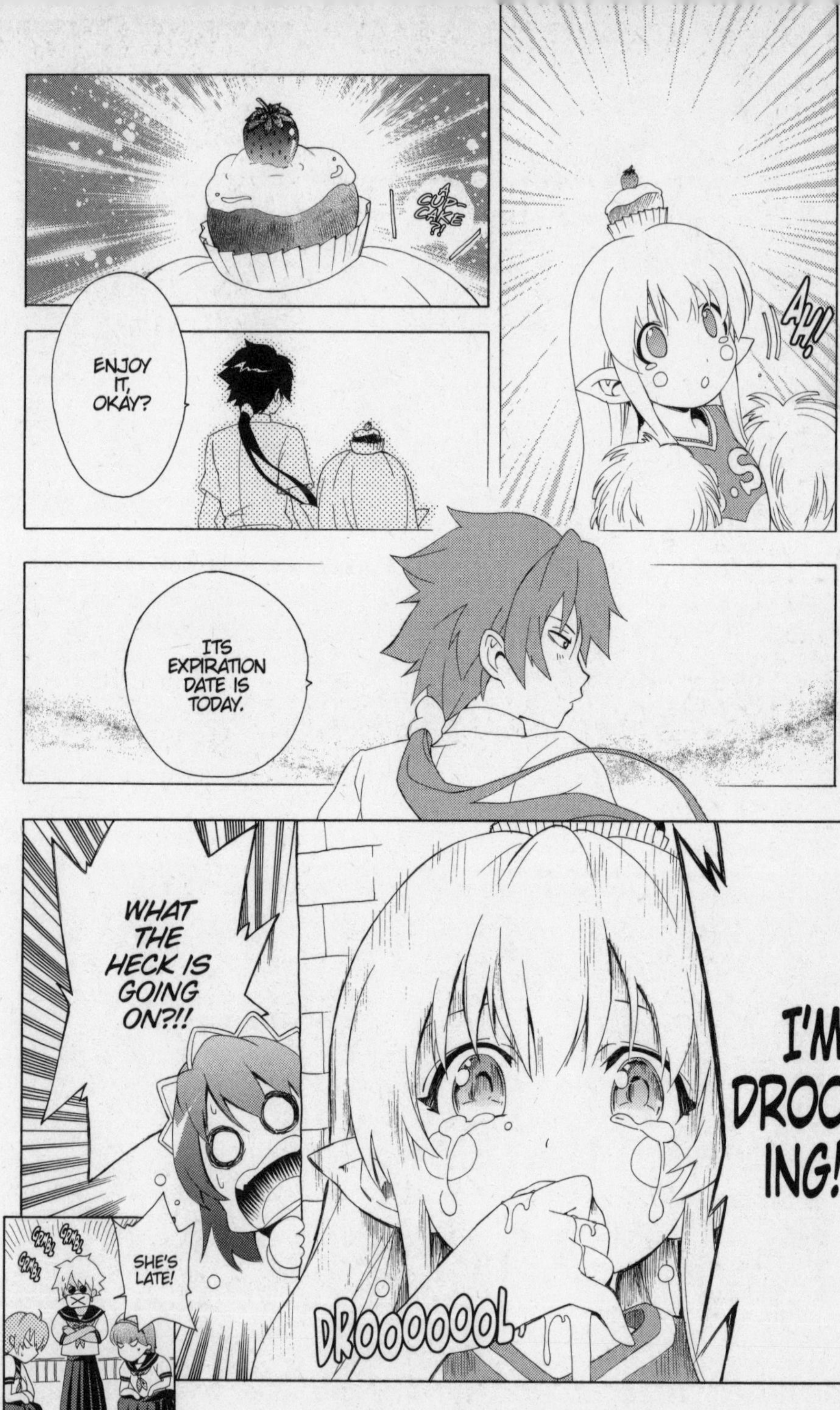
AH!
A CUP-CAKE?!
ENJOY IT, OKAY?
ITS EXPIRATION DATE IS TODAY.
I'M DROOL-ING!!
DROOOOOOOL
WHAT THE HECK IS GOING ON?!!
GRMBL GRMBL GRMBL
SHE'S LATE!